THE AGE OF TITANIC

CROSS-CURRENTS IN ANGLO-AMERICAN CULTURE

The Age of Titanic

Cross-currents in Anglo-American Culture

John Wilson Foster

MERLIN

PUBLISHING

Published in 2002 by

Merlin Publishing
16 Upper Pembroke Street
Dublin 2
Ireland

www.merlin-publishing.com

Text Copyright © John Wilson Foster
Arrangement and design Copyright © 2002 Merlin Publishing
except
Photographs courtesy of: Ulster Folk and Transport Museum, Richard
Howells, Fr. Browne Archive, Camera Press, Mary Evans Picture Library

ISBN 1-903582-37-7

A CIP record for this book is available from the British Library.

Typeset by Artwerk, Dublin

To Benedict Kiely in boundless gratitude

(A dedication too brief to count the ways)

Acknowledgments

Help in writing about *Titanic* is readily come by and many friends, acquaintances and strangers have, since I published *Titanic* in 1999, either supplied me with a fresh quantity of citations, facts and fictions about the ship, its sinking and the cultural phenomenon of the tragedy or offered other kinds of necessary help. These include colleagues at the University of British Columbia: Keith Bunnell, Andrew Busza, Jane Flick, Bryan Gooch, Arthur Lipman, who kindly translated for me the Chilean poem *Solidaridad en el Dolor (Catastrofe del* Titanic), Daniel O'Leary, George McWhirter, Patricia Merivale, Paul Stanwood, Jack F. Stewart, Jerry Wasserman, Jonathan Wisenthal. At Simon Fraser University in Burnaby, Paul Heyer and in Victoria, Ann Saddlemyer.

Farther afield, I would like to thank Peter Björkfors (Abo Akademi University, Finland), Ian and Sally Corry (Edmonton), Alan Finlayson (University of Wales Swansea), Tim Henighan (Carleton University, Ottawa), John Hill (University of Ulster), Rui Carvalho Homem (Universidade do Porto, Portugal), Richard Howells (University of Leeds), Dennis Kennedy (Queen's University, Belfast), Allison Murphy (Ulster Titanic Society), Maureen Murphy (Hofstra University, New York), Gerald Parker (Université du Quebec à Montreal) and Tim Wilson (Kingston).

I would like to thank the University of British Columbia for a number of travel and small research grants over the past few years; Patrick Dunn and David Truelove at Resource Sharing Services, Koerner Library (UBC); the support staff of the Department of English (UBC), especially Dominique Yupangco; and the Media Group (Biomedical Communications, UBC). I am grateful to individuals at institutions for inviting me to give a lecture or conference presentation on the *Titanic* phenomenon (thereby pressing me to quicken the pace of my reading and research), including Pam Cook (University of Southampton), Brian Hanna and Ian Adamson (Belfast City Council), Michael Larsen and Brian Robinson (Saint Mary's University, Halifax), Una Reilly (Ulster Titanic Society), Mark Vessey (Green College, UBC) and Robert Welch (University of Ulster).

I am especially indebted to Brian Cosgrove and Patrick Duffy for enabling me to serve as National University of Ireland Visiting Professor at NUI Maynooth in 2001 and President WJ Smyth for the hospitality the university offered me; the second of my three public lectures was on *Titanic* and the Machine Age. I am equally indebted to Ken MacCrimmon (Director) and his staff at the Peter Wall Institute for Advanced Studies (UBC) for providing me during my stint in 2001 as UBC Distinguished Scholar in Residence with the most stimulating and congenial of spaces in which I finished writing *The Age of* Titanic. Thank you Ken, Chris, Dale and Katie. Above all, I want to thank my wife Gail Malmo for her thousand virtues.

Contents

A SEAMAN, A FOREIGNER — AND WOMEN: THE CREW AND PASSENGERS OF ONE OF THE "TITANIC'S" LIFE-BOAT AFTER THE DISASTER.

Illustration from Illustrated London News *of April 20, 1912. Caption reads 'a seaman, a foreigner – and women: the crew and passengers of one of "Titanic's" life-boats…'*

Introduction

A sudden blow: the event it engendered stretched over tense days and weeks. Details were at first garbled and uncertain and driven by rumour. Those safe elsewhere were at first stunned and disbelieving; the thing was not possible. At first in the United States, and progressively around the world, people clamoured for more information and the media tried to feed their hunger. News organisations competed for scoops and fresh angles. In the days after, there were countless church and memorial services, innumerable sermons preached across the English-speaking world and beyond. There was an outbreak of religious sentiment and it was one of those occasions when ministers and priests were called upon to assuage the pain.

A great many people died, and the horror of this, combined with the unprecedented scope of such a disaster, caused widespread consternation and depression; society had sustained a severe shock and reeled from it. There was an upsurge in patriotic sentiment in America and Britain. There were inquiries and painful self-examinations. The fatalities were only part of the magnitude of the event: a manmade creation, object of pride and even arrogance, and vast into the bargain, had been brought low. Whatever emotions (including anger) came after, at first the dominant feeling was one of stunned humility, a chastening disbelief.

It gives pause that these paragraphs could describe either what befell RMS *Titanic* on April 14–15, 1912, or what befell the World Trade Centre on September 11, 2001. There are, of course, important differences between the twin calamities. We can speak of the *enormity* of the September 11 tragedy but not of the April 14–15 tragedy, since enormity refers to an atrocious crime. And although there were some who thought of the *Titanic* owners and managers as culprits, what happened to the liner was not calculated nor the result of terrorism or dreadful sabotage.

And whereas 1,500 died when *Titanic* went down, 3,000 perished when the Twin Towers collapsed. And yet we have to remember that the population of the United States in 1912 was less than a third of what it is today, and that a death toll of 1,500 in the earlier disaster had if anything a larger impact on society. But both roll-calls of the dead were in fact international; many nations supped sorrow with the spoon of grief when each tragedy occurred. The internationalism of the event in each case enlarged both its impact and its repercussions. In the same manner did the glamour, wealth and prestige of the fallen creation: the World Trade Centre (tallest buildings in North America) and *Titanic* (largest ship in history until then). In ship and towers were men and women of achievement; if in the towers they were not themselves among the wealthiest of citizens, they were the agents of wealth and the means of glamour, which is why the Centre was targeted.

In consequence of both disasters, new laws were swiftly enacted, new rules and regulations drafted, the map of communication re-drawn. The context was international tension and the threat of war. *Titanic* and her sister liners were obliquely engaged in a European competition that declared itself openly and savagely a mere two years later with the outbreak of the Great War. It was a widespread belief when *Titanic* sank that the foundation of the western world had shifted. An era had been shattered and a new fearful episode of human history had begun. If the *Titanic* disaster effectively or symbolically inaugurated the twentieth century, September 11 announced the start of the twenty-first. With both calamities, all was changed, changed utterly, to adapt William Butler Yeats, a poet of the time who specialised in identifying the moments of violence in human history that were cataclysms and after which nothing could be the same again.

But in the case of the *Titanic* disaster, it is possible to see fairly clearly at this range in time how the culture in some ways awaited the sinking. This is the subject of *The Age of* Titanic. The long-term and even the immediate causes lay in the culture itself. The conduct and reactions of the officers, crew and passengers, and those on dry land when apprised of the horror, were in the main culturally determined. The response to the tragedy in newspapers, churches, books, poetry, cinema and song had in fascinating ways already been formulated.

For example, if the calamity was the outcome of the Machine Age, it nonetheless instantly became a case in point for the spiritualist revival of the Victorian Age. Partisans, zealots and opinion-makers of all kinds were ready to receive the facts, or even the hearsay, of the tragedy as evidence for their cause. Christianity reasserted itself, despite the inroads spiritualism and materialism (sometime in cahoots) had made. Perhaps the most surprising example of cultural preparation is the way in which the folk art tradition of African-Americans readily absorbed the *Titanic* disaster and with socially conscious irony, since there were no African-Americans on board. All the while, the language and idioms in which the tragedy was reported and debated in Britain and America were familiar to the culture, as were the images, forces and themes that were deployed. These included ice and icebergs, the far North, the abyss and the ocean deeps, omens and pre-visions, and the marvel of wireless communication, and these all revealed the fascinations and anxieties of the time.

The issues of the relations between the classes, races, and sexes that the sinking aroused were already alive, and were, during that awful night to remember, vexed to nightmare. It was even thought by some in 1912 that there was only one issue, that women, workers and non-whites suffered alike the disadvantages of alleged inferiority to privileged white men. Since in what follows I have not discussed in detail the *Titanic* version of one of these issues, the 'Woman Question' (as it was called) – and which Steven Biel in *Down with the Old Canoe* (1996) has dealt with in an exclusively American context – a few comments of my own here might be in order.

The 'story that came up from the sea', as the first number of the anti-suffragette journal, *The Woman's Protest* (USA., May 1912), put it, was regarded by some as telling against the campaign for female suffrage: boats for women cancelled the need for votes for women. Replying to 'Man', an article in *The English Review* (1912) by the playwright, essayist and suffragette, Cicely Hamilton, 'Homunculus' insisted that 'those men were lovers who put the women in the boats and went down with the Titanic. They did the noble, the beautiful thing. But a woman is always the beautiful thing: as girl, as beloved, as mother. It is her privilege, as the weaker vessel'. There were women on board *Titanic*, some of them strong and successful women, who thought along similar lines. But some anti-suffrage champions turned combative. Charles H. Parkhurst (whom we shall meet again) felt hounded by 'cantankerous viragos' and hysterical termagants and wrote in the New York *Journal*: 'One would suppose that those women who are making it a part of their creed to lampoon the members of the other sex ... would wince a little under the superb courtesy accorded to them at the wreck of the Titanic'.

But Hamilton in *Marriage as Trade* (1909) saw chivalry as a code maintained by a superior on behalf of an inferior and repeated the claim in 'Man' after *Titanic* sank. When, as reported in the *New York Times* of April 21, 1912, the suffrage activist Sylvia Pankhurst was asked if the chivalry on the sinking *Titanic* contradicted suffragette assumptions, she replied that the gallantry displayed was merely a matter of rule, that there was no special chivalry attached to it. The Philadelphian suffragist Lida Stokes-Adams (reported in the same paper) thought that women passengers should have insisted that the lifeboats be filled with equal numbers of men and women; like the anarchist Emma Goldman she regarded events on board as a setback for sexual equality. It was with heavy anti-suffrage irony that the editor of the *Girl's Own Paper* (UK) wondered aloud what happened to the equality claim when the ship was going down. Charlotte Perkins Gilman in her magazine *The Forerunner* (May 1912) identified the 'natural base' of the Women First custom as the value of motherhood and paid tribute to those women on *Titanic* who refused chivalry, who waived 'this sex advantage' and chose to 'die like brave and conscientious human beings, rather than live on a wholly feminine basis'. She might have mentioned Edith Evans, who will play a role in my story.

Rev. Dr Leighton Parks (USA), preaching on the chivalry aboard *Titanic*, thought that complete equality would lead to base Darwinian struggle. The gentleman, the chivalrous male, was not just an idea but a force pitted against bestial struggle. But it seemed to some to require belief in a higher power, and so Leslie Stephen (the father of Virginia Woolf) wondered if it were possible 'to live and die like a gentleman' without a belief in God. The Christian reaction to the *Titanic* disaster was in part a reaction to the growing empire of unbelief in the Age of *Titanic*.

The sailing and sinking of *Titanic* involved relations between the nations as well as between the races, classes and sexes. The discrepancies of Anglo-American culture in 1912 and 2001 betray a difference between the twin calamities. In the immediate aftermath of September 11, the United States and the United Kingdom drew ever closer as allies and partners. This was possible because the growing disparity between the two countries since 1912 in power and influence had by the end of the twentieth century lessened to negligibility the rivalry that was active in the Age of *Titanic*. Around 1912, a fervent Anglo-Saxonism and search for amity (if not unity) by the two nations, juxtaposed with a growing sense of friction, jostle and mutual irritation (with Europe suffering as usual the effects of America's growing pains), caused a rich cultural ambiguity. It was fitting that *Titanic* was steaming westward towards the New World with its luxury, power and artistic talent on board. *Titanic* sailed and sank in the choppy cultural cross-currents of the Atlantic, which became apparent as soon as the United States Senate decided to have an immediate and full-blooded inquiry into the disaster. At least in the short run, April 14–15 prised the two great nations apart as September 11 drew them together again.

The most famous passenger on board *Titanic* sought to bring the two great nations together. This was WT Stead: most renowned newspaperman of his day, tireless editor and reviewer, eminent spiritualist, social justice campaigner. Stead was an admirer of the United States whilst being an English patriot; he advanced the cause of English-speaking union and was on his way to a religious peace congress in America when *Titanic* met the iceberg.

Because of his versatility and because many claimed his spirit returned after his drowning, Stead looms large in this book. He can seem to be everywhere one turns when exploring the *Titanic* disaster. Indeed, Grace Eckley in *The Steadfast* Finnegans Wake (1994) all but convinces me that Stead was the original for that protean Everyman of James Joyce's titanic novel, *Finnegans Wake* (1939) – Henry Chimpden Earwicker, aka Haveth Childers Everywhere. We do know from Richard Ellmann, biographer of Joyce, that the great novelist listened on his birthday in 1928 to his friend Robert McAlmon sing 'a negro blues' about the *Titanic* disaster, and Eckley reminds us that a *Titanic* allusion has been detected in *Finnegans Wake* in the line 'It's our last fight, Megantic, fear you will', which incorporates the name of a White Star liner and the refrain of Huddie Leadbetter's famous song about the ship that is perhaps what McAlmon sang: 'Fare thee well, *Titanic*, fare thee well'. She provides lavish circumstantial evidence for the ghostly presence of Stead in Joyce's novel. If, as Eckley assures us, Stead was warned before his departure from Southampton by Cheiro (the famous palmist Count Louis Hamon) to fear death by water and beware of travel during April, he joins a select band who received the same caution that surfaced in TS Eliot's modern epic poem *The Waste Land* ten years later.

Despite his ubiquity, Stead is only one among several remarkable figures, either on board *Titanic* or safe but shocked on terra firma, who inhabited Anglo-American culture in the Age of *Titanic*. The liner was the product of this culture but also helped define it, and, of course, its loss brought to a powerful convergence many of those preoccupations of the culture that threatened its integrity and helped to usher in the modern era.

1. MR. F. CLARKE, OF LIVERPOOL. 2. MR. P. C. TAYLOR, OF CLAPHAM.
MR. G. KRINS, OF BRIXTON, SOMETIME OF THE RITZ HOTEL ORCHESTRA. 4. MR. W. HARTLEY (BANDMASTER), OF DEWSBURY. 5. MR. W. T. BRAILEY, OF NOTTING HILL.
6. MR. J. HUME, OF DUMFRIES. 7. MR. J. W. WOODWARD, OF HEADINGTON, OXON.

Titanic musicians with Wallace Hartley (centre).

one

A Mechanical Age

for one sad century
machines have triumphed, rolled us hither and thither.
D.H. Lawrence, 'The Triumph of the Machine'

A Mammoth and Marvellous Machine

The novelist Joseph Conrad noted at the time that the sinking *Titanic* was nothing more than a 'holed, helpless, big tank', a monstrous salmon tin, in which heroic death was unlikely if not impossible. The question of heroism aside, we can at least allow what Conrad called 'the unsentimental truth' of his description of the stricken ship, certainly from the terrified perspective of those on board who watched the last lifeboats rowing away.

Yet many passengers had been reluctant to abandon the motionless 'salmon tin'. Its great size and bright lights (kept shining by the engineers to the bitterly cold end) maintained the illusion of safety and comfort, the illusion that they still inhabited the luxury hotel to which transatlantic liners had often been compared. Only when the awful truth sank in must this amazing machine have dwindled in the passengers' frightened eyes. An engineering marvel had become nothing more than an immense tank letting in water. Luxury became, for a while, mere utility (warmth amidst the cold of the subarctic night, light amidst the darkness, terra 'firma' amidst the drowning sea) and then a dangerous and at the last lethal uselessness.

A mammoth and marvellous machine RMS *Titanic* had been. It was almost 300 yards (274 metres) long and over 30 yards (27.4 metres) broad, with a displacement of 60,000 tons and held together by three million rivets; everyone at the time knew that it was the largest moveable object on earth. The ship had, from top to bottom, ten decks. From keel to navigating bridge, it had the height of an eleven-storey building. Its power of motion, its enormous carrying capacity and great speed (25 miles or 40 kilometres per hour) were enabled by its 29 boilers (containing 159 furnaces in all), most of them 20 feet long and 15 feet in diameter (its fuel on departure consisted of almost 6,000 tons of coal). Its two sets of triple-expansion

1

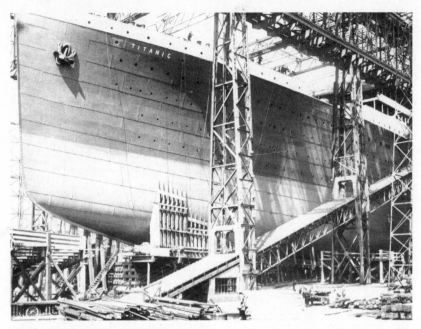

Titanic being prepared for launching.

reciprocating engines generated 30,000 horsepower exhausting into the steam turbine that, with up to 16,000 shaft horsepower, drove the four-bladed central manganese bronze propeller (16 feet, 6 inches or 5 metres in diameter) and the two three-bladed wing propellers (23 feet, 6 inches or 7 metres in diameter).

The propulsion system of *Titanic* was a machine attended by smaller machines. There were sundry contrivances associated with the working of the main engines – circulating and air pumps, heating and ventilation fans, ash ejectors, condensers. On the port side of the reciprocating engine room were the refrigerating engines. The builders of *Titanic*, Harland & Wolff of Belfast, were called in the July 1912 issue of *Engineering*:

> builders in the most complete sense of the word. As in the case of all vessels built by them, not only have they constructed the hulls of *Olympic* and *Titanic*, but also their propelling machinery, while much of the outfit usually supplied by sub-contractors for ships built in other yards has been manufactured in their own works.

In the shops of the vast shipyard, sophisticated tools and machines (some manufactured by other firms) were used to make not only the parts but also other tools and machines. Even so, outside factories did supply machinery and fittings for the ship. Davidson and Co. (Sirocco

Works) made the fans, Trewent & Proctor made the ash ejectors, Ross-Schofield made the boiler circulators, Hoskins & Sewell made the brass cot berths, and so on. *Titanic* was a giant product of an immense manufacturing network, despite the keen commercial competitiveness that drove each firm.

The professional writer Filson Young (BF Alexander), one of the first out of the blocks with a book on the tragedy, may have seemed melodramatic when he likened the *Titanic's* taking shape inside its gantry to 'an evil dream' and described everything about the ship as 'on a nightmare scale', but the famous photographs of the ship being prepared for launch justify the heated metaphors when we note the human figures dwarfed by the giant vessel looming menacingly far above them. The statistics of its inner and outer economy also justify them: the four funnels each 150 feet (45.72 metres) high and up to 24 feet, 6 inches (7.46 metres) across, the rudder 78 feet (23.7 metres) high and weighing 101 tons (102,616 kg), the centre anchor weighing over 15.5 tons or 15,748 kg (each side anchor weighed eight tons or 8,128 kg), requiring a team of 20 horses to transport it from the foundry to the dock. The famous photograph of the team in action resembles a scene in Lilliput from *Gulliver's Travels*, perhaps the one in which the Lilliputians transport Gulliver's hat, a scene in which worlds of different scales collide.

Electricity for light and power on board was generated by four 400-kilowatt (580 horsepower) engines coupled to dynamos collectively capable of 16,000 amps. Electricity was required for 10,000 lamps that

An eight-horse team transporting the centre anchor from dock to shipyard.

lit life aboard *Titanic*. Electricity also powered the ship's automation – working deck cranes, winches, passenger elevators, pantry and service lifts, ventilation and stokehold fans, cabin fans, gymnasium apparatus, workshop machine tools, the marconigram conveyor, kitchen machinery, electric heaters, electric baths, steam whistles, sounding machines, clocks, watertight doors, boiler room telegraphs and the fifty-line telephone system.

Although the engines of propulsion were shut down after the collision with the iceberg, this electrical system, and some of the heavy machinery, kept the ship alive though immobile. The uncustomary quietness in the upper decks (when the sound of escaping steam couldn't be heard) overlay feverish noise and activity below decks. 'Down in the engine room', Walter Lord reminds us:

> no one even thought of getting away. Men struggled desperately to keep the steam up ... the lights lit ... the pumps going. Chief Engineer [Joseph] Bell had all the watertight doors raised aft of Boiler Room No. 4 – when the water reached here they could be lowered again; meanwhile it would be easier to move around ...

Only fingers moved in the Marconi shack, but the energy of concentration there was intense as the wireless sparked and rapped. Lights burned in the ship until it started its downward plunge – the machine in that respect had not failed.

Vast though *Titanic* and her sister ship *Olympic* were, they generated rumours of even greater immensity, rumours that sprouted from a popular impression of unbridled luxury. The *Review of Reviews* told its readers in 1910 that the newly-launched *Olympic* would boast a tennis court and fishpond. In its account of this 'fifteen story floating palace', the *New York Times* of April 16, 1912 furnished the newly-lost *Titanic* with a miniature golf links and tennis courts 'with a coach on board to teach those who could not play'. In his sermon (or article), 'The Tragedy of the Sea' (reprinted in *Wreck and Sinking of the* Titanic, edited by Marshall Everett, 1912), Rev. Andrew Johnson referred witheringly to the 'golf grounds, tennis courts, swimming pools, promenades, elegant parlors and concert halls' on board the lost ship. There was one squash court on board and one swimming pool, but no tennis courts, golf course or concert hall.

The Acceleration of Technology
In mechanical design as well as convenience and luxury of appointment, *Titanic* and her fractionally elder twin *Olympic* were further refinements of the Atlantic liner, the evolution of which, starting with *Sirius*, the 208-foot-long pioneer steamship that crossed

the ocean in 1838, was called by the technical journal *The Shipbuilder* in 1911 'one of the most remarkable achievements in the scientific progress and commercial activity of modern times'. Harland & Wolff, and the company whose ships they built, The White Star Line, played a leading role in this achievement. 'The story of the association between the Belfast builders and the White Star Line', a writer in the journal *Engineering* told his readers in 1912, 'practically involves the story of the development of the Atlantic liner'. Liners designed and built by Harland & Wolff from 1870 (when *Oceanic* was launched) helped to chart the evolution of international shipbuilding. Though the liners became larger, more complex and more effective, they did not lose the aesthetic appeal first generated by the 'ocean greyhounds' of the later nineteenth century.

The ocean liner was only one of the technical accomplishments registered in the years before the First World War. The two and a half decades before the launch of RMS *Titanic* saw a striking sequence of technological breakthroughs that seem in hindsight to have made our contemporary world; when listed they compose an impressive and curious miscellany.

From celluloid film to pneumatic tyres to the internal combustion engine, great technical innovations characterised the years between the 1880s and the Great War. As automobiles, submarines, high speed ships and manned flight made their first appearance, innovations came rapidly. In 1909, Louis Blériot flew a monoplane across the English Channel, followed in 1910 by non-stop flights by other aviators between Albany and New York City and between London and Manchester (by which time the world altitude height had reached 4,100 feet or 1,250 metres) and in 1911 by a flight between London and Paris. By 1912 the oil-driven ship, such as the 300-foot-long (91.44 metres) *Selandia*, was a maritime fact; an 'oil motor' had powered the *Toiler* across the Atlantic the previous year. A backdrop to these often solo or national accomplishments was the huge-scale international engineering feat of the Panama Canal, well under way by the time *Titanic* was built and launched.

In Germany, as Modris Eksteins reminds us, there was a cult of 'technicism' that encouraged technical education and resulted in a far greater number of patents taken out by German industries between 1886 and 1900 than by their British counterparts. Of course, there had been a steady accumulation of scientific and technological accomplishments for some time, and it was Britain that led the way for decades. The same year celluloid was invented, 1887, the famous English biologist and controversialist TH Huxley had claimed that:

the most obvious and the most distinctive feature of the History of
Civilisation, during the last fifty years, is the wonderful increase of
industrial production by the application of machinery, the improvement of
old technical processes and the invention of new ones, accompanied by an
even more remarkable development of old and new means of locomotion
and intercommunication.

But in the quarter century after 1887 these increases, developments,
improvements and inventions accelerated.

The year 1912 maintained the momentum. In April – the fateful
Titanic month – it was reported that a giant Simplia motor car driven
by Louis Disbrow had in Jamaica reached a speed of 180 miles per hour
(289.62 kilometres per hour). On April 22, Corbett Wilson in a
Blériot monoplane made the first successful flight from Britain to
Ireland and four days later Vivian Hewitt repeated the achievement.
That same month, a Farman biplane was fitted with floats (following
Glenn Curtiss' innovation in San Diego, California in 1911), thereby
constituting a 'hydroplane' or 'hydro-aeroplane', capable of 'wonderful
feats.' It could rise from, as well as alight on, the water; indeed, it could
soon become airborne from ships with platforms, the aircraft carriers of
the future. In 1912 a young German-American, Grover Loening,
designed and built the world's first amphibious aircraft. The Fokker
aeroplane was introduced and Sopwith Aviation founded. In May
1912, the imminent attempt was announced to cross the Atlantic from
the island of St Vincent in the 195-foot-long (59.43 metres) dirigible
Suchard. It had been reported in March that the German air force was
to consist of 'cavalry aeroplanes' and 'artillery air-ships', the latter
capable of flying at 45 miles per hour (72.4 kilometres per hour) in a
calm and for 24 hours nonstop. The German-British rivalry gave heady
impetus to European developments in speed and power of locomotion
from around 1908 onwards. Military observers from the major
European nations routinely witnessed experimental displays of
airborne and land vehicles. In 1902 the stratosphere had been
discovered and soon after the German upper-air branch of meteorology
was christened 'aerology' – 'the newest of the applied sciences' – and
described for English readers in 1912 as indispensable to German
'aeronauts' in its practical form of aeronautical meteorology.

The new technology was soon at work in and around the home.
The vacuum cleaner, invented in 1901, was by 1912 a widely advertised
electric promise of the dustless home, and was one of those appliances
that spelled the imminent reduction of maids in the middle-class home,
thereby fractionally altering the class dynamics of English society. (HG
Wells was right when in 1901 he claimed that 'the enormous

development of mechanism' was 'the cardinal feature of the nineteenth century' and that it had changed not only the 'facies' of society but the social, particularly class formations that made up society.) The electric iron was introduced by a German manufacturer in 1912. A process for manufacturing cellophane was invented by Edwin Bradenberger in 1912. In 1912 one could buy 'fount-pens', 'book typewriters' (typewriters capable of writing in bound books!) and 'typograph' duplicators, as well as prismatic binoculars, foldable and capable of up to 25x magnification. The photostat (the early photocopying machine) was announced in 1912 in the United States. Machines, appliances and gadgets were revolutionising everyday life as well as offering exciting spectacles of derring-do by fearless experimenters.

Anxiety and the Machine

mechanical man, in triumph seated upon the seat of his machine…
DH Lawrence, 'The Triumph of the Machine'

The machine troubled the nineteenth century, even as it increasingly dominated it. There were those who were enthusiastic advocates and who had an almost utopian belief in the machine future. Charles Babbage, who invented 'calculating engines' – ancestors of our computers, attacked in his *Reflections on the Decline of Science and Some of its Causes* (1830) what he saw as a British 'anti-industrial spirit' and in *On the Economy of Machinery and Manufactures* (1832) sang the praises of applied science and the efficient organisational system of the ideal factory system. Andrew Ure in *The Philosophy of Manufactures* (1835) maintained that 'the blessings which physico-mechanical science has bestowed on society, and the means it has still in store for ameliorating the lot of mankind, has been too little dwelt upon'.

Ure was answered by John Fielden's *The Curse of the Factory System* (1836) which claimed that the increased avarice of factory owners had accompanied the improvements in machinery. But Ure's vision of a factory (which imagined an immense enterprise such as Harland & Wolff's shipyard or the operating system aboard *Titanic*, with its almost 900 crew members) was of:

> a vast automaton, composed of various mechanical and intellectual organs, acting in uninterrupted concert for the production of a common object, all of them being subordinated to a self-regulated moving force.

Life in the stokehold, however, reflected Fielden's rather than Ure's perception of workplace machinery. But an agenda of anxiety rather more sophisticated than Fielden's was established in Britain by

Thomas Carlyle in 1829. In 'Signs of the Times', the Scottish writer
dubbed his age 'the Mechanical Age ... the Age of Machinery' and saw
the machine's power of change everywhere around him. The sailor, for
example:

> furls his sail, and lays down his oar; and bids a strong, unwearied servant
> [the vapour or steam engine], on vaporous wings, bear him through the
> waters. Men have crossed oceans by steam .... There is no end to
> machinery.

He acknowledges the physical benefits to humanity of machinery, the
'wonderful accessions . . . to the physical power of mankind'. He
thought of the early masters of steam engines as heroes, and of the
Industrial Revolution as a dynamic achievement. He considered the
noise of Manchester awakening on a Monday morning, 'the rushing-
off of its thousand mills, like the boom of an Atlantic tide,
ten-thousand times ten-thousand spools and spindles all set humming'
as 'sublime as a Niagara'.

Yet when human beings war with 'rude Nature; and, by our
resistless engines, come off always victorious, and loaded with spoils',
something is wrong. Carlyle is balanced between pride in the human
subjugation of nature and disdain for the underlying arrogance.
Decades later, HG Wells made plots out of this ambivalence. Wells'
unsuspecting humans at the end of the nineteenth century go about
'serene in their assurance of their empire over matter', as if the war
waged by machines against nature had been won for good, though the
machine-beings from Mars are about to invade them in The War of the
Worlds (1898). In The Time Machine (1895), a remote future in which
nature seems to have been entirely subdued into the appearance of a
garden turns out to be one in which nature's abject compliance has
weakened an unchallenged humanity and allows nature to reassert
herself. Besides, the machinery that enforced the compliance had been
sequestered underground in order that the Eloi could evolve an
aesthetic, life but comes vengefully to the surface in the form of those
dark machine-beings, the Morlocks.

Although he was happier than the Scots philosopher with science
and machinery, Wells confirms, as it were, Carlyle's claim that
machinery alters the social system. As far as Carlyle could see,
mechanization widened the gap between the rich and the poor and
concentrated wealth – these very issues rose quickly to the surface after
Titanic sank – and made mechanical our approach to fields of endeavour
quite distinct from the operation of machinery, made mechanical,
indeed, our very way of thinking and behaving. Wells' demonstration
in Anticipations (1901) of the impact of improved mechanical

locomotion on social relations (particularly through the steam engine) shows him a follower of Carlyle in his awareness of the broader role of machinery. ('Signs of the Times' began life as a review of three books, one bearing the Wellsian title, *Anticipation: or, An Hundred Years Hence.*) The world is no machine, Carlyle declared, and there is more to life than the clank of spinning jennies. 'There is a science of *Dynamics* in man's fortunes and nature, as well as of *Mechanics*', and it is in the 'Dynamical nature of man' that science and art originate.

The 'two cultures' of science and literature that Carlyle's chasm between cultural mechanics and dynamics anticipates has a bearing on the profound ambivalence with which such giant products of industrialism as *Titanic* and other ocean-going behemoths were greeted. Machinery was seen, deplorably, to be challenging nature, humanity challenging God. We associate the forking of the two cultures with Matthew Arnold, author of *Culture and Anarchy* (1868). 'Faith in machinery is', Arnold was sure, 'our besetting danger'. It encourages the confusion of means with end and obscures the true goal of culture which is a perfect spiritual condition, formation of character, the generation of sweetness and light. Those who invest their ultimate hopes in machinery are, in Arnold's word, 'Philistines'. Charles Dickens was also among the opponents of scientism and undue mechanization. With his familiar combination of highly charged realism and sentimental humour, Dickens attacked the tyranny of machines and the mechanical vision in his novel *Hard Times* (1854). Incidentally, Dickens did not enjoy his passage in 1842 across the Atlantic in the flagship of Cunard's first fleet, *Britannia*: with a scathing reductionism, he found his cabin a 'thoroughly hopeless and profoundly preposterous box' and the dining saloon 'a gigantic hearse with windows'.

Samuel Butler in *Erewhon* (1872) was more imaginatively exercised by machines, musing on their superior speed of development compared to organic forms, and their superior powers of calculation as well as stamina. Indeed, they seem on course to become something akin to animate; already they reproduce other machines systematically, a prospect that had caused dismay in Benjamin Disraeli: 'The mystery of mysteries', he wrote in *Coningsby* (1844), 'is to view machines making machines, a spectacle that fills the mind with curious and even awful speculation'. (This happened routinely in Harland & Wolff shipyard.) In the meantime, as Butler saw matters, the stoker, for example, below decks on a steamship, 'is almost as much a cook for his engine as our own cooks for ourselves'; machines such as steam engines are creatures with stomachs that feed like organisms and are therefore alarming. This tendency to see machines as near-animate, as Wells also does, perhaps underlay the intimate relationship some passengers forged with *Titanic*, and which later enthusiasts of the great liner have also done.

More than 20 years later, HG Wells in his short stories 'The Cone' and 'Lord of the Dynamos' and his short novel *The War of the Worlds* created startling fictions out of Butler's concerns, depicting man-eating or man-destroying engines; he even contemplated the effects of a dangerous machine aesthetic. Yet like Carlyle, Wells saw virtue in the kind of work that discovered, invented and applied: work was a bulwark against introspection and doubt. We are familiar with the Victorian gospel of work and it was a motivating force behind the building of *Titanic* and other great machines. It connected in one direction with the almost subconscious desire to refashion the earth and subdue nature, though the scientific project to subdue nature that had found eloquent expression in Francis Bacon more than two centuries before had been a quite conscious one. In another direction, the gospel of work connected with an English conscious desire to refashion the world and further civilization under English leadership. In yet another direction, it connected with the Biblical commandment (translated through Protestantism) to earn our human passage after the Fall by working off our guilt. The gospel held special sway in Protestant Belfast, *Titanic*'s birthplace.

Popularly we associate the gospel of work with Samuel Smiles, he of *Self-Help* (1859) fame, though the gospel was promulgated also by General William Booth, founder of the Salvation Army. Smiles' popular handbook to work and self-reliance exalted experience and practice (which engaged with the *facts* of a matter) over book-learning and theory, neither of which led to wisdom and both of which were devoid of moral force. This too had Baconian origins. (Other Smiles books addressed *Duty* and *Thrift*.) The philosophy of *Self-Help*, at base Christian and Protestant, complicated the simple distinctions between mechanics and dynamics, science and the humanities. It helped to create a climate of ideas inhabited by more complex figures such as Rudyard Kipling and Joseph Conrad, both proponents of work. After all, despite the ideal of virtual leisure for human beings in the factory achieved by machinery which would perform all the work, the most work was, as things stood, demonstrably performed by those closest to the machines.

A Chivalry of Labour
Harland & Wolff began operation in 1858. Smiles dubbed the two men 'the true Watt and Boulton of Belfast.' (This was high praise:

James Watt the famous Scots engineer and inventor stands to Matthew Boulton as Edward Harland stands to Gustav Wolff: Boulton was Watt's partner and introduced Watt's steam engine to Britain.) Harland, the managerial and engineering brains behind the firm, had come from Yorkshire to Belfast in 1853. He said that he was brought up in a house of 'industry and mechanism', an upbringing that Max Weber would have recognised as conducive to the Protestant work ethic. His father was an engineer and inventor who had befriended George Stephenson; young Edward was to serve his apprenticeship under George's son, in Messrs. Robert Stephenson & Co., Newcastle. George Stephenson the famous inventor later provided Smiles with an exemplar of the self-made man schooled in the no-nonsense college of adult life.

Fifteen years before *Titanic* sank on her maiden voyage, Harland contributed a chapter on 'Shipbuilding in Belfast – Its Origin and Progress' to Smiles' *Men of Invention and Industry* (1897). Smiles' own chapter on Irish manufacture shows him to be a hard-headed latter-day Arthur Young, the famous eighteenth-century English explorer of Irish industry and agriculture; Smiles was a firm believer in *national* self-help and his chapter bristles with practical advice for the Irish to this end. Smiles had earlier written *History of Ireland and the Irish People* (1844), in which he extolled the spirit of what he would later have called self-help in Daniel O'Connell's Catholic Association and all Irish attempts to better their lot and escape from the inhibiting government of England. (He would no doubt have praised the later Irish Ireland movement and the self-help movement begun by Sinn Féin, Gaelic for 'Ourselves').

Smiles recognised the growth of machinery as the key to Belfast's success, 'one of the most prosperous and enterprising towns in the British Islands'. When his party visited Harland & Wolff in 1883, 'we passed through the roar of the iron forge, the clang of the Nasmyth hammer, and the intermittent glare of the furnaces – all telling of the novel appliances of modern shipbuilding, and the power of the modern steam-engine'. But these machines simply reflected what Smiles called 'the power of individuality', personal enterprise, an idea that John Fielden, Charles Dickens and Matthew Arnold would have found unintelligible but which permitted a Protestant dimension to mechanism.

Harland's history and the history of his successor at the wheel of Harland & Wolff, WJ Pirrie, are very nearly the history of the heroic age of shipbuilding in Belfast that culminated in *Olympic* and *Titanic*. More than Pirrie, however, Harland was a designer and engineer and

Samuel Smiles

it was these strengths that presumably endeared him to Smiles, author of *Lives of the Engineers* (1878-1904). Smiles in his book on invention and industry is celebrating the achievements of what was virtually an underground culture, as far as an English culture-giver such as Arnold is concerned (and despite the scientific sympathies of such eminent figures as TH Huxley and John Ruskin).

In his fine book, *Travelling Palaces: Luxury in Passenger Steamships* (1913), RA Fletcher devotes an admiring chapter to the engineers who ministered to the machinery of propulsion on steamships. To him, they were men as alert of ear as music conductors or instrument tuners. Self-consciously, Harland prefixes a Baconian quotation from Ralph Waldo Emerson to his chapter (much as Thomas Andrews, co-designer of *Titanic* was later to use a phrase from Ruskin on his Christmas cards):

> The useful arts are but reproductions or new combinations by the art of man, of the same natural benefactors. He no longer waits for favouring gales, but by means of steam he realises the fable of Æolus' bag, and carries the two-and-thirty winds in the boiler of his boat.

But culturally, Harland knew he was coming from behind. It is hardly surprising that the engineering staff from Harland & Wolff, all of whom went down with *Titanic*, are the largely unsung heroes of the tragedy. They are rarely depicted, for example, in the melodramatic screenplays of *Titanic* motion pictures.

But Wells characteristically picked them out as an island of efficiency amidst a sea of slapdashery on board the liner that fateful night. 'In the unfolding record of behaviour', he wrote of the night *Titanic* sank, 'it is the stewardesses and bandsmen and engineers – persons of the trade-union class – who shine as brightly as any'. Conrad saluted the engineers on *Titanic*, when he claimed: 'I know very well that the engineers of a ship in a moment of emergency are not quaking for their lives, but, as far as I have known them, attend calmly to their duty'. Like Kipling and Conrad, Wells praised the efficiency of technical operation that likewise lent meaning to a threatening chaos

Joseph Conrad

Rudyard Kipling

Bram Stoker

HG Wells

Laureates of Efficiency

or hollowness. Well-oiled, well-maintained, smoothly running machines were a kind of model for human effectiveness. Conrad's famous novella *Heart of Darkness* (1902) depicted the dire results when the vigilance, self-restraint and control required by human organisation (including the efficiency of machines) are thrown overboard. This is not to deny that Conrad had severe reservations about the deleterious effects of engines on seamanship; he believed that the 'new seamanship', which blindly trusted the power of steam to surmount obstacles in the way of the ship, had helped to cause the *Titanic* disaster. His reservations had been expressed even more boldly forty years before by Admiral Rous, quoted by Ruskin as claiming that 'Steam has, of course, utterly extirpated seamanship'. But for the engineers themselves, tenders of the engines, Conrad had nothing but praise.

In Kipling, Conrad and Wells, all of whom reacted strongly to the *Titanic* disaster and none of whom could be regarded as liberal humanists, the figure of the engineer is a socially neglected yet necessary and saving presence in modern society. Wells went as far as predicting in *Anticipations* the emergence of virtually a new social class in the re-formations brought about by mechanical advance. He foresaw that 'the unorganised myriads that one can cover by the phrase "mechanics and engineers"' – not just 'the black-faced, oily man one figures emerging from the engine-room' but the sanitary engineer, the mining engineer, the electrical engineer, the railway maker, the motor-builder – would over time 'tend to become an educated and adaptable class'. Out of the 'muddle' which, like Kipling and Conrad, he thought of as 'the enemy', Wells predicted that 'a new sort of soldier will emerge, a sober, considerate, engineering man'.

These anticipations of Wells' have not come to pass, though an impressive number of his have done. The social diversity that has transpired since he made his predictions has not included Wells' distinct class of elite engineers; the post-manufacturing service economy in many previous centres of industry, including Belfast, has made it an impossibility as far ahead as we can see. Unlike Wells, the liberal humanist EM Forster was later to half-embrace the anti-mechanical humanness of 'muddle' (a favourite word of his, and indeed of Wells and Conrad) and seems in retrospect, with *Titanic* sunk, to have been realistic. Moreover, we might read Forster's 1909 short story, 'When the Machine Stops', as both a satire of Wells' technophilia and a minor anticipation both of the fate of *Titanic* as machine and the opinion of some after the disaster that a machine so large and arrogantly fleet deserved to stop (and be stopped). In the story, the 'Machine' controls our future subterranean world (shades of *The Time Machine*); but one day, after a gradual winding down, the Machine stops and the uniform world as we understand it ends. There were those at the time, and commentators since, who believed that when *Titanic* crashed, the incident was symptomatic of a larger kind of crash analogous to the current computer sense of 'crash' (i.e. the 'system was down') and the western world tilted on its axis.

Nonetheless, the engineer, minister to the machine, was an enlarging figure in the culture out of which *Titanic* grew. According to several social historians, there was a working-class elite in Belfast, an 'aristocracy of labour' composed of highly skilled workers, many of whom were employed by the advanced factories and shipyards. Thomas Andrews can be regarded as occupying the summit of this recently emerged aristocracy. The black-faced oily man, of course, was a necessary commonplace and played an intriguing and surprising role aboard *Titanic* as we shall see.

As in the case of several other important Wellsian ideas, the emerging mechanic elite had already been thought of by Carlyle, who, we are told, believed that

> England can be saved only by the emergence of a new, morally responsible, working aristocracy', a phenomenon he sees as much more likely to arise from the new middle classes than from the old aristocracy. His imagination was still fired by the vision of the Industrial Revolution as a grand creative achievement . . .

According to Carlyle, captains of industry could display the old heroic force and energy that was largely gone from civilisation. A captain of industry of whom Carlyle might have approved was Pirrie (later Lord Pirrie). Pirrie was born in Quebec of parents from County Down in the north of Ireland and his mother brought him back to Ireland as an infant. He entered Harland & Wolff at 15, was head draughtsman at 22 and 'master of the concern' by 27. The English journalist, peace activist, and mystic WT Stead, who was to lose his life aboard Pirrie's *Titanic*, considered him the product of a stock 'which was welded into wrought-iron by John Knox, the Shorter Catechism, and the Book of Proverbs'. Pirrie's philosophy – 'merit is becoming more and more the only determining factor in life, so that to-day the invitation to the youth of the world is "Go in and win"' – had an heroic ring. Moreover, it had obvious application to Ireland which had laboured under so many disabilities. Young Pirrie's mother devised a code of laws for her son and a set of maxims which he took to heart. She believed, for example, that 'simple industry and studious exactness would be the

Captains of industry: Gustav Wolff, WH Wilson, WJ Pirrie, Edward Harland

making of Ireland'. They seem to have been the making of Pirrie. Stead hailed Pirrie as the man who had 'built more ships and bigger ships than any man since the days of Noah'. He thought that in Pirrie:

> foresight, optimism, incessant industry, the selection of able lieutenants ... and every combination of mind and body, have been brought into requisition, united with unique powers of organisation, to build up the greatest business of the kind that has existed in the world since men first began to go down to the sea in ships.

Weber might have had Pirrie in mind when he profiled the Calvinist capitalist; Pirrie represented well the Protestant ghost in the capitalist machine.

Carlyle demanded what Walter E. Houghton has called a 'noble chivalry of labour in which the mill owners, united with their workers in mutual loyalty, should march forth to subdue the forces of Nature'. It is true that Pirrie declared for Irish Home Rule in 1911 (in the run-up to the Third Home Rule Bill at Westminster), as he had in 1893 during the debate on the Second Home Rule Bill, whereas the vast bulk of his employees were implacably opposed to it, wishing as unionists for Ireland to remain inside the United Kingdom. In this event, Pirrie did not march as one with his workers but nonetheless stood against sectarianism and refused to allow Catholic workers (assumed by Protestants to be disloyal republicans) to be expelled from his (overwhelmingly Protestant) shipyard. Pirrie's resolve surely made of him a Carlylean figure and he had risen, moreover, through the ranks, from apprentice boilermaker to managing director, accruing his expertise and position fairly and squarely through a good deal of Smilesian self-culture. Like Harland and Smiles, Pirrie was a great believer in the industrial resources of Ireland as a whole, in national self-help, and he was hostile to muddle and sentimentality. It is not a contemptible social vision, and it is a great pity that it later shrank in Ireland into sectarianism and that a sentimental yet often lethal romanticism overtook much of Ireland and helped to divide the island.

Yet, towering figure though Pirrie was, it is still Andrews – beloved by all the shipyard workers it seems – who even better answers Carlyle's conception of the 'right sufficient captain of men. A man without qualms or fantasticalities; a hard-headed, sound-hearted man, of joyous robust temper . . .'

Thomas Andrews, co-designer of Titanic

As for J. Pierpont Morgan, the tireless American plutocrat who owned the International Mercantile Marine Company that in turn effectively owned the Oceanic Steam Navigation Company which in turn owned the ships of the White Star Line, headed up by J. Bruce Ismay, which in turn employed Harland & Wolff to build their liners – well, he had not been purged of Mammonism, Carlyle would no doubt have concluded, and therefore could be no right Captain of Industry.

A Titanic World

The ships themselves, the engines of all this intricate business (and the shipbuilding industry was itself a complex machinery of motive and action), were machines brought to a high degree of efficiency, culminations of the nineteenth-century preoccupation with mechanism and machinery. Later, we would see Victorian and

Edwardian mechanical genius as disguising the pathologies of that age. Perhaps the cultural preoccupation with bigness was one of those pathologies. The world's largest ship, *Titanic*, was launched from the largest single shipyard in the world. It employed 16,000 workers in 1912 and between 1907 and 1912 it *added* 165,000 square feet (15,328 square metres) in the shipbuilding yard and 223,000 square feet (20,717 square metres) in the machinery works.

Efficiency was another preoccupation of the day. Recovering from broken health and the death of Sir Henry Irving whose secretary he was, the author of *Dracula* seized the opportunity of journalism to start afresh, and for a special Irish number of the magazine *The World's Work* in May 1907, he travelled to Harland & Wolff's shipyard in Belfast and wrote a piece entitled 'The World's Greatest Ship-Building Yard'. Stoker visited when the new White Star liner *Adriatic* was nearing completion. He reported: 'The mere appearance of these vessels towering over one makes one exclaim, "Here we undoubtedly find Efficiency".' Efficiency indeed was a dominant motif in Edwardian culture and Stoker saw its embodiment in Harland & Wolff's. He saw 'genius and forethought … experience and skill … organisation complete and triumphant'. He took the dispensing of wages to 12,000 workers *in ten minutes* on Friday afternoons as proof of what he saw as 'the perfection of the establishment's organisation', the most remarkable of many remarkable things. Stead was to call the unwritten story of the yard 'an epic of modern industry' and this before the very different epic of the voyage on which Stead lost his own life. Stoker was greatly affected by the loss of *Titanic*, but died the day before the official American inquiry into it began.

The machines the yard built and the machines used to build them (and to make *those* machines) were steadily improved in the direction of greater reliability and efficiency. That meant, where engine-driven vehicles were concerned, greater and greater size (or carrying capacity) and greater and greater speed (of delivery of cargo, passengers or military payload). Size and speed became highly conscious cultural values. They became cultural imperatives and not just technical ambitions; they were functions of the new cultural engagement with time and space that was a portion of what later became known as Modernism.

Matthew Arnold had complained of the worship of size as early as 1868 but to no avail. The progress in size of White Star steamers between 1871 and 1910 is very nearly linear. International rivalry (behind which loomed military contention) incited greater speed and greater size. 'What *is* greatness?' Arnold asked forlornly, and gave his own answer: 'greatness is a spiritual condition worthy to excite love, interest, and admiration'. Nations were sure it meant the biggest merchant fleet, the biggest ships, the biggest air force, the biggest army. According to the *Review of Reviews*, Pirrie predicted in 1911 that by 1920 the 100,000 ton ship would be launched.

As if to promote his schedule, a mere five weeks after the loss of *Titanic*, the Hamburg-American Line launched *Imperator* whose keel had been laid in 1911, 909 feet long (*Titanic* had been 882 feet long), with a gross tonnage of 50,000 (the White Star liner had been 45,000), and accommodation for 4,000 passengers and 1,200 crew (*Titanic*: 2,400 and 890). But already by then, Cunard had announced that its *Aquitania* would be a foot longer than *Imperator*. This caused consternation in Hamburg, and *Imperator*'s owners replied by attaching a bronze eagle as figurehead, extending the ship by nine feet. The eagle's wing was soon washed away and the rest of the bird removed shortly after. After World War One, the German super-liner became Cunard's anyway, re-named *Berengaria* (after Richard the Lionheart's queen). In April 1913, a year after the *Titanic* tragedy, the Hamburg-American Line launched *Vaterland*, a 950-foot-long behemoth of 54,000 gross tons. In 1914, after a troubled three-month career, the great ship was detained in New York harbour after the outbreak of hostilities and was officially seized only in 1917 upon which it became a dazzle-painted American troop transport, renamed *Leviathan*.

Eksteins is of the opinion that Germany suppressed any anxieties about bigness by embracing the necessity of change, characterizing itself as a nation by a *Flucht nach vorne*, a flight forward. The country had achieved an industrial titanism of its own. By 1912, Germany had well overtaken Britain in steel production. Indeed, by 1914 its production equalled that of Britain, France and Russia combined. The national emphasis on scientism and efficiency, the cult of *Technik*, the hospitality to machinery, reached a peak around the turn of the century.

From the reckless expansion of countries (whereas France physically occupied Morocco in the European colonial fashion of the day, the United States accomplished its expansion simply by renewing the Monroe Doctrine that prohibited European meddling in the Americas) through corporate mergers and monopolies to the alarming enlargement of the ocean liners and aspirations of American skyscrapers, the age was apparently mesmerised by titanism. 'We have arrived at a new time', announced Winston Churchill in 1909, 'and with this new time, strange methods, huge forces and combinations – a Titanic world – have spread all around us'.

We find titanism as a motif in the literature of the time, in Thomas Hardy's novel *The Return of the Native* (1878) with the 'Titanic forms' of Egdon heath; in Wells' futuristic novel, *When the Sleeper Wakes* (1899); in Morgan Robertson's famous anticipation of the building and sinking of *Titanic*, his novel *Futility* (1898). Titanism is an early nineteenth-century Romantic strand in Victorian culture, what has been called 'the Titanic Romantic'. Carlyle was fascinated by the super-hero whose death he called 'Titanic', oddly enough a common misspelling of the ship's name when both the ship's building and its loss were reported. The Titans, after whom the great ship was named, were giant deities in Greek mythology. (*Titanic*'s sister ship, *Olympic*, was also named from ancient Greek culture.) The name *Titanic* was, as Sir James Bisset rightly said, both 'a masterstroke of nomenclature and a challenge to fate'.

The English Romantic poets were attracted to the Titans as rebels, as transgressors against the new gods who threatened to supplant them. Part of the hugely popular appeal, a mesmerising appeal as events proved, of *Titanic* (whose name made explicit the implicit arrogant claim to greatness staked by *Olympic*, *Britannic* and shortly after *Imperator* and *Vaterland*), was the half-conscious idea that the great liners were transgressive in their dimensions and velocity. This idea fed into the notion of *hubris*, a Greek word meaning overweening pride, of which the ship's fate was to many commentators an enactment. In some sense (if one could exempt the poor guiltless passengers and crew), *Titanic* deserved her fate. *Titanic*, then, was a late Romantic manufact, a cultural artifact, even before its tragic sinking. George Bernard Shaw, after the ship sank, attacked what he thought was the reflex and unthinking Romanticism of public reaction, the desire of people to have a narrative of the ship's loss, involving the gallantry of officers and the bravery of the Anglo-Saxon race, worthy of the Romanticism of the ship herself.

The God of Speed
If, despite Romantic associations, increasing size of machine, engine or vehicle was one component of what we might call progressive modernity, acceleration of speed was another. A new intense value placed on time and speed led to what was interpreted after the disaster as recklessness. When Captain Smith in practice ignored the repeated ice-warnings he received, he was (surprising though it was to hear) following the custom of commanders of ocean liners, as Second Officer Charles Lightoller made plain at the inquiries.

'There was no reason, I take it, why you should not go fast; but in view of the abnormal conditions and of the fact that you were nearing

ice at ten o'clock, was there not', he was asked by Thomas Scanlan at
the British hearing, 'a very obvious reason for going slower?' Scanlan,
a lawyer representing the National Sailors' and Firemen's Union,
wished to establish negligence by officers and owners. Lightoller
answered: 'Well I can only quote you my experience through the last
24 years, that I have been crossing the Atlantic most of the time, that
I have never seen the speed reduced'. If that constituted recklessness,
why, 'that recklessness applies to practically every commander and
every ship crossing the Atlantic ocean'. Lightoller took sharp
exception to his interrogator's use of the phrase 'banging on' and
insisted on describing the speed of *Titanic* through the ice-field as
'ordinary navigation, which embodied careful navigation'. RA
Fletcher a year after the tragedy persisted in justifying the fast passage
of the liners: '... speed makes for safety .... If the number of voyages
made and the small number of accidents be taken into account, it will
be admitted that speed makes for safety under practically all
conditions except that of fog' (*Travelling Palaces*). The author's
employment of the adverb 'practically' must have provoked a pungent
memory in his readers since *Titanic* had notoriously been called
'practically unsinkable' by her builders.

There was, added to the pressure of custom, the pressure of
schedule. This began in the shipyard itself on its production line. In
1910 there were 2,083 motors at work in Harland & Wolff; in 1911,
2,138 motors, and in 1912, over 2,200. These crucially speeded up
construction. For example, a five-ton travelling crane that used to
travel at 70 feet (21.33 metres) per minute and lift at four feet, six
inches (1.37 metres) per minute now travelled at 300 feet (91.44
metres) per minute and lifted at 20 feet (6.1 metres) per minute.
Businessmen shared this busy schedule: they wanted, and then
needed, to get themselves and their cargo to their destination as
quickly as possible. The New York *Morning Telegraph* (quoted by
Everett) reminded readers that 'Captain Smith went at high speed
because every one was in a hurry; because the persons on the vessel
wished to get to New York as soon as possible'. Besides, the rugged
competition among the shipping lines for the transatlantic route –
particularly among Cunard, Hamburg-America and White Star –
resulted in the prize for the fastest crossing known as the Blue Riband,
which *Lusitania* had taken from Hamburg-America's *Deutschland* in
1907, with the added satisfaction for Cunard when *Mauretania*
captured the prize from her stablemate.

When we add in the celebration of speed achievements by rapidly
improving engines and machines, the gross result was a general

worship of speed reinforcing the principle of seamanship aboard large transatlantic liners that considered maintenance of speed a contribution not a hazard to safety through icefields. James Bisset, second officer of the rescue ship *Carpathia*, and later to be commander of both *Queen Mary* and *Queen Elizabeth*, writes his memoirs as a man with his hands firmly on the ropes of life, yet he too sees in the *Titanic* tragedy something behind the undoubted recklessness of speed. The disaster:

> was too tremendous to be explained away by finding one scapegoat, or two, or three, to bear the brunt of the blame. It could be explained, and was explained ultimately, as the fatal culmination of a long and complicated sequence of interrelated causes which lay deep in human nature itself.

It certainly lay at least as deep as the widespread values of the time. It has been pointed out by Michael Freeman that by the 1850s in England, Greenwich or 'railway time' had become uniform throughout Britain, throughout the world by the 1880s. 'Ultimately the departure time of the milk train in country districts became the arbiter of milking time. The rhythms of rural life became inextricably part of the new industrial consciousness' (precisely what EM Forster lamented). Being 'on time' became part of the new momentum of life. As speed of travel increased, timetables were constantly revised, uniformity constantly made inadequate. Being on time meant being early, being better than punctual, being on record time, and this meant haste.

In Stephen Kern's reading, Captain Smith's behaviour was cultural rather than personal. 'The age', he writes, 'had its doubts and hesitations, but it was essentially characterized by hubris that ignored the warning messages and pushed the throttle full speed ahead'. He even sees the loss of *Titanic* as 'a simile for the outbreak of the war' two years later. The shortsightedness of the look-outs, the lack of safety precautions, the reliance on technology, the overweening confidence, the flurry of wireless messages, even the icebergs in the path of the liner – Kern finds larger scale analogies in the July crisis of 1914 that precipitated the catastrophe of the Great War.

In 1901, Wells published a short story, 'The New Accelerator', about a man who sets out to seek 'an all-round nervous stimulant to bring languid people up to the stresses of these pushful days'; but in the mind of the narrator (who has 'always been given to paradoxes about space and time'), the inventor Gibberne 'was really preparing no less than the absolute acceleration of life'.

One American cartoon commenting on the *Titanic* disaster depicted a cloaked skeleton (Death) at the wheel of the liner – the

THE HELMSMAN.
—Johnson in the Philadelphia *North American.*

ship's telegraph registering 'Full Speed Ahead' – whose cloak is labelled 'Speed Mania'. That phrase was a commonplace of the day; the *Brooklyn Eagle* observed tartly after the tragedy that 'the glacier's children do not get out of the speed maniac's way like the children of men'. Some identified speed mania as a cultural enemy. 'The trouble nowadays', the New York *Morning Telegraph* complained:

> is that people wish to go with a rush. Subway trains whiz along through the tunnels at top speed; automobiles dash through the streets at a speed of a mile in two minutes, and ocean liners tear through the water, each striving to break a record.

Rev. Andrew Johnson complained after the *Titanic* sinking that:

> People generally are too reckless and restless. There is witnessed on every hand, in all circles and realms of twentieth century activity, an untempered and untamed mania for sped. The regular movements of

modern machinery it seems can no longer satisfy this depraved and abnormal desire.

In 1909, the *Review of Reviews* quoted a writer in the *Cornhill Magazine* who identified 'speed-lust' as an uncomfortable factor in the present condition of things, a kind of 'madness, and whom it seizes it demoralises'. He even saw the contemporary craze for abbreviation in everyday language (*bike, bus, tram, pram, tube*) as another symptom of this disorder, and remarked sadly that in the old days fast living was counted a vice instead of a virtue. EM Forster may have read this observation, for in his novel *Howards End* (1910), he complains about the 'the language of hurry' used by Londoners, 'clipped words, formless sentences, potted expressions of approval or disgust'.

The *Literary Digest* (New York) reported in its April 27, 1912 issue that many editors around the world were attributing the loss of *Titanic* to 'speed madness'. Not surprising, then, the same magazine, when introducing its readers to the new French 'Syllabic typewriter', in its May 25 issue, said: 'The "speed-mania" extends much further than travel, whether on sea or land. Every one, no matter what he may be doing, tries for a speed-record ...' Advertisements may well be reliable

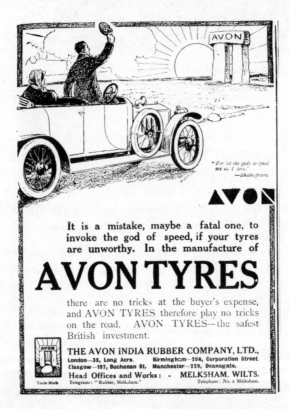

"*For let the gods so speed me as I love.*"
—*Shakespeare*.

AVON

It is a mistake, maybe a fatal one, to invoke the god of speed, if your tyres are unworthy. In the manufacture of

AVON TYRES

there are no tricks at the buyer's expense, and AVON TYRES therefore play no tricks on the road. AVON TYRES—the safest British investment.

THE AVON INDIA RUBBER COMPANY, LTD.,
London—35, Long Acre.　　Birmingham—204, Corporation Street.
Clasgow—197, Buchanan St.　Manchester—229, Deansgate.
Head Offices and Works: - MELKSHAM, WILTS.
Trade Mark　Telegrams: "Rubber, Melksham."　　　Telephone: No. 2 Melksham.

registers of popular notions and phrases. In its April 20, 1912 issue, the *Illustrated London News* carried an advertisement for Avon Tyres which depicts a happy motorist standing up at the wheel saluting with his cap a sunlit henge monument to Avon; there is an epigraph from Shakespeare, 'For let the gods so speed me as I love', while the text of the advertisement begins: 'It is a mistake, maybe a fatal one, to invoke the god of speed, if your tyres are unworthy.'

Speed risked collision. DH Lawrence predicted in his poem 'The Triumph of the Machine' that 'traffic will tangle up in the long-drawn-out crash of collision'. Such a collision had been predicted for a transatlantic liner. Writing in the *Atlantic Monthly* in 1910, Lieutenant CT Delaney drew attention to the laxities on board liners and prophesied that 'until some fine vessel with her precious cargo is sent to the bottom through collision, these things, I believe, will not be rectified'. Delaney gave two examples of near collisions while he himself was on watch, one between a liner travelling at 21 knots and an iceberg which the ship missed by a mere 20 feet (6.1 metres). He considered full speed across an ice-track madness yet it was a regular occurrence.

Collision was in the Edwardian air, we might say. It was already an English literary motif by the time *Titanic* struck the iceberg and sank. Hardy and Forster both depicted unhappy physical coincidences and the fatal collision of incompatibles in human life. Hardy's famous poem about *Titanic*, 'The Convergence of the Twain' (which first appeared in the Souvenir Programme of the Covent Garden theatrical benefit matinee of May 4, 1912), was thus a poem waiting, as it were, to be written, as the iceberg in the poem waited for the ship to rendezvous with it. The collision Hardy terms a 'consummation', congress between 'twin halves of one august event', and the iceberg a 'sinister mate'. But the mating is still a fatal conjunction of opposites and *Titanic* now lies on the ocean floor entirely out of her element, with sea-worms (as Hardy imagines it) crawling over mirrors meant to reflect rich faces on board. Hardy has fish of the dark depths ask: 'What does this vaingloriousness down here?'

Hardy had earlier depicted another fatal collision, between Tess Durbeyfield's slow cart and the morning mailcart, 'speeding along these lanes like an arrow' in *Tess of the d'Urbervilles* (1891), a crash that proves for Hardy's young heroine the blightedness of life and catapults her out of her element into a world suffering 'the ache of modernism', a world of tyrannical machines setting an inhuman pace for agricultural labourers.

Hardy's speeding horse-drawn mailcart is updated to the motor car in Forster's *Howards End* (1910); by 1910 in London, Spufford tells us, 'a declining fleet of fewer than 5,000 hansoms competed against 6,300 taxis.' Forster's car speeds through the English countryside leaving a dust cloud behind it, shattering the rural world depicted in Richard Jefferies, George Borrow, EV Lucas, Robert Louis Stevenson and other popular late Victorian writers, and in one chapter carelessly runs over a cat.

I wonder if Forster realised that this strand of *Howards End* was anticipated, of all places, in Kenneth Grahame's *The Wind in the Willows* (1908). Toad, Mole and Rat are strolling along the high road, leading their horse and canary-coloured cart, when they are overtaken by a 'cloud of dust, with a dark centre of energy, advancing on them at incredible speed'. A magnificent motor car:

> immense, breath-snatching, passionate, with its pilot tense and hugging his wheel, possessed all earth and air for the fraction of a second, flung an enveloping cloud of dust that blinded and enwrapped them utterly, and then dwindled to a speck in the far distance.

The horse rears and the cart crashes into the ditch (the scene in *Tess* echoes lightly). 'Road-hogs!' Rat shouts, an epithet many commentators, though not in so many words, called Captain Smith of *Titanic*. Toad is overtaken by speed-delirium and wants such a vehicle.

> 'What dust-clouds shall spring up behind me as I speed on my reckless way! What carts I shall fling carelessly into the ditch in the wake of my magnificent onset! Horrid little carts – common carts – canary-coloured carts!'

The popular English poet WE Henley in his long poem of 1908, *A Song of Speed*, sounds at moments not unlike Toad (and, as we shall see, the Italian futurist, Marinetti): 'Speed as a rapture:/And integral element/In the new scheme of life ... Speed, and a world of new havings ... The alert, aboriginal/Father of Ships;/And Speed! ... *Speed in the laugh of the Lord.*'

Lord Northcliffe had taken Henley for a drive in his new Mercedes and this was the rapturously anapestic result.

In his national profile, *The Condition of England*, first published a year after Grahame's rural fantasy but revised in the year of *Titanic*, CFG Masterman (a Liberal MP) likewise bemoaned the 'speeding up' of living that has 'charged all our high roads with wandering machines racing with incredible velocity and no apparent aim', driven by those who habitually violate the speed limit and destroy 'the amenities of the rural life of England'. Whole industries and even the growth of cities minister to 'our increasing demands for speed'. Indeed:

in all our mechanical ingenuities we have constructed masters for us,
rather than servants ... We are compelled, for example, to avail ourselves
of the telegraph and the telephone; we are driven to the express train, the
motor omnibus, the various expedients which are adapted to acceleration,
rather than to happiness .... If we do not adjust our lives to such
accelerations, we are swept aside or trodden under ...

Borrowing from HG Wells, Masterman sees the ordinary citizen with
'mono-rails running across his head, flocks of balloons and aeroplanes
clouding the horizon; everywhere on earth and sky the impression of
a hustling, distorted, dissatisfied energy, writhing into fresh forms of
grotesque invention'.

Forster for his part sees real and figurative collisions everywhere in
his Edwardian England. In *Howards End*, Margaret Wilcox shows her
disdain for upper-class contempt, male arrogance, and the new speed
and machine worship by jumping from the car after it hits the animal.
The speed is such that the impact with the cat barely registers, just as
ocean liners of the time ran over small craft without pausing because
they were unaware that anything had occurred. Margaret and the
other women are then treated to the tyrannical 'chivalry' of Charles
Wilcox, her stepson, who wishes immediately to evacuate all the
women from the two cars, as women were later evacuated from the
sinking *Titanic* by order of men.

Oddly enough, jumping from a speeding car was an image that the
American historian Henry Adams had already used in a letter from
Paris in 1905. The speeding motor car was both symptom and symbol
of a menacing eventuality; the American name for it, *automobile*, had
in it the possibility of pun. In his letter, Adams worriedly ponders the
effects of the contemporary acceleration of life.

> I don't know what is going to happen in the world, because the sequence
> of centuries has now brought us far beyond the elements of our old curve,
> and the acceleration of speed is incalculable; but all my figures lead me to
> conclude that the present society must succumb to the task within one
> generation more [i.e. around the 1930s]. Otherwise they will be running
> infinite power, that is, the stellar universe. The break-down must come
> with us, since we hold the mass of energy. Naturally I can help nothing,
> nor you, nor anyone; but at least we might stick together. We are all in
> the same automobile, and cannot jump.

In 1893, Adams had found the ocean steamship a more complex
vehicle for his sense of the future of civilization's energy, as we shall
see in a moment.

The fate of *Titanic* was, on a giant scale, a terminal object lesson in what concerned Hardy, Conrad, Forster, George Moore and other writers of the time. The novels of these writers are but the tips of the iceberg (as it were). Late Victorian and Edwardian culture was preoccupied with a universe of chance from which a jealous God seemed to be withdrawing; with a society in which the social classes collided more frequently; with a world of mal-adaptation that was the everyday reality of evolution; and with an epoch coming to an end not with a whimper but with the bangs of collision.

Chance permitted coincidences, the coming together of disparate events or things, what Hardy (whose novels are full of coincidences) called 'Crass Casualty' in his poem 'Hap', his title meaning happenstance or accident. By 1912 the poet seemed to believe instead that the *Titanic* calamity was evidence of something more than chance: some cosmic Ironist had caused it to happen. This accorded crudely with popular belief that the ship had been doomed. From the start she was referred to routinely as 'the ill-fated *Titanic*' and still is. Equally tenacious has been the idea that things might have turned out very differently, that the disaster was a chance affair, that there were those who had gambled and everyone lost. It may be no coincidence (!) that the Age of *Titanic* was one fascinated by gambling. Card sharps, or 'boatmen', as they were called on board, routinely plied the Atlantic on ocean liners and were for one reason or another tolerated as long as there was no trouble. It was, after all, an era in which gambling for high stakes took many forms, including stocks and shares, corporate takeovers, art purchases, land development, and even daring stunts of extraordinary variety. There was dare-devilry in the air. It was a golden age of reckless enterprise when huge winnings were possible.

Boatmen had already worked *Olympic* just before the *Titanic* disaster, as the *San Francisco Examiner* reported on April 10, winning $15,000 before smoking-room habitués realized they had been 'trimmed'. There were three, possibly four, professional gamblers on board *Titanic* travelling under assumed names in first-class cabins: George (Boy) Bradley who survived under the name George Brayton, Harry (Kid) Homer who survived as H. Haven and CH Romaine who survived as C. Rolmane. According to Walter Lord in *The Night Lives On*, the most famous gambler Jay Yates may have been aboard.

There were commentators who thought that *Titanic* sank because greedy shipowners and reckless officers this time lost a gamble on speed and size that previous shipowners and officers had apparently won. In the aftermath, the Baltimore *Sun* published a cartoon captioned 'The Steamship-Owner Gambled with Death, But Death Held the Cards'; it depicts this titanic head-to-head poker contest in a darkened game room. The *Literary Digest* of May, 1912 reported that in London, editorialists were blaming:

> reckless gambling on board the great liners as infecting officers as well as passengers, and inducing carelessness which spreads from the saloon to the chart-room. 'The travelling world has fallen into the delusion that every big ship is a life-boat herself. Theoretically the Titanic may have been unsinkable. Practically she was not. The Board of Trade has had a rude awakening from its dream of security.'

The machine, which in its automation seemed to grant immunity from trouble, as once God did, was in fact testament to a dangerous world of chance in which human beings had less control and defence than ever before.

Machine Modernism

Churchill's titanic world and the world of rapid acceleration sounded, and was, alarming. In the particular circumstances of the fast and gigantic steamship, the combination of size and speed was especially dangerous. In his second article on the *Titanic* disaster, 'Certain Aspects of the Admirable Inquiry into the Loss of the *Titanic*', Conrad reminded readers that a ship like *Titanic* was for its size:

> about as strong as a Huntley and Palmer biscuit-tin .... Just look at the size of such a tin, and then think of a 50,000 ton ship, and try to imagine what the thickness of her plates should be to approach anywhere near the relative solidity of that biscuit-tin. In my varied and adventurous career I have been thrilled by the sight of a Huntley and Palmer biscuit-tin kicked by a mule sky-high, as the saying is. It came back to earth smiling, with only a sort of dimple on one of its cheeks. A proportionately severe blow would have burst the side of the Titanic or any other 'triumph of modern naval architecture' like brown paper – I am willing to bet.

In his first article, 'Some Reflexions, Seamanlike and Otherwise, on the Loss of the *Titanic*', Conrad added the weight of a 50,000 ton ship to its disadvantages; the great ship is here to stay, but we should be disabused, he believes, of 'the modern blind trust in mere material and appliances' and in bigness and speed.

The repercussions of a collision involving a gigantic steamship travelling at speed were mathematically explained by Reginald Ryves to readers of the *Scientific American Supplement* of June 1, 1912. Contrary to popular belief, increased size, he pointed out, weakens a ship: 'the bigger the structure is, the larger is the proportion of its material needed to maintain itself and the less is the proportion available for service'. While it is true that a larger ship will usually sustain less damage than a smaller, the larger ship is a readier target and is more difficult to avoid (and to navigate out of danger). And speed is of the essence: 'Probably the directors of steamship companies have not yet fully grasped the fact that a ship traveling at 21 knots will, in full collision, do twice as much damage as a ship traveling at 15 knots'.

Ryves bemoaned the 'profound ignorance that exists on the subject of applied mechanics' in the daily newspapers. In those papers, as in the populace at large, was an anxiety that somehow machines had become too big, too fast, too dangerous, too out of control. This anxiety, which communicated itself to some marine engineers and seamen (including the retired seaman Conrad) was not felt by shipowners, and Emil Boas, General Manager of the Hamburg-American Line about to launch *Imperator*, was quoted by the London *Daily Mail* of April 17, 1912 as saying that 'if any lesson is to be learned from this accident it is to build still bigger ships'.

Yet danger, calamity, hazard, even violence, seemed to be unavoidable portions of the modernist project of which *Titanic* was a product. One particular group of modernists, the Italian Futurists, especially celebrated mechanically powered speed and welcomed the interdependence of man and machine. According to FT Marinetti, author of the *Manifesto of Futurism* (1909), and who was in England the month before *Titanic* sailed, the Futurists revelled in the 'morality of speed' and the 'reign of the machine'. The machine that generated speed was best. 'If prayer means communication with the divinity, running at high speed is a prayer', he wrote. One of his other manifestoes was *The New Religion of Speed*. On a visit to England in 1910, he lectured the English on the oddness of hidebound traditionalism 'in a people of explorers and colonizers whose enormous ocean liners have obviously shrunk the world'.

Most Futurists were painters (theirs was a portraiture of motion) but Marinetti was a writer whose 1909 manifesto included the following articles of faith:

> We intend to sing the love of danger, the habit of energy and fearlessness
> .... We affirm that the world's magnificence has been enriched by a new beauty: the beauty of speed. A racing car whose hood is adorned with great pipes, like serpents of explosive breath – a roaring car that seems to ride on grapeshot is more beautiful than the *Victory of Samothrace*.

Incidentally, the first annual Indianapolis 500 automobile race took place in 1911, a race from which almost every factor except speed has been removed: one merely turns left at constantly high speed for 500 miles (804.5 kilometres), as the British race-driver Stirling Moss once scathingly described it. Marinetti recalled a wild ride he and two friends took in three cars the evening they composed the *Manifesto of Futurism*. Their experience echoed that of the animals in *The Wind in the Willows*: Marinetti's car swerved to avoid two cyclists and overturned in a ditch. Retrieved, the car retains its functions of locomotion and speed but has had its ornamentation satisfactorily destroyed. Marinetti's eleventh article identified among the objects of Futurist celebration 'adventurous steamers that sniff the horizon' and 'shipyards blazing with violent electric moons'.

In 1913, Marinetti listed among contemporary significant phenomena:

> Acceleration of life to today's swift pace. Physical, intellectual, and sentimental equilibration on the cord of speed stretched between contrary magnetisms .... Man multiplied by the machine. New mechanical sense, a fusion of instinct with the efficiency of motors and conquered forces .... New tourist sensibility bred by ocean liners and great hotels (annual synthesis of different races) .... Negation of distances and nostalgic solitudes .... The earth shrunk by speed.

The same impatience was expressed by the London-based Vorticists – associated with Ezra Pound and Wyndham Lewis – who recommended the rush of new ideas and who 'blasted' their predecessors: their magazine was indeed called *Blast* (1914–1915), a title made retroactively appropriate by Lewis' later service on the Western Front (1916–1918) as bombardier and war artist, and commemorated in his punningly titled autobiography, *Blasting and Bombardiering* (1937). Vorticist paintings drew inspiration from the dynamic force lines of working machinery and the violence apparently native to machine forms.

The Futurists were well known enough to exasperate Anglo-American editors of such popular papers and magazines as the *Illustrated London News*, the *Literary Digest* and New York *Sun*. But in fact all revellers in machinery and speed, all transatlantic travellers, all users of the telephone and telegraph and the motor car, all privileged pilots or passengers of the early aeroplanes, were futurists. Minds bent towards the imminent future, whether out of materialism or hedonism. First-class passengers on *Titanic* and other liners moved by electricity and ether their stocks and shares via telegraph while they themselves were moved across the earth at 20 knots an hour. The novelty of speed caused men and women fully alive to the times they lived in to lean into the future, to think in terms of immediate effect. Others thought in terms of decades, centuries and millennia, even aeons ahead; it was an age of futurology (though the word was unknown then) and Wells, WT Stead, and Henry Adams were among the more famous futurologists.

Machines and the Spirit World

Little known as a futurologist but very well known as a rich man and controversial figure was John Jacob Astor who perished on *Titanic*. The wealthiest man on board was of the culture of *Titanic* in interesting ways, and it was imaginative of the German writer Robert Prechtl to make Astor the central character of his discursive 1937 novel, published in English as *Titanic* (1940). Astor was of the fellowship of American millionaires who turned first cabin on *Titanic* into the semblance of an exclusive club or board room of a global super-corporation. That fellowship included, famously, Isidor Straus, Benjamin Guggenheim and George Widener. They were eminent players, like JP Morgan, in the heyday of American plutocracy.

The size as well as luxury of *Titanic* must have appealed to Astor, since though he was a landlord of mixed reputation (owning what have been called deplorable slums), he specialised in raising immense and luxurious hotels in New York, the Waldorf, Astoria, Knickerbocker and others. Expanse is an index of corporate success, and his diversity of financial interest led the *New York Times* to refer to Astor's 'vast business activities'. The speed of the ship must also have delighted him: he took pleasure in fast cars. He sailed in his yacht *Nourmahal* through the southern Atlantic with his son in 1909 and a search was mounted when it was thought they had been shipwrecked. After his well-publicized divorce, he married the eighteen year-old Madeleine Talmage Force (who survived *Titanic*). Like the divorce, the marriage was something of a scandal, since the groom was forty-seven, and it was assumed he sailed with his bride to Europe on his new yacht *Noma* to escape the heat of publicity. It was by misfortune he chose to return by steamship.

All of this is compatible with the image of Astor we have inherited. Yet it should come as no surprise to learn that Astor had visited the engine room and boiler rooms of the ship, for Astor was a mechanical engineer of some ability with patents on several inventions including a brake for bicycles. One of his inventions, a pneumatic device for renovating macadam roads, was awarded first prize at the 1893 Chicago Exposition. The enthusiasm of the inventor enlivens Astor's 1894 science fiction novel, published a year before Wells' *The Time Machine*, which proves that in a passion for engineering as well as for the possible scientific future, Astor was a man very much of the Age of *Titanic*. He is caught in cameo in the memory of those who saw him after the collision, in the gymnasium, slicing a lifebelt open with his penknife to show his young wife of what it was made, and in the report that he went to a lower deck, with the presence of mind of a practical man, to release his pet Airedale.

The fiery American Protestant preacher, Alma White, wrote in her belligerent book on the calamity, *The* Titanic *Tragedy: God Speaking to the Nations* (1913):

> If a report had been circulated that there had been an explosion at the centre of the earth, which had moved it out of its orbit, it could not have been more shocking to the civilised world than the news that the *Titanic* ... was sinking by the head.

Ironically, in his novel, *A Journey in Other Worlds*, Astor imagined that by the year 2000, human beings had the technical wherewithal to alter the orbit of the earth. In order to equalize the planet's climate and make fertile the frozen regions, they straighten the axis of the earth, which is done by pumping out the Arctic Ocean in summer and refilling it in winter.

This titanic enterprise is made plausible both by the astronomical and engineering detail Astor offers in the novel and by the tally of technological achievements Astor's US government historian, Professor Cortlandt, presents by way of a summary of twentieth-century applied science. (The summary creaks badly as plot device.) In a preface, the novelist tells us that in the struggle between science and the classics (fought in England between Huxley and Arnold), science won the Blue Riband of culture. The combination of the machine and republicanism has emancipated us, and 'emancipated man goes on subduing Nature' (very nearly Wells' exact phrase in *The Time Machine*).

The past century's achievements that Cortlandt lists are Astor's predictions for the twentieth century from the perspective of 1894, which have come wholly or partially to pass: colour photography, 300 mph electric trains, videophones, live television transmission – through the 'kintograph (visual telegraph)' – universal metrication, electric automobiles, wind turbines, solar power, divided highways with phosphorescent lane-markers and variable speed-lanes, and capabilities very like nuclear energy and the superconductor. In the twentieth century, Cortlandt reminds his listeners, ocean liners eventually exceeded a thousand feet in length (the longest steamer in 1894 was White Star's *Majestic* at 575 feet; *Titanic* seventeen years later measured 882 ft) and generated 140,000 horse-power (*Titanic* would generate 30,000 horse-power); they passed through the triple screw stage to the quadruple and used both electric and solar power to drive half of their screws.

Having accomplished the straightening of the earth's axis, these enterprising Americans wish to improve earth's orbit to perfect our climate. Astor's Americans display that no-nonsense attitude and technical know-how for which Americans were already renowned, especially among themselves. It is an American inflection of the Victorian gospel of work: 'I think that all real progress comes through thorough work', a chief character remarks. This second mega-project involves a reverse gravitational force called 'apergy' by which intrepid pioneers can escape the earth's atmosphere and explore the heavens. The bulk of the novel relates their escapades on Jupiter, Saturn and 'Cassandra', in the spaceship Callisto. The novel combines adventure and extended exposition, Jules Verne-like, but tilts damagingly off its axis while fascinating the reader nonetheless.

Astor is weak on character but impressively strong on astronomy, geology and engineering. His explanations and specifications are more detailed than Wells', to the detriment of the life of the writing.

He has read to good effect AW Drayson's *Untrodden Ground in Astronomy and Geology* (1890), reports of the observations of GW Hough which Hough himself publicized in *The New Dearborn Observatory* (1889), and the work of the English geologist William Buckland (1784-1856). But for his feel for the mega-project and such a masterful character as Colonel Bearwarden, President of the Terrestrial Axis Straightening Company, Astor needed only his experience as a scion of a commercial dynasty.

A Journey in Other Worlds is wooden as a novel if interesting as a tract for the times, but can come alive when science opens the characters' eyes. The human Spirit who visits the explorers and who acts as a guide to the Otherworld, like Dante's Virgil (and Virgil is mentioned in the text), explains the mysteries of deep space in a convincing brief lyricism. There are some lively pages on which Astor imagines singing flowers, liquefied hydrogen rivers, winged lizards with fatal breaths, airborne jelly-fish, and creatures that achieve locomotion by the explosion of opposing gases self-injected into tentacles.

It may seem odd that Astor tempers his applied science with religion, but such an attempted alliance was commonplace in his day. His is an attempt to spiritualise materialism, a task on which WT Stead was also engaged. Astor is a firm believer in the power and potential of the machine and in Darwin's theory of organic evolution. But for him, both evolution and progressive mechanization will enable humanity to transcend materiality, to achieve fulfilment of the soul. Like Stead, Astor wants to bridge materialism, spiritualism and Christianity. 'Notwithstanding our strides in material progress, we are not entirely content', Cortlandt reminds his listeners;

> we feel a need for something else …. The historian narrates but the signs of the times [Carlyle's own phrase] and strives to efface himself; yet there is clearly a void, becoming yearly more apparent, which materialism cannot fill … with the exception of religion, we have most to hope from science.

The Spirit repeats Cortlandt's warning and assures his listeners that advances in science and reason will lead humanity to a proximity with the Creator.

The scientific adventure becomes quite early a projected colonization of outer space. It then becomes a spiritual quest with the Spirit as Guide, and even though this destabilizes the story which is two novels in one, it positions it firmly within the Age of *Titanic* as an attempt to exalt the machine without paying a spiritual price and an attempt to reconcile Darwinism with Christianity. 'Your preparation for the life to come', says the Spirit, 'can also be greatly aided by intercourse with those who have already died'. Here Astor falls into the idiom of Stead, arch-spiritualist as well as thick-skinned journalist and campaigner. Though both Stead and Astor cleave to a strange kind of Christianity, we might at this point recall the description in John Milton's epic Christian poem *Paradise Lost* (1667) of God bidding his angels after the Fall of man to tilt the earth's axis and alter its orbit to create the punitive climate Bearwarden and the others attempt to reverse. Astor's guiding and explaining Spirit resembles in his role Milton's archangels who explain mysteries and guide Adam and Eve. Both the spiritual need and the mechanical capacity intrigue Astor though he cannot convincingly connect them. Of the two, it is the mechanical that more seriously engages him, just as pride outweighs anxiety: 'this is', Cortlandt tells his audience proudly, 'more than ever a mechanical age', one in which the present is instinct with the future.

Titanic: Triumph and Failure

Futurism, wrote Marinetti, and identifying in machinery an effect that Wells and Astor and even Carlyle had identified before him:

> is grounded in the complete renewal of human sensibility brought about by the great discoveries of science. Those people who today make use of the telegraph, the telephone, the phonograph, the train, the bicycle, the

motorcycle, the automobile, the ocean liner, the dirigible, the aeroplane, the cinema, the great newspaper (synthesis of a day in the world's life) do not realize that the various means of communication, transportation and information have a decisive influence on their psyche.

Projecting improvements in machinery and technology were a way of realising and visualising the future, of both imagining it and possessing it.

A man as fond of projecting current trends into the future as HG Wells, WT Stead and John Jacob Astor was Henry Adams, and Adams calculated a simple geometry of time, space, energy and speed that permitted him to escape the notion of history as mere chance and human life a species of gambling. However, since his projection was either of imminent stasis or of imminent breakdown, his philosophy was not much different in effect from that of Thomas Hardy whose depiction of life and universe veered between randomness – 'hap' of the sort that some commentators thought the *Titanic* collision with the iceberg demonstrated – and a controlling cosmic force, neutral at best, malevolent at worst: 'The 'Immanent Will that stirs and urges everything' and 'Spinner of the Years' that pronounced 'Now!' the instant before *Titanic* struck the berg and that decides in 'The Convergence of the Twain' to have the ship and iceberg fatally rendezvous.

In 1893 Adams visited the Chicago Exposition (at which Astor had won his prize) and was astonished by the evidence of the mechanical world and the speed of its improvement, a world that seemed to reduce to 'babbling futility' the society that permitted such as he to persist in a 'childlike ignorance.' Stead too had been so impressed by plans for the Exposition that he devoted the 1892 Christmas number of his magazine *Review of Reviews* to telling his fellow Britons about the wonders of the Exhibition awaiting them. This number, entitled *From the Old World to the New*, contains a fictionalised account of a sea-voyage from Liverpool to the United States aboard the real-life RMS *Majestic* captained by the real-life EJ Smith, future commander of a sister White Star liner, *Titanic*.

Adams found the Cunard steamship company to have one of the best exhibits and he felt compelled to try

to calculate exactly when, according to the given increase of power, tonnage, and speed, the growth of the ocean steamer would reach its limits. His figures brought him [he speaks of himself in the third person throughout his autobiography], he thought, to the year 1927; another generation to spare before force, space, and time should meet. The ocean

steamer ran the surest line of triangulation into the future, because it was
the nearest of man's products to a unity ...

The question was whether this would be a benign convergence or, as
in Hardy's poem, a malignant conjunction. Either way, the modernist
project was courting danger and could clearly unravel or crash. Indeed,
as we saw, Henry Adams seemed to believe by 1905 that cultural
breakdown was entailed in socio-physical laws of acceleration and
power. The building and launch of *Titanic* followed by its break-up,
with all the cultural implications and ramifications, seem almost to
have embodied first the raised hopes and then the dashed hopes of
modernism; the catastrophe was in the richest of ways a modernist
event. This is not to deny that the ship began life as a triumph of
Victorian machine-worship and ended as a symptom of the deep flaws
in Victorian and Edwardian life and values. Modernism fed on that
Victorian machine-worship but turned it to aesthetic and
philosophical ends, trying in the process to distance itself from what
were already seen by the avant-garde as the sickness of Victorianism
and the debilitation of Edwardianism. Whether as Victorian or
modern symbol, *Titanic* induced the sense and sensation of triumph
and failure.

two

The Frozen Deep

Tragedy and Ice

Col. Astor was drawn to military figures. One of his sources, Major-General AW Drayson, formulated an astronomical theory of the causation of ice ages. This theory by the author of *Untrodden Ground in Astronomy and Geology* involved the motion of the earth's polar axis and provided Astor with the premise of *A Journey in Other Worlds*, itself a fictional treading of some new ground.

Drayson dated the climax of the last glaciation in temperate zones to 13,000 years before the present and its retreat at 7,000 years ago. Retreat was caused by a decrease in the obliquity of the ecliptic – that line in the heavens on which the moon must be for there to be an eclipse, and therefore the apparent annual path of the sun, a path which is a circle oblique to the equator. Among other phenomena, Drayson's theory accounts for the recent retreat of the polar ice-caps and what some Drayson supporters thought was an increased production of bergs.

Drayson's was a controversial theory formulated in his works of the 1870s through 1890s. It was from 1911 onwards that his supporters mustered in its defence, and as late as the 1920s the battle among astronomers and geologists was still being waged. In 1912, glaciation and ice activity were much in the minds of the educated, and the *Titanic* disaster sharpened a faintly apocalyptic cold air blowing through the late Victorian era and even the 'Edwardian summer', as the first decade of the twentieth century has been called.

In his draft of what became *After London* (1885), the English nature writer Richard Jefferies imagines the great city brought to its knees by a 'Great Snow'. During a three-week blizzard, a mad preacher asks of the starving and freezing citizens:

> Where now is your mighty city that defied nature and despised the conquered elements – where now is your pride when so simple and contemptible an agent as a few flakes of snow can utterly destroy it? Where are your steam-engine, your telegraphs, and your printing-press – all powerless and against what – only a little snow! (Quoted by Spufford.)

In so far as the elements were the handiwork of God, many preachers in the wake of the *Titanic* sinking asked similar rhetorical questions the next time they occupied the pulpit. In a more Darwinian spirit, the science writer of the *Illustrated London News*, Andrew Wilson, reminded readers a few weeks after the *Titanic* disaster that the aviator, locomotive driver, balloonist, shipbuilder and wireless-telegraph inventor were all at war with nature and that nature frequently retaliates. Nature, he wrote, is a watchful carnivore and man's duty is to keep out of range of its paws; by sailing a too northerly course, *Titanic* had failed to do that. On April 14, steam-engines of the utmost power met 'snow' in its most terrifying form – a looming iceberg – and were indeed powerless against it.

After the enormous loss of human life, the iceberg was popularly respected and feared because of its dumb indifference: nature at its most insentient. *Titanic* could, in contrast, be fancifully regarded not only as animate, but even as a refined female. In his memoirs, Sir James Bisset, Second Officer of the rescuing *Carpathia*, quoted Rudyard Kipling: 'The liner, she's a lady'. By this way of thinking, or imagining, *Titanic* had been the innocent quarry of a predatory force. Yet as an engineering accomplishment the ship had been extolled in part because *it*, not *she*, was a sheer machine of mammoth and neuter power. The collision between inhuman reality and human vanity could be seen as a collision between two kinds of brute monster or, instead, two kinds of machine. In the mid-nineteenth century, Joseph Rene Bellot sailed on two Arctic expeditions in search of Sir John Franklin, and his experience of icebergs led him in his diary to compare them with a manmade inhumanity. Spufford quotes him:

> I cannot find words enough to say of these icebergs, for which I panted so long at the peak of my feverish admiration ... nature no longer feels her heart beat in the slumber of the north; she is like the pitiless machinery which cuts off the arm which is caught between the cogs of the wheels .... Moral nature seems to have abdicated, and nothing remains but a chaos without a purpose.

Alternatively, the *Titanic* iceberg and its companions were like primitive creatures who had strayed malevolently out of their range, imposing themselves on the consciousness of the passengers and readers alike. In his 1930s long poem *The Titanic*, the Canadian poet EJ Pratt saw the melting berg that sank the ship as 'nothing but the brute/And palaeolithic outline of a face', a creature that lurches and shambles 'like a plantigrade'.

Part of the thrill, the attraction, the fear, the horror activated among readers by news of the *Titanic* disaster was the fact that it had occurred in the cold reaches of the North Atlantic amidst icefields, in the stark presence of a rare and elemental nature. People were already intrigued by ice and the frozen ends of the earth, but this disaster was an opportunity for reporters and feature writers to swot up this exciting branch of oceanography – the study of icebergs – and for readers to take a crash course in the origins and behaviour of these strange phenomena. Scientists suggested timely ways of locating icebergs in the paths of ships: in late May 1912 Professor Howard T. Barnes, for example, in a lecture to the Royal Institution recommended the installation of micro-thermometers to detect minute changes of air temperature as a ship neared a berg. The *Literary Digest* of September 21, 1912 quoted at length an illustrated article in the Paris magazine *Cosmos* on the probable shapes of icebergs below the waterline where depicted shapes were even more bizarre and various than known shapes above. Chopin's contemporary cartoon in the *San Francisco Examiner*, showing a bemused Neptune holding in his hand the sunken *Titanic*, might well have represented many readers' erroneous mental picture of an iceberg, depicted in the cartoon as a tumescent island rooted in the seabed. (Perhaps

"UNSINKABLE"

deliberately, the iceberg in the cartoon bears a passing resemblance to the map of Britain.)

As the immediate cause of the collision, icebergs loomed large in the American hearing. Senator Alden Smith, chairman of the Committee on Commerce, introducing the *Report* of his investigation into the disaster in the US Senate on May 28, 1912, waxed eloquent (as he often did, to the irritation of British readers) on the danger to shipping of icebergs that April night.

> Scores of these towering glaciers planted themselves in the very pathway of this ship ... One of these icebergs was nearly 200 feet above the level of the sea, with seven-eighths of its ponderous bulk hidden beneath the surface. They are composed of ice and earth and rock [British journalists had mocked his question to Fifth Officer Harold Lowe, "Do you know what an iceberg is composed of?" "Ice, I suppose, sir" Lowe replied], and old sailors of the coast of Newfoundland usually give them a wide berth .... As they go southward, their journey is slow and erratic, and the influence of spring often causes explosions in the ice, which frequently serve to warn sailors of danger; sometimes the drift of field ice, led by a great berg, has been known to convoy schooners in a calm, while shipwrecked sailors have drifted hundreds of miles in safety upon the irregular surface of the ice.

For some mysterious reason, Senator Smith concluded, Captain Smith chose to ignore a danger that as the senator pointed out, was relatively easy to avoid.

Senator Smith had questioned Captain John J. Knapp who was in charge of the Hydrographic Office (Bureau of Navigation, Department of the US Navy). The monthly Pilot Chart issued by Knapp's office became in time a weekly Hydrographic Bulletin, with the development of radio telegraphy eventually permitting a daily memorandum as well, each tracking, among other marine data, North Atlantic icebergs. An April 1909 pamphlet, *North Atlantic Ice Movements*, was available to shipping companies and shipmasters. In addition, there were the daily memoranda; the memo for April 15, 1912 relayed the now notorious ice warning that was radioed to the Hydrographic Office in Washington from SS *Amerika* (Hamburg-American Line) via *Titanic* and then Cape Race, Newfoundland: '*Amerika* passed two large icebergs in 41°27'N., 50° 8'W., on the 14th of April'. The Hydrographic Office received that day a report of extensive field ice in latitude 42° 6'N and longitude 49° 43'W from SS *Pisa* via Halifax. Reports received by the Hydrographic Office for April 14 from the vessels *Californian*, *Athinai*, *Paula*, *Trautenfels*, *La Bretagne*, *Hellig Olav*, *Meeba* and *Mesaba* testified to an extensive and

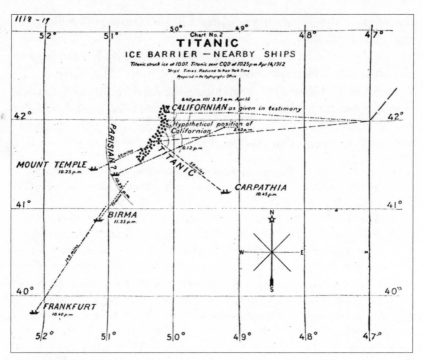

Chart 2 submitted by Knapp

hazardous ice flow. Although none of these reports was received before April 19, we know that *Titanic* had been warned several times about ice in her vicinity. Captain Knapp furnished the investigating committee with a chart entitled 'Ice as Reported near *Titanic*' and one entitled '*Titanic*: Ice Barrier – Nearby Ships' which depict an area of the North Atlantic beset by bergs and resembling a polar field.

We know now, and hydrographers must have suspected at the time, that in 1912 twice the usual number of icebergs came south, because, in 1911, the two fleets of icebergs from the east coast of Greenland and the west coast were kept north by wind and were frozen in. This resulted in the glorious British summer of 1911, but when the ice was released the next spring, it drifted farther south than usual and *Titanic* fatally crossed its path. How odd to think that *Titanic* paid the price for that wonderful summer of British ebullience before the winter of discontent and the decline of the British Empire.

These were the oceanographic phenomena. Meanwhile, the popular imagination was caught by this new tale of disaster and ice. The iceberg, wrote E.S. in an article of that title in the *Daily Sketch* of April 17, 1912, had once been exotic, regarded as a scientific extravagance, as remote as the landscapes of fairy tales, but no longer:

'now our generation will have different and enduring thoughts. The iceberg will not settle back into the oblivion of the school book picture for a lifetime at least.' The 'ice-monster' had become 'one of the most wonderful sepulchres in all history'. The same day, the *Daily Mirror* warned its readers that there was no doubt that the polar ice was advancing southwards, 'slowly but surely'. In 1898, the transatlantic route liners took between Britain and North America had to be amended south; this was bound to happen again. Chillingly, *Titanic* had sunk 14' (or about sixteen miles) *south* of the regular westbound summer route, as the *Literary Digest* informed its readers, quoting *Engineering News* (New York). A day after *Titanic* sank, the established routes were shifted south a further sixty or seventy miles, and on April 19, a *hundred* miles south.

All this might have seemed to confirm for queasy observers the famous French naturalist Buffon's 'sublime but gloomy theory' (in the words of Percy Bysshe Shelley, quoted by Flint) that the Alpine ice-caps were enlarging, evidence that the Earth would one day cool to freezing temperatures.

The *Daily Mirror* of April 18 quoted the description of icebergs encountered by the Allan liner *Tunisian* and witnessed by a London anaesthetist during the period of the sinking of *Titanic*. He had seen 168 bergs within 24 hours, along with field ice. 'The isolated bergs seen from the ship', the doctor reported:

> were far more terrible and impressive than the icefield, for they moved faster and were, of course, more dangerous .... The biggest iceberg I saw was wider than the Thames at Waterloo Bridge, and was at least as high as Big Ben.

Hugh Woolner, son of an English sculptor, and who survived the *Titanic* sinking, said that after the collision, he gazed upon what seemed to be a 'continent of ice'. Mrs JJ Brown (Unsinkable Molly) memorably reported the scene that greeted her fellow lifeboat passengers at dawn:

> Near us was open water, but on every side was ice. Ice ten feet high was everywhere, and to the right and left and back and front were icebergs. Some of them were mountain high. This sea of ice was 40 miles wide, they told me.

A first-class passenger, CEH Stengel, told the American inquiry that from his life-boat he remarked on one iceberg in particular: 'a very large one which looked something like the Rock of Gibraltar'. The *Illustrated London News* devoted whole-page depictions to the 'white foe' on April 27, May 4 and June 1, the first being a photograph of an immense berg thought to have been part of the ice-field *Titanic* entered.

Passengers on board at least three ships claimed to have seen the actual iceberg that sank *Titanic*. In their 1912 books, Logan Marshall and Marshall Everett reproduced a photograph of the alleged culprit taken from the rescue ship *Carpathia*. Charles Hurd, a passenger on *Carpathia*, whose story was included by Marshall in *Sinking of the* Titanic *and Great Sea Disasters* (1912), described the scene as survivors reached the rescue ship:

> At our north was a broad ice field, the length of hundreds of *Carpathias*.
> Around us on other sides were sharp and glistening peaks. One black berg,
> seen about 10 a.m., was said to be that which sunk the *Titanic*.

The London *Daily Sketch* of April 26, 1912 reproduced a photograph of the alleged wrongdoer taken from SS *Birma*. However, on April 30, the same newspaper reported that some on board the steamer *Portland* were convinced the black iceberg 12 feet (3.66 metres) out of the water that they saw six hours after the sinking was a suspect. Walter Lord in *A Night to Remember* (1955) reprinted a photograph of a nearby iceberg taken on April 15 from the German ship *Prinz Adalbert*; there was said to have been a giveaway scar of red paint along the likely offender, but there was little agreement on the matter.

One of the 'culprit' icebergs

One coroner who visited the newly arrived rescue ship *Carpathia* and interviewed Captain Rostron told *The New York Times* that Rostron told him that the iceberg that sank *Titanic* had been '180 feet [54.86 metres] out of the water', though it is unclear who told Rostron that, perhaps Second Officer Lightoller. If so, who then told Dr JJ Kemp, the *Carpathia*'s physician, that the culprit had been 400 feet long and 90 feet high (122 x 27 metres), and reported as such by the same newspaper the next day?

Journalists and experts took the opportunity to investigate afresh this pelagic source of wonder. Marshall Everett (Henry Neil) included in *Wreck and Sinking of the* Titanic (1912) Fred S. Miller's account of bergs, entitled 'The Terror of the Seas'. Miller reported the vastness of the Humboldt Glacier and the Jacobshaven Glacier (the latter putting into the sea four hundred thousand million cubic feet of ice (11,328 million cubic metres) yearly and at an average rate of 42 feet (12.8 metres) a day). Immense sections break off accompanied by deafening roars and the bergs so born compose an 'icy menace' to the mariner. But, he adds, inadvertently explaining some of the fascination of the *Titanic* story, 'if icebergs are terrible they are beyond doubt among the most beautiful and superb manifestations of nature'. Terror and beauty consort in some of the survivors' accounts, referring either to the calm, starry and iceberg-ridden ocean or to the sinking liner illuminated and graceful in her last hours.

Titanic and the Polar Sagas

Francis Spufford writes of the influence of polar material on the collective imagination of Britain and America around the turn of the century, and the material he refers to likewise evoked terror and beauty. It is not far-fetched to suggest that reports of the sinking of *Titanic* in cold latitudes carried echoes of recent and ongoing stories of polar difficulty and loss. Like many of the Arctic and Antarctic explorations, *Titanic*'s voyage ended in disaster; like them, too, her journey was pioneering, since this was the maiden voyage of a much-vaunted vessel and with luminaries of the culture on board. Especially in Britain, the reports struck a national nerve. It seems that the career and fate of *Titanic* composed a story that was an episode in a larger narrative of expeditionary, even heroic patriotism. Another episode of expeditionary patriotism began in the autumn of 1914 and was also a profound national setback in its short-term failure.

The South Pole saga started early with James Cook who in 1773 crossed the Antarctic Circle and reached latitude 67°15' south before being baffled by an ice-field and retreating to New Zealand. In 1823,

James Weddell (whose name adorns the sea he voyaged through), reached farther south than Cook, but he too was forced to retreat by worsening conditions. There was another British Antarctic Expedition in 1839–1843 led by Sir James Clark Ross with the ships HMS *Erebus* and *Terror*, ships that would later be commanded by Sir John Franklin in the ill-fated Arctic expedition of 1845. Ross penetrated as far south as 78°11' south, four degrees farther than Weddell before him. According to Spufford, there was agitation in the 1890s for Britain to resume exploration in the Antarctic, and the British Antarctic Expedition of 1898–1900 led by Carsten Borchgrevink aboard *Southern Cross* was one reply. This expedition, with the aid of steam, located the south magnetic pole and penetrated as far south as 78°50'. The succeeding National Antarctic (or *Discovery*) expedition of 1901–1904, in which both Robert Falcon Scott and Ernest Shackleton took part, was a polar drama. The expedition crossed the 82nd parallel but with Shackleton ill (and one member already killed), the explorers had to race death back to the ship, as one commentator put it. Shackleton returned with the *Nimrod* expedition of 1907–1909. He crossed the 88th parallel and got to within 100 miles of the Pole before admitting defeat. Shackleton's defeat stirred the British. The October 1909 issue of Stead's *Review of Reviews* was virtually a polar number, and it carried a paraphrase of Shackleton's diary, published the same month in *Pearson's Magazine*. The antagonists of the diary are the hundreds of icebergs the *Nimrod* was towed past by another steamer (to save coal), the Great Ice Barrier, masses of ice five or six feet (about two metres) deep created out of frozen wind-driven ocean spray that covered their first camp in McMurdo Sound, and the 'fearful blizzards' that whipped them as they ascended Mount Erebus. Readers seemed to enjoy the polar epics with a fearful delight.[1]

A Scottish National Antarctic Expedition was projected in 1912, but the British imagination was monopolised by what proved to be Scott's last attempt on the Pole, the *Terra Nova* expedition, which began in 1910 and ended in 1913 with the return of the survivors. Scott reached the South Pole but discovered that Roald Amundsen, the Norwegian explorer (who at the last moment had switched his polar interest from the North to the South), had beaten him by a month. Intensely disappointed as the English were, they did, in the cause of fair play, give Amundsen his due. The May 18, 1912 issue of *The Illustrated London News* – one month after the *Titanic* sensation – devoted a photo-essay to 'The End of the Last Great Quest',

Amundsen's discovery of the South Pole showing observations at the Pole between October 11 and December 17, 1911.

Heroism under duress and in defeat was what was called for, it would seem. And that is what influential observers and commentators made sure the *Titanic* disaster provided. It was the return journey that made the *Terra Nova* expedition memorable and turned it into a tragedy. Although Captain Scott died in 1912, it was the following year before the fact was known to the outside world, and in retrospect the South Pole tragedy mingled in popular imagination with that of *Titanic*. The Bulgarian-born Nobel laureate, Elias Canetti, who was taken to Manchester to live when a child, recalled the two events as the earliest causes of public grief in his life. For the young Canetti, *iceberg* (Antarctic, *Titanic*) and *captain* (Scott, Smith) were two of the first powerful English words the future writer registered in his imagination. One commentator has described the polar voyages as 'latter-day chivalric romances, quests endowed with allegorical meaning' and the *Titanic* disaster has been read in similar fashion. Both the shipwreck and the expeditions required an often disputed heroism and an equally disputed chivalry that helped to define their historical period.

There were other Antarctic journeys during the Age of *Titanic*, including the *Aurora* (or Australasian) Expedition of 1911–1913 led by Douglas Mawson who became famous as a result, and the even more famous Imperial Trans-Antarctic (or *Endurance*) expedition by Shackleton of 1914–1916, which intended to cross the continent rather than repeat Amundsen's and Scott's feat. This expedition earned its name, for it became an epic of survival after *Endurance* was early crushed in the ice, and Shackleton led his 27 men across ice with dogsleds and man-hauled sledges and heavy open boats, and across the Weddell Sea in those open boats 850 miles to South Georgia Island. Shackleton's epic return rivalled the posthumous fame Scott earned on his attempted return. On the strength of his experience in Antarctica 1907–1909, Shackleton had been called as an expert on ice by the British Commission of Inquiry into the sinking of *Titanic*. His testimony was damaging to Captain Smith and the White Star Company since he was of the opinion that high speed through an icefield was utter folly.

Glamorous though the South Pole became, during the Edwardian period it lacked the popular appeal of the search for the Northwest Passage and then the race to the North Pole. These produced gripping stories of drama and disappointment, escapade and tragedy amidst snow and ice. The stories begin after the Napoleonic Wars when Sir John Barrow, Admiralty Secretary, planned naval expeditions to the

Arctic. John Ross was sent in search of the Northwest Passage in 1818 on board *Isabella*, and his second-in-command, William Parry, led his own expedition the following year in *Hecla* and *Fury*. An article in *The New York Times* of April 20, 1912, intended to educate readers in the ways of icebergs, remembered that Sir John Ross and Lieutenant Parry had recorded a berg two and a half miles long and more than two miles broad. 'Assuming the form to have been approximately a cone erected upon an elliptic base, the mass above water would be roughly 150,000,000 tons, giving a total mass [since eight-ninths of the berg are beneath the water] of nearly 15,000,000,000 tons, which, according to the records, was by no means of extraordinary dimensions'. The article concludes: 'The hopelessness of the encounter of the little *Titanic* is manifest'. Rarely had the 'iron monarch of the ocean', as the same article had it, been so warrantably reduced in scale.

In 1831, James Clark Ross, a nephew of John, discovered the Northern Magnetic Pole during exploration of Arctic America. Successive failures to find the Northwest Passage, coupled with their success in extending the range of knowledge of magnetism, geography, fauna and other matters, not to mention the range of British jurisdiction, culminated in the dramatic and mysterious failure of Sir John Franklin's expedition to find the Northwest Passage. *Erebus* and *Terror* sailed from England in 1845 and vanished. JC Ross searched fruitlessly for the lost expedition in 1848 aboard HMS *Enterprise*. In 1850, the American Relief (or Grinnell) Expedition (sponsored by the shipping magnate Henry Grinnell) found some relics of the expedition; there was a second American relief expedition in 1853. It was not until Ross' second lieutenant, Leopold McClintock, led the *Fox* search expedition in 1859 that Britons learned through papers McClintock found hidden in a cairn by survivors that Franklin had perished in June 1847. Captain Robert McClure of HMS *Investigator* was credited with finding the Northwest Passage in 1852.

In Britain, the *Titanic* disaster shared some popular elements with that of the Franklin tragedy more than 60 years before. Both were regarded as calamitous failures that were tragic because hardship, death and national pride were involved. Both were thought to exhibit heroism – male heroism, British heroism – of a kind that appealed to women as well as men. Yet in both cases, suspicion was aroused that heroism and moral splendour had been besmirched, by the rumours of cannibalism among the Franklin survivors, and by reports of cowardice and selfish scramble amongst *Titanic* survivors. Both disasters stimulated the literary imagination. Charles Dickens and

Lord Tennyson were creatively disturbed by the Franklin saga, Thomas Hardy and Virginia Woolf by the *Titanic* saga. And in our own time, there has been an intense revival of popular interest in both events through belated revelations: Owen Beattie's discovery of the well-preserved bodies of three Franklin crew members in 1984, and Robert Ballard's discovery of the well-preserved corpse of *Titanic* in 1985. Scott's last expedition joins Franklin and *Titanic* to create a kind of tragic patriotic trilogy.

The search for the Northwest Passage and the search for Franklin gave way to the quest for the North Pole. The 1893–1896 voyage of Fridtjof Nansen in the most famous Arctic ship, *Fram* (which Amundsen later used in the Antarctic), was the prologue to the dramatic dash to the Pole. Robert Peary's failure in 1906 stirred him to renewed efforts in his ship *Roosevelt* and he reached the Pole in April 1909. But meanwhile Frederick Cook, an erstwhile comrade of Peary's on an 1892 Greenland expedition, was being celebrated for having reached the Pole a whole year earlier, resulting in a heated public controversy. Before he was vindicated, Peary was disbelieved and vilified, among others by WT Stead, one of the most famous journalists in the world and a man destined to drown on *Titanic*. But as the evidence accumulated, the influential Stead switched his credence from Cook to Peary.[2] Meanwhile, the most ferocious critic of Cook was Philip Gibbs, *Daily Chronicle* correspondent soon after to write (or assemble, like Marshall and Everett) one of the earliest books on the *Titanic* disaster, the prematurely (but justifiably, as it turned out) titled *Deathless Story of the* Titanic (1912).

What has been called the 'golden age' of polar exploration coincided with the Age of *Titanic* and drew to a close with the heroic defeats of Stefansson's Arctic expedition of 1913–1914 and Shackleton's Antarctic expedition of 1914–1916. Shackleton got off in the nick of time, given permission to set out just before the Great War interrupted unnecessary heroics. But in 1912, crushed ships and tragic loss of life amidst ice, snow, in the far north and the far south, were virtually staples of the popular late Victorian and Edwardian imagination. Yet these old stories and their attendant virtues were inseparable from heroism and the new forward spirit. Introducing his extracts from Shackleton's diary, Stead in the *Review of Reviews* began (joining heroism and the new inventiveness, and inventions):

> We seem to be living in times when men have reverted to the age of the elemental heroes ... Following on M. Blériot's flight over the Channel, the week of aviation at Rheims, and the announcement that the American, Dr. Cook, has planted the Stars and Stripes on the North Pole, comes the

record of our own Polar hero – Lieutenant Shackleton's story of his conquest of the Magnetic Pole.

Stead thought it worth remarking that Shackleton took a motor car with him on his expedition: it could not travel over soft snow inland but could glide over the frozen surface of the sea.

Literature and Ice

It is the drifting icebergs setting with any current anywhere, that wreck the ships.
Charles Dickens, *Hard Times* (1854)

Edwardian fiction drew on the complex of ideas, feelings and settings the polar journeys generated. In *Come and Find Me!* (1908), a novel by the popular Anglo-American novelist and playwright Elizabeth Robins (CE Raimond) and published in the year of Cook's claim to have reached the Pole, a former Cunard liner, *Los Angeles*, is beleaguered in an ice-field in the north Pacific in the year 1900. The passengers feel one mysterious and hardly alarming collision, but when others take place, they realise that it is ice, 'man's arch-enemy of the deep'. Feeling themselves in mortal danger, they gather round a piano and sing 'Nearer My God, to Thee' (the Heinemann edition includes a plate of the hymn-singing), the words of which everyone appears to know. This was, in fictional time, twelve years before one of the most famous and poignant episodes of the *Titanic* tragedy, four years before in the real time of the novel's publication. Towards the end of the novel, the character of John Galbraith, dying (and resembling a figure out of Conrad's *Heart of Darkness*, 1902), recalls being inspired by Nansen's 1893–1896 expedition, and his own reaching of the Pole, evidence for which –his diary – he destroys in the novel's climax, not wishing to damage the wonder of the Pole ('the thing that men had dreamed about before ever they'd girdled the globe') or anger the violated spirit of the North.

This was Robins' second fictional expedition into the far North. An earlier novel, *The Magnetic North*, covers some of the same ground (Bering Sea, Norton Sound, etc.) but extends it inland to the Klondike and supplies readers with an end-map. The North was indeed 'magnetic' for readers in the late Victorian and Edwardian periods. Published in March 1904, *The Magnetic North* went into its fourth impression by September of that year.

But Victorian literature had already warmed to the far North and far South, as it were, though more fitfully. Franklin was the inspiring figure who preceded Nansen, Scott and the rest. *The Frozen Deep* was the title of an immediately popular melodrama written by the popular Victorian novelist Wilkie Collins and staged in 1857 by an even more popular Victorian novelist, Charles Dickens, who supplied a verse prologue. The play was instigated by a desire to defend the memory of Franklin against charges and doubts, and tries to retrieve his heroism amidst the icy wastes with the case of a different Arctic expedition. Dickens was moved by the Franklin disaster as later writers were moved by the Scott disaster and the *Titanic* disaster.[3] His brief productions of and performances in the play impressed the small but highly influential members of the audience and the play clearly tapped into the existing high state of patriotism in the matter of tragedy during British heroics at the edge of the world.

Other Victorian writers exhibited a polar attraction. The author of *Moby-Dick* (1851) who mused on ships inside Antarctic whiteness also anticipated a *Titanic*-like collision in his poem 'The Berg: A Dream', collected in 1888. 'Ice-cubes' crash on the deck, the berg is callously indifferent and the stunned ship goes down. Emily Dickinson's line in her poem 'After great pain, a formal feeling comes' (1862) might best describe the fate of those who jumped off *Titanic* and drowned in the icy cold ocean: 'First – Chill – then Stupor – then the letting go'. It might even describe the fate of Melville's stricken and anthropomorphic ship, and *Titanic* herself. Several critics have pointed out the imaginative force of the start of Charlotte Brontë's novel *Jane Eyre* (1847) which describes the title heroine reading Thomas Bewick's *History of British Birds* (1797) with its incidentally thrilling sketch of the forlorn north – Greenland, Iceland, Nova Zembla, Lapland: 'these death-white regions', as young Jane thinks of them.

Yet the Victorians merely perpetuated the Romantic cultivation of the outlandish and extreme. The imaginative power of Coleridge's 'The Ancient Mariner' (1798), with its ship amidst mast-high ice, was such that the poem sounded through subsequent writing. Robert Walton, the narrator of Mary Shelley's *Frankenstein* (1818, rev. 1831) – virtually a handbook to Romanticism – puts trust in 'preceding navigators' and the accounts of their 'various voyages which have been made in the prospect of arriving at the North Pacific Ocean through the seas which surround the pole'. He wishes to avoid the Ancient Mariner's error in violating nature as he seeks the Northwest Passage near 'the northern pole', avoiding too 'the floating sheets of ice that continually pass us, indicating the dangers of the region towards which we are advancing'. Walton happens upon Victor

Frankenstein who is seeking his rogue creation, the monster. Both men are examples of 'the modern Prometheus', scientists who unwittingly repeat the error of the Titan Prometheus who stole fire; that is, violating or insulting nature for human gain. It was fitting that a ship called *Titanic* should be the object of religious and moral scorn for insulting nature by ignoring it (to her cost) and for challenging the given scale of things in its monstrous size and arrogant speed. If the ship's designers were thought of by some as virtually latter-day Frankensteins, the ship herself was the latter-day monster. (When the thawing ice opens a passage south, Walton, having listened to Frankenstein's tale and been dissuaded from Promethean science, turns towards England, but Frankenstein is set upon finding the monster, only to have the monster find him and kill him. It is the monster who intends to continue north, find the North Pole and there destroy himself.)

The extremes of nature were for the Romantics the intersection of awesomeness and beauty, and paradoxically the sublime centre of meaning in the universe. The powerful scenes of the majestic, terrifying, stupendous, beautiful, 'awful' and ironically tranquil in *Frankenstein* are set in the Arctic regions and in the Alps, and always include ice-fields, 'vast and irregular plains of ice', glaciers and snows. This sense of the sublime – aesthetics and fear commingling – touched some of those who witnessed the sinking of *Titanic*. The more eloquent survivors remembered the ironic calm and loveliness that characterized the fateful night. Elizabeth Shutes, a governess, was unable to sleep before the collision because the odour she smelled was one she had noticed in the ice cave on the Eiger glacier. Later, from her lifeboat, she noted the brilliant sky: 'never have I seen so many falling stars'. She echoes the language and sentiment of Walton when she remarks that 'the brilliancy of the sky only intensified the blackness of the water, our utter loneliness on the sea'. In the morning, the rescuing ship and the dawn come together, 'a living painting'.

Molly Brown (Margaret Tobin) too claimed awareness of the unique and pictorial beauty of that dawn, a beauty more insistent in its appeal, no doubt, because of her receptiveness deepened by the relief at seeing the distant searchlight of *Carpathia* appearing above the horizon.

> Then, knowing that we were safe at last, I looked about me. The most wonderful dawn I have ever seen came upon us. I have just returned from Egypt. I have been all over the world, but I have never seen anything like this. First the gray and then the flood of light. Then the sun came up in a ball of red fire.

After her brief description of the surrounding icebergs, she continues: 'Imagine some artist able to picture what we saw from that boat at dawn in that field of ice, with the red sun playing on those giant icebergs'. Shutes also approaches with justification Romantic hyperbole:

> White was the vessel, but whiter still were those horribly beautiful icebergs, and as we drew nearer and nearer that good ship we drew nearer to those mountains of ice. As far as the eye could reach they rose. Each one more fantastically chiselled than its neighbour. The floe glistened like a never-ending meadow covered with new-fallen snow. Those same white mountains, marvellous in their purity, had made of the just-ended night one of the blackest the sea has ever known.

Second Officer Charles Lightoller recalled 'the impressive majesty' of *Titanic* just before she took her final 'tragic dive'. Lawrence Beesley remembered 'a beautiful starlight night' – 'an ideal night', save for those struggling in the water. The 'perfect sky of brilliant stars' later underwent a change of intensity and was illuminated by the northern lights.

The capacity of these survivors to combine the memory of fear and gratitude with that of clearly genuine and unsolicited aesthetic pleasure is surely remarkable. At such times they sound not unlike Carsten Borchgrevink in his memoir, *First on the Antarctic Continent* (1901), remembering discomfort no doubt, but not a near-death experience and able to rhapsodize about 'the ice as it closes and opens far out towards the horizon, where the sky and ice seem to meet, while here and there icebergs are floating about in halos of the most dazzling pink and crimson'.

In these accounts beauty and fear consort to suggest less the cruelty, or even the indifference, of nature than the ultimate meaning of existence that can contain and condone yet reprehend the human suffering. For thoughtful and sensitive survivors, the *Titanic* experience was a Romantically 'Titanic' experience, furnished actually or in the imagination with the scenery or stage properties (I mean this in no diminishing way) of Romantic sensibility – ice, ocean, mountain, darkness, starlight, snow: natural perfection and elementality found at the drear edges of human habitation.

Yet of course the sublime was formulated as an idea and a sensibility in the eighteenth century, the century before Romanticism. Danger, pain, beauty, pleasure, grandeur – these were bedfellows in Edmund Burke's notion of the sublime. He referred to one early experience of 'great though terrible scenes' (a flood in his native

Dublin) in anticipation of his later theory. The sublime held heightened emotions in tense opposition and, simultaneously, in unity. Shutes' 'horribly beautiful' icebergs are echoed in the 'terrible beauty' of the sinking *Titanic* in Charlotte Collyer's memory of her ordeal: the ironic disparity between the abnormally tranquil night of April 14–15, 1912 in the North Atlantic and the dreadful scenes of fright, suffering and death enacted during it are part of the appeal – itself an ambiguous appeal to our pity and our prurience – of the *Titanic* story. (It was Burke who wrote: 'I am convinced we have a degree of delight, and that no small one, in the real misfortunes and pains of others'.)

The clash of elements that can create the sublime seems graphically demonstrated in the collision of *Titanic* with the iceberg. There were a number of stories and poems that depicted a collision between ship and iceberg before the particular reality occurred on April 14, 1912 and they have been cited as peculiar anticipations of the disaster: Celia Thaxter's poem 'A Tryst' (1870s); Herman Melville's 'The Berg: A Dream' (collected 1888); WT Stead's story (1892) involving the real-life SS *Majestic* commanded by the real-life Edward J. Smith; Morgan Robertson's novella, *The Wreck of the Titan* (1898; in Marshall Everett's *Wreck and Sinking of the* Titanic, 1912, Fred S. Miller entitled his account of the collision 'The Two Titans'); and Mayn Clew Garnett's story 'The White Ghost of Disaster' (in press when the *Titanic* went down). Although they still have to be considered in the light of popular contemporary interest in the paranormal (see chapter 5 below), these anticipations seem less so in the light of the contemporary cultural interest both in collision (see chapter 1 above) and in icebergs.

Literary antecedents also increase the chance of some original anticipation inspiring or influencing a work written after the event but that still seems anticipatory or coincidental. Thomas Hardy's famous poem, 'The Convergence of the Twain' (1912), was of course composed after the sinking; it was much published after it appeared in the Souvenir Programme of the Covent Garden theatrical matinee of May 14, 1912, mounted as a *Titanic* benefit. Hardy's reference in the poem to the sea-worm that now crawls through the wreck – 'grotesque, slimed, dumb, indifferent' – recalls Melville's earlier 'slimy slug that sprawls/Along thy dead indifference of walls', and each poem registers the inhuman neutrality of the iceberg, despite the fact that at the same time both poems (like EJ Pratt's, much later) see the berg paradoxically as a rudiment, a precursor of WB Yeats' pitiless 'rough beast' in his famous 1921 poem, 'The Second Coming': the more

Thomas Hardy

frightening for being proto-human as well as inanimate.

Hardy's poem also recalls a wordier effort: Thaxter's 'A Tryst', written and published in *Atlantic Monthly* in the 1870s. In it, a maverick iceberg 'from out the desolation of the North' travels south while a 'stately ship', 'with matchless grace' and 'with her freight of beauty and delight' sails unwittingly but fatefully into its path. 'What drew the two together o'er the tide,/Fair ship and iceberg pale?' the poem wonders. This minor poem has the power of a middling ballad and a certain impressive relentlessness of narrative. Like the New England poet, Hardy too saw the collision between iceberg and liner as an elaborately prepared tryst, a fateful conjunction – both sexual (gay familiar bride, pale strange groom) and nonsexual – at the behest of some higher inscrutable power. The similarity between the designs of the two poems is striking. But whereas it is likely Hardy knew 'The Berg: A Dream', it is far less likely he read the New England poet. Since Hardy's poem is merely one of a congregation of poems he called 'satires of circumstance', and since the ideas of collision, convergence of the twain (here in its icy parody of sexual congress), and the Doppelganger (the Double) were well entrenched elements of the painstakingly developed philosophy of this elderly writer, the resemblance of 'The Convergence of the Twain' to 'A Tryst' is in all likelihood a pleasing and arresting Hardyesque coincidence.

It might be equally coincidental that Hardy's line about the slimed sea-worm evokes Shakespeare's *Richard III* and Clarence's dream of drowned men with gems as eyes 'that wooed the slimy bottom of the deep'. The echo would be fitting. A contemporary popular enthusiasm for the deep energized the public reaction to the *Titanic* disaster – that mixture of fear, amazement and proxy thrill – as much as did enthusiasm for ice, snow, far North, far South: poles of extreme human experience.

Challenging the Abyss

Biggest Liner Plunges to the Bottom at 2.20am
New York Times, April 16, 1912

Nothing more intoxicating than this attraction of the abyss.
Jules Verne, *Journey to the Centre of the Earth* (1864)

What thrilled readers vicariously in April 1912 was not only that *Titanic* had sunk in the vast icy reaches of the North Atlantic but also that she had plunged, beyond recall, into the freezing deep. The *New York Times* informed its readers on April 16, 'Liner's Grave Two Miles Deep', a correct calculation: the wreck lies on the Sohm Abyssal Plain 12,500 feet (3,810 metres) below the ocean surface. The term 'abyssal' is justified, as the transition from the continental shelf to the deep sea, as the oceanographer CP Idyll tell us, is abrupt: 'After sloping gently down from the shore line to an average depth of some 400 feet, the face of the earth plunges into the abyss, down to depths of 10,000, 20,000, and even 30,000 feet'. The abyssal zone lies between the ultra-abyssal (or hadal) zone and the bathyal (or archibenthal) zone; that is, between two and six kilometres (1.24 to 3.72 miles) down.

It was the sense of irrevocable loss of the ship and the drowned, because of the uttermost dark and nethermost depth into which *Titanic* vanished, that impressed readers with horror and even foreboding: the fate of the ship and the drowned had been an archetypal fate from some tenebrous episodes of mythology. To diminish the horror and ease the minds of relatives, experts assured readers that at such a depth, 6,000 pounds of pressure to the square inch meant that airtight compartments were impossible. On April 18, Professor Robert W. Wood (Chair of Experimental Physics, Johns Hopkins University), was quoted in the *New York Times* to the effect that no passenger was still alive at the bottom of the sea. Less assuring was Wood's prediction that no bodies would float up from the wreck at that depth: the buoyancy achieved by the drowned in shallow water once gases are generated is impossible under such intense pressure. He continued:

> That the bodies sank to the bottom of the sea there is no question. Those who were not carried down with the boat followed until the very bottom of the sea was reached. There was no such things as their stopping in their downward course a half mile, a mile, or at any other point.

There must have been many innocent or wishful misapprehensions on these points. The English writer Virginia Woolf wrote to her friend Ka

Cox and despite the glint of malicious humour might well have believed what she wrote: 'Do you know it's a fact that ships don't sink at that depth, but remain poised half way down, and become perfectly flat, so that Mrs Stead is now like a pancake, and her eyes like copper coins'. (Mrs Stead was not in fact on board with her husband, the famous journalist, spiritualist and peace activist who accompanied the ship to the bottom.)

Woolf of course is hardly typical (except perhaps on matters oceanographic): she was a creative instrument of unusual sensitivity, and she had a pathologically developed fear of and fascination with the subaqueous, the fitting element of the isolated self in crisis. She wanted to write a full account of the *Titanic* disaster, and she and her then fiancé, Leonard, attended the British inquiry. Her first novel, *The Voyage Out* (1915), was almost certainly influenced by those hearings; it involves a transatlantic sea voyage and has a scene of a drowning, metaphoric but with the power of literal truth. In the novel a character says, 'What solitary icebergs we are'. She was equally frightened by and drawn to the abyss; life she thought of as 'a strip of pavement over an abyss'. The fate of *Titanic* almost certainly deepened Woolf's fearful sense of the watery abyss.

There will be time later to consider the metaphoric meanings of the abyss that were in cultural circulation in the years before the *Titanic* sinking re-energized them. It was in the first place the actual oceanic abysses that engaged both the popular and scientific imaginations. Many names of deep-sea explorers are familiar from the polar voyages. In 1817–1818, Sir John Ross from HMS *Isabella* took soundings and samples in Baffin Bay in water deeper than 5,500 feet (1,676 metres). On his British Antarctic Expedition (1839–1843), Sir James Clark Ross from HMS *Erebus* and *Terror* dredged the sea-floor as deeply as over 2,000 feet (610 metres). While surveying the North Atlantic in 1860 for a possible route for a telegraph cable between Britain and North America, personnel on board HMS *Bulldog* took soundings and samples of the sea-floor from as deep as over 10,000 feet (3,048 metres). The naturalist Wyville Thomson conducted dedicated deep-sea exploration (north and west of Britain and off the Iberian peninsula) in 1868 from HMS *Lightning* and in 1869–1870 from HMS *Porcupine* and recovered samples of life in the North Atlantic from as deep as over 14,500 feet (4,420 metres) (even deeper than the floor on which the future *Titanic* would lie). The exploration of the inverted landscapes of the ocean caught public interest. This was partly because the explorers had proven Edward Forbes wrong when he speculated that life could not exist below 1,500 feet (457 metres) or so. Who

knew what might flourish at the darkest depths and in their 'secret
abysses'?

The French fiction writer Jules Verne posed this question through
the mouthpiece of his character Professor Aronnax. Pondering the
possibility of monstrous survivals in the Deep, the Professor asked: 'why
should the sea not conceal, within its bosom, the last of these titanic
species, for which the years are but centuries, and the centuries
millennia?' *Twenty Thousand Leagues Under the Sea* was published in
France in 1869 and translated into English in 1873, the year in which
Wyville Thomson published an account of the *Lightning* and *Porcupine*
operations as *The Depths of the Sea*. *Twenty Thousand Leagues Under the
Sea* became one of Verne's popular classics and was read and
remembered well into the twentieth century; in 1912 Shackleton was of
the gloomy opinion that 'all the work of our modern oceanography ...
has won less of public attention and interest than did a single one of
Jules Verne's heroes, Captain Nemo of the *Nautilus*'. In chapters 13 to
16 in Part Two of this scientific fantasy, Captain Nemo's submarine
voyages under the Antarctic ice (like an advanced precursor of a
twentieth-century nuclear submarine travelling under the Arctic
counterpart) and at one point gets frozen in like *Endurance* and other
hapless expeditionary vessels before it. Nemo recites the roll of those
who have tried to reach furthermost south (from the Dutchman Gheritk
in 1600 to the Englishman James Clark Ross in 1842) and triumphantly
caps their achievements by reaching the South Pole in March 1868.
The prolific Verne was mesmerised, it seems, by voyages amidst ice as
well as in the ocean depths, for he was the author of *A Winter Amid the
Ice* (1853), *Adventures of Captain Hatteras* (*The English of the North Pole*,
1866, and *The Desert of Ice*, 1867), *Earth Topsy Turvy–The Purchase of the
North Pole* (1889) and *The Sphinx of Ice* (1897).

The voyage of *Nautilus* under the Antarctic ice is only one of many
recounted by the narrator, Professor Aronnax of Paris, fictional author
of *The Mysteries of the Great Ocean Depths*. *Nautilus* visits all the oceans
of the world and while doing so takes soundings and conducts
experiments. Since Verne knew his history of oceanography, we do not
need to claim his prescience to explain the fact that the voyage of
Nautilus, regarded in its strictly oceanographic elements, closely
resembles the voyage of HMS *Challenger*, a voyage that was conceived
in 1869, the very year of publication of Verne's fiction, and got under
way in December 1872. It was a voyage that in three and a half years
circumnavigated the globe (sometimes crossing the fictional path of
Nautilus), sounding and dredging and sampling and taking various
readings and adding momentously to human knowledge of the deeps as

well as of climate. Not far from Japan, *Challenger* sounded in over 27,000 feet (8,230 metres) of water (her thermometers broke under pressure). The USS *Tuscarora*, also in the Pacific and taking soundings while exploring a telegraph route between Japan and the United States, did not reach bottom in almost 28,000 feet (8,534 metres) of water. The Germans too were in the area in 1875, conducting their own scientific circumnavigation in SS *Gazelle*.

British readers and those interested in natural history had before the *Challenger* voyage become newly intrigued by the ocean depths, chiefly through the works of Philip Henry Gosse. Gosse contrived to be pioneering and popular at the same time. *The Aquarium: An Unveiling of the Wonders of the Deep Sea* was published in 1854, and he followed this with *The Mysteries of the Great Deep* in 1860 which, on republication in 1880 (and again in 1889), was entitled *The Wonders of the Great Deep*. In 1894, HG Wells, reviewing *The Fauna of the Deep Sea* (1893) by Sydney J. Hickson, registered continuing popular fascination with the ocean depths and 'the mystery of life in the abyss' that provoked that fascination.

Senator Alden Smith read into the record of the US hearings into the loss of *Titanic* a letter from George Otis Smith, Director of the US Geological Survey. It must have gratified the senator since it vindicated his supposedly asinine question to Harold Lowe about the composition of icebergs. The director thought that, while possible, it was unlikely (and unnecessary) that the offending iceberg that tore *Titanic*'s hull had rock embedded in it. In answering, Otis Smith quoted a recent address by Sir John Murray who in turn had referred to the dredging results of the *Challenger* Expedition. He also cited Elisha Kent Kane's 1854 volume on the first American (or Grinnell) relief expedition in search of Franklin, and his 1856 volume on the second Grinnell expedition. On the first expedition Kane served as doctor and on the second as leader. Richard Bevis has recently quoted Kane's work extensively as an example of a scientific account suffused with the aesthetics of Victorian fascination with the Arctic. Otis Smith also quoted Isaac Hayes' *The Open Polar Sea: A Narrative of a Voyage of Discovery towards the North Pole* (1867); Hayes was doctor on the second Grinnell relief expedition and returned to the Arctic in 1860–1861 as a surveyor and explorer in his own right.

The scientific and popular fascination with the Deep continued: the French ships *Travailleur* and *Talisman* surveyed the depths of the Eastern Atlantic; the USS *Albatross* completed oceanographic voyages between 1882 and 1904, dredging in the Pacific as far down as 18,000 feet (5,486 metres). From 1898-1899, the German Deep-Sea

Expedition studied the depths of the Atlantic and Indian Oceans from *Valdivia*, and in 1910 the Norwegian Expedition sampled and dredged deep water in the North Atlantic from the *Michael Sars*. The scientific expenses of the 1910 expedition were defrayed by Sir John Murray. By the time *Titanic* sailed and sank, the oceanic abysses had firmly taken prisoner the fascination of the scientific fraternity and general public, fear and familiarity mingling in the general public's reaction to the tragedy.

Endnotes

1   John Maxtone-Graham (1988) reproduces a drawing from the *Illustrated London News* of December 1910, depicting a family playing a new Christmas board game, *To the Pole with Shackleton*. The public was apparently intoxicated by a potent brew of challenge, patriotism, competition and images of the icy wastes of the distant North.

2   Peary wrote a letter to the *Army and Navy Journal* (New York) when *Titanic* was lost; it was extracted by the *Literary Digest*. He recommended the use of a searchlight to enable liners to detect icebergs, but the greatest menace might still escape detection: 'the last remaining fragment of a berg, usually a mass of dense translucent ice hard as rock, almost entirely submerged, absorbing the color of the surrounding water, and almost invisible, even in broad daylight, until close aboard'.

3   A representative sampling of *Titanic* inspirations can be found in my anthology, *Titanic* (1999).

three

In Memoriam

God and His Comforts

In the immediate aftermath of short-lived, unanticipated disaster in which we are not directly involved, our peremptory questions, our demands to know, displace our deep but unformed emotional response and bring it to the surface as rational concern. They let us assume a retrospective responsibility in place of the shapeless guilt we feel (even the guilt of not caring sufficiently). The rough content of our feeling is transformed into our instant nostalgia for the ideal order of things. It is as though a world tilted on its axis suddenly demands to be righted. On such occasions, the investigating police officer, scientist or lawyer in us comes to the fore.

Questions about the *Titanic* crisis actually began as soon as neighbouring ships received the distress signals Commander Smith ordered transmitted from the wounded *Titanic* just after midnight on the morning of Monday April 15. 'Shall I tell my captain?' asked Harold Cottam, wireless operator of the Cunarder *Carpathia*. 'Do you require assistance? ... What is the matter with you?' inquired the operator of the North German Lloyd steamer *Frankfurt*. (Jack Phillips answered politely but later in the heat of emergency would rudely tell the *Frankfurt* operator to stand by and keep out.) The night crackled with questions, from passengers, officers and crew, from ships stunned momentarily in the water by news of the leviathan's predicament. In the morning, an astonished Captain Rostron of *Carpathia* asked Fourth Officer Joseph Boxhall as he climbed aboard the rescue vessel: 'Where is the *Titanic?*'

By Tuesday morning, April 16, the vicinity of the White Star Line offices in New York City was in tumult, distraught relatives of *Titanic* passengers hurling questions at shipping line clerks and executives. Questions directed at the rescue ship were posed of thin air, for *Carpathia* remained mute in its interminable approach to New York with survivors. 'At every wireless station on the Atlantic Coast from New York to Cape Race', the *San Francisco Examiner* told its readers that same day, 'wireless operators are bending over their

61

wireless instruments feeling for the marvellous Hertzian waves that will bring further details of the catastrophe'. The chief questions, 'How many have been saved? Who has been rescued and who has been lost?' went stubbornly unanswered until *Carpathia* reached New York harbour.

By April 17, the *New York Times* printed two deceptively modest pieces to the effect that the French liner *La Touraine* had warned the White Star giant late in the day of April 12 that she was approaching ice, and that on the afternoon of April 14, *Titanic* had passed on to Cape Race the intelligence from the German steamer *Amerika* that she had encountered two large bergs on the transatlantic route, intelligence which became the basis of a Hydrographic Office (Washington DC) ice report. Quite soon, it was being asked if the ship had been speeding through ice-fields and if so, why? By Friday April 19, when the US Senate hearing began, this question had become a formal inquiry. Other questions followed on its heels: why was the iceberg not seen in time? Why did this ship have insufficient lifeboats to accommodate all her passengers? Why were many lifeboats unfilled? After the ship sank, why didn't lifeboats return to the wreckage while cries for help were heard from the water? Why were a disproportionate number of the lost from steerage? Were third-class passengers prevented from reaching the boat deck? Of those on board, on whom should blame settle? (Captain Smith? *Titanic's* officers? President Bruce Ismay? The White Star Line? The International Mercantile Marine Company? The British Board of Trade?) How far away from the scene was SS *Californian* and did she reprehensibly fail to come to the aid of *Titanic*?

Behind these urgent or specific questions, larger questions framed themselves: had ships become too large to be structurally sound or navigationally safe? Did the ship break in two before she sank? the inquiry wished to know, and the answers were confusingly pro and con. Had society become obsessed with speed at the expense of safety? And an urgent practical question: what steps should be taken to prevent another such maritime disaster? Seemingly smaller questions that nevertheless had large social implications bubbled up from the wreck: how come President Ismay survived whereas hundreds of passengers did not? How chivalrous in their behaviour were first-class men? (Was chivalry desirable in any case? feminists asked each other.) Certain counsel at the British inquiry especially wished to know why emergency boat No. 1 (capacity: 35) was launched with only twelve aboard, seven crew and five passengers, only two of those women. The women were Lady Duff Gordon and her secretary. Lady Duff Gordon's husband, Sir Cosmo, was suspected by some of having bribed the crew not to return to the scene of the sinking to look for survivors. At times during the two inquiries, it seemed as if the British class system with its special treatment for the rich and the ennobled and scant regard for the lower orders was being called into question. The American capitalist system that seemed to encourage the *New York Times* to strike a deal with the Marconi Company in order to secure a monopoly of news from the rescue ship, and to encourage companies such as Marconi to seek a monopoly in their market, was also questioned, though in an inevitably ineffectual manner.

Amidst all of these pertinent questions, one that was apparently trivial gradually took captive popular curiosity. What was the last tune played by the band as *Titanic* sank? Why did this question matter and why did it occupy so much of the attention of commentators?

The *New York Times* of Friday, April 19 printed Harold Bride's testimony, taken down on board *Carpathia* by a *Times* reporter who had brazened his way on board before the ship properly docked and discharged the survivors. The *Times* knew the value of the testimony and posted copyright below the byline. They must have sensed too the incipient romance of the story, entitling it 'Thrilling Story by Titanic's Surviving Wireless Man' and including in the subtitle 'Ship Sank to Tune of "Autumn"'. Having knocked out a below-deck hand who tried to steal radio operator Phillips' life belt, Bride left the radio shack with Phillips, hearing 'the tunes of the band. It was a rag-time tune, I don't know what. Then there was "Autumn". Phillips ran aft and that was the last I ever saw of him alive.' Oddly enough, Bride returned to this tremendous detail in his reported account.

> The ship was gradually turning on her nose – just like a duck does that goes down for a dive. I had only one thing on my mind – to get away from the suction. The band was still playing. I guess all of the band went down. They were playing "Autumn" then.

And a third time: 'the last I saw of the band, when I was floating out in the sea with my life belt on, it was still on deck playing "Autumn". How they ever did it I cannot imagine'. In its Sunday, April 21 issue, the *Times* itself returned to the subject of the last tune. It was sure that Bride had heard the Episcopalian (Anglican) hymn 'Autumn' beginning 'God of mercy and compassion', if he said he did, since his memory of other events aboard the stricken liner was so rich. The paper printed the three stanzas of the hymn by Louis Von Esch (c. 1810) and drew attention to lines in the third stanza of special poignancy and relevance:

When temptations fierce assault me,
When my enemies I find,
Sin and guilt, and death and Satan,
All against my soul combined,
Hold me up in mighty waters,
Keep my eyes on things above,
Righteousness, divine Atonement,
Peace, and everlasting Love.

The reporter surmised that the reference to mighty waters had suggested the hymn to some minister who asked for it to be played at the end. Logan Marshall, whose quick-off-the-mark book, *Sinking of the* Titanic *and Great Sea Disasters* (1912), is really an assembly of secondary sources with commentary, agreed with the *New York Times* (and lifted their surmise verbatim): 'the most authentic accounts' agree that this was the hymn tune played by Hartley and his band at journey's end. It was Walter Lord's choice too in his 1955 best-selling account of the tragedy, *A Night to Remember*.

But little is certain where *Titanic* is concerned. Bride, if he was quoted accurately here, as he was not quoted verbatim elsewhere in the *Times* article, referred to a rag-time 'tune' but did not identify 'Autumn' as a song or melody. The *Times* chose to identify it as a 'song', the hymn called 'Autumn'. But as Ian Jack recently told us, the father of Wallace Hartley, band-leader, had been choirmaster of a church in Colne, Lancashire and his son Wallace was trained as a musician in a hymn-singing and hymn-playing culture. Conceivably Hartley might have played AUTUMN the *tune*, rather than 'Autumn' the *song*. But in the *Penguin Book of Hymns* (1989), Ian Bradley tells us that there are *three* hymn tunes called AUTUMN, to which are set, respectively, Robert Bridges' 'Joy and Triumph Everlasting', George Horne's 'See the Leaves Around us Falling' and William Waltham How's 'The Year is Swiftly Turning', the last bearing the lines 'And life, brief life, is speeding;/The end is nearing fast' which, as Bradley comments, would have had a melancholy appropriateness.

But would Bride have recognised any of these tunes? None is reproduced in Bradley's anthology or discussed in his book, *Abide with Me: The World of Victorian Hymns* (1997), suggesting that none was popular enough to be played by Hartley's group. In any case, since Hartley's father was choirmaster in a Provident Independent Methodist church, was Wallace likely to be familiar with these Anglican productions? Perhaps. But would he have played, and could Bride possibly have recognised, the American Episcopal hymn tune AUGHTON (by WB Bradbury)? According to Bradley in his Penguin anthology, Sir Ronald Johnson believed AUGHTON was what Bride said but was misheard as saying 'Autumn' by the *New York Times* reporter and that this was the last tune heard from *Titanic*. Certainly the words by Joseph Henry Gilmore for which it was the setting had a chilling relevance:

> And when my task on earth is done
> When by Thy grace the victory's won
> E'en death's cold wave I will not flee
> Since God through Jordan leadeth me

Most of those who have pondered the last tune played on board have tended to forget that whatever tune it was had to be readily recognisable to Harold Bride, that it had to be a very familiar tune indeed, given the repetition of his identification of it.

It is possible that Bride was remembering and recognising a tune that had been played during one of the divine services aboard *Titanic* by the quintet which, according to Lord in *The Night Lives On* (1986), Hartley mustered for such an occasion, a trio being reserved for more intimate occasions outside the first-class restaurant and café. However, the *New York Times* of Sunday April 21 distinguished between the 'saloon orchestra' of five players and the 'deck band' of three players, which would imply a rather different separation of functions from that suggested by Lord. Yet there still seems to me the kind of familiarity in Bride's reference to the last tune that implies a secular popularity. It does not seem to me that Bride would have been so familiar with AUTUMN or AUGHTON as to recognise it and mention it frequently yet casually, and assuming equal familiarity on the part of the reporter and his readers. The reporter who felt it necessary to Americanise Bride's speech felt no need to identify the tune other than by its bare title. Admittedly it has been reported that a friend once asked Wallace Hartley what tune he would play on a sinking ship and he replied with the names of two well-known hymns (though not AUTUMN.

Still, Lord is probably correct when he changed his mind between his two books and identified the last tune (or one of the last tunes) not as AUTUMN a hymn but as 'Autumn' the popular waltz, composed by the Englishman Archibald Joyce and popular in the London of 1912. It was a former steamship band leader and contemporary of Hartley's who wrote to Lord in 1957 and informed him that the waltz 'Autumn' was almost certainly the tune in question. Joyce composed several popular waltzes, including 'Remembrance' (1909) and 'Songe D'Automne' (1908), the second widely known as 'Autumn'. The waltz was on the White Star Line playlists used by bands booked for 1912 by the company. No doubt it had been played often during the voyage, which would explain Bride's casual reference to it. Lord's observation that the waltz was not particularly popular in the United States might, however, make the *New York Times*' reporter's failure to qualify Bride's reference to the tune seem a bit odd. Still, in the matter of last tune aboard *Titanic*, 'God and his comforts were in full retreat', as Ian Jack remarks.

The Music of what Happened

And yet. The tunes Hartley told a friend he would play on a sinking ship were hymns: 'O God Our Help in Ages Past' written by Isaac Watts in 1714 and 'Nearer, My God, to Thee' written by Sarah Adams and published in 1841. Almost everyone – readers, film-makers, picture-goers, the man and woman in the street – associates Adams' hymn with the sinking of *Titanic*. In popular memory, it is the music of what happened that fateful night. The Bethel Choir and Colne Orchestra Society sang 'Nearer, My God, to Thee' as Wallace Hartley's body was lowered at his funeral on May 18, 1912 which an estimated 30,000 mourners attended. In Colne cemetery, the first words and musical bars of the hymn accompany the stone violin at the base of Hartley's tomb. It was Hartley's father who had introduced the hymn to Colne when he was choirmaster of Bethel Chapel. Since the hymn retells the story of Jacob who dreams a ladder to heaven and builds a monument on the site of his dream and calls it Bethel, Albion

Wallace Hartley's gravestone   Detail from the gravestone

Hartley's adoption of the hymn could not have been more appropriate. In the *New York Times* of April 21, the same issue in which 'Autumn' the hymn was identified as the last tune, it was reported from London (dateline April 20) that all of England believed that 'Nearer, My God, to Thee' was the tune in question.

Colonel Archibald Gracie, an American first-class passenger, posthumously dismissed the notion that the band played 'Nearer, My God, to Thee' as the ship sank. *The Truth about the* Titanic (1913) appeared after the author died in December 1912 from the lingering effects of his extraordinary ordeal after he swam to safety from the liner. The ever particular and sensible Gracie remembered that the band began to play before the inevitability of the sinking came home to him.

> We considered this a wise provision tending to allay excitement. I did not recognize any of the tunes, but I know they were cheerful and not hymns. If, as has been reported, 'Nearer, My God, to Thee' was one of the selections, I assuredly should have noticed it and regarded it as tactless warning of immediate death to us all and likely to create a panic that our special efforts were directed towards avoiding, and which we accomplished to the fullest extent. I know of only two survivors whose names are cited by the newspapers as authority for the statement that this hymn was one of those played. On the other hand, all whom I have questioned or corresponded with, including the best qualified, testified emphatically to the contrary.

Although Gracie was late off the doomed liner, he was until then busy with launching boats and escorting ladies into them; it could be that he was distracted from keeping note of the band's desperate repertoire. Besides, more than two survivors claimed to have heard 'Nearer, My God, to Thee'. Several were adamant the last strains heard from the sinking liner had been of this hymn. Of course, the vagaries of memory, with its fitfulness, its element of wish-fulfilment, its revisions through time but also its unforgettable and entrenched episodes, are fertilised by cultural desire and a need for appropriate closure. As Ken Kesey reminds us in his novel *One Flew Over the Cuckoo's Nest* (1962), some things are true even if they never happened. The sound of 'Nearer, My God, to Thee' wafting with heart-breaking plangency from the dangerously sloping decks of *Titanic* is one of them.

Vera Dick from Calgary was quoted in the *New York Times* of April 19:

> What I remember best was that as the ship sunk we could hear the band playing 'Nearer, My God, to Thee'. We looked back and could see the men standing on deck absolutely quiet and waiting for the end.

This may be a communal rather than personal memory, a post-traumatic suggestion, a memory that is graphically visual as well as aural. Mrs Dick's image evokes descriptions of the legendary foundering of the British troopship *Birkenhead* which sank off South Africa in 1852 with the troops, once the women and children had been put safely in the boats, standing in rank to attention until the waves overwhelmed them.

Mrs WJ Douton testified later: 'We rowed frantically away from the *Titanic* and were tied to four other boats. I arose and saw the ship sinking. The band was playing "Nearer, My God to Thee"'. The ship's barber, G. Whiteman from New Jersey[1], was reported as having heard the band play this hymn a few moments before she turned tail up and went under. Eva Hart, a long-lived and celebrated survivor, insisted in 1987 that she had heard 'Nearer, My God, to Thee' from the ship's deck: 'I am as certain about that as I am sitting here'. Charlotte Collyer was travelling to the United States in second cabin with her husband and daughter; her husband Harvey who had intended to become a fruit-farmer in Idaho was lost but Charlotte and her daughter were saved. Charlotte wrote a letter to her English in-laws from New York on Sunday April 21 in which she tries to console Harvey's parents: 'But mother we shall meet him in heaven. When that band played "Nearer, My God, to Thee" I know he thought of you and me for we both loved that hymn ...'.

It is impossible to rule out the possibility that the wish to console caused Charlotte Collyer to participate in the general desire that the band had played that hymn at the last and that she used it to provide comforting closure to Harvey's parents. The American *Semi-Monthly* magazine published her lengthy eye-witness account in late May 1912; it is a fine piece of writing and comparing its prose with that of her letter we might suspect a heavy editorial hand at work. A literary quality like a veil lightly covers Charlotte's testimony.

> During the day, a priest, a certain Father Byles, had held services in the second-cabin saloon; and I think it must have been he who stood there, leading those doomed men in prayer. The band was playing 'Nearer My God to Thee'; I could hear it distinctly. The end was very close.

The received elegiac syntax might have smuggled into Charlotte's memory the received wisdom that the band played 'Nearer, My God, to Thee', a hymn which in retrospect could function as a sacred elegy.

This restrained literary quality became self-confident melodrama in the books that quickly appeared, hastily pasted together by Jay Henry Mowbray, Marshall Everett, Philip Gibbs and Logan Marshall.

Restrained or unbuttoned, the literary quality helped enshrine the 'truth' of what tune was played at the last. A dramatic imperative was at work. 'When the last faint hope was gone', Everett in *Wreck and Sinking of the* Titanic intones:

> the eight musicians lined up on deck. Then solemnly and quietly the leader waved his baton, hands flew to instruments and over the ice laden water floated the strains of one of the most sadly beautiful hymns ever written. It was 'Nearer, My God, to Thee'.

In Marshall, the hymn becomes solemn but kitschily rendered accompaniment to two events, one foreground and one middle-ground:

> The band had broken out in the strains of 'Nearer, My God, to Thee', some minutes before [First Officer William] Murdock [sic] lifted the revolver to his head, fired and toppled over on his face. [Sixth Officer James] Moody saw all this in a vision that filled his brain, while his ears drank in the tragic strain of the beautiful hymn that the band played as their own dirge, even to the moment when the waters sucked them down. Wherever Murdock's eye swept the water in that instant, before he drew his revolver, it looked upon veritable seas of drowning men and women .... The strains of the hymn and the frantic cries of the dying blended in a symphony of sorrow.

Rev. Frank Adams, preaching a sermon in Central Universalist Church, Indianapolis in May 1912, saw in his mind's eye a theatrical tableau: 'in the face of the stern reality, standing in the presence of the great mystery that lies beyond the impenetrable curtain we call death, the music became a prayer, and on bended knees the orchestra played "Nearer, My God, to Thee"'.

This particular hymn expresses and evokes what we might call, riskily under the circumstances, rock-bottom sentiment. It is a hymn that expresses such latitudinarianism, such near-universality of human feeling that it expands its appeal beyond denomination, even beyond Christianity. Indeed, in 1923, a theologian, J. Gresham Machen, felt he had to lodge a doctrinal objection. Hymns addressing the Cross, Biel quotes him as writing, are on a scale between a lower and higher view of 'Jesus' Person'. At the very bottom of the scale is 'Nearer, My God, to Thee'. People have been misled by the occurrence of the word 'cross' in the hymn, but:

> the verse simply means that our own crosses or trials may be a means to bring us nearer to God. It is a perfectly good thought, but certainly it is not the gospel. One can only be sorry that the people on the Titanic could not find a better hymn to die by than that.

This criticism (made much earlier by those who objected to the hymn-writer's Unitarianism – but no one objected at the time of the tragedy, for that would have been perilous) indirectly explained the immense popularity of the hymn and why readers wanted it to have been played and sung at the end.

Swansong of the *Titanic*

In any case, 'Nearer, My God, to Thee' quickly became the unofficial anthem of the *Titanic* disaster. One reporter called it the 'swansong' of the *Titanic*. According to the *Literary Digest* (New York), there was a Requiem for the *Titanic* dead towards the end of April 1912 in the Trocadero hall in Paris. The French paper *La Liberté* reported that the Leeds Choir sang the Hector Berlioz *Requiem*, yet this work:

> in spite of its beauties, had less effect upon its hearers than the simple hymn chanted at the beginning of the service by the English choristers. Two hundred and fifty voices of men and women thundered forth the hymn 'Nearer, My God, to Thee' which the unfortunate shipwrecked victims of the Titanic sang at the hour of death in the midst of the ocean.

The reporter felt moved to imbue the hymn with an extraordinary significance and power.

> This Anglican hymn resembles our Catholic hymns. It is broad in meaning and is inspired. It breathes the spirit of profound faith. When we heard it yesterday it seemed to us sublime. When the first notes of this hymn were uttered the whole audience rose. The members of the Calonne orchestra did the same. Every face grew pale; the women, covering their faces with their hands, seemed to pray or weep; a kind of shudder passed through this crowd composed, as it was, in a great measure, of religious skeptics. But in listening to this supreme appeal to the pity of God your imagination mingled with the air, with the night, with the infinite outside, and the terrible solitude of the gigantic ship stricken to death and laden with human beings doomed to die. The hymn arose ardent and serious, 'Nearer, my God, to Thee, Nearer to Thee, Nearer to Thee'. Doubtless among the men and women who listened to it more than one of them felt that this faith which they had neglected, forgotten, or denied, for a few moments regained its power over them, recovered all its empire in the most frivolous hearts, in the most emancipated minds.

Survivors and memorialists ignored the question, 'which *tune* did survivors hear?' The words of 'Nearer, My God, to Thee' have been set to at least five tunes. The most popular (Anglican) British tune has been HORBURY, composed by JB Dykes for *Hymns Ancient and Modern* (1861); in the USA the tune most often heard has been

BETHANY, written by Lowell Mason in 1856; PROPIOR DEO, composed by Sir Arthur Sullivan in 1872, was favoured by British Methodists. Other tunes include LIVERPOOL by John Roberts (1822–1877) and NENTHORN by Thomas Legerwood Hately (1815–1867). Those who insisted that they heard this hymn included Britons, Americans and Canadians, so nationality of memory is no obvious solution. Besides, as Lord reminds us, divine service on British liners was Anglican, during which HORBURY would have been played had the hymn been sung, whereas Hartley was a Methodist and therefore would have been more familiar with PROPIOR DEO: so denomination is no obvious solution either. Does this uncertainty throw a fatal doubt on the role of 'Nearer, My God, to Thee' in the drama of *Titanic?*

Even if it does, the cultural imperative that exerted itself in the immediate aftermath of the disaster is no less fascinating. Clearly 'Nearer, My God, to Thee' is the hymn that many thought ought to have been played as the liner sank. In popular imagination then, and popular memory since, the band played ragtime and waltzes to keep the spirits up and then a hymn when doom was imminent. There was no better candidate than 'Nearer, My God, to Thee'. After early criticism that the hymn, composed by the Unitarian daughter of a radical journalist, did not mention Christ (this made it suitable for multi-denominational occasions, which the last scenes on board *Titanic* would have represented in the bedlam of anguish), Sarah Adams' creation became so popular in late nineteenth-century Britain as to reach number seven spot in a popularity poll run by *Sunday at Home* magazine in 1887. ('Rock of Ages', an eighteenth-century composition, led in popularity, Bradley tells us in *Abide with Me*.) After President McKinley of the United States was shot by an anarchist on September 6, 1901, he was expected to recover but within a week succumbed. When he knew that his end was near, readers of the *Review of Reviews* were told, 'he was heard muttering the first verse of the familiar hymn, 'Nearer, my God, to Thee'. His last audible words were, 'It is God's way; His way is best. God's will be done'.

This description of McKinley's death would have been written by the editor of the *Review of Reviews*, WT Stead. In a despatch by Marconi Transatlantic Wireless Telegraph, readers of the *New York Times* were told on April 21, 1912 that it was believed in England that it was Stead who on board the sinking liner had chosen 'Nearer, My God, to Thee' for the band to play. (To caulk the idea that uncertainty attends all things Titanic: *Etude*, a Philadelphia music magazine in its

June 1912 issue printed a framed tribute to the ship's musicians and ended by quoting 'the last lines of the hymn *Autumn*, said to have been chosen by the much-loved journalist and educator, WT Stead, just before the *Titanic* sank to its grave two miles below'.) The reporter recalled the successful anthology Stead had edited, *Hymns that have Helped: Being a Collection of those Hymns, Whether Jewish, Christian, or Pagan, which have been Found Most Useful to the Children of Men*, published in London by the *Review of Reviews* in 1896, and the following year in the United States by Doubleday and McClure. One month after the *Titanic* sinking, the *Review of Reviews* announced in its May, 1912 number that Stead's anthology was now available again from Stead's Publishing House, London in a reprint Stead had been arranging just before he sailed for America. In the anthology, Stead reprinted about 150 hymns nominated by those who responded to (in effect) his question, 'What hymns have helped you?' He must have selected his own respondents because they included the famous or established.

Hymn number 72, 'Nearer, My God, to Thee', Stead identified as the favourite hymn of the Prince of Wales and printed a letter he had received to that effect from Sandringham. But Stead comments that the hymn 'is as dear to the peasant as it is to the prince'. The universal appeal of the hymn in the English-speaking world must have specified itself with almost subliminal appropriateness during the *Titanic* affair. The exhortation to God of an apparently abandoned soul in darkness ('Daylight all gone') is a desire to rise upwards to the divine vicinity: 'There let the way appear/Steps unto heaven ... Sun, moon, and stars forgot,/Upward I fly'. The opposing and awful trajection, the imminent *descent* into the Deep by the hapless left on board after the last boats had gone, must have virtually required that this be the ending hymn.

Two last comments on 'Nearer, My God, to Thee' and its role in cultural memory and in our difficulty in getting to the truth of the matter. One is on Elizabeth Robins' choice of the hymn for her endangered passengers to sing while the liner they are on is assailed by icebergs in her 1908 novel *Come and Find Me!*

> While the nerves of the people still vibrated under the bombardment, some one started 'Nearer, my God, to Thee'. Strangest of all on that strange evening was the revelation that in this particular company, hardly one but seemed to know the hymn, and few that were not singing it with abandon to the thunderous bass of the ice.

The strangeness of passengers singing a hymn in such circumstances (or perhaps singing *this* hymn) is offset by the familiarity of the words and tune to everyone there. It is as if Robin's imaginary characters have surprised their own creator in their sudden accession of cultural identity. Robins was a popular writer but it is impossible to tell if this scene embedded itself in the English and American collective memory and imagination and came to the surface in April 1912 on a real ship in very real distress.

Might Robins in 1907 (when presumably she would have been at work on her novel) in turn have been drawing upon reports of a real sinking and a real singing of 'Nearer, My God, to Thee' that Richard Howells recently uncovered? On Monday, January 22, 1906, a steamer, *Valencia*, a vessel of the Pacific Coast Steamship Company, sailing from San Francisco to Victoria, ran aground off Vancouver Island on the west coast of Canada. Although the beached ship was only 60 feet from shore, passengers and crew could not disembark because of the rough seas and as time went on, to the horror of helpless onlookers and would-be rescuers on the shore, there were deaths. The ship broke up and the desperate survivors clambered up the rising stern and eventually the rigging. On Wednesday morning, by which time the situation looked hopeless, the survivors began to sing 'Nearer, My God, to Thee'. Howells quotes a contemporary reporter in the *Pacific Monthly* recounting how 'a half-score women lifted up their voice in song' ... after 'long hours of agony that crazed strong men, [they] tremulously sang "Nearer My God, to Thee"'. A group of men who attempted to reach shore on a life-raft looked back and saw women and children:

> over the roaring of the waters the strains of the song faintly floated: 'E'en tho' it be a cross that raiseth me' ... the brave faces looking at them over the broken rail of a wreck and of the echo of that great hymn sung by women who, looking death smilingly in the face, were able in the fog and mist and flying spray to remember: 'Nearer, My God, to Thee'.

The wreck of *Valencia* was widely reported in the *New York Times* and elsewhere, though it seems unlikely that Robins read, specifically, Clarence H. Baily in the *Pacific Monthly*. Yet both the fictional and the historical accounts register a surprise that this hymn was so readily available to those in grave danger, a surprise that is then undermined by the sense of a shared cultural reserve the singing of the hymn expresses.

Those in Peril on the Sea
Not all of Stead's respondents agreed to name the hymns that had helped them: Herbert Spencer the philosopher admitted to a dislike of hymns, while the Bishop of Winchester declined on the grounds that

his cooperation would require his spiritual autobiography: from his pulpit, the bishop would nonetheless be famously and thunderously forthcoming about *Titanic* on the Sunday after the disaster, denouncing the Godless arrogance that built and furnished *Titanic*. But a kind of autobiography is what Stead was after. He volunteered the hymn which had most helped him: 'Begone, Unbelief' by the eighteenth-century poet John Newton. Despite the hymn's bad rhymes and its illogic, 'the verse', said Stead, 'has been as a life-buoy, keeping my head above the waves when the sea raged and was tempestuous, and when all else failed'. Surely Stead must have sung this hymn under his breath as he went under with the great ship.

The good Christian fortune of being 'saved' is, in the Acts of the Apostles and the Epistles of St Paul, as JR Watson reminds us, a maritime metaphor. Newton had experienced danger at sea and in one hymn he writes: 'With Christ in the vessel/I smile at the storm'. Stead used another maritime metaphor in his preface; he interpreted the ostensible modesty of those who refused to reveal their preference as inverted egotism and continued: 'It is not regarded as egotism when the passing steamer signals across the Atlantic wave news of her escape from perils of iceberg or fog', yet individuals repress their expression of gratitude after a hymn has helped him or her to survive a physical or spiritual shipwreck. Regardless of the intrinsic merit of a hymn's poetry, 'if that hymn proved itself a staff and a stay to some heroic soul in the darkest hours of his life's pilgrimage', that hymn was a sacred song. Perhaps in order to make themselves – the safe on terra firma – feel less guilty, many assumed 'Nearer, My God, to Thee' performed that duty just before *Titanic* went under the waves.

Stead considered hymn selection autobiography of a more impersonal kind. He thought hymns provided a superior profile of the British nation – its aspirations and deepest emotions – to that provided by the press, and suspected that the same was true of hymns sung in America. Victorian hymns in particular could overtly reflect English chauvinism. Besides, there had been incidents 'where a hymn has figured conspicuously in some notable episode of human history': even the spiritualist Stead could hardly have anticipated his own role and the role of one of his hymns in just such an episode. Really, the role of a hymn could hardly have been other, given the astounding popularity of hymn-singing, not just in Britain but in the empire; Stead was sure that as he wrote, the sound of a simple hymn somewhere in Canada, India or Australia was transporting its listener back to his beginnings in an English parish. Christian hymns were the foremost music of the British Empire. And many hymns were sung on both sides of the

Atlantic: 'The English-speaking race has presumably no difficulty in recognising its unity when praising its Maker'. Hymns could preach an Anglo-Saxon supremacy, of which we will have more to say later.

Stead identified 269 Anglican hymnals in existence; 35 million copies of *Hymns Ancient and Modern* had been circulated between 1860 and Stead's time of writing. Every important Protestant sect had its hymnal, with the hymn book as important for non-Anglicans as the Prayer Book for Anglicans. The most resonant form of popular religious feeling, JFC Harrison observes, was the singing of hymns; it was a form of British and American folk culture. Hymns sounded from top to bottom of British society, from the lowest to the highest church, from cottages to cabinet-rooms. Gladstone's 1880 cabinet included three hymnodists. Hymns were everywhere, not only in churches and chapels but in schools, house parlours, public halls, hospitals, street corners: at weddings, trade union rallies, political meetings. The Arctic and Antarctic exploration parties regularly held 'church' with hymn-singing. Presumably hymns were morale boosters and expressions of thanksgiving as well as religious obligations. Apsley Cherry-Garrard recalls the hymn-singing aboard *Terra Nova* on Scott's last expedition, and which the expedition's naturalist Edward Wilson as a religious man punctiliously recorded in his diary. Cherry-Garrard remembered the popularity of 'Praise the Lord, ye heavens adore Him' (an early Victorian hymn) at Cape Evans on Scott's last expedition.

Certain events were infused with importance through the singing of hymns over and above the Christian calendar. For example, when the rescue ship *Carpathia* reached New York harbour on Thursday evening, April 18, crowds of relatives and friends of passengers scrambled toward the Cunard pier. A *New York Times* reporter observed that 'On the curb at Tenth Avenue, just outside the police lines, a band of Salvation Army folk stood in the rain singing hymns and praying for those aboard the Carpathia'.

Passengers still on board or on the departing boats, if they heard a hymn, had probably heard other hymns on the day that had recently ended, Sunday, April 14. On British liners, divine service was conducted by the captain according to the rites of the Church of England and included the singing of hymns. The American first-class passenger Archibald Gracie remembered the Sunday morning service. He had been impressed by the 'Prayer for those at Sea', which would have been a reading, or singing, of the 'sailors' hymn', 'For Those at Sea', written by William Whiting (1825–1878) and having as a refrain 'O hear us, when we cry to thee,/For those in peril on the sea'. The shipboard congregation that morning also sang 'O God, our help in

ages past', Watts' paraphrase of Psalm 90. Ian Bradley considers it to
have achieved the status of second national anthem in Victorian
Britain, and its ringing out in divine service would have fractionally
Anglicised the *Titanic* experience, even though the fourth verse
reminds its singers that 'All nations rose from Earth at first,/And turn
to earth again'.

There were other religious services aboard *Titanic* the evening she
hit the iceberg. An English priest, Father Thomas Byles from Essex, and
a German monk, Father Joseph Peruschoetz (or Peruschitz) – both
second cabin passengers – held morning and evening services for the
ship's Roman Catholics; in the dying minutes of the tragedy on board,
when the last boat had gone, they repeated the rosary to a gathering
crowd of the doomed in steerage. Both priests perished. Stuart Collett,
going to America to become a theology student, was saved in well-
laden lifeboat number 9. He told reporters that he had been assisting
Rev. William Carter (a Londoner like Collett) in a hymn and prayer
service (Charlotte Collyer appears to have confused Carter with Father
Byles). At the service, one of the young women later saved on lifeboat
9, Marian Wright, travelling to Portland, Oregon to be married, had
played the piano and sung three hymns: 'There are Green Hills Far
Away', 'For those in Peril at Sea' and 'Lead, Kindly Light'. The first
must have been the Irishwoman Mrs Cecil Alexander's popular 'There
is a Green Hill Far Away', the second was the sailors' hymn, and the
third JH (later Cardinal) Newman's composition, a poem surprisingly
turned into one of the most popular of all Victorian hymns. Rev. Carter
prayed and the 35 travelling worshippers then sang 'Now the Day is
Ended'. This would have been either Sabine Baring-Gould's 'Now the
Day is Over (night is drawing nigh)' or another Victorian hymn, 'The
Day Thou Gavest, Lord, is Ended'. Either would have been painfully
apt unbeknownst to the congregants. During the last hymn, according
to Collett, the worshippers felt *Titanic* collide with the iceberg and
scrambled to the boat deck. This is not Lawrence Beesley's recollection.

Beesley had met Carter, a Church of England vicar, on Sunday
afternoon and befriended him, and it was Beesley who asked the purser
if Carter might use the saloon for the 8:30pm 'hymn sing-song' on
Sunday evening. Before the hymn-sing, the observant Beesley had
noticed the English and German priests talking together. Beesley
estimated 100 singers in the saloon and in his recollection a young
Scotch engineer had played piano accompaniment to hymns chosen
by the impromptu congregation, each introduced by the
knowledgeable Carter. Many passengers according to Beesley chose
hymns dealing with dangers at sea. Singing lasted until ten o'clock

after which Carter spoke of the happiness and safety of the voyage thus far, and all the while, as Beesley remarks, 'the peril on the sea' was but a few miles ahead. Carter and his wife, Lillian, were lost, but Beesley takes comfort in the supposition that 'the sound of the hymns still echoed in their ears as they stood on the deck so quietly and courageously'. Beesley had effected his own escape in a lifeboat.

Hymns satisfied the Victorian thirst for public sentiment, often masquerading as religiosity. They released some of the feeling repressed by what was otherwise Victorian public severity, and even hymns put their feeling in strict harness. Among the major English writers who were moved to comment on the *Titanic* tragedy were Rudyard Kipling and Thomas Hardy, both deeply interested in hymns and the culture of hymns. Stead quoted the writer Alice Meynell's testament to the power of hymns over men's minds, which Kipling and Hardy also acknowledged. (Even the self-avowed atheist George Bernard Shaw admitted that hymn-singing is a 'highly enjoyable, healthy, and recreative exercise', one that he had been caught out performing in October 1912 at a Salvation Army meeting!) The English novelist and poet, DH Lawrence, recognised the power of hymns, and in an *Evening News* article of 1928, 'Hymns in a Man's Life', he recalled the hymns of his Congregationalist boyhood in Nottinghamshire, and how they survived his early rejection of Christian dogma. It is easy to claim that the depths at which hymns 'live and glisten' in a man's consciousness, as Lawrence put it, are those from which the need to sing or hear 'Nearer, My God, to Thee' surfaced on board *Titanic* in its last minutes.

Hymns seemed particularly suited to express the anxiety of wayfarers, especially seafarers. There was good reason for spiritual consolation to be on hand for those who sailed the seas and those who waited for them on land. In 1911 Stead reminded his readers in the *Review of Reviews* of the astounding loss of life and loss of material that took place on the seas. 'Nine hundred and eighty-six vessels of the world's merchant marine – steam and sail – totally lost in the year 1908 ... and this tally recognises only steam-vessels over one hundred tons burden'. In March 1912 he returned to the theme and quoted an article, 'Lost Liners', from *Chambers's Journal* to the effect that between 1841 and 1890, twenty-four large steamers had disappeared entirely without trace, with a complement of human souls numbering from 77 to 480. The exact number of lives lost in this 'toll of the sea' over the years was unknown but vast. In May 1912 Stead's magazine ran a full-page serious *Punch* drawing called 'Toll of the Sea' that depicted Britannia holding the hand of a mourning woman

waiting by a stormy shore for her beloved who she seems to intuit is
drowned.

The anxiety of wayfarers is an intense form of the anxiety that
made easy the idea of life as a hazardous pilgrimage, from which many
hymns appeared to derive. The frequent helplessness of the wayfarer
was like the helplessness of the child (the best hymns had a childlike
quality and established themselves in the Christian's childhood, as
Lawrence knew) which in turn was, writ small, the helplessness of
humankind that like a lost child was painfully nostalgic for home: 'I'm
but a stranger here', one hymn lamented, 'Heaven is my home'.

We will never know what the lost on board *Titanic* felt if and when
they heard or sang a hymn as the ship sank. But we might claim with
some assurance that the living felt it necessary that the playing and
singing of the hymn rose up *de profundis*. 'There is no getting away
from the centrality of death as a theme in Victorian hymnody',
Bradley remarks. What Victorians wanted in hymns, it was said, was
plenty of consolation and not too much theology. Indeed, late
Victorians were plagued with religious doubt, and whereas it would
make sense that the Last Tune on *Titanic* Question was due to the deep
Victorian interest in hymns and deep Victorian faith, it might equally
be the case that the desire for a hymn to have been played at the last
was due to the receding nature of Victorian Christianity, that the
Titanic tragedy troubled religious well-springs because those well-
springs were starting to dry up. If newspapers and magazines wrapped
the tragedy in religion, that may be because a secular age was dawning
in Britain and America. If commentators wanted certainty, including
the certainty of heroism, of chivalry, of Christian faith and a hymn-
singing finale, that may be because doubt was in the increasingly
chilly air. Thomas Hardy was a leading and eloquent doubter and in
his famous poem 'The Convergence of the Twain (Lines on the Loss
of the *Titanic*)' he quickly appropriated the *Titanic* calamity as a
graphic example of the kind of eventuality that showed divine malice
(at worst) or nature's grim neutrality (at best) holing the body of
benign and spiritually optimistic Christian faith and belief. Yet Hardy
was a lover of hymns and his preserved copy of *Hymns Ancient and
Modern* is well-thumbed and his favourite hymns asterisked and
annotated; beside 'Praise the lord, ye heavens adore Him' (beloved of
Scott and his men) Hardy, according to Bradley, scribbled 'AE
Housman', suggesting it was the favourite hymn of that well-known
English poet.

Bradley has observed how often darkness is a theme in Victorian
hymns, and he sees what he calls 'faith-in-doubt' even in

Newman's 'Lead, Kindly Light' that Rev. Carter and his small flock sang as the iceberg bore up on them. The tragic end of *Titanic* took place in darkness amidst the bright lights of the liner that stayed lit long after it seemed they should have, and when they were doused only the mocking points of the stars remained to illuminate those in the boats.

In Memoriam

It might seem far-fetched to see *Titanic* as taking to the bottom much of the Christian certainty that had pervaded Britain and had helped shore up the Victorian nation and its empire, to see it as a sunken symbolic culmination of the retreat of faith that the English poet Matthew Arnold imagined 40 years before as a receding sea. Rather, it is the First World War that is seen as a watershed in the career of a nation-based European Christianity, yet the latter as much as the former is suffused and enveloped with religion. The wish to believe that the lost on board *Titanic* had sought solace in a Christian hymn went beyond payment of tribute to the stoicism of those passengers. Survivors' accounts became quasi-religious testament: there was an assumption of events into sacred legend through the rituals of commemoration. Victorian Britain was a deeply memorial society. A central text of this memorial society was by a Poet Laureate who earned the name of nation's poet more than most and who in a maritime metaphor famously imagined dying as 'crossing the bar': *In Memoriam* (1833–1849) by Alfred, Lord Tennyson. Here is the Victorian instinct to preserve, commemorate and perpetuate, yet an instinct flagging and admitting doubt, and the more brittle for the admission. The ritual career of *Titanic* displays the Victorian love of public commemorative panoply in a perhaps too gaudily triumphant way.

Commemorative observance began at once. On board *Carpathia* Captain Rostron found an Anglican minister among his passengers to conduct a religious service in the first-class dining room – a funeral ceremony for the lost, a thanksgiving ceremony for the rescued. The obituaries of the notables who drowned were appearing in the major newspapers at the same time. Since the lost included some of the wealthiest and most powerful men in America, assorted club-men and society women from the chief cities in the United States, a sprinkling of English nobles, and a variety of actors, actresses, producers, writers and artists, the obituaries were lavish and occasionally fulsome. Astor, Guggenheim, Straus, Hays, Butt and Widener dominated the obituary columns. Astor's funeral took place on May 5, and at the suggestion of King George V, the Prince of Wales sent roses. But Steven Biel in his

Down with the Old Canoe (1996) tells us that a huge female suffrage parade in New York on that day, attracting 15,000 women, elbowed the report of Astor's funeral off the front page of the *New York Times* – not, as we shall see, such an irony since Astor had been widely believed to have demonstrated faultless chivalry, a chivalry that was being weighed in the balance (and found wanting) by many of the women attending the parade.[2]

The many funerals extended the opportunity for mass displays of commemorative mourning, though none equalled in popular attendance Wallace Hartley's funeral on May 18 in Colne, a town of around 26,000 playing host to a funeral party of 30,000 or more. Hartley's body had been brought from the New World to Liverpool by the White Star liner *Arabic*, thence by road to its destination.

Memorial services held at St Paul's Chapel in New York on Friday April 19 and in St Paul's Cathedral in London on the same day were but the opening religious salvoes that reached barrage proportions on Sunday April 21. Not that the London service wasn't impressive. Five thousand mourners, Gibbs tells us, 'a vast, black multitude', packed the cathedral and the neighbourhood; a military band from the Household troops played sacred music and the 'Dead March from Saul'. A caption to a full-page photograph in the *Illustrated London News* for April 27 identifies some of the notable mourners: the Lord Mayor of London, members of the Cabinet, the President of the Board of Trade, the United States Ambassador to the Court of St James, and representatives of the White Star Line. But we are told that no seats had been reserved and 'rich and poor sat together in the vast congregation'. The alleged democracy in grief was a motif in much published comment on the *Titanic* disaster.

But it was on the following Sunday that Christianity roused itself into action and the Victorian and Edwardian memorial culture (that lasted halfway into the twentieth century, as late as the state funerals of Sir Winston Churchill and John F. Kennedy) drew itself up and fully asserted itself. Churches were packed throughout the Western world with services dedicated to the *Titanic* dead in hundreds, perhaps thousands of places of worship, in New York, Washington, Chicago, London, Ottawa, Toronto, Melbourne, Cape Town, Liverpool, Southampton, Glasgow, Belfast and countless other towns and cities. Services were more numerous in the English-speaking world, and they became rallying points for Anglo-Saxon (or Euro-American) Christianity in the British and American empires. 'Nearer, My God, to Thee' received a bountiful hearing, for example at Belfast Cathedral when it was sung during the offertory, which was in aid of the widows and orphans of the disaster. It is fair to assume that gallons of tears were spilled across the world before the first verse of the hymn was through. The hymn was also heard during the evening service at the City Temple in London, but was augmented by a hymn written especially for the occasion by the English novelist Hall Caine, 'Hymn for Survivors of the *Titanic*' and sung to the tune of 'O, God, our Help in Ages Past'.

Ministers of the cloth were well versed in calamity and come the Sunday after the sinking they were more than ready with their sermons, some of them delivered in blistering tones of retribution, but many of them careful not to distract their congregation from their grief by doing other than paying tribute to the chivalry of the men, the nobility of the women, and the heroism of almost all. (Caine's hymn sounded that positive note of regret: 'Beneath the roll of soundless waves/Our best and bravest lie'.) The 'women and children first' rule, largely observed during the ship's evacuation, was easily assimilated to the Christian notion of sacrifice, and the standing aside of many of the rich men in first class easily assimilated to the Christian connection between poverty and purity that made riches a spiritual impediment. 'The man with a hundred million dollars', Rev. Frank Adams reminded his Indianapolis congregation:

> stood aside and made room for his wife's serving maid. The man who has swayed continents with his pen gave place to a woman from the steerage. The railroad magnate remained on the sinking ship that a babe in arms might have his place in the lifeboat .... Then to me, one of the most heartening lessons is that religion is not such a back number, after all.

The demonstration of Christian behaviour aboard *Titanic* was to this and to many another preacher a surprise, a successful spiritual rearguard action. In Christian terms, the outcome had been a fine one. What a splendid thought, Dean Grierson of the Anglican Belfast Cathedral was reported by the *Belfast News-Letter* of April 22 to have exclaimed, that the bond of a common sorrow had turned rich and poor again to God. Mangasar Mugurditch Mangasarian (founder of the Independent Religious Society), and quoted by Biel, said: 'The *Titanic* episode has vindicated human nature grandly'. Yes, said the *Christian Century*, 'it is the moral greatness of man that stands revealed in the picture ... manhood triumphed when the Titanic sank'. The tragedy was both a complete spiritual triumph (with its 'numerous evidences of religious confidence, resignation, and prayer that we meet in the narratives of the unhappy survivors', as James, Cardinal Gibbons put it in his sermon in St Stephen's Church, Washington

DC) and a healthy spiritual prospectus for the future: 'Surely', the *Baptist Courier* of Greenville, South Carolina proclaimed, 'all men will read with a renewed faith Christ's eternal warning "Be ye also ready"'.

The religious grand narrative was too good to overlook. 'The Great Captain is on the bridge of the good ship "Rescue" looking for the souls lost in the night of sin', readers of the *Baptist Record* (Jackson, Mississippi) were told. The *Herald and Presbyter* (Cincinnati, Ohio) found no 'hesitancy' on the part of the rescuers; and indeed, the deeply sentimental response around the Western world to the tragedy derived in sizeable part from the warmth of the spectacle of strangers hastening to the aid of fellow human beings in darkness and danger.

But emotions were mixed nonetheless, even in the heat of public bereavement. On Thursday April 18 it was announced in the papers that Frederick Townsend Martin was organising a mass meeting for Sunday April 21, to be held in the Broadway Theatre, New York – 'A meeting that is to be at once a memorial to the *Titanic's* dead and a protest against the laws and customs which made possible so fearful a toll of lives'. Despite the solemnity of the occasion, the packed theatre resounded with approval of resolutions that were proposed and passed. On the day (as Everett reported), Martin celebrated a heroism 'that only the angels can surpass, far greater than that shown on the greatest battlefield in the world's history' but also attacked policy that encouraged commerce unfettered by safety considerations. The keynote speaker was William Jennings Bryan, the fiery campaigner who had lost the presidential race to William McKinley in 1896. Bryan praised the 'manliness and womanliness' demonstrated during the disaster and that are 'the heritage of our people' but suggested to the 'vast multitude' that 'this great disaster, this greater, this gigantic, this Titanic disaster will result in legislation that will be beneficial to those who come after'. He condemned 'the mania for speed' demonstrated by shipowners. The tone struck by these speakers was that uniquely American combination of inflated rhetoric and hardheaded legalistic resolution that characterised the Report of the US Senate Hearing on the *Titanic* disaster and so irritated the British.

While those on shore wept, mourned, sang, prayed and occasionally protested, a grim scene was unfolding on the ocean and in a Nova Scotian city. The task of searching for bodies fell to a Canadian cable ship chartered by the White Star Line. The *Mackay-Bennett* carried on board Canon KO Hind of All-Saints' Cathedral, Halifax who conducted three burial services at sea. When the ship returned to port with 190 bodies (leaving another Canadian cable ship, *Minia*, to continue the search), a naval band was waiting to play the 'Dead March from Saul'. Church bells rang for days. There was a funeral service for 50 victims (mostly unidentified) conducted by the Evangelical Alliance on Friday May 3 in Brunswick Street Methodist Church. The Royal Canadian Regiment played 'Nearer, My God, to Thee' at the service as well as Hall Caine's new hymn, before the 700 mourners moved to Fairview Lawn Cemetery where the bodies still repose. At the grave-sides, 'Nearer, My God, to Thee' was played by a kilted band of pipers.

However, there were denominational differences in death to be respected as fully as the social class differences (the wealthy dead were expensively transported for burial in their home towns and villages). The major denominations claimed the bodies which were dispersed to their appropriate graveyards in interim divine judgement. Accordingly, three Halifax graveyards have since 1912 been dignified by the presence of *Titanic* dead: Fairview (non-denominational, i.e. chiefly Protestant), Baron de Hirsch (Jewish) and Mount Olivet (Roman Catholic). (One victim buried in Fairview was discovered to be a Catholic and a fortnight after burial was whisked over to the correct destination of his earthly remains.) Absurd though it is to be invidious about graves, the Fairview cemetery offers the most powerful emotional impact, not just because it holds the greatest number of bodies (121) but because, as Jeffers and Gordon tell us, the grave-site forms a giant hieroglyphic, with the graves arrayed to suggest the curvature of a ship's hull tapering towards her bow. By an affecting coincidence, the direction of this landlocked ship happens to be perfectly aligned with the direction of the real forward hull on the ocean bed miles below the surface.

The drawn-out recovery of the bodies and their passage home, the numbers of towns, cities and countries affected by the disaster, the magnitude of the bereavement, the celebrity of many of the first-class dead – these caused the *Titanic* disaster to be commemorated well into May, 1912. There were scores of memorial services for individuals. For example, for Major Archibald Butt (Presidential aide) in New York City's St Mark's Church and again in St Paul's Episcopal Church, Washington with President Taft and Mrs Taft and the Secretaries of the Treasury and War in attendance. Unsurprisingly, the singing of 'Nearer, My God, to Thee' opened the service. The mourners and tribute-payers at the service for WT Stead at Westminster Chapel on April 25 were impressive, including Lords Haldane, Esher and Milner, Earl Grey, Lloyd George, and the Countess of Warwick. Queen

Alexandra sent a message of sympathy. Stead was acclaimed as a journalist and prophet, though there is no record of his being acclaimed at the service as a firm believer in spiritualism.

The Culture – and Industry – of Grief

In many cities, but especially in London and New York, there were pageants and fetes and concerts in memory of *Titanic* victims and in aid of their relatives and orphans. Money cascaded into fundraising agencies: London's Mansion House Fund alone reached the sum of £321,000 ($1,600,000) by the end of July and finally reached the sum of £412,000 (over $2,000,000) and was active until as late as 1958, when it closed, its purpose fulfilled. Impresarios and performers, for whom the disaster was as big an opportunity as it was for preachers, tried to achieve a high profile.

The memorial culture embraced the memorial industry. George M. Cohan, actor-manager, staged vaudeville and theatre stars at the Cohan Theater and raised $2,500. The Shuberts, FC Whitney, Henry W. Savage and other theatre managers staged a benefit performance 'of large proportions' in the New York Hippodrome on Sunday evening, April 28 which featured Marie Dressler, Al Jolson, Weber & Fields, Charles Hawtrey, Forbes Robertson, and numerous other famous performers and companies, including the French Grand Opera Company. A five-hour matinee at the London Hippodrome on April 30 mounted a new operetta, *Arms and the Girl*, by Richard Fall, and presented Cyril Maude in *French as She is Spoke*, CH Workman and Claude Fleming in a duet from *Nightbirds*, Herbert Sleath and WF Grant in *The Littlest Girl*, a lantern slide show brought from the United States showing the arrival in New York of *Carpathia*, and the first-hand experience of condescension disguised as role-reversal and *noblesse oblige*, with Countess Townshend giving out programmes. At the Queen's Hall, London matinee on May 5 (organised by the Amalgamated Musicians' Union and the Sunday League), a 500 strong orchestra played in aid of the relatives of *Titanic*'s bandsmen.

As the 500 strong orchestra suggests, it was difficult to avoid Titanism in commemoration which was both big business and big public theatre (as well as big religion) in those days. But that orchestra was given a run for its money by the combined musical force of the Philharmonic, Queen's Hall, London Symphony, New Symphony and Beecham orchestras, assembled at the Royal Albert Hall on May 24 to honour the memory of Hartley and his fellow *Titanic* musicians. May 24 ('The 24th of May, the Queen's birthday/If we don't get a holiday,/We'll all run away') – was Empire Day; the choice of occasion 'patriated' the *Titanic* disaster, and the ship herself, and claimed them for Britain. The massed orchestras stood to play Chopin's *Marche Funèbre* conducted by Sir Henry Wood. Percy Pitt conducted Sullivan's overture, *In Memoriam*, followed by Sir Edward Elgar's conducting of his own [*Enigma*] *Variations*. Ada Crossley sang 'O Rest in the Lord' which was followed by excerpts of the third movement of Tchaikovsky's *Symphonie Pathètique*. The afternoon closed with the audience of 10,000 singing 'Nearer, My God, to Thee' to the tune by Dykes, HORBURY.

Only Wallace Hartley's funeral had exceeded the Royal Albert Hall memorial in sheer volume of public grief and scale of ritual tribute, and perhaps the open-air service held at the Marlands, Southampton on April 28 to celebrate the return of surviving crew members, which 50,000 celebrants were said to have attended.

Before April 1912 was ended, the Victorian and Edwardian propensity to perpetuate memories in stone, brass or marble had taken three-dimensional form. This propensity would have a second, even greater field day in the aftermath of the Great War when throughout Britain and Northern Ireland life-like and life-sized statues of soldiers would grace town squares and village greens and tablets emboss themselves on interior church walls: the relief that a culture of grief required. Indeed, it was during the Great War that some of the *Titanic* memorial plaques or statues were unveiled and when some of them were absorbed at first by circumstance and then by design into the commemorative cultural work that the war provoked. For example, a Liverpool monument originally intended to preserve the memory of the brave engineers who went down with *Titanic* was broadened in reference, in 1916 when it was unveiled, to incorporate the memory of 'all heroes of the marine engine room'. On the wall of the foyer of the Philharmonic Hall in the same city, there is a bronze wall memorial to the ship's musicians (there is also a wall memorial to them in the Symphony Hall, Boston). Ian Jack reminds us that when the bust of Wallace Hartley (mounted on a pedestal) – proposed in 1912 – was unveiled in Colne in 1915, the mayor took pains to refer to the thousands of other young men 'who were giving their lives freely'. Incidentally, the *Titanic* bandsmen were remembered as far away as Australia, in the pillar above an engraved plinth in Broken Hill, New South Wales.

Other group memorials were erected: to the wireless operators on *Titanic* and other ships, in Battery Park, New York City (proposed in 1912); to the five British and American postal workers on board (a

Belfast Titanic Memorial photographed by Fr. Browne

bronze plaque made from *Titanic's* spare propellor), in Southampton Post Office; to the engineers, in East Park, same city (an ambitious sculpture unveiled on April 29, 1914); and to passengers, officers and crew alike in New York City (the *Titanic* Memorial Lighthouse, raised in 1915). Across America and over Great Britain memorials to the individual dead appeared. The violinist John Law (Jock) Hume and steward Thomas Mullin shared a standing memorial in Dumfries, Scotland, though Hume's body was buried in Fairview Lawn cemetery, Halifax. A wall tablet in Dalbeattie, England commemorates First Officer Murdoch (who some passengers believed shot himself on board); the tablet stipulates that a Murdoch memorial prize is to be contested for annually at the First Officer's old school, Dalbeattie Public. By April 24, it had been decided in Jack Phillips' home town of Godalming, England that a permanent memorial be erected to his memory, to supplement the memorial brass tablet intended for Farncombe Parish Church; there is a John Phillips Memorial Park in Godalming. The American artist Frank Millet and US government official Archibald Butt share a memorial fountain in Washington, DC, and a wall memorial to Harry Widener graces Widener Library, Harvard, a library endowed by young Widener's mother.

The captain of *Titanic* had enjoyed an enormous reputation and was much-loved. This voyage was, with sad irony, to be his last before retirement. Michael Davie tells the story of the monument erected to EJ Smith's memory in Lichfield, England. It was in 1914 that the mayor of Lichfield deemed a memorial appropriate. Perhaps the two-year lapse had softened the memory of Smith's culpability alleged by the US Senate hearing. The widow of Captain Scott of the Antarctic, Kathleen, was commissioned to produce a somewhat larger than lifesize statue. Subscribers and those in attendance at the unveiling included Waldorf Astor, Duke of Sutherland, Dowager Countess of Arran, Lady Diana Manners (later Lady Diana Cooper), the Marchioness of Anglesey, Lord Beresford and Rear-Admiral

Winnington-Ingram. Smith's White Star Line captaincy over the years had enabled him to meet the rich, powerful and ennobled, and on the evening of the tragedy he had dined on board with, among others, Mr and Mrs George Widener and Mr and Mrs John B. Thayer. His memorial statue strikes a rather martial attitude, fitting perhaps for the year of 1914 and the gathering storm.

We will leave for a later chapter and a different context the vast quantity of songs and tunes written in memory of the disaster, the ship and her lost passengers. Most of them were probably sincere even if Tin Pan Alley was where they were marketed and sold, but the line between genuine commemoration and crude commercial bounty-hunting is indistinct. Not that the publishers of postcards could definitely be said to have purer motive. In both forms of popular culture, music and postcards, a blatant sentimentality was simultaneously of its time and a warning sign of opportunism. Mark Bown and Roger Simmons tell us that during the Edwardian period there was a national craze for collecting postcards; the craze subsided with the outbreak of the Great War (though soldiers and their families exchanged postcards even between the trenches and the home fires), and postcard sales dropped with the rise of postage rates and increasing use of the telephone. The collecting craze returned in the 1970s which uncovered many cards in the Age of *Titanic*: 'Amongst the more sought after postcards', Bown and Simmons write, 'are those depicting the "Titanic". The rarest cards are those that were issued and postally used before the date of the disaster. After 15 April, 1912, postcard publishers issued a wide variety of postcards.'

In the golden age of postcards, many were promotions of White Star and other companies, souvenirs from the viewpoint of users and collectors. Just as WT Stead's journal *Review of Reviews* arranged for photographs to be taken during Scott's *Discovery* expedition to the South Pole (including one from 'on board SS *Discovery* during her wanderings among the icebergs of the Southern Seas') and made into postcards and sold to readers, so White Star and Harland & Wolff permitted photographers and publishers to create postcards that promoted their great ships. Extant cards include the departure of *Titanic*'s huge anchor from Hingley's Works in England, final preparations of *Titanic* for launch, and interior depictions of *Titanic*'s luxurious accommodation. Immediately after the disaster, postcards were pressed into memorial service: one series depicted the Marlands, Southampton open-air service of April 28; others jointly depicted Captain Edward Smith and wireless operator Jack Phillips; WT Stead in a multi-view card with a British warship passing an iceberg and a shot of *Titanic* departing from Southampton; and cameos of the bandsmen superimposed on the sheet music of 'Nearer, My God, to Thee'.

Bamforth memorial postcard.

But the memorial postcards that have become most famous are those in the series published by Bamforth & Company, from near Huddersfield. This suite of cards puts 'Nearer, My God, to Thee' to good use and graphically expresses Victorian and Edwardian religiosity, that is to say, the cards exude a combination of piety and sentimentality. Several use what appear to be young women models whose attitudes suggest the stylized postures of the contemporary stage and thus effectively mingle religion with theatricality. These maidens could ostensibly be said to be grieving young widows or perhaps pure symbols of human vulnerability or grief, or even angelic human stand-ins for the dead themselves, soon to be assumed into the divine company. But they also suggest the maidens-in-distress of middlebrow Edwardian drama. Religiosity and theatricality bonded by sentimentality: somehow these cards capture the essence of the memorial culture in which *Titanic* and her tragedy were quickly ambered and preserved.

Endnotes

1   This crewman is identified as G. Whiteman in Mowbray, K. Whiteman in Marshall, and A. Whiteman in computer crewlists.

2   However, the *Literary Digest* (New York), reporting the parade, dates it to May 4.

four

The Goblin Footfall

The Latitude and Longitude of Defeat

The religious doubts entertained by Victorian artists and intellectuals, and the lapse from church attendance that early sociologists recorded among the cities' under-classes, did not prevent late Victorian Britain from being a society still dominated by the outward and inward observances of Christianity. Religion was an immediate and unavoidable circumstance for the sinking and the sunk *Titanic;* the actions of passengers and crew were judged in its light, grief was given form by it, the meaning in such disaster was bestowed by it.

And this was so on either side of the Atlantic. One of the most famous casualties of the *Titanic* disaster was WT Stead, once dubbed 'the Gladstone of the Press'. In 1902 he published a book entitled *The Americanization of the World, or The Trend of the Twentieth Century* in which he claimed that Christianity was one of the forces of Americanization. He saw five chief religious movements in the nineteenth century and found only one of them of English or non-American origin. If Tractarianism was English, the others – revivalism, spiritualism, temperance-feminism, and Christian Endeavour – were American. America had begun with a religious impulse and American life was suffused with religion still. Looking from his posthumous domicile after the *Titanic* disaster (as his daughter and many mediums claimed he was doing), Stead would have been gratified by the religion – if not religiosity – that surrounded the *Titanic* tragedy.

Stead himself had been the son of an English Congregational minister. In 1879 he discovered the Salvation Army and was tempted to abandon journalism and join up in that new movement; in any case, Stead became a missionary of another sort, a 'preacher', as the *New York Times* called him in his obituary, for 'the propaganda of universal peace'. Much of his later life was a crusade for what he once summed up as 'imperialism plus the ten commandments and common sense', but which often adopted quite specific targets, such as child prostitution. Stead's later famous spiritualism was deeply informed by

Christianity, and a little over a week before he embarked on *Titanic*, he met with his co-spiritualists and led a service which ended with the singing of the hymn 'Our Blest Redeemer' with words by Harriet Auber and melody by JB Dykes who had provided the Anglican tune for 'Nearer, My God, to Thee'. It is a hymn that celebrates with poignant ambivalence Christ's farewell before his crucifixion and Assumption and it had been chosen in the light of Stead's imminent departure from England.

Stead was going to the United States 'to preach a single sermon', Marshall Everett tells us in his *Wreck and Sinking of the* Titanic: *The Ocean's Greatest Disaster* (1912). It was to have been delivered on Monday evening, April 22 in Carnegie Hall at the Men and Religion Forward Movement Congress, his daughter reported in her biography of her father, and was on the subject of 'Universal Peace'. The day before, there was a global blizzard of sermons on the subject of the *Titanic* sinking and on Stead himself. These were variations on half a dozen themes. Three of these themes had in common the spiritually welcome, consoling and opportune (if carnally disastrous) nature of the tragedy. Indeed, preachers tried to interpret the sinking of the ship and the loss of hundreds of souls as a scale-model of Christ's death: as a kind of Fortunate Calamity (just as Adam's and Eve's sin was regarded as *Felix culpa*, a Fortunate Fall, because it paved the way for Christ's advent). After all, the democratic nature of the deaths (one theme of the sermons) was a salutary reminder of the essential spiritual equality of all human beings before God. 'Think of the passengers on the vessel', Rev. RM Ker enjoined his congregation in the Grosvenor Hall, Belfast – 'the millionaire with his fabulous wealth, the emigrant with his few pounds; all classes of society, all creeds of religion, and all bowing down impartially before the stroke of death'. (The *Belfast News-Letter* paraphrased many of the sermons delivered in Ulster that Sunday.) How thin are the bulkheads that separate the fortunate from the unfortunate, the rich from the poor, Rev. Samuel H. Greene of Calvary Baptist Church, Washington DC reminded mourners. In the eyes of the preachers, the equality of suffering and loss made social inequality an illusion.

Then there had been demonstrated in the world's reaction to the tragedy 'the bond of a common sorrow and of universal sympathy' (a second theme), as Dean Grierson reminded his listeners in Belfast Cathedral. The Rev. Dr Patterson in May Street Presbyterian Church, Belfast said the same thing differently: the tragedy 'was drawing men's hearts together; it unbuttoned people's pockets, and enlarged their sympathies'. It was doing that all over the world, he said – acting as a global spiritual adhesive. The Rev. Dr MacDermott in Belmont Presbyterian Church, Belfast was sure the disaster was unifying the human race and referred to the rapid development of sympathy. Rev. R. Lee Cole of the Donegall Square Methodist Church, Belfast fastened on the idea of sympathy too; most people were

> so engrossed with their own concerns that they were scarcely ever touched by the feeling of true sympathy. The world was better for anything which helped it to realise the bond of brotherhood which bound man to man.
>
> *Felix culpa.*

These sermons reveal the apparent anxieties of the age. Unification and fellow feeling were important in a world riven by nationalisms and sectarianisms. The democracy of death and grief were important in a world increasingly stratified by social class, with incredibly wealthy haves and incredibly poor have-nots.

Yet many preachers, as we shall see, were quick to praise the Anglo-American passengers for demonstrating White, Anglo-Saxon, Protestant virtues. And paradoxically, the idea that social superiority and superfluous riches were illusory could be regarded as rendering unnecessary any political action to remove them. This was the profound conservatism of mainstream Christianity; true equality lay in death and either salvation or damnation, not in the redistribution or equitable possession of wealth. Moreover, the scale of the *Titanic* tragedy was a godsend for a faltering Christianity eager to see its enduring necessity demonstrated in no uncertain fashion.

A third theme of consolation in the sermons preached across the world on April 21 was the 'splendid heroism' to which the Rev. Dr MacDermott paid tribute. People talked about 'the heroism of the battle-field', Rev. Ker pronounced: 'but had the world ever witnessed more thrilling scenes of heroism than when the leviathan of the deep was sinking?' The *Literary Digest* reported that Dr Manning, Rector of Trinity Church, New York, wished in his sermon to celebrate the

> splendid heroism displayed by sufferers and survivors .... We can give thanks for the heroism, the calmness, and the courageousness shown on that boat in the last few horrible minutes ... their example on board that sinking ship has made the world richer, has given this generation a greater heritage to leave to those generations to come.

It was the heroism not of action but of valorous inaction, the heroism of self-sacrifice, which sermonizers saluted. It was Christlike and redemptive: 'the Son of Man came into a world that was lost', said Rev. Leighton Parks in St Bartholomew's Church (USA), 'and so the men on the *Titanic* sacrificed themselves for the women and children'.

Reading these sermons one gets the impression that whereas men of all classes aboard *Titanic* are commended, it is the men of the first class who are uppermost in the minds of the less recriminatory preachers. 'The man with a hundred million dollars stood aside and made room for his wife's serving maid. The man who has swayed continents with his pen gave place to a woman from the steerage. The railroad magnate remained on the sinking ship that a babe in arms might have his place in the lifeboat': so sang Rev. Frank Durward Adams in the Central Universalist Church, Indianapolis. (Biel reproduces Adams' elaborate May sermon.) Those who had the most to lose materially were those deemed the most self-sacrificial and heroic ... Astor, Guggenheim, Widener, Straus, Hays and the other princes of power and wealth. Astor, Everett reminded his readers, was said by the *Chicago Examiner* to have 'laid down his life as bravely as a soldier, as calmly as a philosopher, and with as sweet and quiet a philanthropy as if his days were without color and his years without hope'.

At his memorial service in St Paul's Episcopal Church, Washington DC, Major Archibald Butt (President Taft's military aide) was spoken of in biblical terms. 'It is not my purpose', Rev. Frank Talbot disclaimed, 'to dwell at length on the life, character and death of the gallant soldier who sacrificed his life for his brother men'. Rev. Talbot endorsed the proposal to erect a monument to Butt's memory and he was sure that 'his name and his valiant death will be treasured in song and story for centuries to come'. Rev. Adams quoted Benjamin Guggenheim's alleged message for his wife given to a powerful swimmer as testament to a heroic self-sacrifice: 'Tell her', he said, 'that this is a man's game, and I played it to the end. Tell her that no woman was left on board the ship because Ben Guggenheim was a coward'. 'Wasn't that splendid!' Adams asks his listeners. 'What a wonderful picture of the human heart in free action!'

It was the vast store of what such first-cabin passengers had to lose that troubled some preachers, as we shall see. But the entire *Titanic* enterprise seemed to some an exercise in hubris, and The Rev. Dr Purves in Elmwood Church, Belfast thought the sinking illustrated 'the impotence of man against nature at his strongest', and this was to be a fourth, unconsoling theme of many of the *Titanic* sermons. A fifth theme, unconsoling perhaps, but profitably challenging for the Christian, was the apparent test of faith and of belief in Providence the disaster constituted. The Rev. Dr McKean, in Assembly Hall, Belfast, imagined (a trifle pedantically) the self-sacrificing men who nevertheless survived asking themselves 'what is there in all the world that can shed any light on this mysterious providence, or explain to us the meaning of the problem of suffering resulting from it?' Rev. Cole admitted that great disasters such as this sometimes brought 'a sense of revolt almost against the providence which permitted them'. He had asked himself, the newspaper on his knee with its dire intelligence of the sinking, 'does God care?' For a moment his faith had rocked. He had no dogmatic answer to give his flock. However, there was something he had to protest against: 'Men were going about saying because the boat had been built on Sunday, or because of the gambling that was allowed on board, or because there was no prayer at her launching, God had permitted this thing to happen'. No; it was a mysterious but ultimately benign Providence that was at work. Rev. RS Donaldson of Milwaukee agreed; it was a matter of Providence, not judgement, though it was true that man's heedlessness could lead, as here, 'to the latitude and longitude of defeat'; he was prepared to strike two notes in his sermon: 'Thanksgiving for man's heroism; dismay for man's improvidence'.

Heroes and Shipwrecks
The claims of heroism aboard *Titanic* were the more strident and insistent because doubts about the possibility of heroism in the contemporary world were as freshly troublesome as widespread doubts about the truth of Christianity. Heroism had become acutely problematical, hedged around with deep reservations in the light of race, class and gender inequality, and the hero was increasingly perceived as having been for too long and too often a white man of social privilege, class distinction and imperialist impulse. Events on board *Titanic* focused the issue remarkably. EM Forster had devoted an important plot-strand of his novel *Howards End* to the possibility and definition of heroism. The novel, with its commercial antagonists who make money from the stock-market and the empire, was published in 1910 while *Olympic* and *Titanic* were raising their heroic forms in Belfast. Forster associates traditional heroism with economic and military imperialism and it is of course male, just as *Titanic* heroism was male, with a couple of exceptions that proved the rule (the 'plucky little' Countess of Rothes and Mrs JJ Tobin, later known as the Unsinkable Molly Brown). Through his central character, Helen Schlegel, Forster lays his mines under heroic triumphalism in an early chapter in which the Schlegel family listens to Beethoven's *Fifth Symphony* and each listener interprets it differently; to Helen, the Andante disconnects 'the heroes and shipwrecks of the first movement from the heroes and goblins of the third'. The ever-present

but often invisible goblins return again and again to undermine shipwreck heroism: 'they were not aggressive creatures; it was that that made them so terrible to Helen. They merely observed in passing that there was no such thing as splendour or heroism in the world' (a pre-echo of the 'splendid heroism' many contrived to see in the last minutes of *Titanic's* life). Doubt, poverty, inequality – each is 'a goblin footfall' that threatens our heroic clamour. Forster wants a quieter heroism divorced from gender, race and class, and for this reason he rejects hereditary aristocracy for what he called in 1939 (amidst the martial noises from Europe) an aristocracy of the plucky and sensitive. But in the short hours left after *Titanic's* collision with the iceberg, there must have been innumerable acts of sensitiveness and pluck – of compassion, courage, selflessness. By all accounts, for example, the behaviour of Thomas Andrews, the co-designer of *Titanic,* was exemplary and unostentatiously heroic in a Forsterian sense.

Joseph Conrad in his powerful novella, *Heart of Darkness* (1902), had already tried to show the empty heroism of the imperial adventurer, so ten years later when *Titanic* went down amidst claims of heroism, Conrad would have none of them.

> I am not a sentimentalist; therefore it is not a great consolation to me to see all these people breveted as 'Heroes' by the penny and halfpenny Press .... There is nothing more heroic in being drowned very much against your will, off a holed, helpless, big tank in which you bought your passage, than in dying of colic caused by the imperfect salmon in the tin you bought from your grocer.

But this is rather perverse. No one claimed that everyone who drowned on *Titanic* was a hero: the claim was that *some* were heroic (because others were not) and that some of those were survivors, some casualties. Moreover, contemporaries thought that one's recorded reaction and conduct during the crisis – whether one helped others at risk to oneself or simply saved one's own skin, whether one exhibited composure or panic – was the issue, not the fact of one's death. These terms seem more outmoded nowadays than they did in 1912, but only because they have largely been driven off the public stage into the private realm where conduct in crises and emergencies is still an occasion for shame or sombre pride.

Besides, Conrad was willing enough to embrace as 'brothers' the crew members who worked valiantly to the end and perished with *Titanic,* and to regard as a contemptible calumny the journalistic conjecture that Captain Smith had deserted his post by committing suicide. The ringing last sentence of Conrad's essay, 'Some Reflexions, Seamanlike and Otherwise, on the Loss of the Titanic' – despite the sting in its tail – belies his previous old sea-dog posture throughout most of the essay:

> Yes, material may fail, and men, too, may fail sometimes; but more often men, when they are given the chance, will prove themselves truer than steel, that wonderful thin steel from which the sides and the bulkheads of our modern sea-leviathans are made.

No more than Forster could Conrad entirely deny heroism, but he demanded that efficiency and competence be the necessary though insufficient criterion of heroic action.

For HG Wells, too, the real heroism aboard *Titanic* was found among 'the stewardesses and bandsmen and engineers – persons of the trade-union class': those whose behaviour was dictated by the discipline of work. J. Bruce Ismay failed to maintain the required standard and justified the common man's distrust of the wealthy and powerful. According to Wells in one of his articles on 'The Labour Unrest' in the *Daily Mail*, 'heroism and a general devotion to the common good are the only effective answer to distrust'. But whereas it is apparently easy for us to derive satisfaction from the notion that wealthy men such as Astor and Guggenheim – superior versions of EM Forster's businessman Henry Wilcox in *Howards End* – were idle men, undisciplined and inefficient, the evidence is that they were anything but idle. Irrespective of our views on the economic system which they dominated, under these men work got done, products made, machinery set in motion, goods transported, investors made happy (or unhappy). Certainly there were acts of bravery among the deck crew and engineers on board *Titanic*, many of them unrecorded. But that some first-class men behaved with commendable *sang-froid* amounting to heroism in the face of imminent death by drowning is beyond doubt. Whereas 42 per cent of third-class women and children were rescued, only 32 per cent of first-class men made it to New York; a far higher percentage of the third-class women and children ought to have been saved, but at least two-thirds of the first-class men accepted the women-and-children-first code.

Of course, the power of *noblesse oblige*, even as late as 1912, seems to have been strong enough that we might think of first-class behaviour less as heroism than as subordination to a code: the heroism, we might say, was of the system rather than of the person. But in either guise, heroism was under sceptical scrutiny by advanced thinkers and writers who inclined to the left rather than the right in their politics. Of these, the playwright and polemicist George Bernard Shaw was one of the most audible in British society. In the London

Daily News of May 14, 1912, Shaw galloped bumptiously into print with an article entitled 'The *Titanic*: Some Unmentioned Morals'. 'What is the first demand of romance in a shipwreck?' he asked rhetorically. 'It is the cry of Women and Children First.' A titanic lie, claimed Shaw: one boat left with more men than women in it. 'Second romantic demand ... the captain must be a super-hero, a magnificent seaman, cool, brave ....' Another titanic lie: Captain Smith showed bad seamanship in going full-steam into an ice-field. 'Third romantic demand. The officers must be calm, proud, steady, unmoved in the intervals of shooting the terrified foreigners.' Yet another titanic lie: one officer was insubordinate to Ismay. 'Fourth romantic demand. Everybody must face death without a tremor.' Another titanic lie: officers reassured passengers (to avoid panic) when they should have warned them. In short: 'What', asked Shaw, 'is the use of all this ghastly, blasphemous, inhuman, braggartly lying?'

The creator of Sherlock Holmes was incensed by Shaw's article and took the famous polemicist to task in the same newspaper. (The patriotic Conan Doyle had previously found himself on the opposite side of the Boer War from Shaw and now they traded fire again over *Titanic*.) Doyle pointed out that Shaw's first 'lie' rested on the case of a single lifeboat: the second boat away had 65 women and five men on board. As for Shaw's second 'lie': Smith's heroism, Doyle reminded Shaw, was earned by his behaviour after, not before, the collision. Shaw's third 'lie' rested partly on Fifth Officer Lowe's celebrated insubordination to the ship's effective owner J. Bruce Ismay, which Doyle took as testifying not to Lowe's dereliction of duty but to his heroic attendance to duty (though the fact that Lowe did not know that he was addressing Ismay somewhat weakens Doyle's case on that point). The third romantic demand, as Shaw understood it, did incidentally provoke one version of the Race Question on *Titanic* – that is, the numerous scathing remarks by surviving crew and passengers about the behaviour of dark-skinned and yellow-skinned passengers. I will broach this and other versions of the Race Question later; they were goblin footfalls behind the shipwreck heroism, and Shaw's point has a disturbing general if not specific validity.

Shaw's fourth 'lie' required him to see the *Titanic* bandsmen as unwitting instruments of the officers' fear of panic and purveyors of dishonest reassurance in a time of lethal danger. Doyle said he failed to see how this, even if true, would detract from the bravery of the musicians. (Few commentators were willing or able to question the bandsmen's heroism.) Whether the passengers should have been early apprised of the true nature of the danger they were in is a moot point.

George Bernard Shaw (left) and Arthur Conan Doyle: in dispute over heroism on Titanic

Shaw suggests that the risk of panic was worth taking in order that the officers tell everyone the truth about the inevitable fate of the ship and many of her passengers. (Just as – by implicit analogy – Shaw was willing to take the risk of offending most of the British public by telling the 'truth' about the 'heroism' on board Titanic.) The decision not to alert passengers early was presumably a judgment call rather than an application of shipowners' policy, and Shaw's certainty on the subject is itself braggartly. Besides, the fear of panic was, as I shall show, a cultural fear as well as a specific fear entertained by the officers that night.

Indeed, Shaw's position seems to me one dictated by his own leftist political subculture rather than by his specific objections, just as Doyle's defence of the officers and public perception of the tragedy is dictated (though rather less so in my opinion) by *his* right-wing political subculture. One can understand why Shaw should have been annoyed by the paeans of patriotic and patriarchal praise that drowned out common sense in the aftermath of the disaster. When he replied to Doyle, Shaw, though aggressive as ever, was wise in restricting his topics to journalists' ignorant hyperbole about the Titanic disaster and Captain Smith's lack of restraint (which the US Senate investigation also targeted for criticism). In a brief riposte in the *Daily News* of May 25, Doyle bowed out of the exchange and accused Shaw of needlessly hurting the feelings of others. Though this must have seemed to readers like surrender and though Shaw had strengthened among the advanced crowd the anti-heroic position, the general public perception of *Titanic*'s shipwreck heroism was not severely damaged. But heroism was no longer so easily demonstrated to have occurred as it formerly had been.

The Perils of Prosperity

The widespread identification of *Titanic* heroism with affluent first-class men bothered leftist intellectuals but bothered also some clergy who likewise associated the ship's first class with unprecedented and deplorable luxury in travel (and luxury implied sinfulness). One of the selling points of the White Star Line's promotion was that *Titanic*, like her sister *Olympic*, was a ship of almost unimaginable opulence, with 'accommodation of unrivalled magnificence', as a richly detailed souvenir number of *The Shipbuilder* in summer 1911 (between the launches of the two vessels) put it. Most *Titanic* enthusiasts are aware of the studied and varied period decor of the first-class bedrooms, saloons and lounges and of the fact that the builders, Harland & Wolff, employed their own upholsterers and their own in-house decorators, including wood-carvers, 180 of whom worked in studios carving the panelling on the two ships. First-class staterooms were fitted with individually controlled electric heaters to allow Americans accustomed to more heat than Britons to supplement the warm-air system already in operation. Everywhere, ventilation and heating removed the horrible conditions of earlier transatlantic travel. Ten thousand lamps lit life on board *Titanic*; first-class staterooms had dimmer lights so that the nervous could sleep with less anxiety. Fifteen hundred bell pushes could summon help, necessaries or more luxury. Passenger elevators and service lifts conserved human energy. Next to the Turkish baths could be found 'electric baths', individual pod-like 'beds' apparently for heat-ray treatment. There was a swimming pool, a squash court and a gymnasium. *Titanic* had her own 50-line telephone exchange for inter-cabin communication and separate circuits for service communication, including that between the crow's nest and the bridge, which proved crucial on the evening of April 14.

Titanic enthusiasts have memorized the legendary ship's stores for the Southampton-New York voyage, and the crockery, cutlery and linen manifest: all contributing to the idea of *Titanic* as the Ship of Plenty. And as though the fittings, facilities and decor were not sufficient, a Southampton horticultural florist, FG Bealing and Son, provided fresh flowers for every White Star liner using the port. Lady Duff Gordon recalled her last meal on *Titanic*: 'We had a big vase of beautiful daffodils on the table, which were as fresh as if they had just been picked'.

In his 1913 study, *Travelling Palaces: Luxury in Passenger Steamships*, RA Fletcher wrote:

> Luxury has been defined as the art of providing edibles out of season, and more things to use than anyone can possibly want combined with the least exertion and the utmost physical comfort if anyone should want to use them. If this definition be correct, then modern liners have certainly provided luxury.

Perhaps a better description of the modern liner, he added, 'is that she is a travelling palatial hotel, combining the best features of the modern hotel with the comfort and luxury generally associated with the palace'. *Titanic* was a ship noteworthy even among the liners of 'the Gilded Age'. The Halifax businessman Samuel Cunard founded the first transatlantic steamship company in 1839, and thereafter rivalry among Cunard and other companies ensured that seductive comfort and competitive speed would be priorities. The rivalry later became international, with numerous British, German and French shipping lines ruthlessly vying for the lucrative North Atlantic passenger traffic. That traffic was a rich prize because of the money floating freely in the late Victorian and Edwardian periods, the springtime of American plutocracy as well as the Indian summer of British aristocracy. For many first-class American passengers on board *Titanic*, the luxury transatlantic liner was a shuttle between the New World origins of their wealth and the Old World occasions for their enjoyment of it.

But such luxurious appointments as *Titanic* boasted amounted to what Rev. Dr Purves called in his April 21 sermon 'the perils of prosperity'. It had been claimed by a marine engineer, Stanley Bowdle (quoted by the *New York Times*) that such liners as *Titanic* were 'degenerate in size, foolish in enjoyment, sybaritic in luxury, and criminal in speed'. Cardinal Gibbons, Archbishop of Baltimore, in his sermon of April 21 in St Stephen's Church, Washington, DC, was certain that 'the remote cause of this unspeakable disaster is the excessive pursuit of luxury ... the undue passion for material welfare and mere earthly enjoyments'. This was a sixth, unconsoling theme in some sermons preached after the sinking. Everett did not shrink from quoting Rev. Andrew Johnson who exaggerated the sufficiently opulent nature of *Titanic* in order to condemn the spiritual delinquency he felt sure accompanied her luxury – the golf courses(!), swimming pools, concert halls, tennis courts. 'The curse of the world and the crime of this age is the spirit of rivalry, the craze for speed, the desire for luxury.' Heroism and self-sacrifice: these were but silver linings to the dark cloud of disaster, in Johnson's metaphor; the goblin footfall (in ours) becomes almost deafening.

The sternest recrimination in sermon came from Dr Charles H. Parkhurst preaching in the Madison Square Presbyterian church on April 21 and reported by the *Literary Digest*. Parkhurst in the way of stout believers seemed almost to relish the calamity. 'The picture which presents itself before my eyes', he publicly confided:

> is that of the glassy, glaring eyes of the victims, staring meaninglessly at the gilded furnishings of this sunken palace of the sea; dead helplessness wrapt in priceless luxury; jewels valued in seven figures becoming the strange playthings of the queer creatures that sport in the dark depths.

This anticipates the prurience of Thomas Hardy's poem 'The Convergence of the Twain (Lines on the Loss of the *Titanic*)':

> Over the mirrors meant
> To glass the opulent
> The sea-worm crawls – grotesque, slimed, dumb, indifferent
>
> Jewels in joy designed
> To ravish the sensuous mind
> Lie lightless, all their sparkles bleared and black and blind.

Hardy too was a stout believer in his own philosophy, of which the *Titanic* disaster was a satisfying verification. Parkhurst saw the tragedy as the inevitable result of love of money and passion for luxury, twin evils 'gnawing into our civilization'.

An even more ferocious attack on the age of luxury came from another famous preacher of the time. Alma White, founder of the Pillar of Fire Holiness Group in the United States, wrote *The* Titanic *Tragedy – God Speaking to the Nations* in 1912; it was published the following year by the Pentacostal Union in New Jersey and is an extended sermon. White began by identifying 'scientific investigation and civil and mechanical engineering' as 'all-absorbing passions' that prevent her contemporaries from acknowledging God as the source of their achievements: the machine age, like the age of luxury, was stupefying the people. Like other fervent evangelists, White was in two minds about disaster. What happened to *Titanic* and her passengers and crew appeared to be a terrible thing but its very awfulness usefully revealed God's anger (as Hardy thought it revealed the existence of some inhuman controller of our affairs) and hastened the day when God would feel obliged to intervene in human affairs once and for all. In those two senses it was in fact a welcome thing. At the very least, it was, in today's parlance, a wake-up call.

The 'floating palace' men called *Titanic* was, White maintained, the progeny of the age of materialism 'when wealth, luxury and pleasure-seeking are swaying the multitudes' and was in reality a 'floating Babylon'. The most egregious example of sinful ostentation among nations is Britain, latterly demonstrated by the royal pomp and religious hypocrisy of the coronation of King George V in 1911. It was hardly surprising, White thought, in a country the established religion of which (Anglicanism) is a mere step from the Papacy (which, like British royalty, is a worshipper of Mammon) and edging ever closer. Unbridled wealth and unsated appetite for the world's goods and luxuries are a sign of decadence and Britain is clearly a waning power, being the builder of *Titanic*: 'in miniature, she perfectly represents the United Kingdom of Great Britain and Ireland ... in this vessel, with all the modern appliances and luxuries that money could secure ... we have a picture of England'. J. Bruce Ismay 'had drunk the Babylonian cup to the dregs, and God's rebuke was at hand'.

According to White, Ismay's behaviour after the collision was in keeping with his character as it had been moulded in an effete society – his 'shrinking and timidity' were the product of an irreligious materialism. Astor was little better, stumbling around bewildered, betraying like other honorary Britons from the USA the weakening influence of excessive affluence. Indeed, Ismay showed superior power of self-preservation by seizing an opportunity to escape whereas Astor submitted to his fate. Curiously, chivalry for White exposed the weakness of anglicised men not their strength of character – and White meant weakness in the most literal sense. Men, she wrote (and demonstrating her muscular Christianity), have ceased to develop muscle, which is necessary to character building. 'In England's manhood there is rapid physical degeneration', not just in the malnourished slums but also among the higher orders. 'A generation has been brought up in her midst in pride and luxury, ignorant of the fact that Ichabod is written upon her escutcheon.' This for White has been the true meaning of Victorianism .

White writes both as an avenging fundamentalist and as an American who sees the mother country as a decadent parent and no longer the adventurous and manly force that discovered and settled America . But despite what would seem to be her fervent eccentricity of vision, she writes also as one of many observers around the time of the *Titanic* tragedy who felt that degeneration (an inversion of heroism, a mockery of splendour) was an alarming and widespread phenomenon. Degeneration (be it social and artistic decadence or moral degeneracy) was the heaviest goblin footfall of them all.

Given the accelerating Anglo-German rivalry after 1908, it may not be surprising that a German writer wrote an article entitled 'England and the Signs of Her Decline' that appeared in a German magazine in 1911 and was reported in the *Review of Reviews*. Queen Victoria's reign had been the zenith of England's powers, but the Boer War had divided the population and weakened the country. The intellectual domain too betrayed signs of decadence, and duty, energy, discipline and moral feeling were in decline. The upper classes led a 'luxurious and indolent existence' without restraint and apparently without ambition beyond marriage to American heiresses. 'Could anything be more enervating', he asked, 'than incessant amusement and entertainment?'

But these sentiments merely echo those expressed by no less an English figure than GM Trevelyan in 1901, the year of Victoria's death. Trevelyan likewise identified decadence as the most worrying condition of England. Chiefly because of the sudden destruction of rural life, in the second half of the nineteenth century, social life, literature, journalism, religion, politics have all deteriorated from the days of Waterloo. Cromwell's Puritans, the Stuarts and the Elizabethan adventurers are all mere memories in the midst of 'material luxury'. Physical degeneration has followed the ruination of country life but worse, 'In the last generation intellectual, moral and spiritual degeneration has set in, due to causes analogous and even related to those corresponding causes of physical degeneration ...'. Trevelyan conceived his article in the context of the widespread fear of 'the Yellow Peril' and ironically termed the continuing degeneration he saw around him 'the White Peril'.

If these allegations of decadence were widespread and well-known, as they seem to have been, one can understand why the behaviour of first-class men on *Titanic* was so closely scrutinised in the press and pulpit and was seized upon in some quarters as evidence of their redemption of English and upper-class vigour and virility.

Criticism of the luxury enjoyed on board *Titanic*, occasionally deepening into revulsion, sprang from the moral, psychological, social and aesthetic reactions against alleged degeneration that had been ongoing for more than a decade before the ship sailed. The father of the reaction was Cesare Lombroso, author of *Delinquent Man* (1875). Lombroso was an Italian psychiatrist who inspired the famously scandalous assault on *fin-de-siècle* decadence (including the work and personality of Oscar Wilde) by Max Nordau in his book *Degeneration* (1892, trans. 1895) which provoked anger in George Bernard Shaw and others. Degeneration was seen as assuming many shapes, from effete society through decadent art forms (created by 'higher degenerates') and mysticism to personal morbidity and criminal degeneracy. In criticising what she saw as John Jacob Astor's disinclination to action, Alma White was identifying one of the traits of degeneracy, as Nordau saw it. Degeneration could be the condition of an individual but also of a group or race (race perception, as we shall see, played a huge role in the *Titanic* inquest) and famous students of zoology, including E. Ray Lankester and HG Wells, felt compelled to draw attention to retrogression in animal forms.

Some, including Flora McDonald Thompson, even saw retrogression occurring in women, paradoxically among those women struggling for enfranchisement and equality with men. (The Woman Question played an even larger role in the *Titanic* aftermath than the Race Question.) For Thompson, end-of-the-century American women had degenerated since De Tocqueville's time for one obvious reason: 'by thus attempting to make one sex equal to the other, both are degraded'; voting and labour rights are species of luxury that spoil and weaken the female sex and deflect it from its domestic destiny.

Several literary works, written after the *fin-de-siècle* fashion for literary displays of decadence had passed, were studies in degeneration. *Heart of Darkness* (1902) by Joseph Conrad was one of the most famous. Conrad, Wells and Kipling, all keenly interested in the *Titanic* disaster, were writers who affirmed the necessity of restraint, efficiency and practicality as antidotes to degradation and decadence. They were writers who were at home in the uncloseted world of power and machinery (actual and figurative) where these virtues could be exercised. Wells expressed a consistent horror of the destination awaiting those who degenerated too far – *the Abyss*. The title of one of Wells' book reviews, 'Life in the Abyss' (1894), anticipated the similar titles of novels and documentaries that would in the near future explore the dark depths of English society; but Wells' abyss in this case was the literal one at the bottom of the ocean. He would in his scientific romances, however, plumb the depths of metaphoric abysses. The fate of *Titanic* was to sink to the bottom of the literal abyss, and by doing so arouse debate about the condition of those who inhabited the figurative abyss in English and European society, which steerage was held by some to symbolize.

The Sinking Classes

We are not concerned with the very poor. They are unthinkable.
EM Forster, *Howards End* (1910)

The depth of ocean into which *Titanic* sank deepened for those safe on land or ship the horrifying thrill of the ship's loss and the fate of her passengers. The widespread interest in the Deep to which I have already referred extended to fiction in the Age of *Titanic*, and it comes as little surprise that Jules Verne was pioneering in his exploitation of the Abyss as an image as well as a geological feature. The journey to the centre of the Earth in his 1864 adventure of that title is a journey into the terrestrial abyss, a physical journey laden with pre-Freudian and pre-Jungian but nevertheless psychological suggestiveness. Wells too was fascinated by the narrative excitements of the real abyss. One of his short stories was 'In the Abyss', the story of the disappearance of a bathyscape in deep water; the explorer fails to return, like the Time Traveller in one of Wells' most famous scientific romances, *The Time Machine* (1895).

Interestingly, the wreck of *Titanic* was found by submersible in a replay of Wells' story. Until then, the abyss was in popular imagination the unvisualizable habitation of *Titanic*: Stygian darkness out of all countenance. Before Robert Ballard, the discoverer of the wreck of *Titanic*, proved otherwise in 1985, the ship was thought to have suffered extinction of the deepest-dyed kind: 'beyond reach', as the Texan Jack Grimm called the wreck after his failures to find it. It had been assumed by many that volcanic eruption in the 1920s had shifted the ocean bed and buried the ship – loss upon loss. The poster advertising *Search for the* Titanic – the 1980 film of Grimm's quest, narrated by Orson Welles – proclaimed: 'Like a sleeping giant, she has rested for seven decades in the unknown abyss of the North Atlantic'. Even without this second possible (but now disproved) descent, one imagines with sufficient horror the interminable plunge of *Titanic* with its captives through the rapidly darkening ocean; it is the peculiar if in this case inaccurate horror of the *submerged* abyss, of the vast mountains and steep rough valleys that lie *under the ocean, out of sight.*

Much was made by survivors of the fear they had of being sucked to their death in the maelstrom created by *Titanic's* sinking. That fear was used by some boatmen to explain why they did not approach the wreck scene even when they heard the cries for help of those in the water. It came as a surprise to the survivors as well as to commentators that no maelstrom had in fact occurred. *Titanic* upended herself, poised for angle, then slid noiselessly and smoothly under the surface leaving little disturbance behind her. But the expectation had been powerfully there, and its disappointment did little to lessen the pain of the survivors' memories of those trapped on the ship who were seen to accompany the ship beneath the waves.

The justified horror evoked by the Abyss made easy its historic passage from earthly to unearthly existence. To Christians, the Abyss from which being sprang (in John Milton's epic poem, *Paradise Lost*, things begin when the Spirit of God broods into life the 'vast Abyss') was the more real for being unearthly. Indeed, it may be that horror of the abyss in Western culture derives from the Christian notion (in Milton's phrase) of the 'darkness visible' of Hell rather than the other way round. (Presumably, though, human beings have a biological fear of falling , especially of falling through air in darkness.) This was the abyss that as far as Alma White and Charles Parkhurst were concerned the drowned rich sinners from *Titanic* (including the extravagantly wealthy, reprehensibly divorced and scandalously remarried John Jacob Astor) sank spiritually into even as the ship sank into the oceanic abyss. White shows less concern for the drowned from steerage (less fodder for savoury retribution there), but the connection between the abyss of poverty and the Abyss of damnation had already occurred to General William Booth of the Salvation Army.

The Salvation Army interested itself in the *Titanic* disaster. Booth sent a cablegram to the *New York Times* on April 18 grieving for his lost friends on *Titanic* and said his heart was 'moved in its deepest sources of feeling concerning that sudden and awful summons into the presence of God'. Eva Booth and a delegation from the Salvation Army met the rescue ship *Carpathia* at its New York pier and offered food and clothes to survivors. On Tenth Avenue, an Army band sang hymns and prayed for survivors as cars and pedestrians hastened by to greet the ship. In 1890 General Booth published an exposé of poverty in London, *In Darkest England and the Way Out*. The title, like the title of Rev. Osborne Jay's reply, *Life in Darkest London: A Hint to General Booth*, 1891, echoed the contemporary picture of Darkest Africa and the ironic parallel provided the frame narrative for Conrad's *Heart of Darkness*. *In Darkest England*, which inaugurated the 'Darkest England' social scheme, was said to have been ghost-written by WT Stead, who wrote an adulatory profile of Booth in his journal, *Review of Reviews*, entitled 'Our One International Man'. Stead was also a social activist in the cause of understanding and solving the problem of deep poverty.

For Booth, the problem was indissolubly social and spiritual. In his book, he devotes a chapter to those 'On the Verge of the Abyss'; that is, on the verge of becoming irreclaimably (in economic terms) or irredeemably (in spiritual terms) destitute. He refers to 'the sinking classes' whom the Army is especially interested in saving, both spiritually and economically. It must surely have occurred to Booth when he read the statistics by class of human loss in the *Titanic* disaster (60 per cent of first-class passengers saved, 42 per cent of second class,

25 per cent of third class) that his metaphor had become nightmarishly literal.

The widespread perception, especially in America, was that steerage had been full of poor European emigrants making their way towards the Statue of Liberty and a fresh start, that the same class-ridden country that had discriminated against its poor continued that discrimination on board its fancy liners, that steerage passengers were not warned about the danger until it was too late, that they had been prevented from reaching the boat deck when they realised their plight, that the lifeboats left without them, that a disproportionate percentage of the lost were from third class – in brief, that the British sinking classes duly sank.

In the background of the *Titanic* sinking were serious and even violent labour disputes in both Britain and the United States, and although many Americans, socialist or no, fastened on the possible class discrimination on board, left-wing groups and organs were especially incensed at the thought. For example, *Appeal to Reason*, a socialist magazine out of Girard, Kansas, saw the deaths as 'sixteen hundred deliberate, cold-blooded murders', many of them of steerage passengers, 'penned in like cattle' and held at bay by officers with loaded revolvers, allowed to make for the boat deck 'only when the rich passengers had been given all the favoured opportunities to make sure of their escape ...'. Unlike many Christian sermonizers, socialists did not have their view of the tragedy clouded by the need for a demonstration by the rich on board of redemptive heroism: the rich were rich and thus were at fault. The American left-wing magazine *The Masses* saw *Titanic* as a model of the exploitative capitalist state driven by the 'insanity of luxury' and the 'insanity of speed'. Ben Tillett, a well-known British trade unionist, protested on behalf of the Dock, Wharf, Riverside & General Workers' Union at the 'vicious class antagonism' shown by officers who forbade the saving of the lives of third-class passengers.

It is unfortunately the case that had the steerage passengers indeed been treated in this way, it would not have been quite so repugnant to middle- and upper-class Britons as to their American counterparts: the 'lower orders' (including both the working class and the chronically unemployed) by definition were regarded in Britain as not so valuable to society as the middle and upper classes. As human beings they were viewed as more primitive – or as degenerate. 'In Degeneration', Lankester said of the biological process, 'there is suppression of form, corresponding to the cessation of work'. Unemployment was for some a moral condition and renewed work its antidote. Manliness was the opposite of degeneracy and fears over British manliness survived *Titanic*. 'John Bull, Junior – Slacker' was an article in the December 1912 issue of *The World's Work* and it mourns the fact that the 'sterner duties' taught by Kipling and others were not being taught to young Britons whose 'sins to-day are slackness, indifference, cynicism, luxuriousness'. The first-class behaviour by some men on the sinking *Titanic* was one such stern duty, but clearly their example had not been immediately followed by young people safe on shore. The writer sought 'a complete and whole-hearted admission of the manly virtues into the moral curriculum'.

Class consciousness, then, had its moral and even psychological dimension: members of one class despised the class below more out of fear and the struggle for survival than out of snobbery *per se*. The neglected lower middle class in Britain, personified by the clerk Leonard Bast in Forster's *Howards End* – 'He was not in the abyss, but he could see it' – led a precarious and largely overlooked existence, ambitious to clamber into the middle class, afraid of sinking into the labouring or unemployed classes. (Their shipboard equivalents on *Titanic* were perhaps the engineers whose fate was largely overlooked by commentators on the disaster.)

The American and British inquiries revealed the issue of the three classes on board *Titanic* and the relations of them to social classes off the ship as more complicated than some observers had thought. Besides, there were other factors. Not only did the gender of the lost and the saved cloud matters, but so too did the autonomous behaviour of third-class passengers: one Swedish third-class passenger thought that more steerage passengers could have helped themselves had their peasant Catholicism not made them passive, inducing them to despair and pray. Daniel Allen Butler has suggested that steerage passengers were not physically impeded so much as psychologically impeded; they were simply acting out their prescribed station in life, believing until it was too late that their betters in uniform were taking care of things on their behalf.

In addition, it is not evident that *Titanic*'s steerage passengers were the wretched and humble whom the Statue of Liberty requested from Europe. The ship was not built primarily for the emigrant market, and White Star relied for the economic success of its liners on well-heeled traffic to and fro across the Atlantic. For example, 113 steerage passengers embarked at Queenstown (now Cobh) in Ireland, probably all of them natives of that country. Half were women and most of those would probably have been going to some eastern American city to enter domestic service already arranged for them. The men were probably going to join Irish kith and kin, possibly because of overcrowding at home or for adventure or fortune. Daniel Buckley was a steerage passenger who testified before Senator Alden Smith; he already had a Bronx address and had gone to the United States 'to make some money'; he had chosen to sail on *Titanic* 'because she was a new steamer'.

Still, even after the hearings and all the magazine discussions, the idea remained popular that the *Titanic* disaster demonstrated the existence in society of sinking classes, some of whose members followed the ship into the abyss. The disaster took its place in a drama already well-developed and scripted. Shipwrecks, drownings, rescues, the abyss, lifeboats – these constituted a floating contemporary complex of metaphor waiting for *Titanic*. The graphic confirmation of social, religious, sexual, racial and even political dynamics (and prejudices) that *Titanic* provided was part of the lure of the ship and its fate.

Booth's answer to the social problems of what we would now call the inner city was the 'Salvation Ship', of which *Titanic* could be seen as a tragic travesty, in the light of the large numbers of European emigrants it carried in steerage. The answer is certainly not, he argued, *laissez-faire*, the laws of human supply and demand. How do these principles look, Booth asked,

> when we apply them to the actual loss of life at sea? Does 'Let things alone' man the lifeboat? .... No desire to make it pay created the National Lifeboat Institution .... We want a Social Lifeboat Institution, a Social Lifeboat Brigade, to snatch from the abyss those who, if left to themselves, will perish as miserably as the crew of a ship that founders in mid-ocean.'

The People of the Abyss

If you gaze for long into an abyss, the abyss gazes also into you.
Frederich Nietzsche, *Beyond Good and Evil* (1886)

The applicability of the *Titanic* disaster to contemporary social concerns is quite remarkable. The language and imagery in which these concerns were being voiced were the language and imagery that had to be employed when the disaster was reported and discussed, simply because it was from the imagining or memory of such disasters that the language and imagery derived. In 1900 HG Wells wrote a series of articles for the *Fortnightly Review*, collected the next year and

published as *Anticipations*. In the book Wells anticipated the main
outlines of twentieth-century society. WT Stead reviewed the book in
his journal, the *Review of Reviews,* and remarked on how many
contemporary thinkers were looking forwards (under the aegis of
evolution) instead of backwards (under the aegis of religion). In
identifying the hazards of this change of perspective, Stead fell back on
an extended nautical metaphor. Wells, he said:

> finds himself adrift in the midst of a generation which has lost both chart
> and compass. It is true there are old charts in the cabin, but they have lost
> their authority. New soundings have revealed not only new rocks and
> quicksands, but vast oceans and continents of which the older
> hydrographers did not dream; and therefore the old charts, although very
> good in their day, seemed to him about as useful as the geography of Strabo
> would be to a navigator of the Pacific.

Wells attempts a scientific prediction that is little affected by 'the
eddies of opinion':

> He has, therefore, approached the question from the point of view of an
> inquirer, who endeavours to ascertain from a scientific measurement the
> force and direction of the winds or the set of the tide, the probable course
> which would be taken by the ships which are drifting apparently without
> any definite aim or in any definite direction.

Among Wells' predictions are advances in applied science, including
the mechanics of future locomotion. He also analysed Edwardian
society, using the language of his scientific romances, including the
image of the abyss. He saw the new urban poor as, 'to borrow a popular
phrase, the "submerged" portion of the social body, a leaderless, aimless
multitude of people drifting down towards the abyss'. It is hard when
reading this not to think of the perceived fate of *Titanic's* steerage.
Here is second-class survivor Charlotte Collyer's account:

> Before the darkness came, I saw hundreds of human bodies clinging to the
> wreck, or leaping into the water. The Titanic was like a swarming bee-hive;
> but the bees were men; and they had broken their silence now. Cries more
> terrible than I had ever heard rang in my ears. I turned my face away ....

Immediately above the hapless multitude, Wells saw the remnants of
the old middle class,

> a vast intricate confusion of different sorts of people, some sailing about
> upon floating masses of irresponsible property, some buoyed by smaller
> fragments, some clinging desperately enough to insignificant atoms, a
> great and varied multitude swimming successfully without aid . . . and an
> equally varied multitude of less capable ones clinging to the swimmers,

clinging to the floating rich, or clutching empty-handed and thrust and sinking down.

The most striking of the new classes he saw emerging was the shareholding class, a development of 'irresponsible wealthy people'. Since Wells put his trust in an emerging professional class of engineers and scientists and since he was pretty cold-blooded about the leaderless submerged, it was little wonder that Wells had sympathy only for the engineers and effectual crew members aboard *Titanic*. The three new classes Wells identified can be recognised in peculiar shorthand on *Titanic* (and more accurately than we can recognise the familiar triad of aristocracy, middle class and working class), just as the social 'deliquescence' Wells saw at work in Edwardian England – with the abyss its likely terminus for many – received its most graphic unsolicited image in the early hours of April 15, 1912.

Wells, of course, knew that even engineers had their hierarchy, at the bottom of which was 'the black-faced, oily man' who occupied, of course, the stokehold, engine rooms and boiler rooms of *Titanic*. When we think of the highly charged world of these portions of the ship, with their infernal machinery – heat, steam, racket: life below the waterline – it is hard not to think of Wells' use of such imagery in stories he wrote a few years before *Titanic* was built, including 'The Cone', 'Lord of the Dynamos' and *The Time Machine*. The last stirs another association. In the widespread (but contested) story of the third-class passengers storming rebelliously upstairs during the sinking of *Titanic*, as well as our knowledge of life below decks in the stokehold, engine room and boiler room, it is hard not think (a trifle guiltily) of Wells' Morlocks who come up from their underground darkness, their abyssal machine life, to alarm their privileged brothers, the Eloi. And the Eloi, decadent and ineffectual, might remind us, under the circumstances, of those whom Conrad referred to as 'the ineffable hotel exquisites who form the bulk of the first-class Cross-Atlantic passengers'. We know that in *The Time Machine* Wells was projecting into the remote future the contemporary and growing gulf (or abyss) between capital and labour.

The notion of a submerged portion of the society (an under-class) was formulated with some precision simultaneously by General William Booth and by his namesake, the sociologist Charles Booth, author of the monumental *Life and Labour of the People in London*, the first volume of which appeared the same year as George Gissing's novel, *The Nether World* (1889). The three-tier class system on *Titanic* was a crude and simple version of the more complicated system William Booth saw at work on terra firma. (Economically determined class on ships and trains in Edwardian Britain, as on airplanes today, is not completely identical with social class outside the vehicle or vessel.) However, the danger of drifting, sinking and drowning was ever-present for the lowermost classes. Gissing explored life in the London abyss from the perspective of fiction. One character in his novel believes he and others 'have to fight against the rich world that's always crushing us down, down, whether it means to or not'. With recourse to what was becoming a popular metaphor and one that the *Titanic* disaster seemed to ratify, the narrator reassures his readers that although his characters are defeated and go down, 'at least their lives would remain a protest against those brute forces of society which fill with wreck the abysses of the nether world'.

The profound gulf between the rich and the poor (indeed, between the modestly well-off and the poor) was recognised as a kind of abyss by Victorian writers even before Gissing and the Booths. Stephen Gill reminds us that James Greenwood investigated the people of the urban abyss in *Low-Life Deeps: An Account of the Strange Fish to be Found There* (1876), and Cardinal Newman (quoted by Bradbury) thought in 1871 that crowds might 'rise up from the depths of modern cities' and be the new scourges of God. In Charles Dickens' novel *Hard Times* (1854), the abyss beckons for those facing ruin – Mrs Sparsit (at the bottom of the narrator's imaginary staircase), Louisa Gradgrind (the ruined woman is the fallen woman, from L. *ruina*, fall or tumble down) and Stephen Blackpool (who dies by falling into a disused mineshaft). The image of the Abyss continued after Gissing, the Booths and Wells. Charles Masterman published *From the Abyss: Of its Inhabitants by One of Them* in 1902, and his population in the abyss at times resembles Wells' Morlocks who attain the surface through shafts ('they have been hurried up in incredible number through tubes sunk in the bowels of the earth', says Masterman of his abyss-dwellers, as though describing Wells' creations). They appear resistless in their spread and Masterman's inhabitant predicts that the suburbs will be engulfed, vanishing beneath the restless, unquiet sea of abyssal denizens. Jack London followed with his own study of the London poor, *The People of the Abyss*, in 1903. (Wells, incidentally, had used London's title phrase in *Anticipations*.) London said he 'went down into the under-world of London' like an explorer. His first chapter is called 'The Descent'. He quotes the sociologists' references to 'the submerged tenth' of the population that are driven downward until they drown at the bottom of the abyss.[1] (After 1912 the *Titanic* iceberg might seem to have loomed in the background of this idea of submerged existence.)

No doubt in ironic allusion to such works as these, Forster expressly declined to depict the very poor in *Howards End* ('They are unthinkable', but not alas unsinkable), opting to hesitate with Leonard Bast on the verge of the abyss. Forster has his heroines, the Schlegel sisters, inhabit guiltily one of the 'islands of money' that the *Titanic* of first-class could be said to have represented. 'Remember the submerged', Forster cautions us in the novel. After all, not everyone has his or her hands on 'the ropes of life' (a nautical metaphor that runs through the novel) and those who don't, sink as a consequence.

Panic and Emptiness

Forster's friend and fellow novelist Virginia Woolf returned time and again to the ideas of submergence and sinkings into the abyss, suggesting a psychological preoccupation. This would have been tantamount to a preoccupation with the unconscious itself, for by Woolf's time the unconscious was seen as a 'world underneath', the *sub*conscious in popular understanding. Max Nordau saw the image of the abyss in the poetry of Baudelaire as a manifestation of the poet's unconscious disorder and interpreted 'cremnophobia' (fear of abysses) as a degenerate obsession. He would no doubt have pounced upon Woolf as fresh meat for his theory. Be that as it may, Woolf's concern with submergence and the subaqueous seems to have been reinforced if not inspired by *Titanic*'s fate. Like the ship in *The Voyage Out* (1915), *Titanic* embarked on 'the voyage out' across the Atlantic but did not return, and those who survived were, like Woolf's characters, sea-changed. A chief character in the novel, Rachel Vinrace, gazes with fascination into the depths of the ocean. Her delirium towards the end of the novel produces a vision of her own drowning that I suspect was inspired by Woolf's thoughts about the drowned of *Titanic*:

> She saw nothing and heard nothing but a faint booming sound, which was the sound of the sea rolling over her head. While all her tormentors thought that she was dead, she was not dead, but curled up at the bottom of the sea. There she lay, sometimes seeing darkness, sometimes light, while every now and then someone turned her over at the bottom of the sea.

Fear of drowning animated Woolf, like many contemporaries who followed accounts of the *Titanic* disaster, allowing the ship to fuel vicarious dread and help turn its horror into thrill.

The voyage in Woolf's first novel starts with a set of socially ranked relationships on board, with stateroom partitions between the travellers, and with passengers 'colliding' rather than truly communicating or connecting. But the novel ends with lethal individualism, not quite balanced by an altruism and mutuality reminiscent of those famously shown by Isidor and Ida Straus who chose to stay on board *Titanic* and drown together rather than separate, with Ida almost certain to be saved, and Isidor almost certain to perish.

The importance of unity in British society was a cultural preoccupation among many politicians and captains of industry in the Age of *Titanic*. As we shall see, many thought that this ship and other great ships, as economic entities and machine entities, were both symbols and forces of racial and national unity: the hardware of unity, as it were. Others (often the same people) saw heroic masculinity, male chivalry and the class system itself as the necessary connectors that held society together and allowed it to function efficiently: the software of unity, as it were. This is why it was important that the *Titanic* tragedy not be allowed to impede the transatlantic shipping trade or the general economy. And why also there was such concern to prove heroism and chivalry on board.

But it was the fracturing unity of society, its disintegration and atomisation, that was a cultural preoccupation among the major writers of the time. Woolf, Forster, Conrad, Wells, Gissing, James Joyce, TS Eliot and others either could not accept the rightness of the class system or could not agree that heroism and chivalry existed or actually worked. Atomisation seemed an all but unavoidable evil and it seems as if Woolf saw the *Titanic* disaster as a vivid case-study in it. Liberals such as Forster and Woolf (at least at the start of her career) thought the best one could do in face of the organic and traditional culture breaking up through cosmopolitanism and subjectivity (both were evident on board *Titanic*) was to move among the fracturing parts of society, making connections where possible. *Howards End* and *The Voyage Out* are novels that try to show us how that might be done, not least by having large casts (or motley crews) of characters and covering a great deal of discursive territory in their pages. The reports of Thomas Andrews, the ship's co-designer, moving through the ship after the collision, helping, advising, cautioning, make of him a rather Forsterian figure, 'only' but effectively connecting. ('Only connect ...' is the celebrated epigraph of Forster's *Howards End*.)

As for the other writers who were not liberals, Gissing was a left-leaning pessimist who thought that the abyss of class division and destitution could not be bridged or plumbed. Conrad, Kipling and Wells in their right-leaning way thought that the kind of efficiency associated with an ideal engineering could hold things together for a while, which aligned them with the gurus of applied science, including the makers of *Titanic*. In the case of Wells (scientist, socialist and right-wing eugenicist all in one), however, efficiency was a solution only this side of large-scale evolutionary transpirations of even deeper abysses; for both Wells and Conrad, degeneration was the likelier undesired eventuality.

Those writers we might call experimental modernists (including the mature Woolf) thought the best one could do in face of culture's breakdown was to shore up its ruins with fragments of the past reconstituted in a new kind of artistic work that would hold the fort, a strategy brought to fulfilment by TS Eliot's *The Waste Land* (1922). Alternatively, it could perhaps be shown how the individual, isolated in his subjectivity, could nevertheless carry the entire culture around redemptively in his head, a strategy brought to fulfilment in James Joyce's *Ulysses* (1922). In any case, the atomised society is represented on board Woolf's ship *Euphrosyne*, though Woolf has her characters early in the novel dreaming at night of each other, the dreams dissolving the thin partitions that separate them and connecting them strangely at sea and by chance. The failure to 'connect' is represented in the sea itself, which in *The Voyage Out* might be Matthew Arnold's 'unplumb'd, salt, estranging sea'. 'What solitary icebergs we are', says one character in Woolf's novel, 'how little we can communicate'. When fieldglasses are trained on *Euphrosyne* from the decks of great liners passing, Woolf's ship becomes 'an emblem of the loneliness of human life', loneliness a goblin footfall amidst the apparent gaiety. Intimations of drowning float ominously in the text, as though death by water were the only possible reunification of the isolated selves.

In a curious early passage, Woolf depicts England as a shrinking island from the viewpoint of passengers on departing ships. The description reads like a transposition of survivors' accounts of *Titanic* before she went under:

> it was a shrinking island in which people were imprisoned. One figured them first swarming about like aimless ants, and almost pressing each other over the edge; and then, as the ship withdrew, one figured them making a vain clamour, which, being unheard, either ceased, or rose into a brawl. Finally, when the ship was out of sight of land, it became plain that the people of England were completely mute.

The end of *Titanic*, the site of panic, is in some sense the end of a nation or country as it has been known. Panic is the condition of extreme breakdown in unity, and it was much feared in the age of *Titanic*.

Woolf by her novel and her interest in the *Titanic* hearings incidentally alerts us to the cultural context of two troubling questions that were urgently posed during the postmortem. Was there panic on board *Titanic* while the passengers were being evacuated (and if so, in what quarter and how was it handled)? What happened in the waters around *Titanic* when the ship disappeared (could the struggling swimmers have been saved)? The ship and the waters of its vicinity were the two sites in which some contemporary cultural beliefs could be tested. The two questions might easily have been posed in the terms of two famous phrases from *Howards End*: had a shipboard post-collision episode of 'telegrams and anger' been followed by an episode in the boats and in the water of 'panic and emptiness'?

The enormous, pro-active interest of editors and readers in possible panic aboard *Titanic*, like the interest in hymns, is of interest to cultural historians. Not surprisingly, reports were contradictory. One of the first survivors off *Carpathia*, a first-class passenger, Robert W. Daniel, a Philadelphia banker, told a *New York Times* reporter:

> Five minutes after the crash everybody seemed to have gone insane. Men and women fought, bit and scratched to be in line for the lifeboats. Look at my black eye and cut chin. I got these in the fight. Then Capt Smith seemed to get some order .... I saw men praying as I struggled to get to the rail. Curses and prayers filled the air.

From the other end of the economic scale, Carl Johnsson (Johnson in the *New York Times*), a labourer, reported to the paper that when he got on deck, he saw, in his own words, 'the first sign of panic among the passengers. Women were screaming with terror and men were rushing this way and that.' There is a dramatic impetus to these accounts that suggests that some survivors felt they knew – with that degree of self-specialness survivors of colourful crises feel – what they ought to say to the lesser mortals who were not on board; or perhaps American reporters doctored their shorthand transcripts to achieve an acceptable dramatic flair.

Many witnesses saw panic that either deteriorated into gunfire or was curtailed by the same gunfire. Johnsson reported: 'Suddenly I hear shrieks and cries amidship, and the sharp reports of several shots'. (Unless education standards have deteriorated astonishingly, what this labourer was reported to have said is suspiciously succinct, symmetrical in syntax and rich in vocabulary.) The City Assessor for San Francisco, Washington Dodge, reported that 'everybody seemed to be panic-stricken, and there was a rush for the boats. I heard a lot of shots, but I do not know where they came from. In fact, it was not until later on the *Carpathia* that I recalled the shots.' Daisy Minahan, a first-class passenger from Wisconsin, was put into lifeboat No. 14. In an affidavit requested by Senator Alden Smith, she wrote that:

> The crowd surging around the boats was getting unruly. Officers were
> yelling and cursing at men to stand back and let the women into the boats
> .... At times when we were being lowered we were at an angle of 45
> degrees and expected to be thrown into the sea. As we reached the level
> of each deck men jumped into the boat until the officer threatened to
> shoot the next man who jumped.

Mrs Mark Fortune, who had travelled in first-class, remembered that
men from steerage tried to rush the boats and that officers had been
able at first to keep them off by 'slugging them' (this sounds like the
Times' reporter's hard-boiled phrase) but that the passengers grew more
terrified, requiring the officers to use their revolvers, firing them in the
air but then aiming 'at the bodies of the men'. A Mrs Alexander Lurch
was reported by the *Times* as having witnessed 'a scene of disorder and
cruelty' that was continued on *Carpathia* when survivors were forced to
sign a paper testifying that there had been no such disorder aboard
Titanic. She claimed to have seen one woman clinging to her husband's
neck as the lifeboats were being loaded and crying to the sailors to save
him. 'Instead of doing this, the sailor drew a revolver and pressing it to
the man's head shot him to death. Several sailors then picked up the
body, tossed it into the ocean and threw the woman into a lifeboat.'
(But who was the originator of this lurid account? Since there was no
Mrs Alexander Lurch on the passenger lists, could it have been a
second-class passenger, Mrs Alice Louch?) Boyd Smith reproduces a
story allegedly given by Lady Duff Gordon to a Reuter's representative
in New York on April 19:

> Just as we were about to clear the ship a man rushed to get aboard our
> lifeboat. He was shot and apparently killed instantly. His body fell in the
> boat at our feet. No one made any effort to move him, and his body
> remained in the boat until we were picked up.

Gracie makes no mention of this horrifying incident in his account of
this lifeboat nor did Duff Gordon recall it at the British inquiry.

The association of shots with commotion was early made. *Times*
reporters in the Friday April 19 edition warmed to the theme:

> According to others of the survivors, shots rang out in the still night, and
> it was reported that an officer of the ship had shot two men passengers who
> had tried to force their way into the lifeboats with the women, thereafter
> shooting himself [an allusion to the fate of First Officer Murdoch]. Still
> others, however, declared that the shots were fired by the Captain, and it
> was reported that both he and the Chief Engineer of the vessel [Joseph
> Bell] had shot themselves.

One senses here, in the early days of the story, the overheated
American medium (that of thriller fiction) as well as the cultural

message (that violations of chivalry were dealt with in the most effective way devisable). Still, the reports persisted. Mrs George Widener insisted she saw an officer put a gun to his own head and shoot. A Dr JF Kemp, a medical instructor in the University of the Philippines (before which he had been a surgeon in the United States Army), was a passenger on *Carpathia* who reported that he had been told by a boy survivor of *Titanic* that he had seen Captain Smith put a pistol to his head and fall down. Kemp relayed the talk among other survivors 'of the use of pistols and the firing of shots'. Harry Senior, a fireman, said Captain Smith had been armed and had threatened to use his gun on any fireman who tried to come up on deck.

The precise nature of Captain Smith's death has never been satisfactorily established. Besides the version of his death which has him shoot himself, there is another that has him save a woman and then a baby but refusing help from lifeboat No. 14 and giving himself up to the sea. In yet another he is washed overboard when the ocean overwhelms the forward superstructure and is never seen again.

Mrs Daniel Marvin of New York, whose honeymoon and marriage were ended with the loss of her husband, said at pier-side after disembarking from *Carpathia*, that she had heard at least ten revolver shots. 'See there powder marks', she was quoted in the *Times*, presumably pointing either to her clothes or her skin. This eighteen-year-old sudden widow was distraught and perhaps an unreliable witness, but her testimony is troublingly graphic.

Yet there were many survivors who denied there had been any panic on board. Seaman Frank Osman was asked by Senator Burton at the American hearing 'was there any panic?'

Mr Osman: No, there was no panic at all. I was helping women and children in the boat and the crew was lowering boats.
Senator Burton: Was there any panic?
Mr Osman: I never seen no panic there.

Max Frolicher-Stehli, a first-class passenger saved with his wife and daughter, claimed that the order maintained on *Titanic* 'was what I would call remarkable. There was very little pushing and it was in most cases the women who caused the commotion by insisting that their husbands accompany them in her lifeboats.' Another first-class passenger, Mrs Thomas Potter of Philadelphia, later wrote to Colonel Archibald Gracie, the American survivor who privately investigated the disaster. Mrs Potter insisted that 'There was no panic. Everyone seemed more stunned than anything else ... we watched upwards of two hours the gradual sinking of the ship.' Dickinson Bishop, a first-class passenger from Detroit, Michigan, and quoted in the *Times*, thought too that 'the people were apathetic at first all through the ship', the absence of panic being due to everyone's certainty that *Titanic* was unsinkable. His wife confirmed that 'there was little or no panic. The behavior of the crew was perfect.' TM Graham, whose wife and daughter were saved, relayed their claim to the *Times* that 'there was no panic and everything was perfectly orderly'.

Neither Mrs L. Davis Parrish nor her daughter, passengers in second class, saw any quarrelling or fighting on the ship; a Mrs Andrews (first class) knew of no panic on board; Elizabeth Allen of St Louis (also first class) reported that 'Although there was plenty of excitement there was no panic aboard that I saw. The men and the officers behaved admirably.' Helen Churchill Candee (of whom more later), a writer in first-class cabin, whose testimony to reporters founded the legend of Ida Straus' choosing to stay with her husband Isidor, praised the first-class men's noble behaviour for the lack of confusion, much less panic. A passenger on *Carpathia*, Jose Mardones, a bass singer with the Boston Opera, relayed different intelligence from Dr Kemp: he had been told by survivors that 'there was no panic whatever. In fact, I was told by several of the survivors that they jested about going into the lifeboats.' When Henry Blank, a jeweller in first class, went to the boat deck he found that 'although there were plenty of people hurrying around, there was no panic'.

So huge was *Titanic*, however, that few if any people aboard, possibly a few officers and crew and probably no passengers, could be sure of what mood and behaviour prevailed throughout the stricken ship. Witnesses' accounts of the lengthy drama were also time-restricted. It may be that first-class women who were early away in the boats had an impression of greater orderliness than later obtained out of sight; the bulk of the steerage passengers had in all probability not appeared on the boat deck yet. One occasionally gets the sense too that first-class women were contriving to preempt any criticism of their men, this forestalling of criticism requiring that there be no panic on the parts of the ship where first-class men held sway.

In any case, the unprompted denial of panic reveals a concern with a phenomenon that was uppermost in people's minds.

A truer picture of the situation on board would probably depict an initial and studied calm on the part of the officers (which George Bernard Shaw disbelieved) – in part professional response, in part an improvised but possibly official policy of withholding bad news from passengers, in part English coolness under fire. The calm of passengers would have been less studied, a combination of shock and of trust both in *Titanic*'s comforting and well-lit magnitude and her officers' competence. Then as the evacuation of passengers progressed and more of those left on board began to realise their plight, the calm would have steadily evaporated.

The *New York Times* identified an AH Blackworth as a young survivor from London who jumped from the ship and managed to make it on to an upturned boat. I cannot find his name in lists furnished by Walter Lord and others, and it is an AH Barkworth whom Gracie identifies on the upset Engelhardt boat 'B' from which Gracie was also rescued; but Barkworth is identified on another list as a Yorkshire Justice of the Peace, which does not suggest youth. According to the *Times*, young Blackworth walked into the Hotel Imperial and was given free accommodation as a *Titanic* survivor. In any case, his story was not unusual, though oddly he described the crash between ship and iceberg as fearful: 'There was, however, at first no panic'. He rushed to the boat deck where 'for the first few minutes a marked calm in the midst of the uncertainty prevailed'. But when the officers began to man the lifeboats 'fear seized upon the women, and the scenes were pathetic and awful in the extreme. I hate to think of them.' According to NK Chambers, a first-class passenger quoted in the *Times*, 'there was nothing like a panic at first', but from his lifeboat (Gracie later identified it as boat No. 5) he watched the panicky rush for the remaining boats. Washington Dodge recalled that 'For a little while the ship's officers had the situation pretty well in hand, but when the water and floating ice began to cover the lower decks there was a wild panic'.

Just as some survivors denied panic, some went out of their way to deny shooting. Ada Clarke, a second-class passenger emigrating to California with her husband (who was lost), claimed that her lifeboat (one of three lashed together) was so close to *Titanic* that 'I could even hear the water entering the funnels as the vessel disappeared' yet 'I heard no pistol shots'. Neither did NK Chambers who was sure there were no shots fired or any violence. 'Charette the French sculptor' (actually Paul Chevré) was quoted in the *New York Times* as denying 'certain wild rumors' that had been

> flying round during the evening as to the necessity of the shooting of some
> of the men passengers to prevent them from clambering into the boats
> with the women. This, M. Charette said, was not the case. All that was
> done in the way of shooting was by a German passenger, who fired a
> revolver in the air in order to summon aid, he explained.

Chevré and two other French survivors from first class elaborated on this incident in a cable sent from America to a Paris newspaper. In their lifeboat (Gracie places Chevré and Pierre Maréchal, an aviator, in boat No. 7) they cried out for aid 'and a German baron who was with them, emptied his revolver in the air'.

Anglo-Saxon Attitudes

In the confusion of testimonies it seems certain only that First Officer Murdoch fired probably twice to deter men from swarming into a boat on the starboard side and that Fifth Officer Lowe fired perhaps three times from lifeboat No. 14 as it was being lowered (the boat in which Daisy Minahan sat) to deter men from jumping into the boat as it passed lower decks. (The question of Captain Smith and his revolver has not been definitively answered.) What is disturbing in Lowe's account and the accounts of others is how the issues of gunfire and race are mingled. Those survivors who told the stories that in turn survived the inevitable transience of much *Titanic* lore and literature were those who believed that what events on board the sinking *Titanic* demonstrated was the sterling comportment of members of the Anglo-Saxon race. In cool reflection, Archibald Gracie was of the opinion that:

> There was not a member of the crew who shirked, or left his post. The coolness, courage, and sense of duty that I here witnessed made me thankful to God and proud of my Anglo-Saxon race that gave this perfect and superb exhibition of self-control at this hour of severest trial.

Lawrence Beesley, a second-class passenger, had a similarly racial explanation for what he saw as the orderliness of the men during the loading of the lifeboats. These men were 'the average Teutonic crowd, with an inborn respect for law and order and for traditions bequeathed to them by generations of ancestors'. This might have been faint praise had Beesley meant to draw the conclusion that these passengers did not act the way they did for reasons of personal character but for reasons that were 'impersonal, instinctive, hereditary' (like suggesting that their heroism was actually due to the impersonal code of chivalry) but Beesley intended only to exalt his race. Panic was a mode of behaviour demonstrated by the darker races (and – if they weren't held in check by their betters – by the lower orders; and also – if chivalry as a kind of preemptive crowd control were absent – by the weaker sex). From our popular perspective today, and from the advanced perspective in the Age of *Titanic*, this racism was a goblin footfall threatening the heroic story of the ship.

In the survivors' accounts, the actions, even the presence, of representatives of the swarthy races and the yellow races almost marred the heroic drama acted out on board – or, perhaps, those representatives were *necessary* to that heroic drama! Fancifully, the *New York Times* of April 19 reported 'Chinese stokers' piling into the bottoms of the boats before the women could get in and attempting violently to wrest a lifejacket from a passenger, the latter surely a garbled version of the Marconi operator Harold Bride's story of the stoker who tried to steal his colleague Jack Phillip's lifejacket. There were no Chinese stokers but this report may have conflated Mrs CEH Stengel's claim to the *Times* that 'Chinamen and stokers' hid in the bottom of lifeboats before they were launched. Second Officer Lightholler testified to the British inquiry that 'a couple of Chinese' stowed away in Engelhardt boat D of which he supervised the launch. In a more sensational report, retailed by Mowbray, two 'Chinamen' who hid themselves in the boat bottom were shot dead by an officer when they were discovered, and their bodies tumbled overboard. The *Times* of April 20 stated:

> When the revised list of survivors was made up at the White Star Line office yesterday it became known that among those saved from the Titanic were six of eight Chinamen who were among the steerage passengers on the big liner. It seems that they climbed into one of the lifeboats without anybody making objection, despite the fact that many of the women in the steerage of the Titanic went down with the ship.

The implication here is that whereas no great fuss would or should be made if some Anglo-Saxon men got away before steerage women, 'Chinamen' ought to have observed the women-and-children-first rule and in doing so acknowledge their inferiority to those lower-class women and children.

A dining-room steward told the American inquiry that two foreigners were found crouching in the bottom of boat No. 10 and who were then pulled out, one apparently 'a Japanese' and the other apparently an Italian but then discovered to be an Armenian. Boat No. 14 happened upon a floating door on which a survivor had lashed himself. According to Charlotte Collyer, Fifth Officer Lowe hesitated to try to save what looked like a corpse: '"What's the use?" said Mr. Lowe. "He's dead, likely, and if he isn't there's others better worth saving than a Jap"'. But Lowe changed his mind and turned the boat around, only to find that the corpse was alive, and when brought on board readily took an oar and performed manfully. 'By Jove!' Lowe was heard to mutter, 'I'm ashamed of what I said about the little blighter. I'd save the likes o' him six times over if I got the chance.' Lowe had expressed racial prejudice in the most literal sense of the phrase, prejudging a 'Jap' to be cowardly if not dead through feebleness. Gracie was surprised enough to refer to this survivor as 'a plucky Japanese', the adjective meaning – as it does in the phrase 'the plucky little Countess of Rothes' – 'surprisingly self-possessed and uncowardly'.

It was the Italian passengers who drew most of the animus of the Anglo-American survivors. This despite the fact that the first-class à la carte restaurant (decorated in the style of the Louis Seize period) was managed by Luigi Gatti, former manager of the restaurant in the London Ritz. Gatti brought with him his own staff, including ten of his own cousins. There were at least 26 Italian waiters on board – from Antonio and Basilico to Valvassori and Viani, not to speak of wine butlers and glassmen. Yet British and American survivors did not recall Italians with fondness. Collyer remembered a steerage passenger, 'an Italian, I think', hurling himself into boat No. 14 and injuring a child. The officer grabbed him by his collar and pushed him back on to the ship. 'As we shot down toward the sea, I caught a last glimpse of this coward. He was in the hands of about a dozen men of the second cabin. They were driving their fists into his face, and he was bleeding from the nose and mouth.' Collyer is approving.

There was a telling casualness and imprecision in references to Italians by survivors. They were damned with the faint praise of being distinguished (barely) from other 'foreigners'. A steward named F. (or G.) Crowe at the American hearings told of a rush for the boats by 'various men passengers, probably Italians or some foreign nationality other than English or American'. British witnesses would have been more likely than Americans to confuse ethnicity with nationality. Hugh Woolner, an English businessman travelling in first class who saved himself by jumping into Engelhardt boat D as it was being lowered, told the American hearing that he had heard two flashes of a pistol on the starboard boat deck and had gone forward to help clear away men who were climbing in so that 'a bunch of women – I think Italians and foreigners' could be made safe. Woolner & co. pulled men ('probably third-class passengers') ignominiously by their feet and legs so that the Italian women could be hoisted up and into the boat; the women proved their unworthiness and foreignness, presumably, when they had 'not much spring in them at all'. John Hardy, Chief Steward, remembered that 'there were Syrians in the bottom of the boat, third-class passengers, chattering the whole night in their strange language'.

The general note is one of contempt. Major Arthur Peuchen, Canadian chemical manufacturer, militiaman and yachtsman, was pressed to crew boat No. 6 in which, he told the American hearing, they found a stowaway, 'an Italian'. Senator Smith then asks him an unrelated question but Peuchen is determined to malign the stowaway: 'He was an Italian by birth, I should think', Peuchen specifies (presumably to distinguish the coward from an Italian-American) 'who had a broken wrist or arm, and he was of no use to us to row'.

It was with some relish that Fifth Officer Lowe recounted for Alden Smith his discovery in boat no. 14 of a passenger 'who was an Italian' who had 'sneaked in' and was 'dressed like a woman'. Smith found this sufficiently colourful to pursue. 'Had women's clothing on?' 'He had a shawl over his head, and everything else', Lowe reported, though later he said he *supposed* the Italian wore skirts since he wore a shawl. Smith seemed pleased to know that Lowe had 'pitched him' into another boat during Lowe's transfer of passengers among the flotilla he assembled and wanted to know if Lowe had thrown him in 'among the women' and used 'some pretty emphatic language' while about it, but was disappointed on both scores. In fact, Lowe by not doing either of these things was showing what he thought was even greater contempt. Smith couldn't resist a later gratuitous reference to 'this Italian in woman's attire'. The experience first-cabin passenger Mrs Mark Fortune, travelling with her three daughters, recounted to reporters, was the ultimate Anglo-Saxon nightmare which composes for us nowadays a comic scene. They were placed in a boat with 'a Chinaman, an Italian stoker, and a man dressed in woman's clothing'. Only one occupant knew how to row, the Italian stoker, and Fortune's daughters had to take turns at the oars. The Chinese

> was of little use. The man dressed in woman's clothing did his best to row, but did not seem familiar with an oar. This man wore a woman's bonnet and a veil, in addition to a skirt and blouse, which he had evidently picked up in a hurry as he ran through the ship.

How utterly unlike these figures – swarthy, injured, impractical, cowardly, transvestite – is 'the brave American man ... our American manhood' for which Elizabeth Shutes, a governess travelling first-class with her young charge and the young charge's mother, was so grateful; 'God's noblemen', the writer Helen Churchill Candee was reported in the *New York Times* as calling the men of first class who saw her safely off the sinking ship. For Anglo-American first-class and second-class passengers, the clustering of foreigners, like the clustering of the working class and of women, meant an incipient panic, a loss of order and, in fact, the endangerment of civilization. Heroism, manly action, was a sacrifice to race, class and gender order. The British in particular nursed a race memory of the French Revolution and Communist agitations, and of the Boxer rebellion and native unrest in the empire; they also brooded on contemporary labour unrest that threatened to degenerate into violence. Unless officers, with the auxiliary power of first-class men (Gracie and others conscripted themselves for the purpose) took charge, it could all happen in miniature on RMS *Titanic*.

The Age of *Titanic* was the age in which commentators became aware of and alarmed by the growth of 'the multitude', as Charles Masterman termed it in *The Condition of England* (1909), the great and potentially restive congestions in the cities (and was not *Titanic* a scale-model town, a 'floating town', as RA Fletcher called it?). Of course, crowds had often in the past degenerated into mobs, but this was the period in which the 'crowd' was coming to the attention of sociologists, as John Carey tells us, and being defined in a quasi-scientific way. Gustave Le Bon published his immensely popular and widely translated study, *The Crowd*, in 1896. Crowds, he thought, display feminine characteristics (as well as the characteristics of children and savages – the working classes were as unruly children and dark races were of course savages), and it was surely because of the symbolic anarchic threat that passengers dressed as women caused such heat of resentment.

Many major writers of the time, including WB Yeats, TS Eliot, Ezra Pound, DH Lawrence, Virginia Woolf and HG Wells, detested mass man and his herd instinct, as we learn from Carey's *The Intellectuals and the Masses* (1992). Fear of mass man was a feature of the period and lay behind the contemporary concern with the behaviour of third-class, foreign and female passengers on board *Titanic*, and with the fact or fiction of panic. It was during panic that the atomised society was critically reconstituted as a crowd. Wells, who had an almost sadistic hatred of mass man, relished scenes of panic in his early scientific romances, and in the chapter entitled 'The Exodus from London' in *The War of the Worlds* (1898) Wells depicts the 'wave of fear' that engulfs Londoners when the Martians invade and the way social organisations break down under the pressure of panic, 'running' – in Wells' graphic metaphor applicable to a major sea disaster – 'in that swift liquefaction of the social body'.

As well as race memory, there was a quite specific memory for many Britons on board *Titanic* of the *Oceana* disaster on March 16, 1912 in which the 'ill-fated' P&O liner collided with the German sailing ship *Pisagua* off the coast of Lincolnshire and sank six or seven hours later with the loss of seven passengers and two crewmen. Bryceson reproduces a *Daily Sketch* article of April 17 that remarks that 'One prominent [*Titanic*] officer is said to have been on the Oceana'.

One issue arising from the earlier disaster was the behaviour of Lascar crew members. Two months before the collision, Admiral Sir ER Fremantle wrote that of 184,000 seamen on British ships, 66,000 were 'foreigners or Lascars' and that in time of war 'most of the foreigners and Lascars would desert'. In fact, Lascars were employed on board British ships trading with the Far East because it was thought they withstood heat and were amenable to discipline. But it seems that discipline broke down during the sinking of the *Oceana* and, according to some eyewitnesses, the Lascars were terrified and hindered evacuation efforts. If others thought Lascars were nevertheless superior in comportment to the average 'Asiatic' crew (more faint praise), it was surely the full-page drawing in the *Illustrated London News* of March 23, 1912 that Britons on board an ailing vessel would have remembered with discomfort. It showed 'terrified Lascars, rescued from the wrecked P. and O. and afraid to leave the tug "Alert", being forcibly dropped into one of the "Sussex's" boats, birdcages in hand'. Reports of the *Oceana* affair would have fuelled suspicion of any reliance on foreigners in a crisis, and perhaps helped even in a small way to distort memories of what happened in the North Atlantic a month later.[2]

Wells, for his opening scenes of *The Island of Dr Moreau* (1896), had drawn upon the case of the French frigate *Medusa* en route to Senegal in 1816 when the shipwreck became 'la theâtre de scènes épouvantables' with the survivors on board the ship's raft resorting to murder and cannibalism. Here was apparently an episode of panic and degeneration that Jules Verne previously drew on for scenes in his novel *The Chancellor* (1874). When the German painter Max Beckmann came to paint his large canvas *The Sinking of the* Titanic (1912), he too was inspired by the *Medusa* disaster, particularly Géricault's famous depiction of it, *The Raft of the* Medusa (1818–1819), and Beckmann foregrounded the disturbing events around the lifeboats and backgrounded the sinking liner.

Titanic, because of misfortune, had her own 'raft', the Engelhardt boat B that had landed in the water upside down and on which men clambered from the water and stood unmoving for hours waiting for rescue. Archibald Gracie remembered what happened as 'this most tragic crisis in all my life'. After a while, no more swimmers were allowed on the boat and petitioners in the water were deterred by words, feet and paddles. Chivalry had given way to a Darwinian struggle for survival. The eminent biologist E. Ray Lankester had

warned in 1880 that even the white race could degenerate
(Trevelyan's 'white peril') and Joseph Conrad had depicted
degeneration in the absence of restraint in *Heart of Darkness* (1902) as
Wells had done in *The Island of Dr Moreau*. But it seems that the
intense race-consciousness in the Age of *Titanic* made for westerners
the threats of panic and disorder the more acute, and they needed
reassurance about order and unity and the particular heroism that
maintained or re-established them when they listened to accounts of
what happened in the early hours of April 15, 1912.

Peace or Peril

Despite the free bandy with race in *Titanic* coverage, Officer Harold
Lowe went too far on the fifth day of the US hearings (April 24) when
he explained why he had resort to his pistol during the evacuation. He
was in charge of boat No. 14 and it was being lowered into the water
past decks from which stowaways could leap.

> Coming down past the open decks, I saw a lot of Italians, Latin people, all
> along the ship's rails – understand, it was open – and they were all glaring,
> more or less like wild beasts, ready to spring. That's why I yelled to look
> out, and let go, bang, right along the ship's side.

The Italian ambassador to the United States protested and on the
fourteenth day (May 9), Senator Smith read into the record a
retraction by Lowe given to the ambassador and signed in his presence
on April 30. Lowe agreed to substitute the phrase 'immigrants
belonging to the Latin races' for 'Italian'. This retraction saved Italian
face but preserved the original race-awareness.

It was a fine balance. The race-consciousness of the 'Anglo-Saxons'
was unretractable. At the same time, Italians in America were
developing clout through numbers in the Age of *Titanic* and this was
regretted in some quarters. An article in a 1907 issue of the periodical
The World's Work (the American edition published by Doubleday in
New York) by Frederic Austin Ogg entitled 'American Immigration at
High Tide' was subtitled 'The Horde of Aliens, Whence They Come,
and Whither They Go'. (Large numbers of unwanted visitors are always
'hordes', the migratory equivalent of the sedentary 'mob'.) Ogg
lamented the shift in immigration from Celtic and Teutonic peoples of
the north and west of Europe to 'the Iberian and Slavic stocks of the
south and east' and acknowledged that the hope of those who wished
to see the Teutonic newcomer ('and therefore ... the more acceptable,
type of immigrant') predominate in numbers was unrealised. The
author offered a pie-chart showing that in the fiscal year ending June

30, 1906, the largest immigrant group was Italian, at 26 per cent of all newcomers. Little wonder the ambassador's protest got some results, whereas no retraction was required from anyone who had uttered anti-Chinese or anti-Japanese sentiments during the hearings or in the newspapers. Even the Socialist Party of the United States could not agree at its national convention of 1911 whether or not 'Asiatic' immigration was a good or bad thing. Although it was putatively the mere fact of accelerating immigration that exercised established Americans, the origins of the immigrants was the sharper issue. The *Literary Digest* of November 1912 noted that 'there are more foreign-born in this country at present than was the total population of the United States in 1830' and printed a map of 'Foreign America' indicating by state the percentages of alien residents. Race, foreignness, immigration – all were much on the mind of Americans in 1912. In Britain, race and foreignness were rarely out of mind because of the empire.

The success of the British Empire was seen to require race-tolerance, if not 'race-unity', but it was observed by an American writer in *The World's Work* that 'wherever there is an Englishman, he regards other races as radically different and as inferior to his own .... There is a deep hostility, too, in some other races to the English – to all white men.' Toleration may have grown with the centuries but the radical 'race-difference' always asserts itself and according to the American continues to threaten 'race-conflict' in the year of 1907. The English edition of the same magazine was even more pessimistic by December 1912 with an article entitled 'The Map of Europe: How Race has Vanquished Union'. The 'romance and pathos' of race has made even failed ethnic movements preferable to unity in the world since in the early nineteenth century 'Racialism' revived itself.

Race-consciousness was the dominant cultural phenomenon in the Age of *Titanic*. It pervaded everyday language. Harold Bride, *Titanic's* surviving wireless operator told the *New York Times* reporter that when he was on *Carpathia*, he ignored requests from shore to give information about survivors and chose instead to send personal messages, and added: 'I feel I did the white thing'. Nowadays this would be assumed to be an unfortunate misprint for 'right thing', but it wasn't in 1912. Race-consciousness was ubiquitous. The report in 1912 that the Arctic explorer Vilhjalmar Stefansson had discovered white Eskimos in Coronation Gulf was extensively carried by the New York *Sun, Harper's Weekly* and *The Literary Digest*, among other media, and discussed in the pages of *Nature*. If this issue was politically and morally innocuous, the fear that German theories of Jewish

inadequacy were gaining a foothold among 'the Anglo-Saxon nations'
was not, as Nahum Wolf wrote in a 1912 issue of *The North American
Review*, expressing his alarm in an article frankly entitled 'Are the
Jews an Inferior Race?'

Race-consciousness could become race-prejudice or race-hatred
when it was motivated by, or caused, fear. Fear was the product of
ignorance only secondarily; in the first instance it was actually the
product of awareness. Around the turn of the nineteenth and
twentieth centuries, in an age of exploration and commercial
expansion in distant parts of the Earth, white people became acutely
conscious of the *complex* of human races of which they were only a
portion. Whereas Euro-Americans sailing on *Titanic* would have been
vaguely aware of other races on board, it was the emergency of the
sinking, an emergency that lasted long enough to permit observation
of others and to evoke a personal and racial competitiveness, that
brought normally submerged racial feelings to the surface and gave
them unpleasant expression. Those feelings included fear, both
personal and communal. The *Review of Reviews* for February 1911
entitled its coverage of an article in the *Contemporary Review* (also
February 1911), 'Will the Race Cease to be White?' In this article,
Professor LW Lyde concludes with this 'dark outlook' (sic): 'If any
White man can settle in the tropics it is [the] tanned White man; but
probably only the Yellow man can settle there, and the blond White
is probably doomed to disappear off the face of the earth'. (It was
thought by Alleyne Ireland that in the Tropics Chinese expansion
would make itself soon evident.) According to a 1907 number of *The
World's Work*, a US Congressional Commission had already concluded
from a summer visit to Europe that there were not enough white men
in the world, that European governments were concerned at the flow
of their young men to the United States and blamed in part the
shipping lines who, flouting European laws, solicited emigrant
passengers. (*Titanic* was not an emigrant ship but like her sister liners
was carrying many emigrants to the New World.) Meanwhile, the
countries of the East had no such relief from overpopulation, since 'No
country held by Europeans welcomes Asiatic immigrants.'

Europeans were realising that the portion of the human race
complex they represented was a small one and shrinkingly so. If they
were outnumbered, it was chiefly by the 'yellow man'. This danger to
the white man was popularly known as the 'Yellow Peril'. The
likelihood of peace or peril was hotly debated around 1912. From one
side, the Yellow Peril was sham or a bogey, but only because the
'Chinaman' was docile and bereft of his former fighting qualities. From

the other side, the Yellow Peril was real. Since China was a potential acquirer of colonies, it was a commercial threat. 'The Chinaman is the coming Jew', as one respectable writer had it in the *North American Review*, and China a nation awakening and quietly arming and capable of eventually boasting an army of sixty million men which in any coming war could afford to lose ten soldiers for every single English or American and remain a powerful fighting force long after the allies had exhausted their manpower. 'No wonder people talk of a yellow peril', remarked William Trant.

No wonder, indeed. A popular book of 1898 was MP Shiels' apocalyptic novel, *The Yellow Danger* which also appeared in 'Grant Richards' Colonial Library'. This is a Wellsian science fiction work of a certain fin-de-siècle subspecies (the 'coming war' fiction) that is propelled by a vicious Sinophobia and enlivened by an unpleasant sadism in the descriptions of torture and atrocity. It is set in its own day, 1898–1899, and although it heatedly imagines the Great War as a global assault by the hordes of the 'heathen Chinee', mighty naval battles like Armageddon (with the promise of 'boats of the air' to come), and an attempt at a worldwide League of Yellow Races, the novel nevertheless is full of the very real geopolitics of its time and has real politicians as characters, including Sir Robert Hart of the Imperial Maritime Customs, and Lord Curzon. Shiels' hero and redeemer, a perfect Englishman, is John Hardy, a combination of Lord Nelson and (the future) Lawrence of Arabia. As it happens, there was a John Hardy on board *Titanic*, Chief Steward, and he reported that First Officer Murdoch had said to him of the ship that sank through 'kismet': 'I believe she is gone, Hardy', which provokes a faintly Nelsonian echo.

Under the circumstances, it was perhaps necessary to survivors of the *Titanic* disaster that they remember cowardly Chinese, stowaways on the grand ship of state in which they were unworthy to be passengers, and who were of course anonymous, befitting the nameless masses they represented. No doubt too, survivors felt that their anti-Asiatic feeling was simply reciprocating anti-white feeling that observers told them was rife in China. The 'large world-fact' that had to be faced was the Western world's fear that 'a race conflict and an economic conflict between Asia and the rest of the world' was in progress. By 1907 a possible breach between the United States and Japan was being talked about. Readers of *The World's Work* (US) were told in 1907 that 'the inevitable race-feeling would assert itself' if Japanese immigration to the US were to become great. Ironically, the Japanese passenger on *Titanic*, Masabumi Hosono, who survived when

Lowe went to his rescue in the teeth of Lowe's own racial prejudice, was reviled in Japan when he returned home because he had violated the race-expectations of the Japanese themselves by not dying with the Anglo-Saxon heroes.

A former American minister to Siam, John Barrett, believed in 1900 that in the current competition between nations, in which 'the principle of the survival of the fittest has its stern and cruel application', particularly in the contest between China and the English-speaking races, 'our Anglo-Saxon race, our Anglo-Saxon religion, our Anglo-Saxon systems of society and government are at stake'. The same year, Lord Charles Beresford, who is a major character in The Yellow Danger, considered 'The Future of the Anglo-Saxon Race' in the North American Review. He acknowledged the success of the race in controlling or dominating nearly one-quarter of the globe's total land surface and representing over a quarter of the world's population. It was the race's capacity for assimilating 'the progressive forces of other nationalities' that has refreshed the Anglo-Saxon peoples and prevented them from following predecessor nationalities down 'the path of degeneracy'. He was confident that the Anglo-Saxon race would persist triumphantly, in part because of its 'cool, calm, almost phlegmatic and critical way of regarding all questions': a set of traits reporters and surviving passengers alike looked for in the conduct of the race aboard the sinking Titanic. The Anglo-Saxon, said Lord Charles, as if foreseeing the disaster, was the protector of chivalry, manliness and purity. But plutocracy, the 'new order of Wealth', he wrote (and anticipating Alma White and others), constituted a new threat larger than the 'angry waters of the Latin races' – the threat of luxurious immorality, the loss of manliness, chivalry, moral courage and fearlessness: the very virtues Westerners were determined to see exercised on board the world's greatest ship.

Alfred Stead, son of WT Stead, while noting the loss of his father on Titanic in the April 1912 issue of his father's journal, the Review of Reviews, was more confident than even Lord Charles that the Anglo-Saxon race would go from strength to strength: of necessity, since the English-speaking race 'is one of the chief of God's chosen agents for executing coming improvements in the lot of mankind'. All that was required was what his father had always advocated, an English-speaking Union. Stead Sr had combined Christianity and geopolitics when he had informed readers in 'The Progress of the World' in the same journal exactly one year before that President Taft had identified the Bible as the 'true Bond of Union' between the two great Anglo-Saxon nations.

The first decade of the twentieth century was a fine decade in which to be an Anglo-Saxon. If you visited the Paris Exhibition of 1900, there was an *Anglo-Saxon Guide* to help you identify the most important exhibits. (In it, Ridways the tea merchants to Queen Victoria called the attention of 'Anglo-Saxons, either visiting or dwelling in foreign countries' to the fact that the firm would make sure that expatriate Anglo-Saxons would not have to suffer without their chosen Anglo-Saxon beverage.) In need of light history, you could read Dugald MacFadyen's *Alfred the West Saxon King of the English* (1901), reviewed in Stead's journal under the title of 'The Most Perfect Englishman'. By 1908 you could celebrate with gusto St George's Day (April 23, also identified as 'England's Day' and 'Shakespeare's Day'), buoyed by the new magazine, *The English Race*, with a 'Foreword for Englishmen' by the aptly named J. Saxon Mills, and a 'Song of Empire' by Professor WW Skeat, the eminent medievalist. Stead promoted during his tenure as editor of the *Review of Reviews* the patriotic pageants taking place around the English countryside. Stead was a cheerleader in what was really – though unacknowledged by cultural historians since – an English Cultural Revival comparable to, though more diffuse than, its well-known contemporary, the Irish Cultural Revival. Stead hoped that St George would become the patron saint of his fondly hoped-for English-speaking Union.

Despite his racially based Anglo-Saxonism and British imperialism, Stead worked tirelessly for international peace. He supported the various peace conferences (at the Hague, in New York, in London and elsewhere) that punctuated and helped to define the Age of *Titanic*. He promoted the Universal Races Congress, held in London in July 1911, the object of which was to encourage understanding between the peoples of the West and the East. He recommended to his readers a little book by his 'good friend', M. Finot, entitled *The Illusion of Race*, which substituted the dividers of nationality and environment for the divider of race, which Finot held to be a figment. Stead would have considered himself a nationalist and not a racist, though the distinction is sometimes obscure. In the following volume of the *Review of Reviews*, Stead gave generous space to Sir Harry Johnston's paper in the *Contemporary Review* on the Congress of Races that advocated a common inter-racial religion and a common human war against 'the blind and heartless forces of Nature', but at the same time was certain that the white or Caucasian subspecies of humanity is superior in brain development and physical development to all other subspecies. The Caucasian race 'seems to stand revealed as the redeemer of the world' and, it was hoped the following year, the redeemer of valuable (if not all) human life when the greatest maritime disaster ever recorded occurred.

Stead would have shared Johnston's sentiments; and as someone who promoted WJ Pirrie and his shipbuilding empire whose metropolis was Harland & Wolff's in Belfast, and as someone who believed that the peace of the world rested on Anglo-Saxon unity and predominant strength, Stead surely nodded in agreement when the White Star Line in a 1911 booklet promoting their new liners, *Olympic* and *Titanic*, claimed that the ships coincided with 'the movement of the British and American people towards the ideal of international and universal peace' and that the consummation of this unity of the Anglo-Saxon race, devoutly to be wished, has been fired by commerce, and preeminently by the commercial contribution of the White Star Line and her builders, Harland & Wolff. In short, these two 'Leviathans of the Atlantic' stand for 'the pre-eminence of the Anglo-Saxon race on the Ocean', symbols and vessels of that transition from the naval to the mercantile marine idea on which global peace and prosperity depend.

The White Star spokesman at a luncheon in the Grand Central Hotel, Belfast, after the launch of *Titanic* on June 1, 1911, J. Shelley, repeated this race-interpretation of the two ships, seeing them as linking the two great Anglo-Saxon nations, the United Kingdom and 'the mighty Republic in the West'. At this luncheon, the popular author of sea stories, Frank T. Bullen, took up the theme of the Anglo-Saxon race and like many Britons, allowed the 'peculiar genius of the British race' to incorporate the Anglo-Saxons of the United States, in distinction to the lesser and more self-advertising virtues of 'Germany or any other Continental country' which would have heard their streets shouting with joy on such an occasion as the launch of *Titanic* whereas the citizens of Belfast went quietly about their business. (However, those citizens had something even bigger on their minds, the constitutional future of Ireland.)

The Assistant Secretary of Harland & Wolff, J. Saxon Payne (another happy appellation) recognised no distinction between nations of the Anglo-Saxon race, the progressive instincts of which were proved by the two giant ships. Like Lord Charles Beresford, he thought that the vessels proved that there was nothing foreseeable that 'need give them alarm, regarding the prospects for the future': as a race they were young and strong and vigorous. In Payne's remarks one cannot help hearing behind the brittle assurance (like Forster's goblin footfall) things kept submerged – a British worry over a widening gap in power and influence between the United States and the United Kingdom, a fear of the yellow peril, an anxiety about a strengthening Germany, perhaps even a mild apprehension about the 'angry waters' of the Latin races. In the nightmare of the humiliating loss of *Titanic* on her maiden voyage, it became essential to ensure what we would nowadays call 'damage control,' and for the correct race-interpretation to be put on events during and immediately after her sinking.

Endnotes

1. In an October 1906 speech to a Liberal Party gathering, Winston Churchill said: 'We want to draw a line – below which we will not allow persons to live and labour, yet above which they may compete with all the strength of their manhood. We want to have free competition upwards; we decline to allow free competition downwards. We do not want to pull down the structure of science and civilization but to spread a net on the abyss.'

2. It was perhaps the memory of *Oceana* and *Titanic* that triggered Kipling's race response to the burning of the American cruise ship *Morro Castle* in 1934. He wanted to know from his friend Sir Percy Bates, head of the (now amalgamated) Cunard White Star lines if in the liner service they have regular watch and quarter bills giving the names of the officers and seamen. He wanted to write a poem on the subject of names on board and written from the point of view of a passenger 'who took more comfort out of the purely English names of the men with whom he had to sail (and, if necessary, sink)' than all the luxurious appointments of the liner's interior. By 'English' he must mean 'British' since his poem, 'Namely' (1935) – discussed by Pinney – cites Kinsella and MacAndrew among the comforting roll. His hypothetical passenger also wishes to know where the ship he has entrusted his safety on was built, and claims that 'Belfast, Southampton, Clyde and Tyne/Are good enough for me.'

five

Baffling Foresight

The Merest Accident?

In the British House of Commons, the Prime Minister Herbert Asquith as quoted by *The World's Work* referred to the *Titanic* disaster as 'one of those terrible events in the order of Providence which baffle foresight, which appal the imagination and make us feel the inadequacy of words to do justice to what we feel'. But before long, dozens of people, survivors, relatives of the dead, commentators of one sort or another, claimed to have had unbaffled foresight, to have foreseen the tragedy, or known someone who did. The air was soon thick with reports of ill-omens allegedly noted as such at the time, of personal premonitions and previsions, of forewarnings from second parties, even of foretellings: fictional stories and historical episodes that anticipated the events of the great ship's destruction.

It is impossible, of course, for any complex event not to repeat or reflect components of previous events and to have been, in that sense, anticipated. The enormity of the sinking of *Titanic* dwarfed all previous sea disasters, yet in essence it was a shipwreck like those that preceded it. The *New York Times* reminded readers in its April 16 edition that the loss of *Titanic* 'recalls the loss of the White Star cargo steamer Naronic in February, 1893, with 74 lives. She left Liverpool on her maiden voyage, and was never again heard of. It is believed that she was sunk by an iceberg.' To this extent, what happened to *Titanic* had been anticipated, and, in an unmysterious way, the disaster was predictable simply because it *had* been predicted. WT Stead had interested himself in merchant and naval shipping for years, particularly in Atlantic shipping, and his wide reading and acquaintance with reports of shipping accidents would have informed his story, 'The Sinking of a Modern Liner', published in 1886 in the *Pall Mall Gazette*, of which he had become editor in 1883. (He did not visit the United States until 1893, so in 1886 Stead had no personal experience of transatlantic passage.) Told from the viewpoint of a second-class passenger on a ship that left Liverpool and picked up passengers and mailbags at Queenstown (as did *Titanic*), this short story is full of circumstances and incidents that anticipate the later, greater calamity. Stead's son, who assumed editorship of the *Review of Reviews* after his father's death on *Titanic*, thought the story prescient enough to reprint in the June 1912 issue in homage to his late father's grasp of affairs.

It was a practical rather than visionary matter, for Stead had appended an editorial footnote in 1886 claiming that 'This is exactly what might take place, and what will take place if the liners are sent to sea short of boats'. The story's narrator counts the lifeboats on the fifth night out and calculates that of the 916 passengers, there are boats for, at most, just 390; and indeed, after a collision and a panicky evacuation from the sinking liner, 700 passengers are stranded on board with only one lifeboat remaining. The narrator is washed overboard but manages to clamber into a passing lifeboat, as Archibald Gracie and some other *Titanic* swimmers were able to do. In real life, it seems as though Stead either went down with *Titanic* or was washed overboard in a way that did not allow him to swim to safety; but perhaps his profound spiritualist belief lent him a passivity in emergency that quickened his death.

Other incidents in Stead's story are also familiar. There is panic around the boats. The captain is forced to brandish and use a revolver. The women are taken off first and some of them resist being separated from their menfolk. Men from steerage, many of them Irish, try to storm the boats. Some of the boats leave with half their proper complement. And the 'agonised clamour' of the multitude left to fend for themselves when the last boat has gone stuns the narrator. Written without real eloquence, 'The Sinking of a Modern Liner' nevertheless impresses by detail confirmed by what befell *Titanic* and her passengers which Stead clearly if not specifically foresaw.

Stead's story is a lightly fictionalised version of the warnings the author and others had been issuing about possible mishap at sea because of excessive speed or inadequate safety provisions. One warning was issued on board *Titanic*.

Archibald Gracie was quoted in the *New York Times* on Friday, April 19:

> Before I retired I had a long chat with Charles H. Hays, President of the Grand Trunk Railroad. One of the last things Mr. Hays said was: 'The White Star, the Cunard, and the Hamburg-American Lines are devoting their attention and ingenuity in vying one with the other to attain the supremacy in luxurious ships and in making speed records. The time will soon come when this will be checked by some appalling disaster.' Poor fellow, a few hours later he was dead!

The suddenness of Hays' prediction becoming true made his warning seem like privileged information, and the notion of privileged information haunted *Titanic* reportage and commentary thereafter.

What happened, however natural and however cautioned against, could seem like inevitability, a kind of fatedness beyond human control and capacity. Observers and commentators retrospectively saw the collision and sinking as having been scripted before they happened: hence the instant and perpetual use of the epithet 'ill-fated' (to this day) to describe *Titanic*. (The phrase appeared in print as early as April 18 1912, when the London *Daily Sketch* used it in a caption to a photograph.) Of course, it is natural to read disaster back into the immediate past through hindsight; in its editions of April 17 and 18, the *Daily Sketch* reproduced photographs of the ship leaving Southampton and Queenstown and each time referred understandably to the 'doomed Titanic'. In such cases, the past is re-read as the present pregnant with the future.

Quite soon after the event, the spoken or unspoken assumption abroad was that the *Titanic* tragedy had been waiting to happen, not just in physical but also in metaphysical terms. Everyone knows now, and knew then, of the claims of unsinkability supposedly made on behalf of *Titanic*. Very early, those claims were regarded as amounting to – though the exact word was unknown to many – *hubris*, the Greek notion of overweening pride which is an element in the downfall of the Greek tragic hero and in his tragic fate. It suggests the prior existence of some force of cosmic judgment which the hero offends and arouses; his end, if not his beginning, is already written once *hubris* is committed. And so, it was widely believed, with *Titanic*; her fate was foregone and deserved.

All of this must have caused a disturbing frisson in those who ought to have travelled on *Titanic* but for some reason didn't – there were almost 50 fortunate truants. Both Lord Pirrie (who always sailed aboard Harland & Wolff's new leviathans) and J. Pierpont Morgan, both of whom had witnessed the launch in 1911, were too ill to join the maiden voyage of the ship they owned, Morgan opting to travel instead to Aix-les-Bains for the cure. The ship's co-designer Alexander Carlisle had also intended to make the trip but decided at the last moment not to. The most famous wireless operator in the world, Jack Binns (he had wirelessed for help from the stricken liner *Republic* in January 1909 and his *CQD* had been heard and answered by a fellow White Star ship, *Baltic*) wanted, writes Marcus, to return to the United States in haste and decided he could not wait until April 10, *Titanic*'s departure date, and crossed in *Minnesota* instead.

Binns, after his stint on *Republic*, had worked under Captain Smith on *Olympic*, then became a journalist who was called by Senator Alden Smith at the American hearings.

There were less well-known fortunates. A sailor called Joe Mulholland later told William MacQuitty, producer of the film *A Night to Remember* (1958), that he had had a row with one of the officers and walked off the ship at Southampton just before she sailed. A stoker named John Podesta, arriving late from a public house with a mate (J. Nutbean) and three brothers, managed with Nutbean to cross a train track and make the ship in time but the Slade brothers let the train go by and found themselves left behind (Nutbean and Podesta survived, however). Three more brothers called Pugh were also engaged in a last minute scramble to get aboard – one turned back but Alfred, a steward, and Percy, a leading fireman, made it (Percy died and Alfred survived). Lawrence Beesley in his 1912 account of the disaster he survived, *The Loss of the R.M.S. Titanic: Its Story and Its Lessons*, describes a scene he apparently witnessed from over the side of the ship: a knot of stokers running along the quay, their kits over their shoulders, waved back and dismissed by a petty officer when they reached the shore end of the gangway which was dragged back despite their protests. (The *Daily Sketch* of April 17 identified the lucky stokers as six in number.) Equally thankful must John Coffey have been, a Queenstown stoker who jumped ship in his home port. In all (in the figures given by Gibbs), at least 26 fortunate crewmen signed on but did not sail, and 13 unlucky crewmen travelled as substitutes.

The ongoing coal strike in England at the time of the sailing meant that train services in the country were curtailed. As a result, at least six passengers who were meant to sail to the United States on earlier vessels were delayed and forced to sail on *Titanic*: of these, five were men, four in steerage and one in second class and they all perished; one was a woman in second class and she survived. Mrs John C. Hogeboom, a first-class passenger, was booked on *Oceanic* and when it didn't sail was offered a berth on *Olympic* but preferred to wait for a cabin on *Titanic*; she survived. Several *Titanic* passengers had originally been booked to travel on the Cunarder *Lusitania* but that ship was under repair. Two British professional boxers, Leslie Williams and David Bowen, were two such passengers, going to the United States under contract; neither made it there. Benjamin Guggenheim chose not to sail in *Lusitania*'s replacement, *Carmania*, but decided, fatefully, to wait for the next fast ship.

There were narrow escapes from possible death among passengers who did not embark at Southampton on *Titanic*. These are still being related: Hilda Greenwood celebrated her 102nd birthday in North Vancouver, Canada in April 1999. She confirmed that her family was booked to travel on *Titanic* but her mother fell ill at the last moment and the family were forced to cancel their voyage. Gardiner and Van der Vat tell us that Mr and Mrs George Vanderbilt, of the railway and shipping family, cancelled on April 9, but their servant, Frederick Wheeler, sailed in second class with their luggage and was lost. Henry Clay Frick, an associate of Andrew Carnegie's, also cancelled his passage, Marcus tells us, as did Robert Bacon who was finishing his stint as US Ambassador to Paris and intended to leave Cherbourg on *Titanic.* Bacon's final audience with the French President was postponed and he was obliged to miss the voyage: he and his family, he said, 'have had a very happy escape'.

So too had the Edgar Selwyns, friends of the English novelist Arnold Bennett, who recorded in his Paris diary for Saturday, April 20: 'Yesterday the Selwyns and Calou came to lunch. Only their anxiety to meet us here and hear the rest of my comic novel prevented them from going home with the HB Harrises on the *Titanic'*. Nice to think that literature, in this case Bennett's novel, *The Regent*, saved lives! Henry B. Harris was a Broadway producer with whom Bennett had lunched on March 23. He said goodbye to his wife on board (she was saved) and he went down with the ship. A fellow theatre manager, Henry C. Jacobs, told a *New York Times* correspondent that it was by 'the merest accident' that he too did not sail from Southampton on *Titanic*, that a visit to Richard 'Boss' Croker in Ireland had mercifully cost him the maiden voyage and compelled him to book passage on the ship's second east-west passage.

It must have been a smaller frisson, but a frisson nonetheless, that was felt by those who had reserved cabins on *Titanic*'s return to Southampton on May 11. Through vivid association, there would have been some sense of a narrow squeak. These included Evangeline Booth, General William Booth's daughter and head of the Salvation Army in the United States, and also the famous English author John Galsworthy who was in America to rehearse his play *The Pigeon*. From a train bound for Chicago, Galsworthy wrote to the celebrated English classical scholar Gilbert Murray, who was also in America, encouraging him to book passage on *Titanic* and to do soon, 'for she's new and popular'. Instead of sailing to England on *Titanic*, Galsworthy found himself attending the Washington hearing at the invitation of Senator Lodge.

'A queer jumbled business', Galsworthy noted in his diary. 'We heard the unfortunate Ismay give his evidence very quietly and well. The system and public is to blame for the miserable calamity; and, of course, the same public is all agog to fix the blame on some unhappy shoulders.

There were those who wished to see these narrow shaves as vaguely providential or the result of extra-volitional forces. Even the hardheaded were unsure. Norman Craig, the Scottish MP and famous King's Counsel, had intended to make the trip 'for a blow of fresh air' and to return on the Cunard liner *Mauretania*, but was quoted by the *Daily Mirror* for April 17 as saying,

> I suddenly decided not to sail. I cannot tell you why; there was simply no reason for it. No; I had no mysterious premonitions, or visions of any kind. Nor did I dream of any disaster. But I do know that at practically the last moment I did not want to go.

In the same newspaper it was reported that one passenger, a wealthy businessman, *did* have a premonitory feeling of disaster, according to his friend, a 'well-known' solicitor. The passenger asked his friend to act as guardian to his children should anything happen to him or his wife; by April 17 their names had not occurred among the saved.

Norman Craig to the contrary, claims of premonition from non-passengers among the British populace arrived at the offices of the *Daily Sketch* every day for weeks after the sinking, but one American claim, reported in the London *Daily Mail* on April 18, carried some weight:

> A confession that a dream prevented him from sailing in the Titanic was made yesterday by the Hon. JC Middleton, vice-president of the Akron-Canton Railway of Ohio. Mr Middleton told the dream to his friends ten days before the tragedy, and this fact is vouched for by several well-known people, one of whom gave Mr Middleton a signed 'affidavit' to that effect. Mr Middleton says: 'I booked a cabin in the Titanic on March 23. I felt unaccountably depressed at the time, and on April 3 I dreamt that I saw the Titanic capsized in mid-ocean and a lot of the passengers struggling in the water. The following night I dreamt exactly the same dream. The next day I told my wife and several of my friends, and afterwards, on receiving cable advice from America that my business did not necessitate my crossing at once, I decided to cancel my passage.' Both Mr JH Curling, the pigeon-shooting champion, and Mr Feddon, to whom Mr Middleton told his dream, confirmed his statement yesterday.

The Joker in the Stack

Even before she sailed, *Titanic* had provoked hearsay, rumour and even mild anxiety. In this she differed from other ships only in degree, since sea lore is, or was, widespread and potent. Superstitious belief adhered to maiden voyages especially, as Lawrence Beesley reminded readers. Even the clerk in the White Star office where Beesley bought his ticket admitted that there were those who were disinclined to take maiden voyages. Beesley, like the good science schoolmaster he had been, gave short shrift to the paranormality surrounding *Titanic* – 'I suppose no ship ever left port with so much miserable nonsense showered on her' – yet took care to enliven his narrative by reminding readers of the kind of nonsense – entertaining rather than miserable – he was referring to. But most of the 'nonsense' surfaced after the fact of disaster and was by some cultural back-formation activated by disaster in a way that folklorists and psychologists could perhaps identify as a recognizable pattern.

Even if there were quantities of humbug generated by the ship, and there were, and still are, it is not the possible truth of what was claimed that interests me here but rather the phenomenon of the claims itself, since it tells us much about Anglo-American culture around 1912. And we are not speaking solely about what we would now call the contemporary 'tabloid' culture (in fact, the 'tabloid' newspapers of the day were far more literate and sensible than their degenerate counterparts of today).

James Bisset, who was second in command of the rescue ship *Carpathia* and who went on to become wartime commander of *Queen Mary* and *Queen Elizabeth*, wrote (as, by then, Sir James Bisset) his autobiography, *Tramps and Ladies* (1960), in which he admitted that *Titanic* was a '"hoodoo ship" from the beginning' only because she was a forerunner of the gigantic super-liners and was the victim and perpetrator of the errors and misfortunes surrounding all pioneer vessels and vehicles. Of several observers' belief that the near-collision between *Titanic* and *New York* when she was leaving Southampton was an ill-omen, Bisset judges that it may have been superstition but may instead have been a seamanlike opinion that the ship was indeed 'unlucky'. He thinks it worthy of comment that so many seamen had deserted the ship before she sailed and wonders if any of them had been 'fey' and had sensed the ship's enveloping misfortune.

Beesley recorded the 'direst' misgivings he heard expressed by crewmen and passengers around him after the near-collision with *New York*, though he himself discounted the episode as ominous. With his usual truculent ambivalence, Beesley records a second bad omen, this one at Queenstown, *Titanic's* last port of call before heading across the Atlantic:

> As one of the tenders containing passengers and mails neared the Titanic, some of those on board gazed up at the liner towering above them, and saw a stoker's head, black from his work in the stokehold below, peering out at them from the top of one of the enormous funnels ... that rose many feet above the highest deck.

Beesley seems to have known at the time that *Titanic*'s fourth funnel was a dummy used for ventilation, but most passengers presumably wouldn't have, and received quite a shock. Even with the knowledge, passengers might still have thought (as some did) that the apparition boded ill for the journey. The stoker's joke certainly took place, for a Mr Whyte of Queenstown took a photograph that shows the tiny head peering above the rim of the giant funnel.

This joker in the stack had a long life and underwent many metamorphoses as we shall see (including that of HG Wells' 'black-faced, oily man'). His Queenstown materialization was not his first. Ellen Williamson was a rich American socialite who wrote a book entitled *When We Went First Class* that relived the era of luxury liners, including the Age of *Titanic*. Her aunt and uncle boarded the ship in Cherbourg after a buying spree in Europe. Uncle Walter told his wife that he had been talking to some passengers who had embarked at Southampton, where they had seen 'a black-faced stoker peering at them through a hole in a smokestack of an adjacent ship, and had made faces at them'. Several passengers were upset and thought it an ill way to start their crossing.

It is difficult to know how much the alleged foresight was really hindsight. Much of it, presumably. Even premonitions that are realised

Photograph of Titanic leaving Queenstown with a stoker's head in the dummy funnel just visible.

by events might only be notable, and noted, coincidences; after all, premonitions that turn out to be baseless are rarely recorded. Even so, when they exceed an undefinably high incidence, omens and premonitions that *are* vindicated by events, even if they are coincidences, achieve a cultural critical mass that is independent of the possibility that they disrupt the time continuum. The answer to the question, 'Why *were* there so many claims that the *Titanic* tragedy had been sensed or seen before it happened?' is a cultural one that I proffer below.

Walter Lord calls Chief Officer Henry Wilde 'the enigma of the night', because his precise fate is unknown (he did not survive) and few of the survivors said much about him. First Officer Charles Lightoller remembered him as a 'pretty big, powerful chap' certainly capable of intimidating J. Bruce Ismay into the lifeboat in the way someone told Lightoller on *Carpathia* Ismay's desertion happened. But this powerful chap wrote his sister (the letter was mailed from Queenstown) with misgivings: 'I still don't like this ship ... I have a queer feeling about it'. Other surviving crewmen remembered uneasy feelings before the ship set sail, including Arthur Lewis, a steward, who told a newspaper that on the eve of departure he asked his wife to put his white star into his cap and that the star fell to pieces while she was about it: 'with a look of dismay she said, "I don't like this"'.

Able Seaman Joseph Scarrott crewed boat No. 14, of which Fifth Officer Harold Lowe was in command, and survived to supply some time later (perhaps with some editorial help, though his testimony to the British inquiry is eloquent enough) a moving account of how he and Lowe eventually manoeuvred their boat among the bodies and wreckage after the liner had gone: 'As we left that awful scene we gave way to tears. It was enough to break the stoutest heart'. Scarrott was stout-hearted, like Wilde, but he afterwards said that he had joined the ship 'not with a good heart'. Never in twenty-nine years of seagoing could he recall 'that feeling of hesitation' that accompanied his preparations for the journey. He thought *Titanic* the finest ship he had ever seen but he bade his sister 'Goodbye' and when asked why, instead of 'So long, see you again soon' he was at a loss to explain. Once on board, he found himself behaving in uncustomary ways, even omitting to don his uniform before fire and boat drill (which didn't take place during the voyage itself). Scarrott and Lewis are quoted in Hyslop *et al.*, *Titanic Voices*.

Among the embarking passengers, Eva Hart's mother had a famous premonition and as a result refused to sleep in bed but rather sat up each night. Lady Duff Gordon claimed she had a similar unease and that her response was the same: she could not completely undress at night and kept her coat, wrap and jewels ready to hand in case of emergency. 'I have never been a psychic woman', she later wrote (and one can believe it),

> and in all my life have never been to a seance or dabbled in the occult, so I am even now loath to call this feeling of acute fear which I experienced a premonition, yet the fact remains that though I have crossed the Atlantic many times both before and since I have never had it on any other occasion. Something warned me, some deep instinct, that all was not well.

Mrs JJ Brown (Unsinkable Molly) told Archibald Gracie after the disaster that Mrs William Bucknell, travelling without her husband (who founded Bucknell University in Pennsylvania), repeated on the ship what she had already told her on the tender as Cherbourg – that she (Mrs Bucknell) feared boarding *Titanic* because, in Gracie's words, 'she had evil forebodings that something might happen'. After the collision, on A deck, surrounded by passengers strapping on their lifebelts, Mrs Bucknell had whispered 'Didn't I tell you something was going to happen?' Unsinkable Molly, ever the practical woman, must have thought the reminder at best unhelpful under the circumstances.

In several incidents, the premonition occurred to a second party, who then warned the prospective passenger. Ellen Williamson's uncle, Walter, relayed the story of the black-faced stoker in order to introduce an omen just as silly, in his mind, as the forewarning which his wife had just received from a shabbily-dressed, grey-haired Frenchman who approached Aunt Mahala and her maid Berthe on the tender at Cherbourg to whisper in a Basque accent, 'Excuse me, madame ... This ship, she is not safe. *Je vous en prie* [I beg of you] not to sail on her'. Then he bowed and vanished and was never seen again. Hustak relates that an Egyptian soothsayer or clairvoyant told young Alice Fortune as he read her palm in Cairo that she was in danger when on the sea. Soon after, the wealthy five-member Fortune family from Winnipeg took ship in Southampton; Alice's father, Mark Fortune, and his son Charles were lost, Mark's wife and two daughters saved (in that boat that caused them some racial unease).

Archibald Gracie told the *New York Times* that among the women he last saw on board was a Miss Evans who, he said, virtually refused to be rescued because, in Gracie's words, 'she had been told by a fortune-teller in London that she would meet her death on the water'. He repeated the anecdote in his book, *The Truth about the* Titanic (1912). Young Edith Evans, aged 25, spoke to Gracie during the early stages of evacuation and said that she had been told by a fortune-teller to 'beware of water' and now 'she knew she would be drowned'. Gracie went on:

> My efforts to persuade her to the contrary were futile. Though she gave voice to her story, she presented no evidence whatever of fear, and when I saw and conversed with her an hour later when conditions appeared especially desperate, and the last lifeboat was supposed to have departed, she was perfectly calm and did not revert again to the superstitious tale.

Gracie had been introduced to Edith Evans only during the emergency and it was the husband of one of the women who introduced her, Robert Cornell, a New York magistrate, who relayed to the *New York Times* Mrs Cornell's account of her last view of her niece, Edith Evans. Mrs Cornell, her two sisters (Mrs Appleton and Mrs Brown) and their niece, were travelling together; Mrs Cornell and Mrs Appleton were assigned to boat No. 2 and Mrs Brown and Edith Evans to another boat that left later. When it was found that the second boat had one passenger too many, Miss Evans left the boat, saying that Mrs Brown had children at home and that she, Miss Evans should forgo her place. She 'left the boat, saying that she would take a chance of getting in a boat later. It seems that this brave girl never got that chance ...'. Mrs JM Brown was rescued from Engelhardt boat D which indeed left after Emergency boat No. 2. According to Second Officer Lightoller, D was the last boat to leave the ship and he had difficulty finding women to enter it. 'When that boat went away', Lightoller told the British inquiry, 'there were no women whatever' (i.e. left on board *Titanic* as far as he could see). Edith Evans must have deliberately made herself scarce, and the supposition that she was honouring the fortune-teller's warning is tempting. Incidentally, anyone familiar with TS Eliot's twentieth-century modernist epic poem, *The Waste Land* (1922), will find the story of Edith Evans and the clairvoyant interesting; the connection is one to which I will return.

At least one person – someone of great interest to *Titanic* enthusiasts – was, it is claimed, and adapting a coinage by Robert Ballard (discoverer of the wreck), 'telepresent' at the tragedy, having been one of those fortunates who was prevented from making the maiden voyage. James Ismay, grandson of J. Bruce Ismay's brother, gave this testimony collected in *Titanic Voices*:

> I once asked my grandmother why my grandfather was not on the Titanic. She told me he was to have been, but had very serious pneumonia so was at home. She then added that on the night of the Titanic disaster, he suddenly came out of the coma and said: 'Bruce is in trouble, Bruce is in trouble'.

Archibald Gracie was in even deeper trouble; when the ship took him under, he had to swim to the surface and find wreckage to cling to, first a plank then something more substantial, until he discovered the upturned Engelhardt B which provided safety for about thirty men. Gracie's wife at the time of the disaster was in New York visiting her sister, but unable to sleep until she seemed to hear a voice that commanded 'On your knees and pray!' 'Instantly, I literally obeyed with my prayer book in my hand, which by chance opened at the prayer "For those at Sea". The thought then flashed through my mind, "Archie is praying for me".' She lay sleepless until five in the morning, and at eight was shown the morning paper (presumably the *New York Times* for Tuesday April 16) with news of the sinking. For his part, Gracie while swimming for his life underwater prayed:

> I prayed that my spirit could go to [my family] and say, 'Good-bye, until we meet again in heaven'. In this connection, the thought was in my mind of a well authenticated experience of mental telepathy that occurred to a member of my wife's family. Here in my case was a similar experience of a ship-wrecked loved one, and I thought if I prayed hard enough that this, my last wish to communicate with my wife and daughter, might be granted.

Even if this later version of Gracie's remembrance (from *The Truth about the* Titanic, in press when Gracie died in December 1912) is rather more literary than the one Filson Young quoted in *Titanic* (published mere weeks after the disaster), what is of interest here is the unfazed reference to telepathy by a man who was nothing if not practical and rational in his pursuit of the truth about *Titanic*.

One of the most interesting letters to arrive at the *Daily Sketch* after the disaster was one from an apparent acquaintance of a psychic, Mrs 'A' (as the newspaper referred to her), who attended a lecture on April 3 in an unnamed British city and was asked by the lecturer afterwards why she was so distracted during it. She had had a vision, she said and later told her friends its details: she had seen in vision a railway accident, a mansion on fire, a colliery explosion, and a four-funnelled steamship in collision with a mountain of ice. The visionary name of the ship was *Tintac* and she heard 'Southampton' called out, but of the real ship at the time she was entirely ignorant. The end of the lecture disrupted her vision. According to her acquaintance, the psychic had foreseen other events, including the Hawes Junction railway disaster at Christmas 1911. When asked why she did not make her vision public, she replied that the public was not ready to accept such visions as genuine.

These Absurd Days

Yet much of the public in Britain was highly responsive to both spiritualism and superstition of various kinds. Spiritualism itself began a long period of popularity in Britain after 1850 and according to George H. Doran (in Orel):

> Just before the end of the Great War and for some years immediately following, there swept over the world, Great Britain in particular, a great wave of spiritualism, or to express it more definitely, a belief in the survival of personality after death.

In 1901, HG Wells was provoked in his short story 'The New Accelerator' to complain about 'these absurd days ... when we are all trying to be as psychic and silly and superstitious as possible!' Lady Duff Gordon may not have attended a seance before she sailed on *Titanic*, but many of her contemporaries had. George Bernard Shaw – who would surely have poured contempt on attempts to give the *Titanic* calamity a supernatural dimension – later, and dismissively, remembered the decades before the Great War as those in which people were:

> addicted to table-rapping, materialization seances, clairvoyance, palmistry, crystal-gazing and the like to such an extent that it may be doubted whether ever before in the history of the world did sooth-sayers, astrologists, and unregistered therapeutic specialists of all sorts flourish as they did during this half century of the drift to the abyss.

As I tried to show, the fate of *Titanic* both anticipated and symbolised the surrender to the abyss, while the stories she provoked and inspired betrayed the addiction Shaw lamented in British culture.

Shaw's list of Edwardian paranormalities can be augmented and rearranged to include telepathy or thought-reading, clairaudience and 'phone-voyance' ('seeing through a telephone wire', as Stead defines it in *Review of Reviews*) as well as clairvoyance; mesmerism, hypnotism and levitation, automatic writing, astrology and astral voyaging as well as crystal-gazing and palmistry; magic and ritual, theosophy and the occult as well as spiritualism – all flourished during the Age of *Titanic*. Stead in his *Review of Reviews* regularly surveyed the pages of *Proceedings of the Society for Psychical Research*, *The Occult Review*, *The Theosophist*, *Hindu Spiritual Magazine*, *Annals of Psychical Science*, *Modern Astrology* and *Occult World*. *The Unseen Universe* was another magazine 'devoted to spiritism, occultism, etc'.; *The International Psychic Gazette* was yet another.

The Goldfarbs are useful on the cultural respectability of

spiritualism in late Victorian Britain. The Society for Psychical Research was founded in 1882 and before long had eminent members, including WE Gladstone and Arthur Balfour (Prime Ministers both), Alfred Russel Wallace (the co-formulator of the theory of organic evolution), Alfred Lord Tennyson, John Ruskin, 'Lewis Carroll', and eight Fellows of the Royal Society. The SPR was preceded by the British National Association for Spiritualists (1873) and followed by the London Spiritualist Alliance (1884), of which latter Major-General Alfred W. Drayson, one of John Jacob Astor's scientific sources for his 1894 novel, *A Journey in Other Worlds*, and someone by whom Arthur Conan Doyle was impressed, was a member.

Eminent literary figures who at least at some point in their career interested themselves in spiritualism or the occult included Arthur Conan Doyle and WT Stead (great champions), Rudyard Kipling – all three associated with the *Titanic* disaster – William Butler Yeats and his Irish literary cohorts.[1] (According to his daughter – reprinted in Orel – the playwright Henry Arthur Jones, Doyle's friend who met the rescue ship *Carpathia* in New York and wrote movingly about it for the *Daily Telegraph*, was never won over to spiritualism despite his friend's best efforts.) Then there was the remarkable figure of Cesare Lombroso, scourge of bohemians and diagnostician of degeneration and author also of *After Death – What? Spiritistic Phenomena and their Interpretation* (1909). On March 2 and March 16, 1912 and again on April 20, the well-known author Andrew Lang wrote open-minded articles on dreams, coincidences and dream-warnings for the *Illustrated London News*, using as his jumping-off point a book by Ivor Tuckett, *The Evidence for the Supernatural* (1911). Lang does not mention *Titanic* forewarnings or foresightings in his last article, but it may have been too soon after the disaster for such alleged phenomena to have been broadcast.

Psychical research was as active in the United States as in Britain, and in the *San Francisco Examiner* for April 15, 1912 – the day *Titanic* sank – it was reported that the head of the American Society for Psychical Research would publish in the association's journal for April an account of his experiments 'proving' that the novelist Frank R. Stockton, who had died in 1902, was still writing stories, using Etta De Camp as an amanuensis. (Stockton was been sufficiently regarded for Scribner to have been published by Scribner as a *Frank R. Stockon Reader* in 1968.)

Not surprisingly, many Christian ministers were hostile to spiritualism (as well of course as to the occult sects) and this maintained the air of heterodoxy and surreptitiousness that enveloped spiritualism and muffled its impact on society, however widespread it was. For example, Stead's journal *Review of Reviews* for November 1909 paraphrased an attack on spiritualism on behalf of the Roman Catholic church by Rev. Hugh Benson in the pages of the *Dublin Review* during which he attributed seances to the work of demons and found spiritualism inexorably leading to the denial of the fundamental clauses of the Christian creed, as Stead, no doubt ruefully, put it. (Benson might have been conscious of the fact that some spiritualist beliefs and practices had kinship with some of those in the evangelical and charismatic Dissenter sects, though Nonconformist churches too could oppose spiritualism.) But Christianity in the Age of *Titanic* was faltering, as we have already noted, and hostility to spiritualism was something of a rearguard action. Janet Oppenheim thinks that spiritualism and psychic research 'served as substitute religions for refugees from Christianity in the late nineteenth and early twentieth century'.

Oppenheim demonstrates, however, that the relationship between spiritualism and Christianity was complicated, and this allowed living-room at least for popular, if fugitive, acceptance of the kind of epiphenomena that 'materialised' around *Titanic*. Spiritualism was an ally of Christianity in opposition to materialism, but spiritualism's opposition was more self-defining and literal. The existence of a spirit world was all that spiritualism needed to justify itself, and there was no prescribed or necessary liturgy, doctrine or dogma, no gospel, no organised or traditional expression of faith. (There were, of course, sects and cults that complicated matters beyond the simple notion of the spirit-world; there were customary ways of contacting the spirit-world – seances conducted by mediums, with table-rapping, invoked materializations out of cabinets, and so on – and spiritualist societies.) 'The educated mind', said Madame Blavatsky, a leader in the Theosophical movement and a hugely influential figure in advanced culture of the time, 'is most undeniably attempting to free itself from the heavy fetters of materialism', a sentiment echoed numerous times by WB Yeats the poet, an equally influential cultural figure. Spiritualism was held to be both a cause and a result of the decline in materialist values: 'materialism has fallen into disrepute', wrote CG Harrison in 1894, 'partly because its foundations have been shaken by the phenomena of the seance room ... and partly because it is felt to be unsatisfactory as an explanation of the universe'. J. Arthur Hill, hitherto sceptical, thought in 1912 that by 'exploding materialism', spiritualism would introduce (or retrieve) a new cosmic view of mankind.

At the same time, spiritualists were at pains to distinguish spiritualism from superstition. Spiritualism, insisted Alfred Russel Wallace, is 'a science of human nature ... an experimental science'. Spiritual phenomena were to be observed, studied and explained in the language, and by the methods, of science. Indeed, Stead complained more than once that the Society for Psychical Research were *too* sceptical and rigorous in their hunt for falsehood and fraudulence among spiritualists. The relations between science and spiritualism were as complicated as those between the Christian churches and spiritualism, and scientists were divided in their attitude to psychical research. But the application of scientific methods by psychical researchers meant that there was a similarity imputed between the material and immaterial world. In fact, some spiritualists rejected the notion of the supernatural as a separate category of being and experience, instead viewing it as an extension of the natural. The anti-materialism of spiritualists was in this way a special attitude that permitted some spiritualists to be advocates of applied science and material progress. We have already seen this bifocal perception in Astor's novel, *A Journey in Other Worlds*. In this novel, as in society, the Machine Age and the Spirit Age comfortably overlapped – or rather, the latter was an extension of the former. In a 1907 issue of the *Review of Reviews*, Stead sympathetically paraphrases an article on 'Animal Electricity and Magnetism' in which are discussed the machines invented to measure 'the discharge of nervous force', including 'sthenometer' and 'magnetoscope', inventions that wouldn't be out of place in the pages of HG Wells, or of Astor.

Astor's attempt to synthesize mechanism and a belief in machine progress with science-based spiritualism was not unique. Conan Doyle too was a champion of psychical research by scientific method, the task of discovering, as he put it in *The Edge of the Unknown* (1930), 'the laws which regulate psychic affairs'. Doyle investigated the spirit life from about 1901 and gradually became a wholehearted believer around 1914; indeed, Harry Houdini, about whom Doyle was to write brilliantly in the book quoted (claiming in 'The Riddle of Houdini' that the escape artist was not a magician and illusionist but a spiritualist and medium who spent his later life in denial) observed in 1924 that Doyle's name 'comes automatically to the mind of the average human being to-day at the mention of Spiritualism'.

Although he did not possess Astor's knowledge of engineering, Doyle too was interested in what the future held for material advance and the progress of nations. It was the concern with the future that helped to bridge science and spiritualism. 'The doctrine of a future state and of the proper preparation for it as here developed, is to be found in the works of all spiritualists', said Russel Wallace. Doyle's 1914 story, 'Danger', imagined in detail a blockade of Britain by submarine, and there were those who were fearful that the story would put ideas in German heads. This story of the future was meant to serve as warning to Britain and joined other 'warnings of the Great War' fictions, including the most famous of these cautionary fictions, Erskine Childers' *The Riddle of the Sands* (1913) and perhaps the most egregious, MP Shiels' *The Yellow Danger* (1898).

It is not surprising, then, that *Titanic* as (short-lived) machine triumph should rest enveloped in our imaginations as a ship of almost supernatural aura, and that her innumerable commentators should appear as mediums 'transposing down', as electrical engineers would say, her enormous voltage for us.

The Human Marconigram

Doyle met Stead in London in 1890 and kept in distant touch for the rest of Stead's life, and though Doyle was in collision with Stead, as he was with Shaw, over the Boer War (Shaw and Stead opposed British policy), he recorded his opinion in *Memories and Adventures* (1924) that Stead in psychic knowledge was a generation ahead of his time. Stead was intensely interested in inventions and scientific innovation and in the future, and until his death was greatly concerned with the threat to British sea supremacy, particularly from Germany. He combined his fervid attention to political realities and scientific developments – he was a journalist of polymathic interest – with an unshakeable faith in (he would have said *knowledge of*) the spirit world in all its manifestations. His spiritualism, like his empiricism, was progressive and forward-looking. Hill reminded readers that spiritualism banished the static destinations of heaven and hell and substituted the notion of stages in spiritual development, of which death was merely one. Spiritual progress replaced the finality and retroactive judgement of human beings in Christianity.

Stead referred to the dead as 'the great majority' into whose company we 'pass over'. He was almost smugly convinced of 'the reality of spirit return', he considered death 'the great change', and he spoke with casual familiarity of life on 'the other side'.

For years Stead was the amanuensis for Julia A. Ames, an American woman who had lived in Chicago and who had died ('what we call died' – Stead) in December, 1891. In 1897 he published a series of her messages communicated to him through automatic writing; in 1909 there was a new and enlarged edition which Stead's daughter Estelle published in 1914 as *After Death: A Personal Narrative*. In her biography, *My Father: Personal & Spiritual Reminiscences* (1913), Estelle Stead reveals that it was 'Julia' who chose the hymn 'Our Blest Redeemer' to be sung at the farewell service of 'Julia's Circle' on April 3 before Stead embarked for New York City on *Titanic*, bound for the Men and Religions Congress on Universal Peace to be held in Carnegie Hall. In her message of that evening, 'Julia' failed to foresee Stead's drowning and instead wished him a good journey.

The *Irish News and Belfast Morning News* for April 19, 1912 carried an article about Stead entitled 'First Visit and Last' in which it reported that the day before he left London the 'Napoleon of newsmen' said to a friend, 'What a magnificent chance I have got in making this trip by the Titanic on her first voyage'. He intended, he said, to prepare an article on his experiences for publication in the *Review of Reviews* to replace the usual character sketch. Something of the same benign opportunism motivated 'a big London paper', judging by a report in the *New York Times* of April 17. A Marconigram 'which it has been impossible to deliver' was addressed to Stead via the wireless station on the lonely outpost of Sable Island, 120 miles south-east of Halifax, Nova Scotia, 'asking him to Marconi back to them a story of the disaster of any length he might decide and at his own figure'. But by then, Stead had passed over and achieved a cosmic view of the spot of bother in the North Atlantic.

Years before, Stead had published an account of his first visit to the United States in the *Pall Mall Gazette*, of which he had been editor in the years 1883–1890, which the *Irish News* reproduced. It is datelined *SS New York*, March 10, 1894 (the vessel which almost put paid to *Titanic*'s maiden voyage before it began) and in it the author marvels at the speed of the liner and the effort put into increasing the speed of these transatlantic ships, but complains of the resulting vibrations and wonders if the need for

WT Stead, the 'Napoleon of Newsmen'.

passenger comfort will cap the upward trend of speed. More importantly, he introduces an analogy that he would never abandon. The loneliness of the Atlantic crossing, days going by without another vessel being seen, 'was very like human life. We pass from the cradle to the grave in solitary life, meeting perchange but two or three in the course of our pilgrimage with whom we can exchange signals of friendly intercourse.' When the fog came down, the ship's foghorn sent its tidings through the darkened air, 'much as the voice from the unseen falls upon the ear of the clairaudient'.

The analogy was developed by Stead in a 1909 article in the *Fortnightly Review*, 'How I know the Dead Return', published in Boston that year as a slim book and reproduced as a preface to *After Death*. He imagines a modern liner reaching the shores of America, equipped with contemporary wireless, but in this scenario, no ship has reached the New World since Columbus; the crew and passengers discover the Spaniard's innumerable descendants and wish to relay the astounding news to the Old World. Only later is the telegraphy developed sufficiently to communicate clearly by Marconigram the first message, from, in Stead's scenario, one Captain Smith! The message is disbelieved until further messages are sent and received from both sides of the ocean. In an analogous way, Stead believes, communications from 'the other side' have been sent, received and returned. The telegraphy has now been perfected, the ship's passage is now uneventful.

In the light of Stead's analogy – an analogy that connects science with spiritualism – it is a graphic coincidence that Stead should drown on a transatlantic liner, thereby fusing metaphor and reality. The fusion grew stronger when it was reported that Stead, like his imagined passengers on his imagined liner, was sending messages by spiritual Marconigrams from the New World of the 'other side'. (Indeed, Stead was ubiquitous even in death, 'laid on like the gas', one is tempted to remark, borrowing the description of Mr Browne in James Joyce's story, 'The Dead', 1907.) According to the deceased Stead, his posthumous destination was as described in the title of the book his daughter published in 1922, *The Blue Island: Experiences of a New Arrival beyond the Veil, Communicated by W.T. Stead*. Conan Doyle supplied a somewhat wary letter to Estelle as foreword, welcoming the book but remarking that he had never come across the blue island in the numerous descriptions of the afterlife he had read.

But in fact, years before 1922 Stead's messages from the Beyond had been offered to the world. Indeed, they were also offered to 11 publishers who declined before a twelfth accepted them for a book. *Has W.T. Stead Returned? A Symposium* was published in 1913, edited by James Coates. Doyle cited this book in a letter to the *Nation* in February 1919, regarding it as furnishing 'enormous' evidence for the occurrence of posthumous messages from accidents at sea. (Perhaps by 1922 Doyle had cooled to the Stead phenomenon.)

Coates describes the occasions at which Stead communicated or even 'etherealised' in 1912, his earliest spirit return being recorded on April 19, as an 'impression' of his drowning conveyed to Coates' wife, who is his chief medium or 'sensitive'. Mrs Coates felt the presence of Stead on Sunday, April 21, and on April 26 at a seance Stead unbosomed himself through her mediation.. He took credit for suggesting to the band that they play 'Nearer, My God, to Thee'. He had already taken credit for the suggestion in a seance on April 24 with different clairvoyants (one of them his secretary). At the same session, the spirit of WT Brailey, the band pianist, spoke and confirmed Stead's selection. (However, since the *New York Times* on April 21 had reported the possibility that Stead had chosen the hymn, this was not in itself new or convincing evidence of spirit return.) He warned of the terrible work to be done to save 'laden and helpless men, women, and children sinking in the moral slums of life', a commonplace notion of the time (as we have seen), and a familiar cultural analogy between literal and spiritual death by drowning, and between drowning and dying by descent to the social depths of impoverishment, starvation and addiction.

In a seance on April 23, through a different medium, a Mrs Frith, 'Stead' drew on another familiar analogy, that between the actual ocean deep and the 'spiritual deep'. It is in this message that he describes himself as 'the human Marconigram' and explains the difficulty of communication, despite what he thought in 1909. It is possible that the well-known limitations and difficulties of wireless communication, indeed of applied science generally, helped to persuade some that the apparent impossibilities, improbabilities and incredibilities of communication from the grave were mere technical difficulties. In this way, the credibility of spiritualism would actually be advanced by science, including the fitfulness of communication (wireless and otherwise) from ships in peril. The *Titanic* was not bad news for 'Stead' and the psychic circles.

On May 3 'Stead' draws on yet another commonplace reaction to the *Titanic* disaster:

> I noted that [on the ship], as in the greater world, there was a great gulf
> fixed between those who possessed wealth, demanding luxuries, and for
> whom the mighty vessel was designed, and others there were who were
> permitted to travel and serve on the same floating world. When in the

'Titanic's' clutches, there was no gulf. Think of it, and let it burn into your
souls. A terrific lesson on equality in the sight of God.

But by Sunday April 21, the preachers had said this until they were
very nearly blue in the face.

As though someone – 'Stead', Coates or medium – sensed the
possibility of readerly disappointment, 'Stead' explains in one return
that 'it is a curious thing that on this side it is almost impossible to
remember clearly – I have been told "until a very long time has
passed" –things as they looked to one while on the physical side'.
There are very few details of his death that are vouchsafed and they
too are unconfirmable. He reported at one of the sittings led by Etta
Wriedt (June 9):

> Everyone said the ship was unsinkable but it came to me that we were
> doomed ... I helped all I could ... I remember Butt's threatening to shoot
> ... I took hold of Butt and another man, and I said, "Let us pray,
> gentlemen". And we prayed ... and the ship went down ... I did not
> struggle in the water. I was struck. My head was struck ....

He concluded with another cultural motif: 'I used to say I would be
kicked to death by the mob'. On May 14 a photograph of the spirit
Stead (a 'skotograph') was taken and reproduced in the *International
Psychic Gazette*.

The messages that constitute *The Blue Island* were communicated
through Pardoe Woodman, a young man who had met Stead only
once and who was a member of Estelle Stead's Shakespeare Company,
which was on tour when *Titanic* sank. Woodman foretold the wreck on
the Sunday it happened and Estelle recognised his psychic powers as a
result. Through Wriedt, a 'well-known direct voice' medium, Stead
appeared to his daughter a fortnight after his death and was in daily
touch with her thereafter. (The Wriedt sittings lasted from May 5 to
July 5.) When Woodman came to live with Estelle in 1917, he wanted
to get in touch with a comrade who had been killed in the war and did
so through a medium. Later, Woodman discovered his own gift for
automatic writing and Stead allegedly exploited this to talk to his
daughter. Two major communications had been published before *The
Blue Island*, messages for the world delivered, fittingly, on Armistice
days, 1920 and 1921. Soon after the latter date, Stead conveyed his
desire to relay the messages that compose *The Blue Island*, describing
his death and his posthumous experiences.

Unfortunately for those more interested in this life than in the
putative afterlife, Stead is again parsimonious with his details of his

Stead was everywhere, it seemed – even in death.

death aboard *Titanic*. The precise manner of his death had been a matter only of speculation in the press; as the London *Daily Mirror* put it on April 20, 'Of how William Thomas Stead, the great world-journalist and the greatest man on the *Titanic* met his death there is no certain account'. It was thought that AH Barkworth, whom we have met before, was the last man alive to have spoken to Stead, who told him he had seen the fo'c'sle full of powdered ice from the iceberg. According to the *Mirror* and *Daily Mail*, some survivors were said to have seen Stead returning to bed. Survivors failed to mention him in their published accounts. Stead himself is not much more forthcoming. 'Of my actual passing from earth to spirit life I do not wish to write more than a few lines'.

After he died (by drowning?) he found himself able to help people (how?) and was already in the company of friends who had passed over years before (who?). The journalist in him regretted not having a telephone at hand: 'I felt I could give the papers some headlines for that evening'. But the journalist's literalism instantly becomes the spiritualist's metaphor: 'Here was I, with my telephone out of working order for the present'; so near to earth and yet so far, the life-and-death communication system not yet set up or mastered. The end came, and the old analogy is put to use again:

> it was like waiting for a liner to sail; we waited until we were all aboard. I
> mean we waited until the disaster was complete. The saved – saved; the

dead – alive. Then in one whole we moved our scene. It was strange
method of travelling for us all, and we were a strange crew, bound for we
knew not where.

The picture of the wreck scene is brief and generic:

hundreds of bodies floating in the water – dead – hundreds of souls carried
through the air, alive; very much alive, some were. Many, realizing their
death had come, were enraged at their own powerlessness to save their
valuables. They fought to save what they had on earth prized so much.
The scene on the boat at the time of striking was not pleasant, but it was
as nothing to the scene among the poor souls newly thrust out of their
bodies, all unwillingly.

Off they go then in something akin to the medieval Irish flying boat
that transported souls (or Astor's space capsule), to 'a different land'
which turns out to be a blue island. How one waits for one detail of
Stead's experience that would be both realistic and indisputably his,
one incidental solution to some *Titanic* puzzle, but waits in vain! It was
privately disappointing, I suspect, for contemporary spiritualists
(perhaps including Doyle) who might have wished Stead to *prove*
something. But it as though Stead had already written or imagined the
account before his death and what we have is a dull *pro forma*
corroboration requiring no freshness of fact, no unique earthly
perspective. 'Stead' like Stead before him is at pains to show just how
alike life and the afterlife are: only the body is shed, everything else is
retained and, blue island apart, life, as it were, goes on. In comparison,
the sinking of *Titanic* may have been vulgarly extraordinary and thus
to be passed over quickly. But the ship itself Stead would have relished,
perhaps at the end regarding its sinking as its last machine triumph:
carrying him and others safely to the Other Side.

Yet Stead was fascinated by shipwrecks, both literal and
metaphoric; but because he had imagined them so fully, perhaps
'Stead' – or his daughter – thought it unnecessary to describe one
again, though this one was real and personally fatal. There had been
'The Sinking of a Modern Liner' in 1886. Then, more oddly, there was
a story his daughter called 'A Dramatic Incident' when in her 1913
biography, *My Father*, she excerpted it from the 1892 Christmas annual
of the *Reviews of Reviews*, an issue entitled 'From the Old World to the
New' devoted to the Chicago World's Fair scheduled for 1893 and
which Stead visited. The previous annual had been dedicated to the
Invisible World, this one to the New World, the modern liner by
default becoming a vessel of communication of real and figurative
importance. Stead imagines the voyage of a group of English tourists

from Liverpool to Chicago, and juxtaposes this narrative with a 'dramatic representation of conclusions arrived at after twelve months' experimental study of psychical phenomena; and an exposition of the immense political possibilities that are latent in this World's Fair'. The three most important components of Stead's public life are thereby conjoined – politics (especially the future role of America), spiritualism, and material improvement (especially in the technologies of shipping and telecommunication).

The dramatic incident is fictitious but the ship and its captain were real – *Majestic*, the White Star liner, and Captain Smith, with whom Stead had sailed on that liner and who came naturally to Stead's mind in *How I Know the Dead Return*. On *Titanic* Stead resumed acquaintance with Captain Smith and it seems possible that Stead sought him out after the collision; but how either of them died has never been ascertained. In Stead's story, *Majestic*, with the tourists on board, follow another ship that strikes an iceberg in mid-Atlantic. Six men and a boy succeed in reaching ice alive. The shipwreck had been foretold by one of the *Majestic* passengers through what the spiritualists called a 'spontaneous' phenomenon: she hears a sudden cry of danger and sees the wreck in vision. She tells another passenger (perhaps Stead in disguise) who happens to be gifted in automatic writing and has already received a message from one of the stricken survivors. In the company of Captain Smith, Compton receives a second message; four survivors have been swept away when the iceberg parted, three remain on a diminished ice-floe. The spiritualist agenda continues. In order for the captain to be convinced and turn the mighty *Majestic* off its path to mount a rescue mission, Compton's friend, the Professor, hypnotises the captain's niece into a clairvoyant state who then precedes the liner and describes what she sees; Smith is still unconvinced; Compton receives more messages: one survivor remains; an ice-warning sounds on *Majestic*; the ice-fog lifts; the last man alive is at last seen by Captain Smith and is saved.

White Ghosts of Disaster

Given the increased flow of traffic in the North Atlantic and the increased speed of that traffic, and widespread awareness of icebergs in the region, it is hardly surprising that writers should include in their fictions episodes of collision or that similar episodes should then take place in real life. The well-known writer H. Rider Haggard said that it was curious how often imagination is verified by fact, but that perhaps it is because the lines in which imagination must work are narrow and based on fact. Besides, we have already seen how speed and collision were cultural motifs of the time that would naturally find themselves recruited by storywriters. Our interest in such fictions is proportional to the similarity between the imagined and the future reality. On this score, interest is high in the case of Thaxter's poem 'A Tryst' and even higher because of the resemblance between her poem and Hardy's poem 'The Convergence of the Twain' written about the *Titanic* disaster, a resemblance we can explain either by imitation (not to say plagiarism) or by coincidence of treatment (certainly not of subject, since Hardy was reacting to a real event). Hardy's poem is irrelevant to our somewhat troubled enjoyment of Thaxter's apparent prescience. But again, conditions in the North Atlantic in the days of sailing ships, as late as the 1870s, made Thaxter's imaginary scenario a natural one.

Nor is it surprising that commentators should predict a catastrophe if conditions in the first decade of the twentieth century were maintained, especially if there continued to be insufficient lifeboats aboard liners. In 'The Sinking of a Modern Liner' Stead made a commonsensical short-term prediction which was merely the extension into the near future of knowledge arising from experience, what we call induction. (Wells made a large number of long-term predictions of the same kind – which because of the time involved seemed more prophetic than predictive – as well as creating purely fanciful pictures of the present and future.) Just as Thaxter's poem accrues added interest because of Hardy's, so Stead's 1886 story accrues added interest through the irony of Stead's own death in an accident of just the kind he said was inevitable; the story is otherwise unexceptionable. Haggard put a similar kind of prediction into fictional form two years after Stead. In his 1912 preface to a story entitled 'Mr. Meeson's Will' (1888), Haggard wrote about the episode in which a new and splendid liner is lost:

> I believe it to be a fair and, in the main, accurate account of what must and one day will happen upon a large and crowded liner in the event of such a collision as that described, or of her rapid foundering from any other cause. It is a remarkable thing that people who for the most part set a sufficient value on their lives, daily consent to go to sea in ships the boats of which could not on emergency possibly contain half their number.

Haggard in 1912 reminded readers that the tragedy he had predicted had just happened.

Leaving aside those predictions that seemed to violate the laws of physics (of matter and temporal sequence) – dreams, premonitions and the like – it is still the cumulative incidence of predictions of what befell *Titanic* that gives pause. The Age of *Titanic* was an age of predictions; the future was a cultural preoccupation. Among all the predictions, those about liners and icebergs were recalled because of *Titanic* not because of *Naronic* or any other casualty. The *Titanic* disaster in its magnitude – it was, in Hardy's phrase, an 'august event' – activated modern memory, retrieved, perhaps even created, its own precedents. Not all of these precedents were explicit warnings as were Stead's and Haggard's; some were simply coincidences, the accidental realisation of a prediction by an event. One was a precedent by the skin of its teeth.

In May 1912 a story by Mayn Clew Garnett called 'The White Ghost of Disaster' was published in *Popular Magazine*. However, in American custom, a May issue of a magazine, then and now, appeared at least the month previous, and the *San Francisco Examiner* alerted readers to the story as early as Tuesday, April 16. Some reporter or reader was awake, and extracted from the story what coincided with elements of the *Titanic* story.

It is not a good story but the first half is of interest to *Titanic* enthusiasts, though the *Examiner* reporter goes too far in claiming that 'the fiction is so remarkable as to seem more a prophesy (sic) than a coincident (sic)'. In it, a liner 800 feet long (*Titanic* was 882 feet in length) tears through a smooth sea at twenty-two and a half knots (*Titanic's* speed) despite the conviction of the second officer (Mr Smith!) that there is ice in the foggy vicinity. The captain ignores the warning and ploughs on. The lookout sees too late an iceberg and the liner plunges headlong into it. There is panic among the thousand passengers while the officers and crew try to maintain discipline; Smith himself when in charge of his lifeboat resembles Fifth Officer Lowe, cold, hard, inflexible, but a good officer. The captain returns to the chart room while the ship sinks, retrieves his revolver and shoots himself. This is where the interest of *Titanic* students halts. The coincidental elements of the story are amusing, but the story's chief interest for this reader lies in something that we cannot know is accurate but nonetheless rings true: the portrait of the captain appalled by his own arrogance, pondering the necessity of his own suicide, wondering about how he will be judged after the disaster. As a foretelling, Garnett may have got this more significantly right than even the other circumstantial details, but we shall never know.

Coincidence is the *subject-matter* of Hardy's poem; it doesn't involve Hardy's utterance, since the poem was written after the event. Hardy need not have seen in the *Titanic* disaster anything more than an appalling accident. This is how most people saw it; they thought that it had been preventable by practical steps and that it was this needlessness that made it the more appalling. But then Hardy would not have written his poem. He wrote the poem because to his way of thinking, certain accidents were more than accidental and were not preventable by human beings because the 'accidents' were fated. Because there was to him a pattern of such 'accidents' in human experience (which he had lamented in previous poems), there had to be a larger answer that explained these august events, these personal or communal tragedies. Hardy in his poem and his philosophy imbued coincidence with cosmic import – what *caused* the coincidence? he asked himself, and answered – 'the Immanent Will'.

At that point, human experience of accident, the collision of objects in space, the coinciding of events, becomes a species of religion, of a kind of faith in a reality beyond human consciousness and the world of physics. Hardy would probably have argued that it was by reason of induction that he came to his philosophy: experience made it impossible for him to accept an exclusively material explanation of human affairs. Since he had written other 'satires of circumstance', in novels, stories and poems, he had himself foretold the *Titanic* disaster in its essentials or constants; only the variables were different in the *Titanic* story. His poem, 'The Convergence of the Twain' (the title identifies the general phenomenon, the subtitle its specific demonstration, the loss of *Titanic*), is by back-formation still a foretelling of the disaster, which would account for its definitive, almost fatigued, I-told-you-so tone of expression. Haggard did not follow Hardy that far, but it was because he had found several of his fictions 'coming true' (including an episode in *Allan Quatermain* in which a mission station is attacked by Masai in the very spot in which a mission station *was* attacked subsequently) that Haggard wondered if imagination could possess 'some spiritual insight of its own'.

Certainly the author of the most famous foretelling of the *Titanic* calamity believed that his fiction was more than just coincidentally predictive, more than just an accident of narrative. After all, this lengthy story had, he claimed, come to him unbidden as automatic writing. As such, it would appear to be an extended if distorted prevision, a message from the future in the guise of a magazine story. The life, or at least the legend, of the author deepens the suggestion of something out of the blue.

Morgan Robertson was born in Oswego, New York in 1861, son of a sea captain, and went to sea at 16, serving in the merchant marine until the age of 25 when he left the service at the rank of first mate.

He took odd jobs in New York City until what a writer in 1947 in the worrisomely titled magazine, *True*, called 'the miracle' occurred. Robertson fell asleep on an elevated train, tired from delivering circulars, and when he awoke he was changed utterly. He was overcome by the desire to write, hurried home, grasped a pen, and wrote an 8,000 word story in one sitting. The author had no formal education beyond high school and had barely written a letter. He took the story to the editor of *Spun Yarn*, a fiction magazine, who declared it a masterpiece and published it without revision of any kind. Robertson said the story came from the 'Unknown' (Stead-style) but Walter Lord, who rescued the story from oblivion in 1955 when he began his celebrated book, *A Night to Remember* with reference to it, preferred to see Robertson as a struggling writer who 'concocted' the story. Robertson went on to write 200 stories in 14 books. He died in 1915.

Robertson's story appeared (with three others) in 1912 as *The Wreck of the Titan, or Futility.* (The 1914 reprint identifies The McClure Publications Inc. and *Metropolitan Magazine* as copyright holders and Robertson himself as copyright holder in 1912. Sam McClure, editor of *McClure's Magazine*, fell on hard times around 1895 and his magazine was bailed out, providentially in McClure's eyes, by no other than Conan Doyle, a mere acquaintance during Doyle's American visit.) The anticipations of the *Titanic* disaster in Robertson's story are so startling that I felt sure that the 1912 and 1914 editions had been doctored after the event and sought out the 1898 edition, published and copyrighted by MF Mansfield, the New York publisher, only to find that Robertson, from whatever source, had anticipated so accurately that Martin Gardner was driven to wonder if any of those involved in the building and naming of *Titanic* had read *Futility*, causing life to imitate art.[2] But no one in his right mind, Gardner concluded, would name a ship after a fictional leviathan that strikes an iceberg and sinks.

These are the anticipations: a ship called *Titan* is the largest craft afloat 'and the greatest of the works of men. In her construction and maintenance were involved every science, profession, and trade known to civilization.' Her officers are the pick of the marine service. Built entirely of steel, she boasts watertight compartments with automatic doors and she is regarded as – Robertson uses the exact phrase that was used by *The Shipbuilder* magazine to describe *Titanic* in 1911 and that became notorious in its abbreviation – 'practically unsinkable'. The captain of *Titan* is under orders to move at full steam whatever the conditions, and that means at 25 knots. *Titan* is 45,000 (in the 1898 version) or 70,000 *and* 75,000 (oddly, in the 1914 version) tons displacement (*Titanic* was 66,000), and 800 feet long. *Titan*'s horsepower is 40,000 (1898) or 75,000 (1914) There are two orchestras on board; indeed, 'she was a floating city – containing within her steel walls all that tends to minimize the dangers and discomforts of the Atlantic voyage – all that makes life enjoyable'.

Titan leaves New York in April with almost 3,000 passengers, the same number a full *Titanic* would have carried. During the chilly, star-speckled but foggy night, the lookout cries 'Ice' but it is too late as the iceberg meets the giant liner in the vicinity of where *Titanic* would meet her fate 14 years later. As in the case of the later calamity, had the ship hit the iceberg foursquare she might have survived. Robertson's imaginary liner, like *Titanic*, carries 'as few boats as would satisfy the laws', meaning in her case that only 500 passengers could be saved in the event of shipwreck. In the event, far fewer survive from *Titan* than from *Titanic*. In each case, Lloyds and the 'City' are in an uproar because of the disaster, underwriters and brokers thrown into disarray, offices besieged by anxious relatives of passengers.

Most readers will shake their heads at the coincidences involved, content to be amused, or bemused, by the human capacity to imagine in great detail a future that then transpires and by the power of induction to reason out the shape and content of some future episode. A future involving machinery and its attendant dangers is perhaps one of the more easily imagined futures; the *speed* of development in applied science must have made it easier still for short-term forecasting, especially in the field of transportation and locomotion. This would not explain, of course, such a coincidence as the names of Robertson's ship and Harland & Wolff's ship, *Titan* and *Titanic*. Most readers would simply see this as an odd coming together that cannot be explained but must be accepted ... i.e. these things happen, peculiar, entertaining, even disturbing as they are.

A smaller number of readers will believe that the coincidences in Robertson's story are such that they can and must be explained, and then only through recourse to the idea that the *Titanic* came to the author as some kind of prevision, as Robertson's account of its origin claims. We can let HG Wells stand as an exemplary version of the kind of writer who gets the future right by a richly inductive imagination, and Conan Doyle as an exemplary version of the reader who sees psychic foreknowledge at work in what seem mere coincidences (though oddly, Doyle, having been exercised enough about *Titanic* to take Shaw on in debate, seems not to have addressed the psychic emanations from the story of the disaster). Of Wells,

Doyle wrote in his 1924 autobiography, *Memories and Adventures*:

> I have always had my doubts as to those elaborate forecasts of the future in which Wells indulges. He has, it is true, made a couple of good shots which have already materialized in the tanks and in the machine which would deliver news in our own houses. But he has never shown any perception of the true meaning of the psychic, and for want of it his history of the world, elaborate and remarkable as it was, seemed to me to be a body without a soul. However, this also may be given him, and it will make his equipment complete. I remember discussing the matter with him, when George Gissing, [William] Hornung [novelist and creator of Raffles], he and I foregathered in Rome early in this century, but apparently my words had no effect. (Doyle's use of the word 'equipment' suggests the scientific nature of his spiritualism.)

But at least Doyle shared with Wells a consuming passion for knowing the future, a state of affairs that did not yet exist but was knowable one way or another. Indeed, this passion characterised the Age of *Titanic* and helps explain the otherworldliness that surrounded the ship and her loss.

Spiritualism was an aspect of the mysticism that flourished at the turn of the twentieth century: the fashion for magic, occult societies, exotic religious sects, folklore of the supernatural. Max Nordau, who dedicated his notorious book *Degeneration* (in English, 1895) to Lombroso, saw in mysticism 'a principal characteristic of degeneration'. But if in mysticism we include spiritualism and psychical research, then it was not always hostile to the progressive materialism that produced *Titanic* and other machines. Degeneration and regeneration required each other, the former measured by the latter. The contemporary *Titanic* phenomenon is a case-study startling in its elegant compass.

Superstitious belief, Stead maintained, is something else again. It may have thrived in the Age of *Titanic* because of the late blooming of the British Empire during the Victorian period when exploration was at a feverish pace and all kinds of outlandish customs, beliefs and lore were being reported, all kinds of relics, ornaments and ritual objects were being carried as booty and study materials to Britain. It was the age of Sir James Frazer's monumental catalogue of primitive practices and beliefs, *The Golden Bough* (1895–1915), the heyday of early modern anthropology and Egyptology, the years of growth in the exotic collections of the British Museum and Natural History Museum.

On April 4, 1912, *The Irish News and Belfast Morning News* carried an article on items in the Victoria & Albert Museum that had been donated by aristocrats disturbed by their haunted quality. They included a teakwood Buddha owned by a Mrs Evans (indeed) whose father, a sea-captain, stole it in Burma and killed a priest while doing so. Ill-luck dogged every white man who came in contact with it. The ship carrying it to Liverpool caught fire and the frightened crew threw it overboard. It washed up in Wales and the captain reclaimed it. Misfortune persisted in its vicinity; there were unusual deaths and reports of its wandering around the house at night. Mrs Evans, after her father's death, gave it to the Victoria & Albert where it is still (in 1912) causing disturbances. A large part of Pierpont Morgan's collection we are told, was housed in this museum, including a sixteenth-century Flemish copper ewer in the form of a human head that is heard uttering unearthly groans at night.

The article discusses 'another prominent British hoodoo', the mummy case of the Egyptian high priest Nes-Amsu with a magnificent representation of the priest on it. Walter Ingram, a noted traveller, gave the case to Lady Meux, 'the original discoverer of the artist Whistler'. Deaths kept it company. 'The case bears an inscription stating that a curse will fall upon him who removes it from its resting place'. Lady Meux left it to Admiral Sir Hedworth Lambton, a Boer War hero and brother of the Earl of Durham and who, unnerved by the case, turned it over to the museum. Another mummy case according to the article excited 'all England', that of the priestess of Amen-Ra.

> This priestess, Hetare by name, belonged to the royal family of Egypt. In early life she was ordained a priestess of Amen-Ra; but on the accession of her brother as Pharaoh Amen-hotep IV, she followed the new religion to which he belonged and left the temple of Amen-Ra. Thus she may have incurred the wrath of the ancient gods.

She died in Thebes in 160 BC, In the 1880s, four young Englishmen acquired her mummy in its case but the mummy itself was stolen from the case before they left Egypt. All four men suffered misfortune, three of them dying young (one violently), the fourth being crippled. The sister of the last survivor hastily gave the mummy case to the Victoria & Albert. After violence continued to mar human contact with the mummy case, the museum withdrew it from public view.

These two mummies appear to have become conflated when they became associated in legend with *Titanic*. Geoffrey Marcus, the author of one of the best books on *Titanic*, repeated soberly the story Stead was said to have told to eight companions late on Friday April 12.

> The story he told concerned the finding and translation of an inscription on a mummy case discovered in an Egyptian tomb. The inscription

warned the finder that whoever should repeat the story narrated in its mysterious hieroglyphics would, without doubt, meet with a violent death. Stead thereupon proceeded to tell the story. 'To prove that I am not superstitious', said Stead in conclusion, 'I call your attention to the fact that it was Friday when I began this story and the day of its ending, my watch tells me, will fall upon the thirteenth'.

One version of the legend connects Stead with the mummy even before he embarked on *Titanic*: it was his own curse. In another, the mummy herself was said to be on board *Titanic* en route to New York in defiance of the inscribed proscription against her being moved. This version re-surfaced as late as 1998 in the *Guardian* newspaper, which quoted Dr John Taylor, senior curator of the British Museum's Department of Egyptian Antiquities on the lid of a mummy case in the museum since the 1890s (the British and Victoria & Albert museums are conflated in the legends): 'There is a coffin lid which has a mythology surrounding it, that it is supposed to bring misfortune. It has been said to cause problems if you photograph it or if you show disrespect. It is supposed to have caused the sinking of the *Titanic*.' This quote reappeared, as a novelty item perhaps, in the pages of *Archaeology Ireland*, Autumn, 1998.

But such stories were not novelty items in the Age of *Titanic*, as the sobriety of the *Irish News* article testifies. Not only were the years from, say, 1880 to the First World War a golden age in the ghost story (between RL Stevenson through Henry James and WW Jacobs to MR James, all of whom drew on exotic times and places and, in the latter's case, antiquarianism) but they were years in which the supernatural was thought to envelop the real world and not just the world of the imagination. There was even a subspecies of the ghost story which has been called 'mummy fiction', inspired by a curious, occasionally morbid fascination with Egypt. Remarkably, *Titanic*, ship and tragedy, magnetically gathered to itself much of the spiritualist energy and superstitious beliefs and practices that were a significant part of Anglo-American culture of the time.

Endnotes

1. The name of 'W.B. Yeates' (sic) is given by James Coates (see Sources) as having been present at a seance at which Stead returned in spirit from the dead (see below) and as having signed a document attesting to Stead's having spoken to the assembled spiritualists.
2. Although MF Mansfield indeed published *Futility* in 1898, World Catalogue lists an 1893 edition by the same publisher; there is said to be a microform copy of this edition available.

six

From the Old World to the New

The Ghost in the Machine

Spiritualism detected, as it were, the ghost in the machine. Much of the language generated by psychical research was pseudo-technical, but the reality of the spirit life, though it could materialise itself under certain conditions, was rather different from the materiality of the world with which engineering was productively engaged. In prose as rich as most of the imaginative literature of the period, textured by fluent argot and technical nomenclature, the anatomy and physiology of *Titanic* were described in *Scientific American Supplement* (June 1911), *International Marine Engineering* (July 1911), and *The Shipbuilder* (Souvenir Number, Midsummer 1911: *The White Star Triple-Screw Atlantic Liners 'Olympic' and 'Titanic', 45,000 Tons, The Largest Steamships in the World*). Joining these considerable but overlooked cultural documents of the Edwardian period is a painstaking and lavishly illustrated two-part report, 'Harland and Wolff's Works at Belfast', *Engineering* (July 5, 12, 1912), a report that nonetheless manages (out of professional and commercial discretion, I assume) to make only one glancing mention of the sunken *Titanic*.

The author of *Dracula*, laureate of the undead, was impressed by the inventory in Harland & Wolff's shipyard, by the rich things and stuff of the world, ordered and arranged and yet in living and transformative motion.

> In this shipyard it is possible to follow the whole process of construction, from the reception of the raw material, in itself a big work, to the departure of the registered ship. All day the sound of clattering metal is heard on the stone pavement of the Queen's Road; great waggons are carrying lengths of flat or angle steel. Brass, copper, lead, iron, tin, even costlier metals pass along. There comes an endless procession of tree-trunks—English oak and Irish ash; paint; rubber; cement; canvas; goods for upholstery in every form; and in addition to raw material, anchors and chains, cables and hawsers of steel or hemp or coir, ventilators, lamps, and electric and other fittings.

Stoker thought the timber section of the shipyard worthy of attention in itself.

> Here may be seen fine-grained yellow pine from Canadian slow-growing forests, great teak balks from Rangoon; enormous trunks, roughly squared by the axe, of giant mahogany from Honduras; hardwoods of beautiful texture and pattern, suitable for panelling and veneering, from Californian mountain woods, from Pacific Islands, from tropical rivers. The odour of the dry dust of yellow pine and the damp dust of teak blend and give a strange and unique aroma to the place.

Had the great modern Irish novelist James Joyce hailed from Belfast rather than Dublin, such catalogues of plenty and activity might have found their way into his epic novel of June 16, 1904, *Ulysses* (1922). But Joyce grew up in an Irish city that had lost its manufacturing and mercantile zeal and he captured instead the idle energy and post-industriousness of that city in his suite of stories, *Dubliners*, 1914, and inventories them in the later novel. Joyce was also, for all the modernism and realism of his narrative strategies, a Victorian Romantic when it came to the modern, industrializing world. That world did not in his imagination progress beyond 1904. Other moderns took on that world. Jonathan Rose quotes Richard Ellmann's observation that the Edwardians wrote more tightly than the Victorians: 'Their sentences grew more vigorous and concentrated', and Rose instances the taut prose of George Bernard Shaw, HG Wells and Rudyard Kipling. Those writers – *English* modernists, we might call them – inhabited the same world as the engineering journalists. (Note that all were exercised by the fate of *Titanic* whereas the two Irish literary giants, Yeats and Joyce, both from the agricultural south of Ireland, ignored it.)

The futurist FT Marinetti also inhabited it, if in a highly charged, even Romantic way. In a piece entitled 'Geometric and Mechanical Splendour and the Numerical Sensibility' (1914), Marinetti extolled the *noun* in Futurist prose.

> Many times I have demonstrated how the noun, enfeebled by multiple contacts or the weight of Parnassian and decadent adjectives, regains its absolute value and its expressive force when it is denuded and set apart. Among naked nouns I distinguish the elementary noun and the motion-synthesis noun (or node of nouns) .... I see every noun as a vehicle or belt set in motion by the verb in the infinitive.

One thinks of the 'verbalism' of machinery in motion and of the mastery of the noun in such a passage as the following from *Scientific*

American inspired (that surely is the word) by the internal dynamic economy of *Olympic* and *Titanic*:

> The gearing of the engines is of the double helical or herringbone type, cut from the solid-Citron gear. It is designed for silence and strength, and we were informed that it is perfectly noiseless, and entirely does away with backlash. The pinion on the gear shaft meshes with the teeth on the quadrant, which is loose on the rudder head, but the quadrant is connected by springs to a double tiller below, which is keyed to the rudder head, so that the engine and gearing should be relieved of all shocks, which, in view of the fact that the rudder weighs 100 tons and is 15 feet broad, will not be inconsiderable. An emergency tiller is also fitted, which can be connected up to the two warping engines in the wings, in case of damage to the quadrant, the teeth of which are in interchangeable sections bolted to the casting. The control is by means of a Brown's telemotor from the bridge actuating the steam valves. There is also fitted a Brown's Economic valve – or, 'get-out-of-the-way valve', if we may be allowed to coin a word – to prevent leakage of steam while the engine is standing, due to the absence of lap on the piston valves.

Here language and dynamic function mesh (any apparent surplus is really provision for inefficiency or wear, in both machine and language) and the authority of common nouns is capped by the authority of proper nouns, brand names that act as guarantees of efficiency – Brown's telemotor, the Aspinall governor, Railton and Campbell ash hoists, Napier Brothers steam windlasses, etc.

The machine generated in the Age of *Titanic* what we might call 'machine prose', a language with its own stylishness as well as solidity:

RJ Welch's photograph of workers leaving Harland & Wolff

at its best it re-creates the aesthetic pleasure of pure functioning, the joy of the efficient solution of the technical problem, both in succinct explanation and in working demonstration. In his book, *Making the Modern: Industry, Art, and Design in America* (1993), Terry Smith writes of the 'machine aesthetic', and in Harland & Wolff could be found plentiful examples of that. Early ships of theirs, built in the 1860s, were known as 'ocean greyhounds', and in the words of Jonathan Bardon, *Oceanic*, built in 1899, was 'the most elegant vessel ever launched by Harland & Wolff'. Wyn Craig Wade remarks the 'sheer aesthetic satisfaction of *Titanic*'. In his novel, *Psalm at Journey's End* (trans. 1996), Erik Fosnes Hansen registers the first sight of the ship on one of his fictional ship's musicians:

> Her name was right. The very sight of her vast shape–the cranes, the masts, the wires, and four enormous funnels–made David feel almost faint. The ship had a wonderful supernatural unity that made him think of music, of Bach, of sequence of notes extending and growing together into one vast structure.

We could speak also of the sensory impact of parts of the ship (boilers, rudder, propellers, funnels) that we can appreciate even in photographs. We can appreciate it in reality as well. For example, outside the Ulster Folk Museum (Transport section), there is a Harland & Wolff propeller screw on display. Here reality is re-contextualized by the museum in order to make an aesthetic statement. The screw is reminiscent of a Henry Moore sculpture; it is both machine part and work of art. But in their original working contexts, such machine parts must still have exercised aesthetic appeal to those who took a moment to gaze. Indeed, it is hard not to imagine that the more skilled shipyard workers were impressed aesthetically, even below the level of consciousness, by the objects and material they were fashioning or manoeuvring and that in being so impressed were living a daily life of at least fractionally intensified sensibility. Ezra Pound was later to claim (in the 1920s) that 'Machine plastic is already equal to other plastic. The object exists; the man in the shop may or may not be able to see it, or he may have too many associations with it to judge it clearly.'

Depictions of *Titanic* are images of modernity. The still photography most closely associated with the liner is that of the Ulsterman RJ Welch. Welch is thought of chiefly as a visual chronicler of the Irish countryside, but many of his commissioned photographs of Harland & Wolff shipyard, including those of *Titanic* under construction, bear comparison with the photographs of the Ford automobile plants taken in the 1920s by Charles Sheeler and reproduced by Smith (who calls Sheeler 'the Raphael of the Fords'). According to Smith, a certain iconography seems fundamental to the imagery of modernity: industry and workers; cities and crowds; products and consumers. Many of Welch's portraits of Belfast and Harland & Wolff offer such imagery with an iconographic gravity, including his celebrated photographs of a torrent of workers leaving the city-sized yard at the end of a shift, with the growing *Titanic* and *Olympic* receding in the distance behind them. One might think of Dante's words famously quoted by TS Eliot, and in the arch-modernist poem *The Waste Land* (1922) re-contextualized as crowds flowing over London Bridge: 'I had not thought death had undone so many'.

The Futurists were much taken with the interdependence of man and machine, while the chief English modernist theorist, TE Hulme, advocated 'machine forms' and 'hard mechanical shapes' in art which Butler tells us Hulme saw in the Cubist works at the Brighton exhibition in 1913. Hulme is associated with the poetry movement called Imagism, and *hardness* has been identified by Zach as 'the commonest, widest-ranging concept in the movement's vocabulary'. I have already referred in an earlier chapter to the importance of machine shapes to the visual art movement of Vorticism. It was not until the late 1920s that Pound, chief Modernist thinker, wrote on *Machine Art*, but the Vorticist ringleader Wyndham Lewis thought that Pound had been secretly influenced by Marinetti at the time of the Futurist manifestos. Among other observations, Pound wrote that:

> the beauty of machines ... is now chiefly to be found in those parts of machines where the energy is most concentrated .... Interest for the critic of form will lie mainly in the mobile parts and in the parts which more immediately hold these mobile parts in their loci .... It seems possible that any man intending to practice the plastic arts ... might, in our time, more readily awaken his eye by looking at spare parts and at assembled machinery than by walking through galleries of painting or sculpture .... Among the remarks about beauty that I have come upon in diverse works on philosophy, art, aesthetics, etc., I recall with pleasure the simplest: we find a thing beautiful in proportion to its aptitude to a function .... I suspect that the better a machine becomes AS A MACHINE, the better it will be to look at.

And more:

> The engineering mind is about the most satisfactory mind of our time; like all other mind types, it has its borders, but the practice of engineering seems to me less stultifying than most other contemporary practices. It

does not seem to me, and I do not see how it can be, built up by layer after layer of bunk.

Pound thought that Ford's organisation was, in a good sense of the word, feudal (produce plus service plus obligation); he thought that Ford was experimenting with tempo and that the acoustics of machinery were worth contemplating: 'there is no reason why the shop noise shouldn't be used as stimulus and to give swing and ease to modern work ...'. Pound concluded that *'Modern man can live and should live in his cities and machine shops with the same kind of swing and exuberance that the savage is supposed to have in his forest'*. Whatever we think of Pound's particular points, it seems clear that the machine aesthetic deserved, and deserves, attention and that *Titanic* and the Atlantic liners helped create the imaginary of the modern art world. They were, in a way that hardly stretches the imagination, themselves vast works of cooperative art.

Titanic As Culture

Filson Young in his prompt book on the *Titanic* disaster noted an odd thing about the architecture of the ship. The first-class cabins referred to as such were, he thought, indistinguishable from luxurious apartments on shore, save that sea-breezes kept their air always fresh. Instead of ports he saw windows, and open grates in place of stoves or radiators. 'For there is one thing that the designers of this sea-palace seem to have forgotten and seem to be a little ashamed of – and that is the sea itself.' True, he conceded:

> there is a smoke-room at the after extremity of the deck below this, whose windows look out into a great verandah sheeted in with glass from which you cannot help looking upon the sea. But in order to counteract as much as possible that austere and lovely reminder of where we are, trellis-work has been raised within the glass, and great rose-trees spread and wander all over it, reminding you by their crimson blossoms of the earth and the land, and the scented shelter of the gardens that are far from the boisterous stress of the sea. No spray ever drifts in at these heights, no froth or spume can ever in the wildest storms beat upon this verandah. Here, too, as almost everywhere else on the ship, you can, if you will, forget the sea.

Titanic life constituted itself as *culture*, and there is irony in the fact that it was nature at its purest and simplest – as iceberg – that destroyed this floating (and where its human component was concerned, temporary) culture. Seaborne hotels, travelling palaces, floating towns: these were early metaphors used to describe (and sometimes deplore) luxury liners of the period. Whilst most of the 'townspeople' were 'visitors', hundreds of them were 'resident': the vastnesses between Boat Deck and stokehold included chefs, nurses, library stewards, orchestra members, page-boys, lift-boys, post-office clerks, bath attendants, barbers, butchers, bakers, window-cleaners, scullions, a ship's printer, interpreter, racquets professional, gymnasium instructor.

Passengers formed their own complex and transient society. Far beyond the expected bulkheads of social class and occupation separating first-class from second class and both of these from third class, and all classes from officers and crew, there were other divisions and connections, some of them improvised during the voyage. Captains of the great liners, for example, would consort with selected first-class passengers; they were ambassadors of the Line to some extent, and took the time to acknowledge the importance in society of certain travellers. It became a matter of debate whether Captain Smith might have consumed alcohol when he dined on Sunday evening in the first-class à la carte restaurant as the guest of Mr and Mrs George Widener of Philadelphia, members of the streetcar magnate's family. High-ranking officers might pass the time of day with distinguished passengers, but generally officers and crew kept their distance from the paying travellers and also from each other.

Inside first-class, families were an important cultural unit and were often enlarged in the social space they occupied by maids, manservants, nannies and governesses. Tightly-knit though these families were when the going was good, it appears that crises could necessitate re-formations. Bruce Ismay saved himself, but his manservant Richard Fry was lost in unknown circumstances; so was Mr W. Harrison, Ismay's secretary. In the Ismay case, the gentleman and manservant apparently composed a professional unit, not a family unit as such. Under the social code of the time, maids were usually saved with their mistresses, governesses with their charges, whereas manservants had to take their chances either with their masters or alone. Victor Robbins, John Jacob Astor's manservant, went down with his master (while the Astors' maid, Rosalie Bidois, was saved with her mistress); Benjamin Guggenheim's valet, Victor Giglio, shared his master's sad fate, as did John Farthing, Isidor Straus's manservant and EH Keeking, George Widener's manservant. Other manservants were likewise lost, often separated from their employers.

Beyond families, cliques formed, the more readily among first-class passengers, some of whom knew each other, having already met in the Southampton hotels on the eve of embarkation or on the train from Waterloo station, or even back in New York, Chicago, Boston or

Philadelphia, the chief cities in the United States to where they were returning. It was Walter Lord who remarked that a transatlantic crossing was a kind of reunion for many first-class passengers who regularly vacationed or did business in Europe. Although he was much in the company of Isidor Straus and his wife, Archibald Gracie, for example, identified James Clinch Smith, the sportsman and Paris habitué, and Edward A. Kent, as the chief 'men of my coterie' who would typically sit in the palm room after dinner over coffee and then repair to the smoking room where they would see or talk to such lights as Archibald Butt (Presidential aide), Clarence Moore (Washington banker and Master of Hounds), Frank Millet (artist), John B. Thayer (railroad vice-president) and George Widener. Lord observes that during the evacuation, the Astors, Wideners, Thayers, Carters and Ryersons stuck pretty much together around lifeboat No. 4. In the emergency, friendship and cliquishness would have been reinforced by a natural adhesion of communally acknowledged importance – *like*, in this regard, gravitating to *like* in corporate bonding.

Gracie was an admirer of good-looking women; in the palm-room, when full dress was always, as he said, '*en regle*', he and his cronies would remark on the fact that 'there were so many beautiful women – then especially in evidence – aboard the ship'. Gracie thought of himself as something of a chevalier on such voyages and in Southampton he offered his services as protector to three sisters, Mrs Appleton, Mrs Cornell and Mrs Murray Brown, all of whom we have met, friends of his wife's. The Washington writer, Helen Churchill Candee, also ornamented Gracie's coterie and when the collision occurred and the lifeboats were readied, Gracie sprang into action, as good as his word, shepherding his charges and marshalling the men.

There were cliques in second class as well, but one assumes that in steerage, families and ethnic groups were the chief conglomerations, serving not as enjoyable occasions for reunion as in first class but as protective rings during this worrisome voyage that was always going to be one-way for most of the passengers. One imagines the Swedes, Irish, Greeks, Armenians and other immigrant races and nationalities not just consorting but huddling, perhaps exaggerating their ethnic traits out of early homesickness – talking, singing, gaming, to keep their spirits up during this strange and alarming adventure. Then the deluge: cliques, families, friends, ethnic fellowships – all came under intense pressure during the ship's evacuation, divided, re-formed, broken (in many cases, forever).

Some, mostly among the crew, retained their fellowship to the end. The Harland & Wolff engineers, crew in a special sense (their names appear in the passenger not crew list), all perished while working in concert until it was no longer possible. Another group who enjoyed an odd status were the ship's musicians (who appeared on the second-class passenger list); Hansen has imagined the eccentric society of the *Titanic* bandsmen in *Psalm at Journey's End* . The familiar camaraderie of music combos by all accounts kept morale high among passengers, crew and musicians alike, until the inevitable end.

To some degree a true reflection of class and labour structures on land, ship society (both paid and paying) as was found on *Titanic* and other giant liners was nevertheless highly unusual in its alignments and hierarchies. The argot and slang, the prescribed (and unprescribed) modes of address, the vocabulary and diction, the body language and gestures, the physical and mental attitudes: these all varied by class and occupation. All permutations were made possible (though many were forbidden) by uncustomary proximity in a restricted compass. On *Titanic*, ship society changed soon after the collision and by the end had sea-changed: Harold Lowe's impoliteness to a gentleman (whom he did not recognise as Bruce Ismay) was an early and mild symptom of the small temporary social revolution to come that night.

The first-class gentlemen who stood back while second- and even third-class women went ahead of them in the lifeboats were perhaps asserting their social and 'political' superiority by doing so, and actually shoring up gender and class inequality in Britain and America. However, because of the magnitude of this emergency and the wholesale nature of the suspension of the usual power outcome when women and men had conflicting needs (here men actually lost their lives), something revolutionary was nevertheless going on. It is generally acknowledged that the incomparably greater 'crisis' of the Great War four or five years later permanently altered social and class relations in the United Kingdom, through wartime's critical pressures; but if so, then we see a glimmer of this in the early hours of April 15, 1912. Life aboard *Titanic* was a human society that was recognizably contemporary in its elements, unusual in its brief composition, and unique in its fateful, and fatal, dynamic.

Society (with a capital 'S') survived the night, of course, and the heroism of the first-class men was affirmed in the newspapers to make sure it did. (It was not first class *per se* that was reaffirmed but Society. 'First class' was both an honorific (noun) and an obligatory kind of behaviour (adjective), not a merely economic category; first-class men were supposed to be first-class fellows whose actions were therefore first-class, as befitting gentlemen.) It was not necessary to do for the distaff side anything other than praise the vague nobility of the ladies. Records of actual bravery among the women, such as the Countess of Rothes and Margaret Tobin (Molly Brown), ran the risk of making such women look like overgrown tomboys; hence the Countess was 'plucky', an adjective that attributed delicacy of manner as well as a winsome intention to be valorous of the sort found among Anglo-American schoolboys. Society was as a whole given a female sex and marital status; ladies were married women who carried their husbands' forenames or daughters who carried their fathers' surnames. Mrs FJ Swift, Miss EM Eustis, Mrs J. Snyder, Mrs Figler, Mrs Ettlinger were said to be 'well known in New York society', Mrs GM Stone 'well known in American society', Mrs Stengel 'an American society hostess'.

Their male counterparts were men of industry; whereas men who were identified as socialites, clubmen or sportsmen, such as William Carter (he with the brand-new motor car on board and who left the ship with Ismay) or Clinch Smith, ran the risk of appearing as playboys or even wastrels. When Carter's wife divorced him on the grounds that he had looked out for himself and not his family during the sinking, it somehow suited his description as 'polo player and clubman'. Society faltered on April 15 and on the succeeding days of the official inquiries and unofficial tribunals of the press, but regained its composure, at least until the Great War and then the Depression. But until the collision, *Titanic* played splendid hostess to it, and its culture.

The famously luxurious appointments of *Titanic* formed an appropriate temporary habitat for Society and were suitable expressions of the 'Gilded Age'. Harland & Wolff had their own upholsterers and their own in-house decorators who worked in studios; one hundred and eighty-six men worked on the carved panelling on *Olympic* and *Titanic*. Here is a fragment of the lavish inventory furnished by *The Shipbuilder*:

> the reception room, which adjoins the forward end of the dining saloon, has a length of 54 feet [16.45 metres] and also extends the full width of the ship. The style adopted is Jacobean English similar to the dining room, but the furniture is, of course, different. The dignity and simplicity of the beautifully proportioned white panelling, delicately carved in low relief, will indeed form a fitting background to the brilliant scene when the passengers foregather before dining. The main staircase rises directly from this apartment, thus greatly increasing the palatial effect produced. Facing the staircase is a large and very beautiful panel of French tapestry adapted from one of a series entitled 'Chasse de Guise' at the national

Artist's impression of the grand staircase: an intentionally theatrical space

Garde Meuble, and specially woven on the looms of Aubusson. The floor is covered with a dark, richly coloured Axminster carpet. The furniture includes capacious Chesterfields, grandfather chairs upholstered in a floral pattern of wool damask, comfortable cane chairs, and light tables distributed at intervals, and there is also a grand piano.

Whereas the reception room and dining room were Jacobean, the famous grand staircase was in William and Mary, but the balustrade was Louis XIV; the restaurant was Louis XVI, the lounge Louis XV (Versailles), the reading and writing room late Georgian, the smoking room early Georgian.

It does not seem incongruous that those dedicated to material progress should seek to relax in nostalgic re-creations of a pre-industrial past. The interior of first-class *Titanic* must have given the impression of a mixed-period stately home or possibly museum. It may also have induced the impression of a series of floating stages, with the ship a kind of theatre, in which passengers could not but help but sense themselves as actors, or characters as well as travellers in the real world. The maiden voyage was in any case a quasi-theatrical event, with many first-class passengers reserving berths for 'historic' reasons (passage on the maiden voyage of the world's largest liner was a notable 'first' equivalent to a 'premiere' of a major play or opera) or because the necessity of travel could coincide with the publicity value of appearance. From our perspective, the whole may appear dangerously like early post-modern *kitsch*, historic culture literally unmoored from its context, the ship turning that culture into moveable images in a way that anticipated the theme-imagery and simulacra of hotels and parks in our own day.

If passengers were in some sense actors they were also audience for the music on board *Titanic* which must have added to the cultural experience of first class. Walter Lord when he revisited *Titanic* in *The Night Lives On* (1986) identified two musical units on the ship: a quintet and a trio. Lord has the quintet playing Puccini and Dvorak in the Jacobean reception room on Sunday evening, finishing the concert with *Tales of Hoffmann*. After the collision, the orchestra moved to the foyer of the Grand Staircase and then to the Boat Deck, becoming a smaller ensemble that played 'Alexander's Ragtime Band', 'In the Shadows' and other ragtimes, waltzes and comic songs before the last disputed tune..Ian Whitcomb has brilliantly imagined a posthumous soliloquy by Wallace Hartley for his compact disc, *Titanic: Music as Heard on the Fateful Voyage* (1997). He has also researched the music of the time, and reminds us that the White Star music book listed 352 tunes which ships' musicians learned by heart and by number (hence our reference to tunes as 'numbers') and that the music of *Titanic* drew on a huge hinterland. Just as Britain resounded with sermons and hymns during the Age of *Titanic*, so 'the British Isles were filled with music – from grand operas and symphonic concerts to brass band contests between rival factories and coal mines; from rude and racy music hall songs to genteel drawing room ballads'.

With a reconstituted 'White Star Orchestra', Whitcomb has recorded music passengers would have heard in April 1912 including the two numbers Lord mentioned. Apart from anything else, travel on *Titanic* was a musical experience, itself a portion of an entire cultural experience that was familiar to a select few and an eye-opener and ear-opener to numerous others.[1]

Luxury Lost

If *Titanic* and the life aboard her could be seen as art, as theatre, as culture, it is unsurprising but entertaining to know that amongst the cargo, personal luggage and portable property on *Titanic* were items of real interest to the cultural historian. It was reported in *The Times* of London on April 22, 1912, and more fully in the London *Daily Telegraph* on the same day that:

the jewelled ['Ruba'iyat of] Omar Khayyam' [translated by Edward Fitzgerald and published in 1859], which caused a stir recently in London book circles, has been lost in the Titanic. The original cost of the binding was £500. It was studded with 1,050 jewels set in gold. The example is a copy of the original edition, and the cover is the most remarkable specimen of binding ever produced. There were beauty, extravagance, and splendour of Eastern decoration in every portion of the volume. The 1,050 stones comprised rubies, turquoises, amethysts, topazes, olivines, and garnets, so interlaced that not one could possibly fall out. Each stone was in a gold setting .... The binding took nearly two years of incessant work to produce .... The binder worked to no plan, and a record of how the coloured stones were placed was not kept.

Other details emerged elsewhere. The illustrations were by Eliku Vedder, according to Sir Philip Gibbs in *The Deathless Story of the Titanic* (1912); the binding was by Sangorski and Sutcliffe, famous British bookbinders, according to the Toronto *Globe and Mail* of May 19, 1998. A Piccadilly bookseller named Isaacs had bought the volume on March 29 for £405 at Sotheby's and it was en route to a new owner in the United States.

For my purposes here, it is not necessary that this report – which surfaced in several places – be true, though if it is, the popular interest in, even demand for, the luxury of *Titanic*, even of its private property, is a kind of willed legendry double-plated with fact. *Titanic's* luxury was and is important for the popular imagination, and it was and is even better if items of that luxury were unique, irreplaceable, irrevocably *lost in the abyss* and the more valuable for it. *Luxury lost* – that was a recurring desire in reportage and reception of the *Titanic* catastrophe.

Another rarity, and possibly a unique specimen as well, went also to the bottom: a 1598 edition of Francis Bacon's essays, recently bought in London by Harry Widener, a 27-year-old bibliophile and heir to part of the vast fortune amassed by the Widener and Elkins families through street trams and real estate. Harry and his father George perished, his mother and her maid were saved. Harry inherited the collecting zeal of his grandfather, PA Widener, and at the time of his death Harry owned one of the finest private libraries in America. The famous Philadelphia bookseller AWS Rosenbach had recently bid on young Harry's behalf $18,000 for a first folio Shakespeare in a London auction, a record price for this rarity. The *New York Times* of April 17 reported the ongoing Robert Hoe library sale and, aware that Widener was among the *Titanic* missing, told its readers that he had attended Part I of the sale and been the under bidder for the Gutenberg Bible on vellum, that his bid of $49,000 was bettered by

$1,000 by Henry E. Huntington (the Huntington Library in California is today a prestigious research library). About five o'clock on the evening before he sailed east, Harry looked over the books in the auction rooms and expressed interest, particularly in the Caxton edition of John Gower's *Confessio Amantis*, but he felt Huntington's determination would thwart him. Harry sailed for Europe on the Cunard liner *Mauretania* but expected to return on *Titanic* in time to attend the latter half of Part III.

Harry Widener was reported to have said goodbye to his mother just before *Titanic* sank and told her: 'Mother, I have placed the volume in my pocket – the little "Bacon" goes with me'. And so it did. Harry had left his collection of books to Harvard University and his mother decided to commemorate her son by funding the building of a library to house it at that university – the Widener Library that was dedicated in 1915.[2]

The connection between *Titanic* and New York cultural institutions is oddly rich. In the nineteenth century, an ancestor of John Jacob Astor (who like Harry Widener was a Harvard graduate) had left the Astor library to New York City where it became the nucleus of the New York Public Library. The smelting millionaire Benjamin Guggenheim, lost with honour, was of the family behind the Guggenheim Museum in New York; the name Guggenheim is warmly familiar to every academic and artist in the United States who seeks a prestigious grant for research. J. Pierpont Morgan, head of International Mercantile Marine, by good fortune did not travel on the great ship he effectively owned; he was founder of the J. Pierpont Morgan Library in New York City which grew out of Morgan's opulent collections of books and manuscripts.

Morgan might have been interested in a manuscript on board his ship that was on its way to John Quinn, the celebrated New York book and picture collector. This was the manuscript of Joseph Conrad's story 'Karain' which the writer posted on Tuesday, April 9, a day before *Titanic*'s departure: 'I think there can be no doubt that they went by the Titanic'. Conrad admitted to his being upset by news of the tragedy 'on general grounds, but also personally': he was to get £40 from Quinn for his packet of manuscripts which was to include 'Karain'. 'I depended on that sum', Conrad lamented to the agent JB Pinker, 'but only registered without insuring so as to avoid the trouble of getting the consular certificate'. Conrad sent Quinn the manuscript of another story, 'The Informer', in its place.

Quinn's biographer tells us that 'Karain' indeed went on *Titanic* and 'sank with Lady Gregory's seal ring and her rosary'. This is an initially puzzling reference, and not just because it implies (inadvertently no doubt) that all three objects travelled together. In the next paragraph of his biography of the collector, BL Reid notes that Quinn was sending Conrad two volumes of Lady Gregory's *Irish Folk-History Plays* (1912), the second volume dedicated to Quinn. Lady Gregory was a friend and patroness of WB Yeats, and they were colleagues in the Irish Literary Revival, in which Quinn was very interested. The dedication to Quinn would explain the destination of the ring and rosary: John Quinn. According to a biographer of Gregory, Mary Lou Kohfeldt, the rosary was for Quinn's sister (Gregory herself was a Protestant), the seal ring for Quinn himself. Quinn and Gregory (a widow) had an affair when she toured with the Abbey players in late 1911, early 1912. Although he wrote to Gregory that the manuscript and the ring were a deep personal loss, later he remarked to the painter Augustus John, 'unchivalrously' (to use the word of another Gregory biographer, Ann Saddlemyer), that he was perhaps better off without the ring.

Besides these cultural artefacts lost with *Titanic*, there were to a notable degree living embodiments and representatives of culture, of art and entertainment on board the liner. Two fashion correspondents survived, their eye for style intact.

Edith Russell (her real name was Rosenbaum and she is accounted for in Lord and Geller) wrote columns for *Women's Wear Daily* and the *New York Herald*. She was returning in first class from France where she had covered the Easter races at Auteuil, which commission caused her to cancel an earlier passage on board *George Washington*. That spring she was attempting a new role as fashion buyer and was travelling with trunks of European couture for American clients, all destined for the bottom of the ocean, as it happened. She is remembered as a comic bit player in the *Titanic* drama, sending her cabin steward back for her good-luck musical toy pig with which in lifeboat No. 11 she amused children by having her pig play *La Maxixe*, a pop tune of the day. Fashion-conscious even in crisis, she dressed incongruously for the evacuation in a woollen frock with hobble skirt, light broadtail coat, silk stockings, no underwear and embroidered velvet slippers with diamond buckles. Later on, she recalled what Bruce Ismay was wearing when he ordered her into the lifeboat, and thereby, she claimed, saved her life: 'black evening trousers and a nightshirt with frills down the front'. Less than a week after her rescue, she recorded for *Women's Wear Daily* Lady Duff Gordon's apparel when abandoning ship, another triumph of fashion consciousness (with its echoes of Oscar Wilde) over the appropriate, tastelessness and absurdity redeemed only by a kind of plucky survivalism: 'Lucile, Lady Duff Gordon, made her escape in a very charming lavender bath robe, very beautifully embroidered, together with a very pretty blue veil'.

Her plucky survivalism was verified during the Great War when Edith Russell became one of the first women war correspondents, seeing at first hand the second (and incomparably the greater) of the two disasters of the second decade of the twentieth century.

Edith Russell recalled for *Women's Wear Daily* readers that she and Lady Duff Gordon exchanged compliments about their costumes and swapped fashion news after boarding the rescue ship *Carpathia*.

> All her models, as well as my own, had gone to the bottom of the sea, and we both acknowledged that pannier skirts and Robespierre collars were at a discount in mid-ocean when you are looking for a ship to rescue you.

(The *New York Times* of April 16 reported that 'much of the Titanic's cargo was destined for New York stores for their Spring display of European fashions. These goods comprised expensive laces, the finest silks, and an immense consignment of cotton material from Manchester.') Duff Gordon ('modiste') had written approvingly and at length about pannier skirts and gowns in her fashion column for the *San Francisco Examiner* that appeared the very day *Titanic* struck the iceberg. ('But', she added delicately, 'the woman with individuality will see her limitations and if at all inclined to embonpoint will eschew waistcoat and pannier and cling to her modification of the narrow, clinging fashions'.) The newspaper identified her as '"Lucile" of London and foremost creator of fashions in the world' (she had opened a branch of her business in New York); she was the sister of Elinor Glyn the well-known Society figure and novelist.

Duff Gordon's name had a certain piquancy. Two theatre historians, Kaplan and Stowell, describe her as 'West End London's most notorious couturiere' who had earned a reputation for the risqué by the time she was commissioned in 1897 to design *The Liars*, a play by Henry Arthur Jones, the famous English playwright who was to witness the return of *Carpathia* to New York with *Titanic* survivors. (Duff Gordon fittingly called her autobiography, published in the 1930s, *Discretions and Indiscretions*.) In the Age of *Titanic* fashion and theatre were in symbiosis, and Lucile provoked theatregoers with designs that then became fashionable. Just as stages of the 1890s sometimes resembled couturier's shops, so Lucile turned her showroom into the resemblance of a theatre.

For a couple of days in May 1912, Lady Duff Gordon and her husband Sir Cosmo did something of the sort to the august rooms of the Scottish Hall where the British *Titanic* inquiry was conducted. It had been suggested that Sir Cosmo had bribed the crewmen of emergency lifeboat No. 1 not to return to the wreck scene where the hapless were struggling in the water. In No. 1 there were only five passengers, three of them the Duff Gordon party (they travelled with Miss Francatelli, a maid), and seven crew in a vessel that could have accommodated at least ten more people. (Fireman James Taylor thought they could have had 25 or so more on board.) At the British inquiry, Charles Hendricksen, leading fireman, testified that Lady Duff Gordon objected to the boat's going back to help the swimmers and that her husband supported her. The Duff Gordons defended themselves vigorously – the so-called bribe was simply a donation to help the crew replace their lost kits; they heard no cries in the water after *Titanic* sank; and it would have been dangerous to return before the boat in fact did. With what appeared to be class complicity, Lord Mersey, Wreck Commissioner (chairman) of the hearing, cleared Sir Cosmo Duff Gordon of the allegation of bribery and merely suggested in his report that some lives might have been saved if Sir Cosmo had encouraged the crew to go back.

Because she was a woman, what Lady Duff Gordon had to say about the matter was relatively unimportant. At any rate, the London *Daily Sketch*, reporting on May 21, said that her testimony 'was the briefest appearance of any material witness who had so far been called'. But her appearance was extended enough to help make the British inquiry fashionable. The *Sketch* reported on May 15 that the ladies' gallery was 'sparsely tenanted', but three days later began its report on a patronizing note:

> It was Ladies' Day at the Titanic inquiry yesterday [May 17]. Expectations of hearing more about 'the Money Boat' had excited keen interest in the day's proceedings, and the prospect of seeing Sir Cosmo and Lady Duff Gordon in Court relating their version of the incidents of that tragic vigil in mid-ocean was a compelling attraction to the fair and always curious sex.

British editors readily turned the *Titanic* disaster into Society Drama. Among witnesses, physical appearance and wardrobe were seen as telling, and the perspective of social rank rarely absent; it was entirely different from the procedure and reporting of the American inquiry. Mr Duke, KC, MP by cross-examining Hendricksen 'lifted the curtain on this day's drama', announced the *Sketch* on May 18. Sir Cosmo was, readers were told, 'wearing a black frock coat and light striped trousers, and Lady Duff-Gordon, who is, of course, familiar to the West End as

Mme Lucile, the Court costumier, was in black with a cloak faced with purple'. Sir Cosmo took his place 'with hair brushed well back, and wearing the clothes and the manner of a well-groomed, self-possessed Society man'. (Ismay when he testified was seen by the same paper as a 'commercial monarch' who did not look like one but instead looked like a 'cultured cosmopolitan'.)

The day Lady Duff Gordon gave witness, 'feminine interest was again accentuated', with liberal numbers of 'prominent Society people again putting in an appearance'. (In her autobiography Duff Gordon remembered the fashionable opportunity of the hearing and added: 'I caught sight of the Duchess of Wellington and Lady Eileen Wellesley, Margot Asquith, Prince Maurice of Battenberg, Prince Albert of Scheswig-Holstein'. The *Sketch* offered Prince Leopold of Battenburg [sic] and Count Benckendorff, the Russian ambassador.) 'The ladies wore light costumes, flower-decked hats and white blouses .... It was noticeable that the fashionable cerise colour which had prevailed among the fair listeners last week was now superseded by shades of purple and mauve.' Duff Gordon herself retained black but with 'a touch of white at her neck and bosom, and from her black hat fell a black veil over her shoulders'. Years later she maintained that *Titanic* had been a boon to her business and had made her thousands of dollars.

Although the Duff Gordons travelled on *Titanic* under the pseudonyms of 'Mr and Mrs Morgan', they helped ensure that the British hearing became what life in first class on board the ship had been: fashion parade and Society dramatically on view. The juxtaposition of aristocratic fashion and minor European royalty gives from our vantage point an odd foretaste of the First World War.

The Arts on *Titanic*

There were other theatrical presences on board *Titanic*. The 'well-known' Californian actress Margaret Graham was reported missing by the *Daily Sketch* on April 18 but was reported rescued by the *Daily Graphic* two days later. The serial movie star Dorothy Gibson also survived – indeed, she starred in a movie released on May 14, one month after the disaster. Judith B. Geller has summarised the eventful life of a woman from New Jersey who came to fame as 'the Original Harrison Fisher Girl', her face familiar from magazines, newspapers and advertisements illustrated by the prolific and popular Fisher. In 1911 she was snapped up by the American (New Jersey) division of the French film company Eclair, for which she starred in short escapist films. She finished *The Easter Bonnet* in March 1912 and travelled with her mother to Italy for a vacation, only to be recalled by the studio almost immediately. They returned on *Titanic* in first class and after the collision were the first women to be put into lifeboat No. 7, Dorothy wearing a silk evening gown underneath a woollen sweater. Scarcely missing a beat, the Eclair studio refitted a script they already had and released *Saved from the Titanic*, starring Dorothy, wearing the very same silk evening gown she wore in lifeboat No. 7. This was art imitating life but also, through Gibson, life re-enacting itself as art. In July the film opened in packed British picture-houses as *A Survivor of the Titanic*. In 1913 Gibson killed a man in New York City while recklessly driving a car belonging to a married Eclair financier, Jules Brulatour, with whom she was having an affair; they married in 1917 but were soon divorced amidst wrangling over the legality of the marriage and the alimony settlement. Dorothy lived in Europe as Dorothy Brulatour and died in a Paris hotel room in 1946. A fire at the Eclair studios destroyed the prints of *Saved from the Titanic* in March 1914; only the studio poster remains.

Nineteen year-old Daniel Marvin from New York was returning from his honeymoon on *Titanic*; he died while his pregnant eighteen year-old bride (one of eleven bride-widows to survive the ship) lived to tell the tale to waiting reporters when she disembarked from *Carpathia*. He was the son of Henry Norton Marvin, President of the Biograph Film Company who as a wedding present had had his son's wedding filmed, a novel thing to do in 1912. The *Daily Mail* of April 17 ran a lengthy story under the headline 'Tragic Sequel to the First Wedding to be Cinematographed'. The ceremony was performed twice, the second time for the camera (life re-enacting itself as art). The *Daily Sketch* called young Marvin a business associate of Thomas Edison.

One passenger list describes a second-class casualty, William Harbeck, as 'film producer', but more information about him than that I have not seen. Likewise with Mr A. Stewart (or Stuart) whom Dickinson Bishop recalled for the *New York Times* knocking at the Bishops' cabin door after the collision and exhorting Dickinson to 'Come on out and amuse yourself'. Stewart, said Bishop, had charge of Buffalo Bill's Wild West show on tours abroad.

There is, however, plenty known about another producer, who also died – Henry B. Harris, with whom Arnold Bennett's friends, the Selwyns, might have travelled on *Titanic* had not Bennett's novel-in-progress detained them. Harris had managed the Hudson and Hackett theatres in New York, and at the time of his death managed the Harris and Fulton theatres; and among his actor clients with names that have endured had been Lily Langtry. Not long before the *Titanic* disaster, Harris had no fewer than 16 theatrical companies on tour in the United States in a single season. He owned the Hudson and Harris theatres outright and was said to have been a millionaire twice or three times over. His widow filed a claim for $1,000,000 and when the award diminished to $50,000 she decided, against the advice of her father-in-law, like his son a theatre producer, to become a producer herself, using the Hudson theatre she now owned. She was a success, and gave starts to several actors and playwrights who became famous – Barbara Stanwyck, Moss Hart and Judith Anderson. Her fortune vanished overnight with the Wall Street crash of 1929, and when Walter Lord interviewed her for his 1955 book, *A Night to Remember*, he did so in a welfare hotel, where she was happy to recall the *Titanic* disaster.

At first it had been thought that Henry B. Harris had been rescued by a ship other than *Carpathia* and that he had wired his New York office to that effect, but it proved to be one more unfounded *Titanic* rumour. George Brayton, an asphalt manufacturer from Los Angeles, recounted how he stood beside the Harrises and how when the couple approached the lifeboat (Engelhardt boat D), an officer stepped between them, ordering 'Ladies first, please!' 'Mr Harris bowed and smiled, saying "Of course, certainly, ladies first". After bidding his wife farewell, Mr Harris mingled with the other passengers who remained on board.' This recalls the story (also in the *New York Times*) of how John Jacob Astor likewise went to get on board, was reminded of the rule, and graciously stepped back and lit a cigarette. Renee Harris remembered being beside the Astors by the lifeboats and being told, like young Mrs Astor, that she had to leave her husband: both husbands stood aside quietly and waved goodbye to their wives. Harris, like Astor, was recruited as a dramatic motif in the narration of the disaster: important man gracefully accedes to the gentlemanly rule of the sea, Women and Children First.

In our imaginations, the scene around the lifeboats was a kind of improvised theatre and if so, Harris was a fitting participant. The *Daily Sketch* of April 19 quoted a Mr Hammerstein about his meeting with Henry Harris in London just before *Titanic* sailed: 'He told me he was taking back with him the moving picture films of "The Miracle" which he had secured for £10,000 and a royalty. Those have all been lost now.' But the same newspaper reported in June 28, 1912 that Max Reinhardt, the German director and playwright, who had mounted *The Miracle* in Olympia, Greece in January 1912, was going to muster his actors in July in Vienna to film his production of the vast work.

Harris, then, must have been returning with permission to stage the work, and perhaps the script joined the other cultural artefacts on board at the bottom of the ocean. *The Miracle* was a Christmas mystery play 'adapted to modern conditions', as Reginald Buckley reported in January, 'to be played by a company of two thousand before an audience of ten thousand'. It was said to be the largest production the world had seen. Buckley identified Reinhardt along with Gordon Craig as of the '"artistic" or aesthetic advance guard' in drama. A full-page sketch of the director appeared on the front cover of the *Illustrated London News* on Saturday, March 12, 1912. Reinhardt, claimed Buckley, was the first man to emphasize drama 'as a gigantic spectacle', and it is hard not to see some irony in the potential American mounter of Reinhardt's gigantic spectacle losing his life in one of the real-life gigantic spectacles of the twentieth century, on a ship that was herself the largest production of her kind the world had seen, a ship of the advance guard in nautical modernism and at the same time – as Reinhardt's spectacular drama must have been – a gigantic throwback to Victorian aggrandizement.

The world of art was almost as well represented on *Titanic* as the world of theatre. One of the two artists of distinction on board, Francis Millet, must surely have known, or met on board, another passenger, Henry Sleeper Harper (who survived with his wife, manservant – an Egyptian dragoman – and Pekingese dog, Sun-Yat-sen); Harper was of the well-known New York publishing family, though of late, he had, contemporaries were told by Logan Marshall in what would now be a puzzling reference for readers, 'active in the work of keeping the Adirondack forests free from aggression'.

Millet had been a correspondent for *Harper's Weekly* in Manila during the 1898 Spanish-American War. Millet (b. 1846) had been a war correspondent before that, for the *New York Herald* and London *Daily Mail* during the Russo-Turkish War of 1877–1878, and before that, he had served as drummer boy for the Sixtieth Massachusetts Volunteers during the American Civil War. Millet was a variously decorated public figure whom the Japanese, Russians, French and Romanians saw fit to honour. Before his war-time exploits, he studied in the early 1870s at the Royal Academy of Fine Arts in Antwerp. After the Russo-Turkish war he studied also in Paris and then returned to the United States where he became a mural decorator and stained glass designer as well as an easel painter. He grew restless, went back to Europe in 1881, making sketches for *Harper's*, then settled in England where he enjoyed the company of JS Sargent, Alma-Tadema and other painters. At the request of J. Pierpont Morgan he became director of the American Academy of Art in Rome and had accompanied Major Archibald Butt, President Taft's military aide, on his visit to Rome from which he was returning. The *Daily Sketch* of April 19 reproduced a painting by Millet, 'Between Two Fires', then in the Tate Gallery in London, and the *Literary Digest* of July 13 reproduced a portrait of Millet in bas-relief by Saint-Gaudens in the Metropolitan Museum, New York, and a mural, 'Thesmophoria', on a classical theme.

Millet's fate was like Harris' the victim of rumour: it was believed that Millet's wife (who was not with him) had telegraphed to report a Marconigram from her husband telling her he had survived, but this proved false. His body was among the 190 corpses that the Canadian cable ship *Mackay-Bennett* retrieved and returned to Halifax, Nova Scotia at the end of April.

The other artist of distinction survived the disaster, though he suffered the mild humiliation of having his name reported as 'Charette' in the *New York Times* and 'Cheveret' in the *Daily Sketch*. Paul Chevré escaped in lifeboat No. 7, the first boat away from the starboard side in which Dorothy Gibson and her mother sat. Although First Officer Murdoch was said by Archie Jewell (a lookout) at the British inquiry to have ordered women and children into the boat, nonetheless, 'three or four Frenchmen, passengers, got into the boat'. Mrs Dickinson Bishop at the inquiry complained that there were more male passengers than female in the boat, some of the men unmarried (in which case they had no business being there) and 'three or four of them foreigners', clearly an affront. She was on thin ice here, for her husband Dickinson was, she said, pushed into the boat along with her, whereas he testified that he fell in. He also said that he heard no order on the starboard side for men to stand back and women and children only to come forward. Chevré himself had told reporters that he had been forced to enter the lifeboat. In any case, he was saved along with his friends Pierre Maréchal, an aviator and son of a French admiral, and Fernand Omont, a businessman. Mrs Bishop told the *New York Times* that Monsieur Maréchal's monocle stayed in place until they were rescued by *Carpathia*, though whether this oddly graphic detail was reported in admiration of French *sang-froid* or disdain for French *amour propre* is not clear.

Chevré divided his time between an office in Quebec City where he obtained commissions and a studio in Paris where he executed them. He was travelling in the entourage of Charles M. Hays, President of the Grand Trunk Railway (later to become the Canadian National Railway). On the last evening of the voyage, Chevré played poker and drank with Maréchal, Clinch Smith (Gracie's pal who kept polo ponies and trotters), and Omont, the businessman from Le Havre. Nearby were Hays, Gracie, Clarence Moore and Major Butt. Chevré's patron was a significant figure. In its obituary, the *New York Times* quoted the Canadian Prime Minister Wilfrid Laurier's 1911 assessment of Hays as 'the greatest railroad genius in Canada'. Hays had convinced Laurier of the need for a second transcontinental railroad to break the monopoly of the Canadian Pacific, and Hays proposed to run it from Montreal to Prince Rupert on the west coast (Mt Hays outside that British Columbia port commemorates him). Grand Trunk Railway's majority shareholders were in England and Hays was returning from a meeting with them. He and his wife (and maid) were on board *Titanic* as the guests of Bruce Ismay, who happened to be a director of the London North Railway. On his return Hays was to have opened his new flagship hotel, the Chateau Laurier in Ottawa, on July 1. Making its way to New York on another ship, *La Bretagne*, was Chevré's huge marble bust of Laurier, destined for the chateau's lobby where according to Hustak it stands to this day.

Chevré's experience on the night of the sinking was variously and confusingly reported. In the *New York Times* of April 19, 'Charette' was quoted as knowing that the iceberg had sliced *Titanic* open the length of the keel, that the new watertight doors had failed to work properly, and that a German passenger had fired a pistol in the air to summon aid. The next day there was a more sensational account of Chevré's experiences in the Montreal *Herald* (Hustak tells the story), in which he suffered the loss of his Laurier bust and witnessed Captain Smith use a revolver on himself, having cried out 'My luck has turned!' On April 22, Chevré burst into the offices of *La Presse* to get them to set the record straight.

With his fellow survivors, Omont and Maréchal, Chevré cabled his story to a Paris paper, *Le Matin*, which the London *Times* and the *New York Times* picked up in translation. In it, the Frenchmen are quietly playing bridge (not poker) with Clinch Smith when a violent noise occurs. There is momentary panic which then subsides, and a nervous Captain Smith then takes charge. Half-filled boats depart because passengers are reluctant to leave the giant ship; Chevré and his fellows watch the ship sink without the expected suction, doing so from the vantage point of a lifeboat, but they neglect to explain how they came to be in the boat. The German baron firing his pistol is confirmed. Officers and crew are praised, and those, such as John Jacob Astor, who gave their lives to save women and children. 'What have we saved from the wreck?' they ask themselves. 'Omont has a hair-brush, Maréchal a book, "Sherlock Holmes" and Chevré nothing. We all three send to our families resurrection greetings, and it is with immense joy that we cry from this side of the Atlantic "À bientôt".'

Like Gracie, Chevré never truly recovered from the events of April 15. Having crossed the Atlantic twice a year for 14 years, he crossed but once more (and dreaded the prospect), home to France, and never sailed again. He died in 1914 at the age of 47. The monument to Samuel de Champlain (with Lecardonnel) in Quebec City, his sculptures 'Waking up of Flora' (1895) and 'Young Woman of Bacchanal' (1900), and the statue of Marianne in Viger Square in Montreal, are said to be noteworthy works by this Brussels-born son of French parents, who studied under Cavalier de Barrias and exhibited with the Society of French Artists from 1897 onwards.

One of the survivors who remembered the kindness shown to her by Francis Millet before she got away in boat No. 6 was the writer Helen Churchill Candee from Washington DC. She was returning from Paris where her son was recovering from an aeroplane accident (a novel misfortune in those days, as Lord remarks). It was feared by her friends that she had drowned and that it was a Mrs Kantor who had been saved, not, as the *New York Times* tentatively listed her on April 17, 'Mrs Cander'. Clambering into the lifeboat she broke one ankle, in Gracie's account, both her legs, in the *New York Times* account.

Candee, before she was taken off to hospital, recalled for reporters that all the women were saved except those such as Mrs Straus who gallantly (if mistakenly, one senses her saying to herself) preferred death with their husbands and that the men (including Astor) behaved nobly. 'The last she saw of the vessel was the sight of Mr. and Mrs. Straus standing on the upper deck, and until a few minutes before the end the band was playing.' Candee avoided the heightened realism of such accounts as Chevré's and seemed even as she was carried off *Carpathia* already to have tuned the music of what happened to a pleasant melody.

Her lengthiest reminiscence, a short story called 'Sealed Orders', published in *Collier's Weekly* on May 4, 1912, is a lightly fictionalised account of the shipwreck that tries through poetic effect to lift the disaster beyond pleasant melody to a high romance. It will be worth looking at again later in the book. Suffice it to say here that the lesson in 'Sealed Orders' is of the irresistible power of God, but also of the 'virility immortal' exhibited by the noble (first-class) men on board *Titanic*. Like 'Lucile', Candee enjoyed the company of attentive men – she was the centre of an admiring male circle in first class that included Archibald Gracie who styled himself her protector. In a short article in the *San Francisco Examiner* of April 20, Candee paid tribute to the heroism of Astor, Harris and Isidor Straus; Major Archibald Butt she too identified as among 'God's noblemen' who came selflessly to the aid of women and children.

Like Lady Duff Gordon, Candee combined the professional confidence of the 'New Woman' who emerged in the 1890s with the anti-feminist posture of what became known in the late twentieth century as the 'Real Woman'. Both were among those women who thought that to accept the chivalrous sacrifices of the men was to display a higher nature, not a weaker nature. Candee was the author of *How Women May Earn a Living* (1900), as well as *An Oklahoma Romance* (1901). She overcame her ordeal to enjoy the publication in 1912 of *The Tapestry Book* (popular enough to be published in Britain the following year and reprinted in 1935) and lived to visit and describe exotic places in *New Journeys in Old Asia* (1927). She survived until the age of 90.

Father Browne and 'Sherlock Holmes'

It is mildly ironic that Pierre Maréchal was reading Sherlock Holmes stories on the voyage and saved the book when he got off the ship, for he might have seen on board 'the American Conan Doyle', Jacques Futrelle. The detective writer was one of 'God's noblemen', as Candee defined them. 'Futrelle Refused to Enter Lifeboat', the *New York Times* headline said. 'His Wife Tells How He Parted With Her on Titanic, Commanding Her To Save Herself'. Mrs Henry B. (Renee) Harris said she saw Futrelle standing near her husband and Colonel Astor as her lifeboat was lowered. All three men were lost.

Futrelle had been a journalist with the *Boston Post* and *New York Herald* and a theatre manager before turning his hand to fiction; his first novel, *The Chase of the Golden Plate*, appeared in 1906. He studied Edgar Allan Poe's C. Auguste Dupin and Arthur Conan Doyle's Holmes and invented his own version of these two super-sleuths, Professor Augustus SFX Van Dusen, whom he introduced in book form in *The Thinking Machine* (1907), though stories of Van Dusen had appeared in such magazine's as TP O'Connor's *P.T.O.* Other crime novels followed: *The Simple Case of Susan*, *The Thinking Machine on the Case*, *Elusive Isabel* and *The Diamont Master*. The Professor's most famous case (a self-imposed problem of escape from a confined space) was 'The Problem of Cell 13', which combines the machine-like logic of Holmes (including the breaking of a code) with the actual machine-worship of HG Wells' scientific romances. How Van Dusen would have escaped from another, doomed space, the sinking *Titanic* denuded of lifeboats, must surely have at least flitted through his creator's mind. But then, Van Dusen represented pure mind in action without the cultural impediments of social value; chivalry was one code Futrelle could not break.

Moreover, it is possible that thoughts of escape did *not* occur to Futrelle or to any of the other gentlemen aboard. Indeed, practical thoughts of escape once it was realised that there were insufficient lifeboats – thoughts one would have imagined would intensify once the last of the lifeboats had gone – were not recorded even if they occurred. Gracie seems to have thought of fashioning a raft only when he was in the water. Given all that practical know-how on board (there were among the crew and passengers carpenters, engineers of several kinds – mechanical, marine, mining and electrical – painters, architects, bricklayers, farmers, miners, blacksmiths, tinsmiths, plumbers – all manner of men good with their hands), one is surprised that nothing more ingenious than lashing oneself to a door (in the case of one Japanese passenger) or throwing deck chairs overboard for swimmers to cling to (co-designer Thomas Andrews' contribution) appears to have been attempted. Clearly the culture of the time, at least as it expressed itself on board a giant sinking liner with various social classes uncomfortably juxtaposed in crisis, did not permit a Swiss Family Robinson or Robinson Crusoe reaction, even in the face of imminent and almost certain death. So perhaps after the boats left, Futrelle like many other men chose by cultural reflex heroic passivity over heroic action.

By coincidence, Futrelle's last and posthumous novel, *My Lady's Garter* (1912), included a shipwreck scene and Futrelle enthusiasts (for example, Seymour and Kyper) were moved by this to credit Futrelle with prophetic power – forgetting that Futrelle's mental 'science', like Wells', was opposed to prophecy as the gift of prescience, and accepting of prophecy only as the extrapolation of the real and empirical. Indeed, Van Dusen's strength like Holmes' lay in deduction, not in Wellsian induction. Here, as elsewhere, *Titanic* has imbued thought and event with a significance they would not otherwise have, rescuing and redeeming the ordinary into the numinous.

And then – then – there before his eyes came a great gushing flame from the placid bosom of the ocean; and with it a thunderous crash under his very nose, and the sea seemed to rise in a mass and envelop him. In one fraction of a second, he had seen the *Pyramid* leap clear of the water and turning, bow down, plunge into it again. The next thing Meredith remembered, he was in icy cold water, swimming. Von Derp was here beside him, and on the far side of the overturned dory were the two Boston

men. Gigantic waves flattened out placidly. Where the *Pyramid* had been
there was – nothing!

According to the *Daily Sketch* of April 17, 1912 Futrelle (though he
had tired of his detective as Doyle had of Holmes) had finished a new
series of lucrative Van Dusen stories during a stay in England and they
were bound for an American magazine. A recent anthology of
detective fiction edited by Douglas G. Greene claims there were four
such stories, and prints one of them, 'The Tragedy of the Life Raft'.
The story could make a stronger case for Futrelle's prescience than *My
Lady's Garter*. It concerns the murder of a ruthless businessman, Peter
Ordway, a man so successful that the richest man in America, the
great John Morton (a combined Astor and Rockefeller), had once
sought his aid. The murder is at first wholly mystifying (it is another
'closed room' puzzle) until Van Dusen ingeniously proves it to be the
result of a botched attempt by someone to make Peter Ordway make
good on a pledge made decades before on the cast-off lifeboat of the
sunken transatlantic liner *SS Neptune*. Ordway, it turns out, had
promised a fellow survivor a million dollars if he would toss overboard
the third survivor, thereby stretching their rations and increasing their
chances of being saved. Ordway reneged on the promise and his fellow
survivor has come to collect. Events on the raft might lightly echo
those on the raft of *Medusa* or, because of one word, the upturned
Titanic Engelhardt. A vision comes back to Ordway when he receives
the first anonymous demand, 'One million dollars!' 'Slowly, as he
looked, the sky became a lashing, mist-covered sea, a titanic chaos of
water; and upon its troubled bosom rode a life raft to which three
persons were clinging.' Twice more in the story Ordway remembers
this vision and the 'titanic' chaos of water.

Futrelle struck up shipboard acquaintance with an Irish priest who
explained to a confused author that, no, he wasn't watching France as
Titanic crossed the English Channel, but rather the Isle of Wight.
Frank Browne SJ was a keen photographer and snapped Futrelle
standing outside the ship's gymnasium, just one of many photographs
Browne took on the liner and one of 42,000 he took in his lifetime.
Browne's photographs of life on board *Titanic* are an essential part of
the ship's memory and his collection as a whole a notable British and
Irish cultural legacy.

Father Browne (sharing his name with GK Chesterton's ordained
detective) had sailed on *Titanic* from Southampton and disembarked
at Queenstown (Cobh) by an order of his Provincial Superior in
Dublin denying him permission to travel on to New York at the
generous expense of an American family. He was later to quip that it

was the only time Holy Obedience had saved a man's life. What Fr Browne did not live to know was that the great ship (as discovery of the wreck showed) broke in two as she slipped under the waves and that the line of severance cut through staterooms A36, occupied by Thomas Andrews, and A37, which belonged for two days to his fellow Irishman, Browne.

Father Browne recalled his time on *Titanic*, including the *New York* scare in Southampton, for *The Belvederian* for 1912, the annual magazine of Belvedere College in Dublin. Browne had attended Belvedere (where he was later to teach and found *The Belvederian* and the Camera Club) and then the Royal University, Dublin. At both institutions he was an exact contemporary and acquaintance of James Joyce, and in the Honours BA examinations in 1902, Browne beat the future great novelist both in English and in Latin. During World War One, the Irish religious orders were asked by the British Army to supply chaplains and Fr Browne joined the Irish Guards in 1916. He went to the front in France and Flanders and stayed there until the end of the war. He was five times a casualty and was gassed; he was awarded the Military Cross. His commanding officer, Colonel (later Field-Marshal Earl) Alexander – an Ulsterman of Scots stock – called Browne 'the bravest man I ever met' and remained a lifelong friend. A year after the war, Fr Browne met Rudyard Kipling, whose Irish

Fr Browne's photograph of Jacques Futrelle on Titanic

Fr Frank Browne SJ

Guardsman son was killed in action. Kipling (whom Browne photographed) pays tribute to the chaplain in his history of the Irish Guards in the war.

Although hardly comparable to James Joyce's or Rudyard Kipling's clutch of fictional masterpieces, Browne's *oeuvre* of photographs is formidable and his reputation as a documentary photographer, as a photo-reporter of both *Titanic* and the Great War, is growing, thanks to their select publication by a fellow Jesuit and Irishman, Fr EE O'Donnell.

Titanic Times

Fr Browne disembarked in Queenstown from a floating and temporary island of culture. It comes as a surprise to read what RA Fletcher told his readers in 1913. Every large steamer, he wrote, publishes:

> a daily newspaper on board with columns of news from the world's centres, and the latest important Stock Exchange quotations from London, Paris and New York .... On the big ships the wireless telegraphy room has a small apartment attached to it with thick walls and a double door, so as to be as sound-proof as possible. It is specially devoted to the reception of messages intended for the next day's paper. For some hours during the night the operator will receive messages for publication the following morning ... besides being a telegraphist, the operator has to know something of public affairs, and also be able to act as a journalist to the extent that he may have to sub-edit the telegrams in preparation for the following morning's paper.

The first newspaper printed on board ship was the *Transatlantic Times*, published on *St Paul* in 1899. The *Cunard Daily Bulletin* began in 1904. Geoffrey Marcus tells us that *Titanic* passengers would have read the *Atlantic Daily Bulletin*, a paper in magazine format, printed ashore before sailing, with news added day by day at sea.

> In addition to the news, the *Atlantic Daily Bulletin* contained articles of literary, artistic, and scientific interest, the latest social and theatrical

gossip from London and Paris, and a good many advertisements, together with the menu of the day's dinner, and the previous day's run. It was society and culture in capsule form. The *Atlantic Daily Bulletin* was eagerly sought after by the passengers and was considered very good value at several shillings a copy. The news appearing in its column was discussed at length in the smoking-room and on the promenade decks.

And what *was* the news of the world in which *Titanic* was fitted out, readied, manned and sailed? Both Britain and the United States were experiencing labour unrest during the Age of *Titanic*, and a lengthy, militant and costly coal strike in the former threatened to delay *Titanic*'s departure from Southampton and enveloped her sister ship *Olympic* before the waters over *Titanic* settled. The Labour-and-Class Question surfaced at likely moments in post-mortems on both sides of the Atlantic and in both the American and British inquiries. Many Americans, socialist or no, fastened on the possible class discrimination aboard a British ship during evacuation. Militant trades-unionists in Britain thought a vicious class antagonism had been practised on the sinking ship and Thomas Scanlan, the lawyer representing the National Sailors' and Firemen's Union, tried at the British inquiry to prove negligence by owners and officers at the expense of the crew. For the committed left in both countries, the ship herself was seen as the product of an exploitative capitalism.

The two English-speaking nations bound, as well as separated, by the North Atlantic were also asked the Woman Question (as it was often called) that joined the Labour Question to vex the entrenched sources of power. Its noisiest replies, by the questioners themselves – the smashing of windows by militant suffragettes, the rallies, the gaolings and forced feedings of prisoners – dominated much of the news in Britain in 1912. (It was less dominant in the United States where nevertheless a vocal feminism loudly asserted itself.) The Woman Question established itself as a context for *Titanic* as quickly as did the class issue. Indeed, the sinking ship on immediate hindsight became a floating arena in which the nature of gender equality was contested. Did male chivalry ('boats') render full suffrage ('votes') redundant or was it still an instrument to keep women from complete equality? Was the 'Women and Children First' rule welcome to feminists? Did events on board *Titanic* advance or retard the cause of female suffrage? Answers came pell-mell in letters, editorials, interviews and articles in the weeks after the disaster.

An equally vexing issue for the British was the Irish Question. Designed and built in Belfast, fitted out there and bade farewell from there, it was impossible that *Titanic* should escape embroilment in the heated politics of the island. *Titanic* was built by an overwhelmingly (but not exclusively) Protestant workforce intent like their co-religionists on retaining an unqualified British citizenship in defiance of the strenuous wishes of Irish nationalists, most of them Catholic. That the ship should founder during the crucial stages of the third Home Rule Bill's passage (the bill granted Canada-like autonomy to Ireland) is a coincidence to warm the heart of any cultural historian. Home Rule and the loss of *Titanic* shared tense headlines in Irish newspapers for weeks and many of those who built the ship promised armed resistance to the constitutional proposal, a resistance made unnecessary in the longer term by its own strength and by the outbreak of the Great War.

That war was engendering itself in 1912. The balance of military and political power in Europe maintained by the counterweights of the Triple Alliance (Germany, Austria and Italy) and the Triple Entente (Britain, France and Russia) was threatened by Russian behaviour in Persia and by French and German behaviour in Morocco. Germany had fared worse than her European competitors in the imperial scramble for territories and markets (and empire as we have seen posed one version of the Race Question) and a sense of grievance influenced her foreign policy. 'So long as Germany piles up armaments', Caryl Jordan wrote in June 1912, 'so long must England do likewise'. The race between Britain and Germany for supremacy in transatlantic passenger service barely concealed the commercial competition between them, behind which was the race for naval supremacy, begun around 1907 and heating up in 1912, lending the Blue Riband a faintly ominous significance. By 1910 an article entitled 'The Danger of an Anglo-German War' was not outrageously provocative. WT Stead tried hard to improve Anglo-German relations but at the same time launched a newspaper campaign to maintain British naval advantage: 'two keels to one!' was his muscular advice to the British government in the matter of shipbuilding.

From a British point of view, then, we can speak of a German Question. The Germans had fallen behind in transatlantic passenger service in part because they had underestimated the power of the Parsons marine turbine that Cunard used to propel its $24^1/_2$ knot liners, but then rallied themselves. Vast though *Olympic* and *Titanic* were, they were superseded by the German liner *Imperator*, launched on their heels (or sterns). On the eve of *Imperator*'s maiden voyage, James Armstrong in his article, 'The Mercantile Fight for the North Atlantic' (*The World's Work*, February 1913), outlined the past and summarised the present state of affairs, seeing hope for a British comeback in Cunard's *Aquitania* and White Star's *Britannic*. As it happened, the story of *Imperator* accounted for a considerable chunk of First World War naval history, since like *Olympic* it was recruited from peacetime passenger service into wartime military service.

Titanic was not built primarily as an immigrant ship, though it served as such and carried hundreds of would-be immigrants towards the New World. Many of those were Irish who boarded in Queenstown, but their presence had no British political significance and was not interpreted as having such. But since there were other ethnic groups on board and since race, as we have seen, figured in Anglo-American survivors' accounts, *Titanic* gave fresh impetus to the Race Question that taxed unattractively some of those survivors and often underlay international politics. But the chief significance of the immigrants on board *Titanic* was their illustration of the contemporary pattern of European relocation, in Stead's phrase, from the Old World to the New.

Titanic and the Sceptre of Power

The rapid growth of the United States was not only in population but in political, economic and military power and this caused friction in its relations with Europe from the late nineteenth century. One manifestation of American muscle-flexing was the reactivation from 1895 onwards of the 1823 Monroe Doctrine. This doctrine (which Secretary of State John Hay in 1901 declared 'the golden rule of American policy') preached that European powers had no political business in the western hemisphere, a doctrine which the first crisis in Venezuela (1895) helped to revivify. The American and British periodicals were enlivened in 1901 by energetic debate of the doctrine, and again in 1902 during the Alaska boundary dispute and the second Venezuela crisis. Economically the doctrine had its aggressive translation and in 1904 Theodore Roosevelt enshrined American interference in other sovereign states to protect commercial interests in the Corollary to the Monroe Doctrine. The United States was quickly developing the armed strength to impose its will even on Britain (which repeatedly deferred to its independent offspring) and from 1890 onwards was expanding its navy to the point of implicit challenge to British supremacy at sea; by 1906 (Dobson tells us) the US was ranked second after Britain in naval power.

In 1912 the issue was joined once more with an international crisis in Nicaragua and American intervention in Honduras (to protect railway properties). Opposition to the doctrine was growing in Europe, especially in Germany. In August 1912 the American Senate adopted a resolution forbidding indirect European footholds anywhere in the Americas and this was seen as an expansion of the Doctrine. In the face of Mexican 'anarchy' and European restiveness about the Doctrine, former President William Taft was moved to explain and defend the policy in December 1913 in the pages of *The Independent*. The hastiness of the American *Titanic* inquiry and the placing under virtual arrest of the ship's officers and crew seemed to some Britons to be a small-scale application of the Monroe Doctrine.

As the sceptre of power crossed the Atlantic from east to west, surplus wealth crossed from west to east, exchanging wealth for culture. For well-off Americans, the luxury liner was a shuttle between the New World origins of their wealth and the Old World occasions for their enjoyment of it. During the Age of *Titanic*, wealthy Americans with class pretensions spent a lot of their time in Europe, especially Britain, especially London, living like upper-class Britons and enjoying the same culture. Many first- and second-class passengers on *Titanic* were returning Americans: there were at least 33 distinguished Philadelphians alone on board. Geoffrey Marcus has re-created for us in *The Maiden Voyage* (1969) the European destinations of the American rich and the kind of culture they sampled – the favoured resorts, clubs and hotels, the plays, dance performances, sporting events and spectacles they went to see in 1911 and 1912.

The arts and entertainment offered to first-class *Titanic* passengers were transatlantic, aimed at Britons and Americans at the level on which they shared them, for in terms of culture that could not be bought or transported but merely enjoyed, there was a good deal of mutuality and reciprocity in the American and British ways of life, and more at the higher reaches of society. Despite the diplomatic tensions between Britain and America, there was widespread belief in a cultural amity, if not unity, that rested upon a common Anglo-Saxon civilization. This was the wellspring of Winston Churchill's pride in what happened aboard the sinking *Titanic*. Gilbert quotes a letter Churchill wrote to his wife from the Admiralty in London: 'The Titanic disaster is the prevailing theme here. The story is a good one. The strict observance of the great traditions of the sea towards women & children reflects nothing but honour upon our civilization.' Two days later he wrote again:

> The whole episode fascinates me. It shows that in spite of all the inequalities and artificialities of our modern life, at the bottom – tested to its foundations, our civilization is humane, Christian & absolutely democratic. How differently Imperial Rome or Ancient Greece wd have settled the problem.

Churchill of course had personal reasons of kinship for viewing the *Titanic* disaster in an Anglo-American perspective. It was Anglo-Saxon civilization, the society of the English-speaking peoples, that he was extolling, and it is true that in those days there was a great deal of respectful mutuality in the lifestyle of Britons and Americans. It would be odd to find today a cricket-loving American colonel resident in the United States, but such Archibald Gracie was. He recalled the racquet professional on board *Titanic*, Fred Wright, with whom he had played cricket, Gracie's favourite game, and which he credited with his physical development, which stood him in good stead when he abandoned ship. (Wright was lost.) One of the Philadelphians, John B. Thayer, was also a cricketer. (One imagines that in those days upper-crust Americans spoke with less of a twang than their descendants; you can hear *their* contemporaries and children in movies of the 1930s, speaking rather like upper-class English men and women.)

American heiresses took to marrying British aristocrats, some of them less than well off and glad to trade lineage and title for beauty and a robust bank account. The three sisters whom Gracie sought to protect during the evacuation (Mrs Appleton, Cornell and Brown) were returning from Europe where they had buried a fourth sister, Lady Victor Drummond, no doubt one such American heiress who had become a British noblewoman. In *Titanic: The Full Story of a Tragedy* (1986), Michael Davie, in the context of the ship, remarks on some of the cross-Atlantic upper-class friendships and marriages that wove Britons and Americans together. Many on both sides of the Atlantic, but perhaps rather more on the British side, encouraged Anglo-American friendship. This is not surprising given the entwined histories of the two countries, but friendship went beyond mere feeling. Conan Doyle went to the United States in October 1894 and the summer before he went he said in an interview, 'I have always longed to see America, and I have always longed to see a warmer friendship between the two great nations of the English-speaking race. There is no subject on which I take so keen an interest.' He resented what he saw as the attempt by the press to drive a wedge between these two natural allies and kin. Some time after his American trip, Doyle wrote to Major James Pond who organised Doyle's lecture tour: 'Has not the Anglo-American *entente cordiale* which I preached when I was in the States grown since 1894? It is the best and healthiest sign in the waning century'.

When Rudyard Kipling (a no-nonsense writer and practical man of the world of the kind Doyle liked) made some anti-American noises to drown out the anti-British noises Doyle admitted were coming from the United States, Doyle wrote to Kipling in reproof. Doyle was a self-proclaimed 'passionate believer in Anglo-American union' and feared that Kipling was pouring oil on flames (*Memories and Adventures*). Doyle told Bram Stoker that when he was in America 'a strong wave of anti-British feeling was passing over the country' which saddened him.

If Doyle's belief in Anglo-American cultural unity was in part a sentimental affair – he told Stoker that he had come away from America 'with a deep admiration for both the country and the people, and much touched by all the kindness and even affection' which he had encountered – his belief was also a geopolitical agenda, albeit a simple one: Anglo-American friendship was a prudent thing. Stead's interest in the matter was more complexly geopolitical: the ongoing 'Americanization of the world' (the title of his 1902 book) made an English-speaking union all the more urgent.

From the other side of the Atlantic a partnership seemed more attractive than a union, since the US required no such union to reinforce its power. When John Jacob Astor predicted events until the close of the twentieth century, and did so from the same year Doyle visited America, he was presumably engaging in wishful thinking. He foresaw in *A Journey in Other Worlds* (1894) a hard-headed partnership having evolved, with the English-speaking peoples dominating half the globe and doing so through the partnership of North America (the US having absorbed Canada) and the British Empire. In 2000 AD things look rosy, 'all danger of war being removed by the Canadian change' and healthy competition having taken its place. There were political observers who pointed out (the chief editorial writer for the *New York Journal* did so in 1901) that Anglo-American relations were indeed endangered by 'the unfortunate situation of Canada' that prevented the Unites States from having the clear hegemony over the western hemisphere that would ensure peace. In 'How America Really Feels Towards England', Samuel E. Moffett reported to English readers of *The Nineteenth Century and After* that Americans were pro-Boer, vexed by British intervention in Nicaragua and Venezuela, and irritated by the Britishness of Canada: he dubbed the last 'the Canadian question'.

So there were several motivations behind the nurturing of Anglo-American union, one of them being the desire to ease the tensions that existed between the two nations. Those tensions were peculiarly exacerbated less by the presence in America of thousands of influential and disaffected Irish than by the historic nature of the British-American relationship and its basis in colonialism, paternalism and filial rebellion. Now geopolitical developments made the easing of the tensions rather urgent. In the early years of the twentieth century the British were trying to ally themselves with the USA through racial identity in order to distinguish themselves from, and counterbalance the power of, Germany. Pride in Anglo-Saxonism and the call for English-speaking union often disguised a geopolitical and perhaps ethnic xenophobia. I believe the English-speaking races', wrote Doyle,

> must either coalesce, in which case the future of the world is theirs, or else they will eternally neutralize each other and be overshadowed by some more compact people, as the Russians or the Chinese.

We have already seen how the events on board *Titanic* seemed to some to illustrate the necessity of a mutual Anglo-Saxon front to preserve civilization and express the highest values of the culture.

TIME TO GET BUSY

—*St. Louis Republic.*

St Louis Republic cartoon: American impatience at European bungling in the transatlantic shipping trade betrayed shifting power relations.

But the United States did not always behave as though she needed such cultural union, or even amity, with Britain. Events after *Titanic* went down refreshed and refocused UK–US frictions. The British were shocked and dismayed by the punctuality of the American hearings into the loss of *Titanic*. American response occurred at government level without official consultation with those in power in Britain. American determination to keep British officers and crew in the United States against their will if need be stung Britons. The vindictiveness with which American newspapers uttered Bruce Ismay's name – J. *Brute* Ismay in some quarters – is one of the familiar epilogues of the *Titanic* drama. The British public allowed their objective consideration to be sidelined by national pride. Under normal circumstances they might have been expected to come down hard on Ismay themselves but when he returned to Liverpool after his inquisition he was cheered by well-wishers at the pier, having become a conduit for mutual British-American resentment. British commentators had attempted to discredit the US Senate hearings by belittling their chairman, Senator Alden Smith, accusing him of gaffes and stupidities; but 'Smithisms' were fewer than his British enemies imagined and in fact he was a patient and courteous inquisitor.

One of the distinguished (naturalized) Britons smarting at American insouciance was the eminent novelist, Joseph Conrad. In his article for the *English Review* of May 1912, he protested against 'these Bumble-like proceedings' carried out needlessly by a US Senate who aped demi-gods in what he saw in reality as their 'provincial display of authority', revealing their ignorance of ships and shipping, and engaging in the 'ruffianly abuse' of the hapless Bruce Ismay. On one level he affected indignation as an 'effete' European, but on another he was genuinely insulted as were many of his English compatriots by the insolence of another country questioning the actions and behaviour of Englishmen, particularly Englishmen belonging to a proud professional tradition 'why an officer of the British merchant service should answer the questions of any king, emperor, autocrat or senator of any foreign power (as to an event in which a British ship alone was concerned, and which did not even take place in the territorial waters of that power) passes my understanding'.

Conrad overlooked the fact that the ship was, in the end, American despite its British registration, management and crew, and that it carried many more Americans of influence and importance than it did influential and important Britons. The illusions and realities of northern hemispheric power, including the superficies of

English social graciousness which concealed the fact of American financial potency, and the dynamics of exchange and supersession going on in 1912, were wonderfully represented on and by *Titanic*.

Another distinguished English writer knew that what he called the 'cross-criticisms' between Britain and America unleashed by the US *Titanic* inquiry were caused by the cross-currents of British-American power, with the tide turning in America's favour. As a result, GK Chesterton gazed at the American inquiry with a cooler eye than Conrad could cast. In his *Illustrated London News* column on May 4, 1912, he expressed sympathy with British impatience (and more) with Senator Alden Smith and the way American newspapers were baying after Ismay, but reminded English readers that whereas American newspapers could be vulgar and vindictive and often hunted their quarry as a pack, the English 'national evil' was to hush everything up and damp it down. He put words into the mouth of an imaginary educated American addressing the British: 'I know you and your gentlemanly privacies and hypocrisies. You will shirk this inquiry into the *Titanic* tragedy, just as you shirked the inquiry into the Jameson Raid.' (Lord Mersey, Wreck Commissioner for the British inquiry, had been a member of the Jameson Raid committee of investigation that cleared the government of the accusation that it had been involved in a Cecil Rhodes-inspired conspiracy to instigate a rising against President Kruger of the Transvaal.) Chesterton advised fellow Britons not to despise that which hardly existed in the UK: an impatient, inquisitive, often ferocious Public Opinion that he assured his readers has its uses.

Chesterton interpreted the transatlantic frictions over the *Titanic* hearings as worrisomely symptomatic of British misunderstanding of the US, following hard on the heels of British misunderstanding of France and Ireland, misunderstandings now being righted. He began his column by sensing a ruinous coming crisis in US–UK relations, one being facilitated by British blindness to those real differences between the two countries obscured by the shared language. (Chesterton appears to have anticipated Churchill's famous remark that Americans and Britons are divided by a common language.) Were the British not careful, the *Titanic* hearings could become both cause and symptom of a deepening of the misunderstanding. 'We are in danger of getting at fatal cross-purposes with the great nation called the United States.' The danger was increased by the fatuous assumptions of racial and political unity and amity.

> For this reason, I am inclined to think that it might not be altogether a matter of regret if such phrases as 'the Anglo-Saxons', 'Blood Thicker

than Water', 'Hands across the Herring Pond' and all the rest of it, had
gone to the bottom of the sea with the great ship that was their symbol.

In that symbolic regard (and in that regard only), loss of *Titanic* was
abstractly no bad thing.

One expanding difference between the countries was the alarming
wealth of the United States, concentrated in a few hands. The riches
of Andrew Carnegie, John D. Rockefeller, JP Morgan, William K.
Vanderbilt and a handful of others were such that 'the best use of great
wealth' became a topic of debate. At the turn of the century it was
arranged by an American Joint Stock Company for every voter in the
UK to receive a pamphlet and questionnaire asking him to suggest the
most beneficent ways in which Carnegie could spend his money
philanthropically: 8,000,000 were asked, 11,000 returned 45,000
suggestions. Carnegie had already given bountifully in the United
States. American capital in the Age of *Titanic*, an age of plutocracy,
was surplus to the purchase of goods from abroad, and one editorial
writer, almost certainly WT Stead, feared in 1901 that since America
produced almost everything it needed, capital was crossing the
Atlantic to be invested in British enterprises, requiring the remittance
of that capital to be returned in the other direction. More and more,
American machinery was driving transportation in the old country.
The nineteenth century was the Steam Age and belonged to England.
The twentieth century would be the Electric Age and belong to
America. 'Will the New World Buy up the Old?' the editorial writer in
the *Review of Reviews* anxiously wondered.

His anxiety was stimulated by the Morgan combination's purchase
of the British Leyland steamship line (the notorious *Californian* that
caused such waves during the *Titanic* hearings was a Leyland vessel)
which made British journalists 'shudder at the thought of the
tyrannous power of American capital'. He was afraid that in the new
financial way of things, the appearance of British ownership after
American takeover would be maintained like a façade. For example,
the Leyland steamers would continue to fly the British flag but behind
the unchanged exterior American control would exercise itself. A
decade later, *Titanic* was more or less in the position of the Leyland
steamer, and the ambiguity of the exterior and the hidden confused
and angered many Britons.

The writer wondered if the Americans, there being little
industrially on offer in Britain, 'will buy up England itself'. Already, he
warned:

> we see this process going on in the purchases of the famous country seats
> in the old country by wealthy Americans. Mr Astor, by the might of his

millions, supplants the Duke of Westminster at Cleveland. Mr Carnegie
establishes himself at Skibo. Mr Phipps, of the Carnegie firm, succeeds
Lord Lytton at Knebworth.

As it is with palaces and castles, he lamented, so it is likely to be in an
ever-increasing ratio with titles and all manner of 'bric-à-brac'. Yet
oddly (and the oddity proves Stead's authorship), the writer, against
the run of argumentative play, ends on an exhortatory and even
optimistic note, not just by observing that 'it will take some time
before all the treasure trove of centuries goes up the spout to pay our
debts to the New World' but also by encouraging his fellow Britons to
'start in and hustle round' for fear of being left without a foothold on
the slopes of the modern Olympus. Truly, Stead's take on the American
Titanic inquiry would have been fascinating had he lived. One imagines
that it would have been a more strenuous and outspoken version of
Chesterton's. He would no doubt have registered dismay at American
procedure and then wholeheartedly pitched in to try to sway events
more in favour of British sensibilities and sensitivities.

Some of the costly 'bric-a-brac' Stead – if it was he – referred to
was on *Titanic* on its way to the New World. Certainly, as in the case
of the latest Paris fashions, such bric-a-brac was an extension of
European cultural power. In the cases of the Omar Khayyam and the
Bacon essays – irreplaceable or extremely rare items – it could be said
that products of European culture were simply being relocated without
loss of their essential provenance. However, the *volume* of cultural
transfer from Europe to America suggested an exchange of the *settings*
and *contexts* of culture (for which *Titanic* was a vehicle) with a
significance beyond mere relocation in new libraries and galleries.

British reportage of *Titanic*'s on-board culture betrayed a tone that
implied as such. Of the Omar Khayyam, the London *Daily Telegraph*
remarked that it was to have gone to America on April 6 (the coal-
strike delayed its departure from Britain) 'in all probability to swell the
library of some wealthy American collector, a fitting addition to
splendour of adornment'. It was reported in error by the London *Daily
Mirror* on April 17 that the Philadelphian millionaire PA Widener,
Harry's grandfather, had been a passenger on *Titanic*; this enabled the
paper to retail an interesting story about a man:

> known in London chiefly as the purchaser of 'The Mill' – Rembrandt's
> picture about which there was so much talk a little time ago. Mr. Widener
> has for long been a great traveller. His interest in art, though recent, was
> as enthusiastic as that of many another millionaire. Already his collection
> of fine pictures is well known to the connoisseurs. It may be remembered
> [the writer adds with a tincture of acid] that, some time ago, he purchased

from Genoa certain celebrated Van Dycks in defiance of the Italian law aimed against the exportation of such things.

This was seen as an age of predatory American collecting, with art and books crossing the Atlantic as cultural emblems of the east-west passage of political, economic and military power. In February, 1912, the *Illustrated London News* devoted an illustrated feature to the transfer to the United States of the Pierpont Morgan Loan Collection at South Kensington: £600,000 worth of art treasures. These might have been Morgan's and Morgan might after all be an American, but the passage of European artifacts across the Atlantic ('lost to England') seemed to Britons all too darkly familiar and symbolic.

Endnotes

1   It must remain unconfirmed that an opera was performed aboard *Titanic*. In 1984 a librarian in the National Library of Canada wrote to Solomon Goodman in Long Island City, NY, in reply to his request for details of any *Titanic* music held by the NLC. Goodman had supplied additions to the list compiled by Joseph C. Hickerson (Head of the Archive of Folk Song in the Library of Congress, Washington DC) of '*Titanic* disaster music', i.e. music composed in response to the sinking. (This list, and the letter in question, reposes as an archive, Titanic *Disaster Music* in the American Folklife Center, Library of Congress.) The Canadian librarian had no fresh material to report but added an intriguing footnote to the effect that a colleague had told her that Smareglia's 'ill-fated' opera *Le Nozze Istriane* had been played on board the even iller-fated liner on its last evening afloat. I contacted her colleague in 1999 who told me that the work would have had to be performed 'in some re-orchestrated pit form' and directed me to the *Enciclopedia Italiana de Scienze, Lettere ed Arti* (1929–39). I can alas find no printed connection between Antonio Smareglia's opera (premiered in Trieste in 1895) and *Titanic*. The connection between one rumour-encrusted work and a rumour-encrusted vessel must itself remain a rumour. However, it is almost sufficient consolation to find out that Smareglia (1854–1929) was fascinated by the sea and in 1903 wrote an opera called *Oceana* (La Scala that year) and in 1911 one called *The Abyss* (La Scala, 1914). The literary work on which Smareglia based *The Abyss* was written by Silvio Benco (1874–1949), author of *James Joyce in Trieste* (1930).

2   A fuller report of Widener and the little Bacon has recently appeared: Nicholas A. Basbanes, *A Gentle Madness: Bibliophiles, Bibliomanes, and the Eternal Passion for Books* (1995).

seven

Imagining *Titanic*

The Medium and the Message

The distinction between the reality of the *Titanic* disaster and its imagining was blurred when the actress, Dorothy Gibson, a survivor, wore the dress she had worn in the lifeboat when she was filmed for scenes in *Saved from the Titanic*, an American dramatic re-enactment that reached its first picture-house before a full month had elapsed since the liner struck the iceberg. But in fact, for some the imagining of the tragedy began *almost simultaneously with its happening*. Of the sinking, one woman survivor recalled that 'it all seemed like a play, like a drama that was being enacted for entertainment, it did not seem real'. Fellow-passengers, after all, had the appearance of a holiday crowd, some in casual dress, some in tuxedos or evening gowns; Mrs Stengel wore a kimono, Officer Charles Lightoller wore a jumper and trousers over pyjamas; J. Bruce Ismay wore carpet slippers while he impatiently shepherded starboard passengers into the lifeboats; Lady Duff Gordon and other first-class ladies dressed as finely as they could manage, perhaps believing that entering the lifeboats was an unnecessary and merely temporary inconvenience which they may as well turn into a fashion opportunity.

At first it must have seemed to the observant like casual comedy, carnival almost. The three rescued Frenchmen, Maréchal, Omont and Chevré, told their Paris readers (and in translation, readers of the London *Times*) that 'when our boat had rowed about half a mile from the vessel the spectacle was quite fairylike. The Titanic, which was illuminated from stem to stern, was perfectly stationary, like some fantastic piece of stage scenery.' In this, the ship was merely fulfilling its daylight promise of theatrical unreality.

But then the carnival grew ghoulish and the motley and casual comedy began turning into the makings of tragedy. Points of view diverged. Those in the lifeboats could afford to register the impressive spectacle of the illuminated sloping liner in a calm starry night, though I find the Frenchmen's remarks in doubtful taste.[1] Those still on board had no such luxury – all became foreground for them;

humanity shrank from a reassuring company into one's vulnerable and frightened self. There were no aesthetics, metaphors or long gaze save for the exceptionally brave, composed and prepared. Only those who survived by swimming or paddling or clambering aboard the overturned Engelhardt could later share the point of view of the lost with those safe in the lifeboat or far away on land.

As we know, it was the long view that triumphed in the representation of the *Titanic* disaster. The lost knew before their death that this was no theatrical illusion or mere spectacle. But commentators appealing to less cultivated tastes early resumed the crudely aesthetic perspective. The editorialist in the *Daily Mirror* of April 17 saw in the tragedy a sensation that outdid the romance writers at their own game: it was one of the 'true romances'. In its account of the career of the late Thomas Andrews, the *Belfast News-Letter* of April 20 described what happened as 'a disaster that has *thrilled* and startled the world' (my italics). Joseph Conrad came to detest 'the false, written-up, Drury Lane aspects' of the event which he saw as 'neither drama nor melodrama'.

But in fact it was inexorably turned into both drama and melodrama and in a huge variety of artistic and sub-artistic forms, to such an extent that serious artists seemed chary of tackling it as a subject for serious work. After all, from the point of view of the 'audience' (and it was millions strong, thanks to newspapers), the sinking was, despite what Conrad and George Bernard Shaw insisted, a moving and even terrifying dramatic occasion, the real time of which was roughly that of a theatrical performance. The evacuation of the fortunate and the abandonment of the unfortunate abounded with stories and anecdotes, and the whole assumed a terrible shape that we can only call tragedy, even when we keep in mind how that word can be debased. What happened struck a deep bass chord in many. As much in the body of Anglo-American society as in the individual reader, some kind of catharsis was at work as in all true tragedy.

But even in the early responses to the *Titanic* sinking there were alert sensibilities at work. Just as the technical majesty of *Titanic* and other such ships inspired experts and informed journalists in their prose anatomies, so the sinking in its own awful majesty inspired instant prose impressions. Despite the speed at which reports had to be written and filed, the best reportage of the time has an unfamiliar stylistic composure that must have derived from the reporters' education in the tradition of the English essay and English drama. Reporters for the *New York Times*, for example, gave themselves – and must have been permitted to do so – broad elbow-room: setting the scene, reproducing dialogue, re-creating a dramatic intensity generated by the grief of relatives of the missing, by the relief of relatives of the saved, by the commotion and clamour around the White Star offices in New York, by the tense and interminable waiting as *Carpathia* maintained a stubborn silence as she steamed towards New York with survivors.

On Tuesday April 16, the *New York Times* carried a report indifferently entitled 'Women Sob as News Bulletins Appear' but that described in a dignified and stylish way the human congregations in Times Square of the evening before. Bulletins early in the evening announced that *Titanic* was under tow to Halifax with her passengers safe, but later bulletins changed their tune and bewildered New Yorkers. 'Some of them stopped as if transfixed as they caught sight of the bulletin declaring the Titanic had gone down and all on board except the women and children had been lost.' From about a hundred earlier watchers 'the crowd in Times Square sprang within fifteen minutes to something over 4,000'. The medium was somehow confusing the message:

> With the synchronized bulletin machines flashing the news to immense throngs north and east of the Times Building on three separate bulletin boards, and to another throng far down-town from another bulletin board, all operated from a single centre, the spectators realized that they were receiving news of an overwhelming event in a manner that only a little time ago was unthought of.

The message was new in its enormity as well as its medium but provoked reactions as old as people, as old as drama, and the reporter recaptured some of them as impressive vignettes:

> Conversations, sometimes half hysterical, sometimes filled with sobbing, were heard on every side. Many women, when asked why they were crying, said they had no relatives aboard and no reason to sob except that the bulletins overcame them. Above the hum of conversation occasional phrases were caught indicating the tense strain which every one felt .... Two men and a woman came to the bulletin board together and crowded close to the front of the throng. The woman screamed as she read the bulletins and the men brought her inside the Times Building. One of the men said the woman was his sister and that relatives were aboard the Titanic. The man remained calm for a few minutes, then, rushing to William J. Masse, who was printing THE TIMES bulletins on the machine that was sending them to all the bulletin boards simultaneously, he shouted: 'How dare you – how dare you say they're all lost now when they were saying all day they were all saved? How dare you do it?' Refusing to give his name, he seized the woman by the arm and led her back into the crowd.

Another exchange was turned into a notable vignette in the *New York Times* of the following day. According to the reporter, the White Star Line offices in Bowling Green were under siege by grief-stricken relatives of *Titanic* passengers, including Vincent Astor, son of John Jacob and who was described as almost hysterical from grief and willing to give all the money that could be asked for if he only had news of his father's safety. (He soon after inherited $87 million, an astounding sum in 1912 terms.) Another distraught relative provided the reporter with a dramatic moment. One of the first men to appear at the company offices was Edward Frauenthal who had two brothers on *Titanic*.

> When he was told that his brothers' names appeared on the Carpathia's list of survivors Mr. Frauenthal was so overcome that he hardly could walk to the telephone to send the good news to his home. In a voice that was scarcely audible to those near him he called his home number. When Mrs. Frauenthal answered he broke down and sobbed. 'I tell you they are saved!' he cried in a hoarse voice. 'Yes! yes! They are safe! Do you hear what I say?' The telephone receiver fell from his hand and Mr. Frauenthal sank to the floor, completely overcome by the good news. Helped to his feet, he turned to the reports. 'Young men', he said in a broken voice, 'pardon me, but I could not help it. My nerves are all unstrung'.

The *San Francisco Examiner* reporter in his April 16 despatch, '1,500 Perish on Liner Titanic', had one eye on the tragedy and the other eye on another kind of new technology from that of the bulletin boards but upon which those boards were dependent, a technology that was both marvellous and unforgiving. This too was a finely written report, taut, expectant and controlled (with syntax we do not find in even the best newspapers nowadays) and yet spacious like the seas which remained up to then newsless:

> After the first desperate calls of the Titanic for help had been sent flying through space and brought vessels for hundreds of miles around speeding to the scene, what seems to have been an impenetrable wall of silence was raised between New York and the ocean .... Along the entire Atlantic coast, wireless instruments were attuned to catch from any source the slightest whisper of hope that possibly one of the many steamships which rushed to the assistance of the Titanic bore other survivors. But from the ships reported to be at or near the scene of what, viewed in the light of the possibilities, may be recorded as the world's greatest marine horror, came not the slightest syllable of encouragement to the anxiously waiting world .... At every wireless station on the Atlantic Coast from New York to Cape Race, wireless operators are bending over their wireless instruments feeling for the marvelous Hertzian waves that will bring

further details of the catastrophe. The stations, which are faithfully recording every piece of information that comes from the deep, hear nothing.

The speed at which the events were taken in and described for readers (and described almost as if the events being reported were already historical) was impressive in the great newspapers, and, dependent as despatches were on telegraphy by 1912, puts one in mind of the 'wireless imagination' that Marinetti encouraged into existence. But the times were out of joint. These reports capture wonderfully the human bemusement that results from the inadequacy of otherwise tremendous technology in the face of age-old calamity, that results indeed from the failing attempt to divert intense emotion away from the calamity and its implications to the means by which news of the calamity can be received and processed. Men are at check, and somehow it is a defining moment in the Age of *Titanic*.²

When *Carpathia* finally docked at New York, among the reporters gathered to greet her was Henry Arthur Jones. Jones was a distinguished playwright; indeed he had been the most popular English playwright of the 1890s, writing comedies and plays of social theme, such as the double standard of behaviour expected of men and women, a theme that the *Titanic* sinking brought into high focus. Jones filed his report, 'Arrival Scenes on New York Pier', with the *Daily Telegraph* on Friday April 19 and it appeared on April 20. *Carpathia* had docked on Thursday evening after days when 'the wildest rumours gained credence of fearful scenes, of panic, of injuries, of widely-spread pneumonia, and of dementia amongst those who had been rescued'. Jones cap-tures the sensation of aftermath, of epilogue, in the interminable docking of the ship and the slow disembarkation of survivors.

Survivors on the deck of Carpathia

But it is still a dramatic re-creation, the first hint of which is his early reference to leading New York 'citi-zenesses' who met the ship on a relief mission: 'Amongst those who had come on this errand of mercy was the beautiful and graceful

figure whom English and American playgoers will always
affectionately remember as Eleanor Robson'. Robson (1879–1979),
the English-born American actress for whom George Bernard Shaw
wrote *Major Barbara* (1905), had left the stage in 1910 on her marriage
to August Belmont, a widowed banker who owned the Belmont racing
stables. She became active in the Metropolitan Opera Guild and
threw herself into charitable organisations, including the American
Red Cross. Henry Arthur Jones's name occurs among the
correspondents listed among the Eleanor Robson Belmont Papers
lodged with Columbia University in the City of New York.

From pier-side, Jones tells off the arriving survivors as if they were
a troop of exhausted players, all with stories, and together composing
the human procession. His eye is that of the casting director and the
dramatist.

> Had they not for the last three days filled our imaginations like those who
> had been present and had escaped from some great battle in the past?
> Every figure, every face seemed to be remarkable, while it was passing.
> One face had a startled, frightened look, a look that seemed as if it would
> always be there. Another had a set and staring gaze. Another showed an
> angry rebellious desperation. This one was dazed; the next one seemed as
> though it had upon it some shadow of the dread event …. Another
> woman came down, giving hurried and anxious glances on all sides. She
> uttered a great cry of joy, burst from her friends, and fell into the arms of
> a man who rushed up the line to met her. They kissed each other again
> and again, and uttered extravagant, delighted cries as they staggered
> together down the line in each other's arms, quite unconcerned and
> unconscious of those around.

At length, Jones seeks the meaning of this coming into harbour of the
distressed, of the saved with their memories of the drowned. It is a
Victorian meaning, perhaps, expressed as by some Greek chorus.

> It is only in transcendental calamity, in war, in famine, in pestilence, in
> tempests that shake and rend a State – it is only in these transcendent
> calamities that the heart of man can show itself possessed of a yet more
> transcendent courage, and in face of them all can steadily keep its
> undaunted way.

Ephemera to Remember

As literature, as the written word worth preserving, despite their usual
classification as ephemera, these reactions to the *Titanic* disaster in the
pages of newspapers strike me as being as good as any later, more
pondered reactions. The catastrophe has freshly impressed itself.

Settled or dogmatic opinions have not yet arrived. Those came very soon after. As we know, hundreds of sermons were delivered throughout the Western and English-speaking world on the Sunday following the sinking. The *Belfast News-Letter* in its Monday April 22 issue, reported on the services that took place in the churches around the north of Ireland and gave lengthy precis of the chief sermons delivered in Belfast. These were considerable efforts, and the spoken word here appears at its most deliberated, in the sermonisers' hopes, one imagines, of their words' rising above the weekly Sabbath ephemera. Either *News-Letter* reporters fanned out across the province, or ministers sent copies of their sermons to the newspaper (the texts are in indirect rather than direct speech). Either way, they are proof of the substantiality of Edwardian sermons in times of spiritual crisis, which is clearly how the *Titanic* disaster was interpreted by men of the cloth.

The mission of the Sunday sermon is to remind the congregation of Christian tenets and to shepherd them back into the fold of right Christian thinking, but both the tenets and the opportunities for rhetoric are sufficiently various to allow the sermon to participate in an oral and written tradition while at the same time allowing individual talent among preachers to show itself. One would hear such sermons nowadays as rarely as one would read daily newspaper reports as well-written as those in the *New York Times*. The Age of *Titanic* was a more eloquent (if not more generally literate) age than our own.

Rev. John Pollock (St Enoch's, Belfast), for example, delivered a sharply focused homily. He convincingly re-created the last minutes of the great ship for purposes of grim irony.

> Her stern, holding the largest piece of metal ever cast, rose perpendicular against the stars, light still gleaming from every porthole. Then an awful rumbling sound was heard, and the lights flickered and went out. The ship's engines, the largest and heaviest in the world, had broken loose and gone smashing through the vessel ....

Then he sprang his trap and indulged in the lavish rhetoric of retribution.

> 'Titanic' forsooth! The very name breathed the spirit of human self-conceit, the pride that cometh before a fall. How devils must laugh, and angels weep, at the bombastic impertinence! And they were all parties to it. None of them ever found fault with the name. But did not the catastrophe condemn their blind conceit, their sinful pride? The great Queen's Island plates of steel torn, as one had pithily put it, 'as with a gigantic can-opener!' ... Oh, the irony of it! 'Let him that thinketh he standeth take heed lest he fall!'

Rev. RM Ker (Grosvenor Hall, Belfast) took as his text Psalm 39:9, 'I was dumb – I opened not my mouth because Thou dids't it' and delivered a sermon that deserves preservation amid the literature of *Titanic*. He recalled their dumb impatience as they imagined the wireless operators sending out 'their mute appeals hither and thither across the ocean'; their dumb grief when it became known 'that the wonderful liner which some of them helped to build, which most of them saw launched, which was the pride of Belfast, and one of the wonders of the twentieth century, had sunk, her first voyage never completed, a mass of ruin'. He noted the imperfection of speech for the expression of sympathy and loss and the way the nations in the face of the calamity 'had been awed and silenced by its terribleness'. Ker saw what certain writers and thinkers of the time had been seeing and saying:

> They were living in an age of transition; they had passed away from their standing ground in the old; they were not yet sure of their place in the new. They had a new theology, a new astronomy, a new chemistry, a new biology, and there were those who told them that all that had wiped out their old-fashioned belief about the soul.

But their pessimism over the 'gospel of materialism' had been 'rebuked and silenced' by the tragedy. The accusations of decadence had likewise been rebuked – the heroism of the final scenes of the tragedy had 'silenced the statement on their lips and rebuked the shortsightedness which tempted them to make it'.

Ker's sermon, while maintaining the text of the dumbstruck, impressively registers certain tensions and cross-currents that characterise the Age of *Titanic*. He ends by acknowledging the unfathomable mystery of God's ways (the ship's loss we can understand – but the passengers'?) and offers only the consolation of death's democracy ('all classes of society, all creeds of religion, and all bowing down impartially before the stroke of death') and the certainty of God's final irradiation of the heavens in time to come.

The *Titanic* tragedy permitted Anglo-American and imperial Protestantism, especially such a muscular branch of it as Ulster Protestantism, to flex its rhetorical muscles and to do what it did best – re-create God's displeasure so well that congregants felt the tremor of the aftershocks. Only the heroism of the passengers was allowed to displace, if only temporarily, God's retribution with the sense of a mixed blessing. But Catholic Belfast too was moved, and I have found no evidence that Irish Catholics at the time took any pleasure or consolation from what befell a 'Protestant' ship built by unionists (those who wished to remain United Kingdom citizens) and sailing between two 'Protestant' countries (England and the USA). In any case, Irish Catholics knew that many Irish co-religionists were on board, bound for the New World that had given them succour during and since the Famine of the 1840s. In the Catholic church of Ardoyne (a Catholic and Irish nationalist area of Belfast), the *Belfast News-Letter* reported:

> The choir rendered as an anthem Tennyson's beautiful lines 'Crossing the Bar' to a setting by Herr Werner, the organist, which by a strange coincident (sic) was composed and dedicated some years ago to Miss Andrews, sister of the late Mr. Thomas Andrews, jun.

The Andrews family was Protestant and pro-Empire but there is not a whisper of sectarianism in Ardoyne that Sunday of remembrance.

Across the nations, newspapers and magazines of April 1912 were full of ephemeral accounts, analyses and editorial opinions of the *Titanic* disaster. A fraction of them are worth retrieving and a fraction of those were reprinted in my 1999 anthology, *Titanic*.[3] The worthwhile are those which see and recount *Titanic* and her fate through the lenses of imagination and artistry, or which at the very least consciously add *Titanic* and her fate to the sum of Anglo-American culture. A few writers of real substance responded to the sinking or to the debate and inquiries that followed. They included in Britain Thomas Hardy, Joseph Conrad, HG Wells, GK Chesterton, Virginia Woolf, Arthur Conan Doyle and George Bernard Shaw, in whose biographies *Titanic* merits at least a lengthy footnote. I have represented in *Titanic* the polemical contributions of Conrad, Chesterton, Doyle and Shaw (the latter two locking horns in the pages of the London *Daily News*) and discussed them in *The Titanic Complex* (1997), and they are by now established portions of *Titanic* literature.

So too, though they aren't yet, should be the more dramatic passages from the *Hearings before a Subcommittee of the Committee on Commerce United States Senate* (Sixty-second Congress, Second Session), printed by the Government Printing Office (Washington, DC) for the American public in 1912. (Tom Kuntz edited a selection of the accumulated testimony in 1998 as *The Titanic Disaster Hearings*.) The testimonies, though transcribed for posterity and as matter of official record, were meant to be ephemeral in so far as they were taken down merely to provide the evidence the Subcommittee of the Committee on Commerce required to write its *Report*. However, to read through the original *Hearings* is to learn a very great deal not only about the ship and its sinking but about British and American societies at the time; the *Hearings* in their entirety are a valuable cultural resource.

For example, the testimony of Philip Franklin, American Vice-President of International Mercantile Marine (a New Jersey corporation that owned the White Star Line), was heard in order to assess a possible attempt by IMM to suppress news of the destruction of *Titanic*, presumably (the inference was) for re-insurance purposes. The silence of *Carpathia* was regarded as fair game for investigation by the Subcommittee. Bruce Ismay's attempt from on board the rescue ship to detain the White Star liner *Cedric* in New York was suspected darkly of being a ruse by which to spirit guilty officers and owner alike out of the United States to avoid interrogation. Franklin returned to this topic towards the end of his testimony in order stoutly to defend Ismay and whiten his motives.

The more dramatic evidence of Frederick Sammis (General Engineer of the Marconi Wireless Telegraph Co.) was used to assess possible collusion between the *New York Times* (assumed to be seeking an exclusive story) and the Marconi Company to ensure that the wireless operators on *Carpathia* (including, after his rescue, Harold Bride) would speak to no reporter except a *Times* reporter. Sammis admitted that Guglielmo Marconi had agreed that the wireless operators should be allowed to sell their stories. Indeed, Sammis depicted the agreement as a corporation's way of rewarding a faithful employee. The telegram Senator Alden Smith read to the inquiry, and that Sammis purported was a junior Marconi employee's rendition of Sammis' telephoned instructions that were to be relayed to Harold Bride, has the authentic period ring. Sammis describes it as 'the vernacular of the wireless men' but oddly it suggests the lingo of American gangster films in the next couple of decades or of F. Scott Fitzgerald's creation, Jay Gatsby, in *The Great Gatsby* (1925). The telegram read: 'Say, old man, Marconi Co. taking good care of you. Keep your mouth shut and hold your story. It is fixed for you so you will get big money'. Sammis then recalled his meetings in a New York hotel with *Carpathia*'s operator, Harold Cottam, where a deal was struck and which caused Smith to refer acidly to 'injunctions of secrecy ... and the hope of private reward' as dubious ethics among mediators of information such as wireless operators and newspapers.

John Bottomley, General Manager of the Marconi Company, was also questioned about possible Marconi control of information about the disaster. Should operators be encouraged to regard monetary reward for exclusive stories to newspapers as a normal part of their service? (Bride admitted receiving $1,000 for his *New York Times* April

19 interview, Cottam $1,250 for his published in the same issue: good money in 1912.) Bottomley thought not. Did Bottomley arrange for the operators to give their stories exclusively to the *New York Times*? He denied doing this. Was the wireless niggardliness of *Carpathia* due to a Marconi Company policy of withholding information from ships not equipped with a Marconi wireless system? 'It is absolutely untrue.' When the operator on board the Russian ship *Birma* was told to 'shut up' when he offered help in caring for survivors, was the rude operator on *Carpathia* following Marconi Company general orders? 'Most certainly not.' How could Bottomley account for the wireless silence maintained by *Carpathia* when information was sought about survivors? 'I am unable to account for it at all.'

The silences and rebuffs during wireless transmissions both before and after the sinking unsettled Senator Smith. Bride was asked why Jack Phillips, the senior *Titanic* operator, called the *Frankfurt* operator a fool and told him to 'stand by and keep out' when the operator of the German ship asked if any ships had already reached the stricken liner? True, *Frankfurt* had been apprised of the plight of *Titanic* an hour before, but wouldn't it have been as quick to re-inform *Frankfurt* of the seriousness of the situation? Could Phillips have been following Marconi Company policy in any way? Apparently not, since Marconi, sitting beside Bride during the hearing, identified *Frankfurt* as a ship of the North German Lloyd Line of which he, Marconi, was a director and as a ship equipped with a Marconi system. It was hard for Smith to disentangle policies from employees' personal decisions under tense circumstances.

Behind these lines of inquiry lay a widespread American worry about the anti-democratic concentration of power in trusts and monopolies and also (by analogy) about the possible anti-democratic control of information. The unspoken subtext lends the hearings a submerged tension and in the broadest sense, political anxiety. Of the junior colleague's messages and affidavits, Sammis remarked that 'they were not gems of English literature', prompting Smith to remind him that 'we are not passing upon the literary character of these productions'. But in any case, the exchanges are dramatic stuff, in that way American government hearings have. They (like the stories of several passengers) provide material for potentially greater drama than anything the screenwriters have imagined in their paltry versions of the *Titanic* disaster. Even without 'treatment' of the Hollywood kind, they surpass as literature any extant screenplay. As in the case of the sermons, the spoken word has under the necessity of carefully chosen but avowedly sincere expression, achieved the quality of the written word, and memorably so.

To read the *Hearings* is also to glimpse the human side of individuals as well as the impersonal side of American capitalist organisations, and, more especially, individuals recalling their actions and feelings where, to quote WB Yeats, 'life is at tension'. Second Officer Charles Lightoller's account to the American hearings was brisk, confident and informative, including his account of how he saved himself by clambering aboard the upturned Engelhardt boat B, but whereas Senator Smith had the neutral aim of uncovering facts, Thomas Scanlan, the lawyer representing the national Sailors' and Firemen's Union in Britain, interrogated Lightoller hard at the later British Commission of Enquiry. Scanlan wished to establish negligence at the levels of officers and owners. Lightoller later remarked: 'I am never likely to forget that long-drawn out battle of wits .... Pull devil, pull baker, till it looked as if they would pretty well succeed in pulling my hide off completely, each seemed to want his bit'. But Lightoller sat firm, at bay but defiantly cool, and the result is spontaneous courtroom drama of a high order.

At the US hearings, Fifth Officer Harold Lowe (who admitted to firing warning shots as he was being lowered in lifeboat No. 14) faced Smith's implication that the lifeboat he commanded had lain by for an hour, 150 yards from the fatally wounded liner, while hundreds struggled and cried out in the water. Lowe readily admitted it and brazened out the imputation of callousness. He waited, he said, 'until the drowning people had thinned out'. He went in among the bodies only when the cries 'had subsided a good deal' and claimed it would have been suicide to have done otherwise; he was prepared to pick up only a swimmer who had 'struggled out of the mass'. (None did so.) Only after herding several boats together and transferring passengers did Lowe ask for volunteer oarsmen to go with him to the scene of the sinking where he found and saved four survivors, one of whom died soon after.

According to an affidavit by a first-class American passenger, Daisy Minahan, Lowe had to be persuaded to return to the scene of the wreck and was rude into the bargain. Yet a second first-class woman passenger in lifeboat No. 14, Miss S. Compton, wrote to Gracie telling him that Lowe's 'manly bearing' gave the survivors confidence, and that it was a few women who protested when he expressed the intention of remaining near the sinking liner in order to save those he could. There is no necessary contradiction between the accounts of Lowe, Minahan and Compton: Lowe wanted to stay closer than 150 yards to the ship but pulled away at the request of some women passengers. However, he didn't wish to venture in among the struggling swimmers, despite the appeals of other women. Yet a faint air of self-righteousness attends Lowe's self-exculpation, and he seems happiest when discoursing on the uselessness and obstructiveness of anonymous Italians in women's clothes. It was Gracie's belief that Lowe's language but not his behaviour was intemperate and that he was a first-class officer. In any case, Lowe's testimony is a highlight among *Titanic* survivors' accounts.

So too is the lookout Frederick Fleet's testimony in Washington which, like Lowe's, I excerpted in *Titanic*. Like Lightoller in England, Fleet sensed himself under attack and at both inquiries was an awkward customer: 'Is there any more likes to have a go at me?' he challenged. Perhaps he felt exposed as the man who first saw the iceberg, but not soon enough, as it happened, and anticipated being made to carry the can for superior officers. His was a blighted life from start to finish, the finish coming when he hanged himself in 1965. His dialogue with Senator Alden Smith, the soul of patience with this prickly witness, resembles a scene in a Harold Pinter play: repetitive, pointless and unintentionally humorous all at the same time. Fleet denies he was possessed of any of the qualities we would associate with being a lookout and affects to knowing nothing while answering all questions. It is a remarkable performance that establishes a subtext of painful human frailty and composes a poignant document of the *Titanic* tragedy. Indeed, the transcripts of the American *Hearings* are at once a mother lode of Titanica, significant cultural documentation in their own right (often with the properties of imaginative literature), and untapped sources for *Titanic* fictions.

Before leaving the American *Hearings*, one would wish to enter as exhibit Alden Smith's spoken (but stenographed or transcribed) introduction of his *'Titanic' Disaster: Report of the Committee on Commerce United States Senate* to his colleagues on May 28, 1912. Stung by what they saw as American violation of British jurisdiction and Anglophobe sentiment in the American press, British commentators attempted to discredit the Senate Hearings by belittling its chairman. but 'Smithisms' were fewer than his British detractors supposed. The 'extravagant rhetoric' in Smith's *Report* of which British newspapers complained was, for example when he spoke of Captain Smith, an impressive way of condemning in sorrow rather than anger. Senators today would not, and could not, risk such eloquence; Smith knew he was reporting on a momentous event and his powers of commemorative as well as descriptive and analytic expression rose to the occasion.

Nor would the literature of *Titanic* be complete without the transcripts of the wireless messages that were exchanged between the

Senator SMITH. I want to get on the record the place where you were stationed in the performance of your duty.

Mr. FLEET. I was on the lookout.

Senator SMITH. On the lookout?

Mr. FLEET. At the time of the collision.

Senator SMITH. In the crow's nest?

Mr. FLEET. Yes.

Senator SMITH. At the time of the collision?

Mr. FLEET. Yes, sir.

Senator SMITH. Can you tell how high above the boat deck that is?

Mr. FLEET. I have no idea.

Senator SMITH. Can you tell how high above the crow's nest the masthead is?

Mr. FLEET. No, sir.

Senator SMITH. Do you know how far you were above the bridge?

Mr. FLEET. I am no hand at guessing.

Senator SMITH. I do not want you to guess; but, if you know, I would like to have you tell.

Mr. FLEET. I have no idea.

Senator FLETCHER. You hardly mean that; you have some idea?

Mr. FLEET. No; I do not.

Senator FLETCHER. You know whether it was a thousand feet or two hundred?

Senator SMITH. Was there any other officer or employee stationed at a higher point on the *Titanic* than you were?

Mr. FLEET. No, sir.

Senator SMITH. You were the lookout?

Mr. FLEET. Yes, sir.

Senator SMITH. Where are the eyes of the ship?

Mr. FLEET. The eyes of the ship?

Senator SMITH. The ship's eyes?

Mr. FLEET. Forward.

Senator SMITH. At the extreme bow?

Mr. FLEET. Yes, sir.

Senator SMITH. And on the same level as the boat deck or below it?

Mr. FLEET. Below it.

Senator SMITH. How far below it?

Mr. FLEET. I do not know, sir.

Senator SMITH. Mr. Fleet, can you tell who was on the forward part of the *Titanic* Sunday night when you took your position in the crow's nest?

Mr. FLEET. There was nobody.

Senator SMITH. Nobody?

Mr. FLEET. No, sir.

Excerpt from lookout Frederick Fleet's testimony to the US Titanic hearing

liner and other ships after the collision. Their real existence was as taps in the wireless shack and waves in the ether, but written down they assume a new identity. Composed into one document, the flurry of messages constitute a peculiar but strangely affecting shorthand poetry in which the tautness of operators' argot seems decreasingly able to convey the worsening plight of the ship. Again, here is found literature under the pressure of uniquely human circumstances. Some of the last messages:

1.45 a.m. *Titanic* to *Carpathia: Come as quickly as possible. Engine room filling up to the boilers. TU OM GN (Thank you old man goodnight.)* Last message from *Titanic* to *Carpathia.*

Mount Temple hears *Frankfurt* calling *Titanic*. No reply.

1.48 a.m. *Asian* hears *Titanic* SOS, answers but receives no reply.

1.50 a.m. *Caronia* hears *Frankfurt* working *Titanic* to no avail.

1.55 a.m. Cape Race to *Virginian: We have not heard Titanic for about half an hour. His power may be gone.*

2.00 a.m. *Virginian* hears *Titanic* call faintly.

2.17 a.m. *Virginian* hears *Titanic* call *CQD*. Then signals end abruptly. Calls *Titanic* but no response.

3.15 a.m. *Mount Temple* hears *Carpathia* message *Titanic: If you are there we are firing rockets.*

3.30 a.m. *Carpathia* calling *Titanic.*

3.48 a.m. *Birma* believes she hears *Titanic* and calls: *Steaming full speed for you. Shall arrive you 6.00 in morning. Hope you are safe. We are only 50 miles now.*

RMS *Titanic* foundered at 2.20 a.m.

The Professional *Titanic*

With a speed worthy of the ship herself, and the contemporary technology of communication, the imagining of *Titanic*'s fate accelerated after the essential information was available. In the summer of 1912 a writer in the *Literary Digest* (New York) noted the publication of Lawrence Beesley's *The Loss of the* S.S. Titanic, Filson Young's *Titanic* and J. Bernard Walker's *An Unsinkable* Titanic, and remarked: 'There seems to be no abatement in the production of books about the ill-fated *Titanic*'. Before the year was out, other well-known books appeared, including *Wreck and Sinking of the* Titanic by Marshall Everett, *Sinking of the* Titanic *and Great Sea Disasters* by Logan Marshall, and *Sinking of the* Titanic by Jay Henry Mowbray.

Then and now, *Titanic* was a magnet for the professional writer. Judging only by their large output, the American writers, Everett (Henry Neil), Marshall and Mowbray, were nearly identical. If they were drawn to war and disasters as recurring themes, that says something about the times, when wars and disasters were plentiful and when trouble spots were becoming physically more accessible and the means of reporting technologically more advanced. The world was an unstable place when seen, as it was in the Age of *Titanic*, in a freshly global perspective, and the instability could only be rectified, it was thought in the appropriate quarters, by the steadfastness of the Anglo-Saxon race, especially of its American branch. This American view of the world has become firmer in our own time than it was in its beginnings around the start of the twentieth century. It is still the basis of American foreign policy.

Neil wrote *The Tragic Story of America's Greatest Disaster: Tornado, Flood and Fire in Ohio, Indiana, Nebraska and the Mississippi Valley* (1913) while Marshall the same year wrote *The True Story of Our National Calamity of Flood, Fire and Tornado: How the Whole Nation Joined in the Work of Relief*. In 1909 Mowbray wrote *Roosevelt's Marvelous Exploits in the Wilds of Africa, Containing Thrilling Accounts of his Killing Lions, Rhinoceri and Other Ferocious Beasts of the Jungle* and the same year Neil wrote *Roosevelt's Thrilling Experiences in the Wilds of Africa, Hunting Big Game, Illustrated with a Large Number of Exciting Hunting Scenes and Photographs of the Strange Natives of Darkest Africa*. Also in 1909, Neil wrote *The True Story of the Cook and Peary Discovery of the North Pole* and Mowbray wrote *The Discovery of the North Pole by Cook and Peary*. Unusually – since punctuality is the hallmark of the professional writer – it was a full six years before Marshall counter-punched with a haymaker, *The Story of Polar Conquest: The Complete History of Arctic and Antarctic Exploration, Including the Discovery of the South Pole by Amundsen and Scott, the Tragic Fate of the Scott Expedition and the Discovery of the North Pole by Admiral Peary*.

All three were laureates of horror and calamity, and the contemporary enthusiasm for Arctic and Antarctic exploration to which earlier in the book I connected popular fascination with the *Titanic* disaster, has to be seen in the light of such sensationalism. Marshall's *Horrors and Atrocities of the Great War, Including the Tragic Destruction of the* Lusitania (1915) and Mowbray's *Italy's Great Horror of Earthquake and Tidal Wave, Containing Vivid Descriptions of this Overwhelming Calamity* (1909) were from the same stable as Neil's *The Complete story of the Martinique Horror and Other Great Disasters* (1902). Thrills and horror, disasters and wars: it is hard to quell the idea that these three ambulance chasers of book-length journalism were the same author, or perhaps a limited company. In any case, there was clearly a great market for sensationalism, as though the years leading up to the Great War were full of a mild hysteria and were blunting sensitivities in a way that made the outbreak of war not unthinkable when it came, and the war itself just another 'exciting experience' to be welcomed. (Neil in 1904 had written *Exciting Experiences in the Japanese-Russian War, Including a Complete History of Japan, Russia, China and Korea*). A popular literature of disaster awaited the *Titanic* sinking and Mowbray, Neil and Marshall, who were stalwarts of that literature, plunged in enthusiastically.

Filson Young (BF Alexander, 1876–1938) was a higher-browed British counterpart of Mowbray, Neil and Marshall. Still, his interests included lurid criminal trials; for example, *The Trial of Frederick Bywaters and Edith Thompson* (1923) recounted a famous adultery-and-murder case of the day, while *The Trial of Hawley Harvey Crippen* (1920) involved a notorious killer, arrested on disembarking from a fast transatlantic liner through the superior speed of wireless telegraphy. Young's enthusiasm for motoring (*The Complete Motorist*, 1904, *The Happy Motorist*, 1906, *The Joy of the Road*, 1907) was set firmly within the cultural context of contemporary fascination with speed and engines that I have already discussed. But war profitably drew him also: *The Relief of Mafeking* (1900), *With the Battle Cruisers* (1921) and *With Beatty in the North Sea* (1921), the latter two allowing Young to combine war and ocean, as he had done in *With the Fleet: Studies in Naval Life* (1913).

Besides punctuality, the professional journalist who writes books prides himself on his field work, and Young's seems to have been very good. His *Titanic* is both a highly readable and well-researched book. The prose is overheated at times, and he occasionally chooses legend over fact in order to keep the literary temperature high, but he seems to have been familiar both with Ireland and with *Titanic* before the tragic maiden voyage. Indeed, his ties with Ireland seem strong, for he wrote a novel set there, *When the Tide Turns* (1908), that exploited his knowledge of sailing, as well as a political work that saw three editions, *Ireland at the Cross Roads* (1903).

Versatility is another quality of the professional writer and Young was nothing if not versatile. He was a serious appreciator and populariser of music, to which *Mastersingers: Appreciations of Music and Musicians* (1902), *Opera Stories* (1912) and *The Wagner Stories* (1909) testify. The sea, ships, speed, wireless communication (*Shall I Listen: Studies in the Adventure and Technique of Broadcasting*, 1933) courtroom inquiry, music, Ireland – all were elements of the *Titanic* phenomenon, and Young took to it like, well, a boat to sea. In his description of the building and launch of the liner (quoted anonymously by Wyn Craig Wade in 1980), Young employed two metaphors – the ship as a cathedral, the scaffolding and gantries as a forest – that provided an early context for the later claim that *Titanic* had defied both God and Nature.

The Terrible Beauty

The other two books mentioned above, by Beesley and Gracie, are set apart because they are accounts by survivors of their ordeal but written by men who were well qualified to conduct their own inquiry into the disaster. Gracie was an amateur historian who had recently published a book whose title was repeated in his *Titanic* work: *The Truth about Chickamauga* (New York: Houghton Mifflin, 1911) while Beesley had been a science teacher at Dulwich College. Both books have the bifocal value of survivor's story and sleuth's report privileged by personal contacts and recollections.

But the first survivor's account was Harold Bride's, spoken to, and transcribed by, a *New York Times* reporter in the radio shack of *Carpathia* as soon as the rescue ship docked. It is a famous piece and despite the fact that its verbatim accuracy has been questioned (for example, Bride is quoted using Americanisms such as 'through sleeping' for 'finished sleeping', 'back of' for 'behind', 'off of' and 'I guess' for 'I suppose') it is, as the subeditor's title suggests, a 'thrilling story' (using a word popular at the time). Bride's account established three *Titanic* legends: the tenacious resolve of Jack Phillips, reluctant to leave his wireless; the incident of the thieving stoker (about whom more later); and the equally tenacious resolve of the band. The disappearance of Bride after 15 minutes of extraordinary world fame somehow renders his story starker and shapelier. He returned to Scotland, his hair white with the trauma of it all, and lived in seclusion, amusing himself as a ham radio operator. This was not known at the time; in fact, nothing was known of him until a private investigator discovered in 1987 that he had died in Glasgow in 1956, having concealed his past even from his family through marriage.

The columns of the major newspapers, especially the *New York Times*, added to the autobiography of survival. For example, the survivors' tales gathered after survivors disembarked from *Carpathia* and excerpted in the April 19 issue of the *Times* make for gripping reading. This must have been the early heyday of what we now take for granted, the intense interview on location as close as possible in place and time to the scene of the newsworthy, of news still happening and not merely being remembered and reported. The American and then British inquiries likewise added to the literature of recollection, though only occasionally were witnesses given more elbow-room than those interviewed dockside to develop their memories or finish their anecdotes.

Survivors needed peace and quiet to order their recollections, though Beesley showed under the circumstances great powers of concentration when he wrote an account 'at intervals on board the *Carpathia*' which was published in the *New York Times* of April 19. In that account he captured well two potent formulas of survivors' accounts.

One, the irony of the loveliness of the night on which this tragedy had chosen to occur:

> a beautiful starlight light, with no moon and not very light. The sea was as calm as a pond, just a gentle heave as the [life]boat dipped up and down in the swell: an ideal night, except the bitter cold for any one who had to be out in the middle of the Atlantic Ocean in an open boat.

Two, the horrifying cries of swimmers in the sea once the ship disappeared under the waves:

> there fell on us the most appalling noises that human being every (sic) listened to. The cries of our fellow-beings struggling in the icy-cold water, crying for help with a cry that we knew could not be answered.

Five weeks after landing safe in New York, Beesley was encouraged by the editor of the *Boston Herald* to write a history of the disaster. Beesley was reluctant, he says, and when the editor accompanied Beesley to Houghton Mifflin, they too were at first discouraging, but both parties changed their minds some days later.[4] Installed in a Boston residential club by Houghton Mifflin, Beesley wrote his book in six weeks. He did so, he claims in his Preface, to calm public opinion (as he considered his newspaper article had already helped to do), presumably by establishing fact in place of speculation and hearsay. Indeed, Beesley shares with Gracie a tenacity in pursuit of fact, the way things actually happened, and reproduces a letter he wrote to the London *Times* offering observations detached from value-judgement and making practical suggestions, all in the cause of future safety at sea. Interestingly, this preoccupation with fact requires him at times to re-create conditions on board so that the relevant perspective can be regained:

> if the reader will come and stand with the crowd on deck, he must first rid himself entirely of the knowledge that the Titanic has sunk ... he must get rid of any foreknowledge of disaster to appreciate why people acted as they did. Secondly, he had better get rid of any picture in thought painted either by his own imagination or by some artist, whether pictorial or verbal, 'from information supplied'.

But regaining perspective for himself, he offers observant vignettes that achieve something more than fact.

> Looking down astern from the boat-deck or from B deck to the steerage quarters [early in the voyage], I often noticed how the third-class passengers were enjoying every minute of the time: a most uproarious skipping game of the mixed-double type was the great favourite, while 'in

and out and roundabout' went a Scotchman with his bagpipes playing something that Gilbert says 'faintly resembled an air'.

On the fatal morning with under two hours to go before the sinking, Beesley noted the cellist (Roger Bricoux or Jack Woodward) rounding the vestibule corner of the staircase entrance and running down the deserted starboard deck, 'his 'cello trailing behind him, the spike dragging along the floor. This must have been about 12.40 a.m. I suppose the band must have begun to play soon after this and gone on until after 2 a.m.' And this recollection of a laden moment:

> Suddenly a rush of light from the forward deck, a hissing roar that made us all turn from watching the boats, and a rocket leapt upwards to where the stars blinked and twinkled above us. Up it went, higher and higher, with a sea (sic) of faces upturned to watch it, and then an explosion that seemed to split the silent night in two, and a shower of stars sank slowly down and went out one by one. And with a gasping sigh one word escaped the lips of the crowd: 'Rockets!' ... It is no use denying the dramatic intensity of the scene: separate if you can from all the terrible events that followed, and picture the calmness of the night, the sudden light on the decks crowded with people in different stages of dress and undress, the background of huge funnels and tapering masts revealed by the soaring rocket, whose flash illumined at the same time the faces and minds of the obedient crowd, the one with mere physical light, the other with a sudden revelation of what its message was.

In his book Beesley expands upon the beauty of the night that he had briefly noted in his *New York Times* article. Now the stars have increased their brilliance 'tenfold' and the sky become a mere setting for the display of their wonder. Now the stars are imagined as seeing the calamity below them and flashing messages concerning it to each other (like celestial Marconigrams). Now when *Titanic* disappears and he is in the lifeboat, he remembers 'looking up at the perfect sky and realizing why Shakespeare wrote the beautiful words he puts in the mouth of Lorenzo [in *The Merchant of Venice*] – 'Jessica, look how the floor of heaven/Is thick inlaid with patines of bright gold', and so on for eight lines. It strikes a false note though it is possible Beesley really did think of the passage and remembered it verbatim but thought the memory unsuitable for a daily newspaper if not for a book. Now in retrospect Beesley retrieves metaphors he implies he fashioned at the time: the ship like a stricken animal, the ship losing courage after the collision like an assaulted human being, the sea like a quiet inland river like the Cam. In short, Beesley's account is being transformed into literature but by an amateur writer, whereas the practical side of his version of events has a more professional ring, befitting a science master.

It would have been difficult to avoid literary touches given the nature of the survivors' experiences and the general awareness that what was happening involved the largest ever liner, at night, amidst icebergs at the latter end of the world and with hundreds of fellow human beings facing imminent death. Such accounts were good copy and editors inevitably got involved. We have already met Charlotte Collyer who was saved with her daughter while her husband was lost. Charlotte was looked after in New York and, perhaps to make ends meet, told her story to the *Semi-Monthly Magazine* where it appeared on May 26 (the editor asked readers each to send Mrs Collyer $5 via the magazine). The letter from Charlotte to her late husband's parents shows a shaky command of punctuation and there is little literary flair, so it is probable that the magazine editor ghost-wrote her fine account.

There are several notable vignettes. During the evacuation she recalls that:

> suddenly there was a commotion near one of the gangways, and we saw a stoker come climbing up from below. He stopped a few feet away from us. All the fingers of one hand had been cut off. Blood was running from the stumps, and blood was spattered over his face and over his clothes. The red marks showed very clearly against the coal dust with which he was covered. I started over and spoke to him. I asked him if there was any danger. 'Dynger!' he screamed, at the top of his voice. 'I should just sye so! It's 'ell down below. Look at me! This boat'll sink like a log in ten minutes.' He staggered away, and lay down, fainting, with his head on a coil of rope.

A second involved a boy who leapt into Lowe's boat as was it was being lowered and in which Charlotte and her daughter were already safe. Lowe ordered him out but the boy begged for his life so the formidable Lowe:

> drew his revolver, and thrust it into his face. 'I'll give you just ten seconds to get back on to that ship before I blow your brains out!' he shouted. The lad only begged the harder, and I thought I should see him shot as he stood. But the officer suddenly changed his tone. He lowered his revolver, and looked the boy squarely in the eyes. 'For God's sake, be a man!' he said gently. 'We've got women and children to save. We must stop at the decks lower down and take on women and children.' The little lad turned round and climbed back over the rail, without a word. He took a few uncertain steps, then lay face down upon the deck, his head beside a coil of rope. He was not saved. All the women about me were sobbing; and I saw my little Marjorie take the officer's hand. 'Oh, Mr. Man, don't shoot, please don't shoot the poor man!' she was saying; and he spared the time to shake his head and smile.

Like Beesley and the Frenchmen, Collyer recalled the ironic aesthetics of the scene that offered itself to those in the lifeboats, and in doing so used a phrase that would soon become famous. The oarsmen in Lowe's boat stopped rowing and the boat stood by.

> I shall never forget the terrible beauty of the Titanic at that moment. She was tilted forward, head down, with her first funnel partly under water. To me she looked like an enormous glow worm; for she was alight from the rising water line, clear to her stern – electric lights blazing in every cabin, lights on all the decks and lights at her mast heads.

A 'terrible beauty': four years later the Irish poet WB Yeats was to immortalise the phrase when responding to another catastrophe, the crushed rebellion against British rule in Dublin at Easter, 1916. He is unlikely to have read Collyer's account and she did not coin the phrase, but it retroactively adds a curious literary touch to her memories.

Another famous phrase occurs in the account which Elizabeth Shutes sent to Archibald Gracie for reproduction in the book he was then writing. Shutes, a governess, embarked with her charge, 19-year-old Margaret Graham, who was travelling with her mother (some lists have the Grahams embarking at Southampton), all three saved in lifeboat No. 3. Shutes recalls that after the ship disappeared under the waves 'across the water swept that awful wail, the cry of those drowning people' and is moved, now, to exclaim: 'the horror, the helpless horror,' echoing the celebrated exclamation of Kurtz in the novella, *Heart of Darkness* (1902), by Conrad who was to take such interest in the loss of *Titanic*. Shutes was clearly an educated woman who did not require the help of an editor, and she may well have been familiar with Conrad's quite famous book.

Dante's Fancy-dress Ball
It was events in the water once the ship sank that most threatened the survivors' peace of mind, and among the cultivated they constituted a painful memory that required above all other memories to be both commemorated and purged by means of literature or at least by a gesture towards literature. Any panic on board was that of a crowd that became a mass of individuals despite their numbers – for Collyer they became 'bees' and for Robert Daniel a 'throng of insane, struggling persons at the rail of the doomed ship'. This was panic seen from the distance of a lifeboat. (Filson Young was to see the terrified passengers who clustered at the raised stern and fell when the ship assumed the vertical as mice shaken from a trap into a bucket of water.

In her novel, *The Voyage Out*, Woolf was to see the passengers on her liner as 'aimless ants almost pressing each other over the edge'.) Once in the water, the crowd further lost its identity and became reduced to mere sound – a chorus of souls. From the safety of the Waldorf, Mrs Dickinson Bishop remembered the screaming of those in the water that carried a mile to her lifeboat and gradually became fainter and died away. She and her husband shared the lifeboat with the three Frenchmen, amongst others, and the latter were more graphic than Mrs Bishop in their recollection of the panic in the water, published in *Le Matin* and summarised in English in the *New York Times*.

> A terrible clamor rose on all sides and for an hour anguish (sic) cries rang out. It was, say the narrators, like a great chorus, chanting a refrain of death with wild persistency. Sometimes the cries died out and then the tragic chorus began again, more terribly and more despairingly. Those shrieks pursued us and haunted us as we pulled away in the night. Then one by one the cries ceased and only the noise of the sea remained.

Little wonder that WT Stead's son, writing the regular section of *The Review of Reviews* entitled 'The Progress of the World', the month following his father's death, should reach for a suitable literary allusion.

> First in the throng of memorable events that have accelerated progress in April, 1912, must be ranked the tragic occurrence henceforth for ever associated with his name. The sinking of the *Titanic* was an assemblage of horrors. As the story is slowly ground out, the horrors deepen. To conceive them all, and to narrate them all, would require the imagination of a Dante. What Inferno could equal that tangled mass of fifteen hundred men and women and children struggling for more than an hour in the ice-cold water, and sending up to Heaven vain cries for help, their shouts and groans blending in a long-drawn chorus of anguish that slowly sank into the silence of death?

Dante was to be invoked again, by Archibald Gracie in *The Truth about the* Titanic (1913). When he broke the surface of the water, having been taken under by the submerging ship, he was surprised to see everything – the sea, sky and wreckage – veiled by a smoky vapour that lent the scene an unearthliness.

> At any rate it produced a supernatural effect, and the pictures I had seen by Dante and the description I had read in my Virgil of the infernal regions, of Charon, and the River Lethe, were then uppermost in my thoughts. Add to this, within the area described, which was as far as my eyes could reach, there arose to the sky the most horrible sounds ever heard by mortal man except by those of us who survived this terrible

tragedy. The agonizing cries of death from over a thousand throats, the wails and groans of the suffering, the shrieks of the terror-stricken and the awful gaspings for breath of those in the last throes of drowning, none of us will ever forget to our dying day.

And when Gracie threw his leg over the wooden crate to which he was clinging but overturned the crate and did a somersault in the water, another memory came to him, this one historical.

What may be of interest is the thought that then occurred to me of the accounts and pictures of a wreck, indelibly impressed upon my memory when a boy, because of my acquaintance with some of the victims [Gracie seemed to know everybody] of a frightful disaster of that day, namely the wreck of the *Ville de Havre* in the English channel in 1873, and I had in mind Mrs. Bulkley's description, and the picture of her clinging to some wreckage as a rescue boat caught sight of her, bringing the comforting words over the water, 'We are English sailors coming to save you'.[5]

Like Beesley's book, Gracie's is both an attempt at factuality and the recollection of a personal ordeal. If Gracie's is the more powerful, it is because his experience was the more powerful and more rivetingly recounted. Like Charles Lightoller, he gained the roof of the officers' quarters but before he could get to his feet the ship took him down. His error in leaving the scene of the Engelhardt boat B – which he later met overboard – was rectified only by his astonishing swim under water, a swim that must have taken its toll of this 54-year-old man who died that December. But his book is an essential *Titanic* text because of Gracie's grasp of shipboard life in first class and its unfolding in the hours of crisis. Having survived, he stalked the disaster that nearly did for him, hunting down its details less in revenge than in a passion to set the record straight. The monomania of the amateur historian had been aroused and was now overwhelmingly personal and not to be diverted.

One of Gracie's table companions was Helen Churchill Candee of Washington DC, centre of an admiring male circle. She escaped in lifeboat No. 6 which had among its three crew Frederick Fleet, the lookout. In her remarks to the reporters in New York, she helped establish the legend of Ida and Isidor Straus' heroism. The tribute she paid to the heroism of the first-class men ('God's noblemen') in her lengthier report for the *San Francisco Examiner* of April 20 resurfaced in Candee's short story, 'Sealed Orders', that appeared in *Collier's Weekly* on May 4. In the story, events and personalities are alluded to rather than identified which is part of a technique by which Candee tries through poetic effect and elliptical phrasing to lift the disaster to a chivalric romance in a way familiar to Candee's writing. It is one more example of a transaction we have already noted in other contexts: established cultural expressions and practices awaiting their local version in the tragedy of *Titanic*.

The philosophy of Candee's story resembles that of Celia Thaxter and Thomas Hardy in their poems. A magnificent ship, a 'titan', sails proudly west from Europe while a modest ship (the unnamed *Carpathia*) slips quietly eastwards from New York (not named either); simultaneously the third 'sinister craft set out from the north with an insolent indifference that transcended even the magnificence of the greatest ship afloat'. The titan arrives at the 'tryst', a 'virgin cleanly running to the unknown bridal across the starlit sea' while 'down from the silent north that other sinister craft had slipped into her destined place'. The sealed orders all are under are about to be revealed and followed independently of human choice. It was much in the minds of Candee's contemporaries that humanity's appreciation of its own daring and ingenuity, though these were startling of late, was tempting providence in its conceit. Hardy was of his time in imagining a power above and beyond humanity that felt it was necessary to thwart human grandiosity. (Where Hardy differed was in gloomily seeing this power as at best indifferent to us, at worst malevolent. Something of the same grim sense of humans as playthings came to the soldier poets of the Great War, three or four years later.) Brand Whitlock's poem, 'The *Titanic*', which also appeared in *Collier's Weekly* on May 4, sees 'the dark Ironic Spirit' at work in the tragedy, playing 'Its sublime, stupendous, bitter joke'.

'Sealed Orders' demonstrates the irresistible power of God (not Hardy's brooding cosmic force) but equally the 'virility immortal' exhibited by the noble men who saved Candee and other women. Candee's pride of race ('We are Anglo-Saxons', remarks a character, to explain the calmness with which he and his woman companion are facing death) effaced her pride of gender. Whitlock too sees victory in the way 'our intrepid Northern race' accepted the sealed orders of the Ironic Spirit. This combination of Anglo-Saxon race-pride and human race-humility (in the face of nature's irresistible power) was an Anglo-American cultural posture of the time.

Perhaps Candee's friend Gracie remembered her description of the scenes on board the sinking titan as 'a fancy-dress ball in Dante's Hell' when he came to write his own book, though he claimed that the resemblance struck him as soon as he broke the surface of the water. And it may be indeed that in those days the Dantesque (like the Shakespearean) was part of the cultivated person's cultural perception

Illustration of lifeboats leaving Titanic, *April 28, 1912*

that came unbidden to mind in certain circumstances. The Dantesque was certainly an apt complex of metaphor for the contemporary preoccupations with the abyss, with panic and with social atomisation that we have already noted and which the *Titanic* disasters reinforced. George Gissing, whose fictional image of the Abyss we have commented on, read the whole of the *Divine Comedy* in Italian in 1885 while frequenting the squalid areas of London on which he drew for *The Nether World* (1889). However, of *Titanic's* contemporaries, it was TS Eliot who most memorably inspired Anglo-American culture with the spirit of Dante.

Inevitably, the *Titanic* disaster set the poetasters immediately to work. Newspapers around the world, especially in America and Britain, were flooded with verse elegies and poets' corners became clearing-houses for bad, deeply felt verse. Rather more ambitious was Edwin Drew's *The Chief Incidents of the* Titanic *Wreck Treated in Verse*, a compilation of 27 poems published a month after the tragedy. The poetry is of indifferent quality so that the self-advertisement is accurate in its implication: 'may appeal to those who lost friends in this appalling catastrophe'. Equally punctual (both poems appeared in May) and more interesting is the long poem in Spanish published in Santiago, Chile: *Solidaridad en el Dolor (Catastrofe del* Titanic*): Poema Filosofico-Moral en tres Partes y en Romance Heroico* by Blanca Vanini Silva.

According to the poem's dateline, Silva began his poem on April 21 and finished on May 6. In his prelude he has the ship declare its arrogance and invincibility and draws on indictments that were familiar to informed Anglo-American readers: 'I am *Titanic!*, masterpiece of Progress,/prodigy of Industry and Labour,/manifest proof of man's power'...etc. In his entracte, Silva has the iceberg puncture the ship's (and man's) pride and send it into the 'deep abyss of death' ('profundo abismo de la muerte'). In his finale, Silva sees the ship's unwitting approach to the abyss as representative of the approach of those who do not acknowledge a higher power ruling the universe and guiding mankind, who do not recognise the deeps beyond human understanding and thus plunge into their own terrible deeps beyond recovery. This lesson applies to nations as well as individuals, and Silva adduces recent calamities, including those involving Martinique, Italy, America and Chile (some of them falling prey to the professional appetite of Everett, Mowbray and Marshall), as the fruit of human vices and passions. The ship is evidence of the wrong kind of progress, the right kind being spiritual, through which men will become gods and the firmament their dwelling place.

The *Titanic* disaster allowed the spiritually inclined to oppose the material progress with such vehemence (as here) that their spiritual concerns seems translatable into a reactionary social philosophy.

Poets of greater stature were also drawn to *Titanic*, including Thomas Hardy and Harriet Monroe. Monroe, a well-known American poet, was to become the editor of the celebrated journal, *Poetry*, and to fall under the modernist influence of Ezra Pound. She published 'A Requiem' in the April 21 issue of the *Chicago Tribune*. The poem betrays not a shred of modernism and is an upbeat hackneyed Victorian hymn to the Union dead who sank with the liner: 'Your fathers, who at Shiloh bled,/Accept your company ....//Daughters of pioneers!/Heroes freeborn, who chose the best,/Not tears for you, but cheers!' Hardy also wrote his poem almost immediately, but this haste was offset by the fact that what befell the ship merely confirmed a philosophy of life that the poet had already matured over years of verse. TS Eliot was wiser in allowing the disaster to settle into a larger view of life and culture that was still unformed in 1912.

If the famous opening line of Eliot's modernist epic, *The Waste Land* (1922), is remarkably applicable to the *Titanic* disaster – 'April is the cruellest month' – another line already quoted in this book is just as applicable: 'Fear death by water'. I have already connected this line to the death of Miss Evans and the warning she had received from a fortune-teller. The line entitles one of the sections of *The Waste Land*, a section that consists of ten lines in the published version but in draft form was 83 lines longer, abbreviated by Ezra Pound's fierce blue pencil. The jettisoned lines tell of a schooner that sets out eastwards across the Atlantic and is blown north towards a line of Arctic icebergs.

> And dead ahead we saw, where sky and sea should meet,
> A line, a white line, a long white line,
> A wall, a barrier, towards which we drove.
> My God man there's bears on it.
> Not a chance. Home and mother.
> Where's a cocktail shaker, Ben, here's plenty of cracked ice.
> Remember me.

Graham Nelson notes that the penultimate line recalls an incident recounted by Lawrence Beesley in The Loss of the Titanic, in which after the collision a card-player turns to an onlooker, points to his whiskey glass and says 'Just run along the deck and see if any ice has come aboard: I would like some for this.' Nelson also notes that Walter Lord drew on the anecdote in A Night to Remember and that the incident became part of Titanic legend. (The version I have heard has Lady Astor – a famous member of the English branch of the family, who had the misfortune of becoming a stock character in formula jokes, often off-colour, but who was not on board the liner – saying after the collision: 'I asked for ice in my drink but this is ridiculous'.) And although Eliot's widow identified 'Ben' as 'an obsolete nickname for a sailor', Nelson prefers to see in the apostrophe an allusion to Ben (Benjamin) Guggenheim. Indeed, Nelson goes so far as to posit Eliot's identification with his fellow-schoolmaster, Beesley, as the man on board most like Eliot.

Larger than any such allusion is the pervasive influence on The Waste Land of Dante's great medieval poem, The Divine Comedy, sharpened in Eliot's use of a line from Dante (which I have already pressed into service) when he depicts the crowds flowing over London Bridge: 'I had not thought death had undone so many'. It is easy to imagine an allusion also to the Titanic dead in that line. When one reads the roll of death in the newspapers of the day (or the computer print-outs in our own day of the lost), one can the more imagine it.

One can also see an element of the Dantesque in Max Beckmann's large expressionist canvas, The Sinking of the Titanic (1912), as well as an allusion to Géricault's famous and disturbing painting, The Raft of the Medusa (1818–1919). The disaster immediately produced numerous paintings and sketches commissioned by newspapers, in an age when photographs were not so readily available.

For example, the *Illustrated London News* in its May 4 issue reproduced what looks in black and white like a swift oil painting 'drawn from material supplied by Mr. H. Senior, a survivor' and depicting 'the end of the "Titanic's" captain'. (Beesley was in his book to warn against taking these newspaper depictions as truth.) Captain Smith is seen handing a baby to a crewman (H. Senior, a stoker) lying on top of an overturned lifeboat (the Engelhardt boat B), after which, according to Senior, Smith, who was swimming alongside the collapsible, was hauled aboard the Engelhardt but slipped off, apparently by his own volition, asked to be let go, said he was going down with the ship, and took off his lifebelt in order to accomplish that task. Bride told the Traffic Manager of the Marconi Company that he saw Captain Smith dive from the bridge into the sea at the moment the Engelhardt boat B fell into the water, and Filson Young gave credence to the stoker's story, but Smith's end nevertheless remains a mystery. (In other versions of events, Smith shot himself or was washed overboard and vanished.) Neither Bride nor Gracie nor John Collins (an assistant cook from Belfast), who were saved on top of the Engelhardt, made any mention of Captain Smith and the babies. But by the time Bride managed to free himself from inside the collapsed boat, 'there was a big crowd on top'; when Collins got on board 'there were more than fifteen or sixteen who were then on it'; and when Gracie got himself on board the Engelhardt there were more than a dozen already there; so it is possible that the Smith incident happened before Bride, Gracie and Collins were safe on top of the collapsible. But the story of Smith and the baby made a fine anecdote and worked to exonerate Smith from any culpability. It also made a very dramatic sketch, and one that is a benign echo of Géricault's painting (with self-sacrifice replacing lethal individualism and group savagery) and resembles a detail of Beckmann's later, less benign artistic version of what happened.

Sight and Sound
If there was a host of contemporary paintings and drawings made for journalistic purposes, there were even more newspaper and magazine cartoons; they too are part of the contemporary visual 'literature' of *Titanic*. Of the dozens, probably hundreds, of cartoons published, many of them were sardonic or hostile comments on the disaster, and a good number of them have been reproduced in later books about *Titanic*. It took a little time for postcards (and for commemorative statuary) to augment that 'literature', but photographs, most notably those taken by Fr Frank Browne before *Titanic* left Cobh, and the few taken by

Carpathia passengers of passing icebergs and the survivors on board, were dramatic additions to the imagery of *Titanic*.

The contemporary *Titanic* phenomenon was a highly visual affair, to which the headlines and photographs in newspapers also contributed, an affair that from our perspective seems pioneering, as if the media of visual information were in process of development and of emancipation from the erstwhile dominance of the written word. To immerse oneself in the phenomenon from our vantage-point is to participate in that process, to stand at an early cross-roads in our culture. Perhaps this is part of the lure of *Titanic*.

Moving images of *Titanic* likewise have a curious and poignant effect. Cinematography was much younger than photography and in 1912 was still a callow documentary medium and art form, despite the fact that the industry was thriving and growing. Only days after the sinking, there were silent newsreels in American and European picture-houses purporting to show *Titanic*, though the footage was in fact of *Olympic* with Captain Smith on board, so that the names of tenders had to be scratched out on the prints in order not to give the game away. This odd fusion of fact and fiction was a feature of a cinematic genre already flourishing: enacted documentary films called 'actualities' or 'sensation films'. The shipwreck was a favourite subject and so the *Titanic* disaster was simply absorbed into a prior set of expressive circumstances, a process of which we have seen numerous other examples.

In the light of this, *Saved from the* Titanic, the film which the survivor Dorothy Gibson starred in and which premiered on May 14 (as 'the film marvel of the age'), can be seen as a re-enactment of the tragedy but also a step towards a freer fictionalisation, since Gibson was a film star as well as survivor and her persona must have had the effect of turning the disaster into a movie script. No prints of this film survive so it is impossible to know what liberties were taken by the director and whether fictional events and relationships (such as steadily proliferated as *Titanic* continued its movie career) were used to enliven proceedings. Hard on the heels of the Gibson film came a 30-minute silent entitled *In Nacht und Eis (In Night and Ice)*, a film made in Berlin by Mime Misu; filmed in June, it was released on August 17. It would appear to have been a further step towards free fiction, since according to Michael Wedel it combined 'melodramatic elements and live musical accompaniment with a semi-documentary mode … drawing upon authenticating and legitimating devices from the early actuality genre'. Its special effects were of course primitive but of interest is the way in which it shows tensions between the wealthy in first class and the poor in steerage: this became a fictional motif in later films and rested upon a problematic actuality.

The process whereby an existing mode (the 'actuality' or 'sensation film', itself a combination of fiction and fact through a faked reality) encountered a fresh reality and was absorbed and enlarged by that reality, could extend to mixed media. Deniz Gokturk tells us that:

> Gerhart Hauptmann's novel *Atlantis* about the wreck of a transatlantic liner, inspired by the author's own impressions of a voyage to America, was being published in serialisation in Berlin and Paris newspapers when the news about the real disaster hit. This brought great publicity for the novel, and the Nobel Prize for its author. Without delay, the Danish film company Nordisk acquired the film rights and produced *Atlantis* in 1913, one of the most costly films of the time.

In this way, a fact-inspired fiction was shaped to imitate a subsequent reality. There was, it seems, an animated film made in New York in 1912 entitled *Titanic Wreck* but it must remain in darkness for the purposes of this book.

The *music* of what happened, the *Titanic* sinking as soundscape, is almost as potent as the visual representations. I have already discussed the hymns that compose a virtual contemporary soundtrack and accompany the images in the theatre of our imagination. The services at which those hymns were sung prolonged and replayed the supposed soundtrack of the actual sinking. The hymns were almost instantly swelled by songs issuing from Tin Pan Alley. The first commercial song was copyrighted in the United States ten days after the sinking and sheet music and gramophone records followed in its wake. Before 1912 was out, 112 pieces of *Titanic* music (excluding blues, ballads and gospel songs) were registered in America. These American efforts have been discussed by Steven Biel in *Down with the Old Canoe: A Cultural History of the* Titanic *Disaster* (1996) and their registration details can be found in the Titanic *Disaster Music* archive in the American Folklife Center (Library of Congress).

There were British songs, too. Edwardian sentimentality dominated the sheet music, and contemporary cultural beliefs and prejudices were to the fore. For example, two songs released on record in 1912 were 'Stand to Your Post (Women and Children First)' and 'Be British (Dedicated to the Gallant Crew of the *Titanic*)'. Both wade shamelessly in the opportune shallows of two kinds of chauvinism (national and male), though the writer of the first could claim that he was merely honouring a law of the sea that Second Officer Lightoller called at the American hearings a law of human nature. The writer of the second could claim that he was merely commemorating the alleged last words of Captain Smith to his crew as he released them from service when the end was imminent. Both proved resilient notions for much of the twentieth century: the first has not been entirely discredited or jettisoned as a code of behaviour in emergencies, while Smith's exhortation was repeated a couple of years later and helped mobilise an army, and there may have remained in the call to arms some echo of *Titanic* and her sad captain. Still, much of the music of the disaster was both opportunistic and, not surprisingly, bad.

Some of that music was instrumental. 'A Descriptive Musical Sketch (Piano, Chorus and Reciter)' was staged soon after the sinking. There was also a recording of 'The Wreck of the *Titanic*' ('Descriptive Piano Solo, right from the scene where the ship's bell rings for departure to the pathetic "burial at sea" ... reminiscent of the sad disaster which will live in history as long as the world rolls on'). What the quality of this was I do not know, and it is possible that the sales pitch betrays the artistry of this unknown work. Also unknown, because lost, was an unperformed 'music drama', *Titanic*, composed by Platon G. Brounoff (1863–1924), a Russian-born American composer and pianist of some contemporary renown. The musicology reference books tell us that he studied in St Petersburg with Anton Rubinstein and Rimsky-Korsakoff, going to the United States in 1891. His compositions include *Ramona*, 'an Indian opera', an oratorio: *The Glory of God* and another music drama, *Xilona*. Perhaps the prospect of his 'patriotic song', 'America, My Glorious Land' (words by B. Dahl) does not raise the heart but it is nonetheless a great pity that *Titanic*, advertised on the cover of the sheet music of this song (which is in the Titanic *Disaster Music* archive), has been lost.

Fare thee well, *Titanic*

We have already discussed the race-consciousness that informed the *Titanic* tragedy, and the class-consciousness and gender-consciousness that were likewise never far away. However, the depth and creativity of black American reaction to the tragedy is surprising. To understand it, since there were no black passengers or crew, we have to leap some cultural gaps. That reaction is perhaps the most extraordinary artistic response the tragedy provoked at the time.

In 1928, Newman White wrote that:

> Within the last twenty years the events which have most impressed the Negro folk-singer's imagination have been the sinking of the Titanic, the advent of the boll weevil, the spurious discovery of the

North Pole (strangely, the authentic discovery moved him not), and the World War.

It was disaster that seemed to move the black singer, and disaster could so easily be given a religious construction. White tells us that the black religious songs arose mainly as a result of the missionary activities of the Methodists and Baptists among the slaves in the early and middle nineteenth century. Some slave-owners were opposed to proselytism on grounds that religion lowered morale among slaves, others encouraged it on grounds that religion 'helps production and discipline'. Some owners banned melancholy songs and promoted cheerful music and senseless words. Either way, White remarks that the black spiritual is 'in origin a product of exploitation'. The consolations of Christianity for the poor and oppressed are obvious, and disaster too is an indirect consolation, a reminder that men, even white slave-owners, are powerless and that the world is guided, and good rewarded, from above. Disasters were caused by irreligiousness or arrogance or badness, and the most instructive were those that reduced even temporarily the rich and wicked to the stature of the poor and oppressed.

The religious disaster song took its place beside gospel music as black musical expression, and Levine explains that the former 'became an increasingly common feature of twentieth-century Negro sacred music'. The songs were composed by an individual who had the lyrics printed on paper and sold the sheets for a nickel each. They were circulated by the composer and itinerant singers and from the 1920s, by recordings. Levine instances Charles Haffer Jr who wrote over 100 songs from 1909 onwards and supported himself by doing so. Haffer wrote about hurricanes, storms, fires and both world wars: he was a kind of musical Everett, Marshall & Mowbray Ltd. His first *Titanic* song sold 3,000 copies in 1912. One week after the maritime disaster, AE Perkins boarded a train and found a blind black preacher selling a ballad he had written about it; disaster was God talking in language humanity should be able to interpret: 'God Almighty talked like a natural man,/Spoke so the people could understand'. Levine concludes that no other contemporary event was as celebrated in black religious song as the loss of *Titanic*.

'The Great *Titanic*' was collected in Alabama in 1915 ('Sung by Negro on streets of Hackleburg in Northwest Ala.') but was surely composed and sung in the year of the tragedy. It has since become famous – the chorus is 'It was sad when that great ship went down' – and uses some of the motifs that inhabit both the religious disaster song in general and the *Titanic* song in particular composed by the serious or professional 'ballet' (or ballad) singer.

The first motif is the arrogance of the rich and dispensability of the poor:

> The rich had declared that they would not ride with the poor.
> So they put the poor below,
> They were the first to go

The second motif is the pride of the builders:

> We will build a ship that water can't go through;
> But God with power in hand
> Showed the world that it could not stand

A third motif is the vulnerability of the passengers that must have struck a chord with black listeners with their consciousness of exile from their distant homeland. Perhaps it provoked memories of the slave-ships:

> Those people on that ship were a long ways from home,
> With friends all around they didn't know that the time had come;
> Death came riding by,
> Sixteen hundred had to die

'The Great *Titanic*' also deals with the helpless recourse to one hymn in particular:

> They say that they were singing 'Nearer My God to Thee.'
> While some were homeward bound,
> Sixteen hundred had to drown

The homeward-bound journey with its religious and allegorical freight of meaning is a huge motif in black 'ballet' and blues songs.[6]

An equally famous *Titanic* song is 'God Moves on the Water', said to have been written by Blind Willie Johnson and recorded in December 1929 in New Orleans, though it is probable that the song existed in some form before that year and that Johnson was availing himself of extant versions, in the folk way. The famous collectors, Lomax *père et fils*, collected it from Lightnin' Washington with a group of black convicts in Darrington State Farm (i.e. prison), Texas, in 1933. The futility of earthly grandeur and riches, as Levine puts it, is a recurring idea in the *Titanic* (and religious disaster) songs and in 'God Moves on the Water' it is embodied in 'Jacob Nash,' clearly John Jacob Astor, and a reminder that the fitfulness of communication in 1912, especially across continents and ethnicities and in oral communities, resulted in garbling. In Rabbit Brown's 'The *Titanic*' (see my *Titanic*, 1999, for the full text), Southampton becomes 'South Hamilton'. As Nash, Astor sees the uselessness of money in a calamity:

> Well, that Jacob Nash was a millionaire,
> Lawd, he had plenty of money to spare;
> When the great Titanic was sinkin' down,
> Well, he could not pay his fare.[7]

In these songs, Astor, the fabulously wealthy white man cannot adapt to the circumstances of the disaster, unlike his opposite, a poor black man who can adapt even to the extent of being an escape artist. According to White (whose tone of condescension jars nowadays),

> The sinking of the Titanic was a shock great enough to penetrate even the comparative insulation in which the folk Negro lives; moreover, it was a wreck, and Negroes will always thrill to wrecks. The 'ballet' singer was sobered by it and tuned it to tragedy after the manner of his kind, but the folk Negro soon turned it to jest. He was not there, but on the back of a mule; his alibi is convincing, so why worry.

The transformation of the black non-passenger in this way is far more interesting and complex than White realises.

The black man on a mule's back was usually singing 'Alabama Bound', itself a song and not just a motif in a refrain to other songs. The other songs in which 'Alabama Bound' figures share a formulaic situation. In the version of 'The Great *Titanic*' mentioned above, the lucky passengers are homeward bound but in other versions by black singers (White gives us them), in the penultimate line of the verse the singer is asked the question 'Oh! Where was you when de old Titanic went down?' and replies in the last line of the verse, 'I wus on de back of er mule singing "Alabama Bound"'. This question and reply appear to have lived a semi-independent song existence, as in the version:

> O, what were you singing
> When the Titanic went down?
> O, what were you singing when the Titanic went down?
> Sitting on a mule's back,
> Singing, 'Alabama Bound'.

Sometimes, the answer relocates what seems like an accusation and alibi: 'I was with my honey in the heart of town.' This reply predates the *Titanic* disaster and was given in a song collected in Mississippi and printed in the *Journal of American Folk-Lore* in 1909, three years before the sinking; it is the Captain's alibi and self-exculpation:

O where were you when the steamer went down, Captain?
O where were you when the steamer went down, Captain?
O where were you when the steamer went down, Captain?
I was with my honey in the heart of town.

(This motif occurs more familiarly in the spiritual, 'Where were you when they crucified my Lord?' There is an accusation implicit in the question.) It is extraordinary how the *Titanic* case fits the existing formulas. Where *was* Captain Smith when the steamer went down? And, indeed, no black man *was* on *Titanic* and therefore was somewhere else.

The identification of the truant captain and the truant black man through their mutual need for an alibi is unusual and purely structural. The black man with an alibi derives perhaps from the sociological fact of black men's being routinely suspected and accused of crimes, after the civil war and their emancipation, and having to provide alibis. That the black man is apparently on the run derives perhaps from the fact of slavery itself, while the motif of 'moving on' (requiring all those 'travelling shoes' in the country blues) derives perhaps from the unstable mobility of post-slavery America and the prizing of motion after the enforced sedentariness of plantation living.

One exemplar of the black man with an alibi, but a man too quick for his pursuers and therefore without real need for an alibi, is the figure known (with what would now be regarded as great offensiveness) as the 'Travelling Coon'. One version in the Frank C. Brown Collection of North Carolina Folklore begins:

Once there was a travelling coon
Who was born in Tennessee.
He made his living stealing chickens
And everything else he could see.

Pursued by the police, he hopped a freight train no matter how fast it is going. And before he was finally cornered and shot down, he availed himself of the world's largest, and one of the fastest, liners.

That coon got on the *Titanic* steamship
And sailed across the ocean blue.
When he saw that iceberg a-comin',
Right overboard he flew.

The people standin' aroun'
Said that nigger was sure a fool,
But when that Titanic ship went down,
He was shootin' craps in Liverpool.

A note to this version tells us it was 'sung by travelling minstrel at King's Mountain, Cleveland County, NC' in 1919. Many songs in the Brown Collection were obtained from white informants who had learned them from other white people who regarded them as black songs. This one belongs to the blackface minstrel repertoire. The minstrel show was a white man's interpretation of black people that started in the 1840s and lasted until the movies drove it out of business around the time of the Great War. (It spread to the British Isles – there is a reference to the minstrel show in James Joyce's 1907 story, 'The Dead' – and even experienced a new lease of fragmentary life on BBC television in the 1950s and early 1960s.)

But the figure of the Travelling Coon travels beyond the limits of the minstrel show. The chorus runs:

> Well, he travelled and was known for miles around,
> And he didn't get enough, he didn't get enough,
> Till the police [*police*] shot him down.

These lines, White tells us, seem to be based on the chorus of the modern minstrel song, current between 1905 and 1915: 'He rambled, he rambled, he rambled all around town./He rambled, he rambled, he rambled till the butcher cut him down' (which New Orleans jazz fans will recognize as 'Didn't He Ramble'). The Coon is one version of those ubiquitous figures in American folklore (and society), the Outlaw and Fugitive but also the Trickster whom we find in white, black and red folklore. When the crime or calamity happens, he is often to be found gaming, drinking or dancing. Abbe Niles, in the *Bookman* in 1928, reminded readers of a *Titanic* song that Carl Sandburg had not included in his *American Songbag* (c.1927), remembered for Niles by WC Handy ('Father of the Blues') and which had been sung at the Monogram Theatre, Chicago by 'String Beans', 'a Negro entertainer of high and odoriferous fame':

> I was on dat great Titanic
> De night dat she went down;
> Ev'ybody wondered
> Why I didn't drown–
> I had dem Elgin movements in ma hips,
> Twenty years' guarantee!

My guess is that the singer's prowess in a contemporary dance form allowed him to swim his way to safety.

When Huddie Ledbetter ('Leadbelly', b.1885) offered his musical contribution to Titanica, he moved across from the religious disaster song to the secular song of sharper social comment. But in 'De *Titanic*', he drew on the figure of the black absentee when he had Jack Johnson, the heavyweight champion of the world, refused embarkation on *Titanic*:

> Jack Johnson wanted to get on board,
> Captain said, 'I ain't haulin' no coal'
> Cryin', 'Fare thee well, Titanic, fare thee well'.

Leadbelly wrote in a letter to Moses Asch: 'There was not no Negroes died on that ship. But Jack Johnson went to get on board. "We are not hauling no coal", (they said) ... it was so much Jim Crow he could not have no go'.[8] This incident has never been verified, but in any case Johnson is in Leadbelly's song a preexisting jokester folk figure who could have been found dancing when the ship sank:

> Jack Johnson heard the mighty shock,
> Might 'a seen the black rascal doin' th' Eagle Rock.
> Cryin', "Fare thee well, Titanic, fare thee well'.[9]

It is extraordinary but true that the protean black man established a presence on *Titanic* on the testimony of those who presumably had never heard of the Travelling Coon or String Beans or the black man on a mule singing 'Alabama Bound'. In her book, *When We Went First Class* (1977), Ellen Williamson, whose aunt and uncle were first-class passengers who embarked at Cherbourg, reported (via her aunt who survived) that her uncle had told his wife that some friends of theirs had seen a black-faced stoker peering at them through a hole in the smokestack (funnel) of an adjacent ship while they were docked in Southampton. 'Several *Titanic* passengers took it as bad luck and were upset.' A later report was of a grinning stoker peering down from Titanic's fourth (dummy) funnel while the ship was in Queenstown, the one a Mr. Whyte seems to have photographed on another occasion from shore.

It is hard not to connect these apparitions with the mysterious crewman who Bride told the *New York Times* reporter had tried to steal Jack Phillips' lifebelt in the Marconi radio shack in the last minutes of the ship's life:

> While he worked something happened I hate to tell about. I was back in my room getting Phillips' money for him, and as I looked out the door I saw a stoker, or somebody from below decks, leaning over Phillips from behind. He was too busy to notice what the man was doing. The man was slipping the life belt off Phillips's back. He was a big man, too. As you can see, I am very small. I don't know what it was I got hold of. I remembered

in a flash the way Phillips had clung on – how I had to fix that life belt in place because he was too busy to do it. I knew that man from below decks had his own life belt and should have known where to get it. I suddenly felt a passion not to let that man die a decent sailor's death. I wished he might have stretched rope or walked a plank. I did my duty. I hope I finished him. I don't know. We left him on the cabin floor of the wireless room and he was not moving.

At the American Inquiry, Bride said simply and with different detail: 'We forced him away. I held him and Mr. Phillips hit him.'

There's a disturbing ardency in Bride's accounts: there is a needless machismo explicable perhaps by the exhilaration of his experience but also a less pleasant class or even race animus. In any case, Logan Marshall apparently found it easy to turn the stoker into a 'negro' stoker and irresponsibly to invent appropriate dialogue between Phillips and Bride and unpleasantly mangle Bride's testimonies.

> An hour later, when the second wireless man came into the boxlike room to tell his companion what the situation was, he found a negro stoker creeping up behind the operator and saw him raise a knife over his head. He said afterwards – he was among those rescued – that he realized at once that the negro intended to kill the operator in order to take his lifebelt from him. The second operator pulled out his revolver and shot the negro dead.

Oddly enough (but this is not to exonerate Marshall of racism), there is a song, 'De *Titanic*' (different from Leadbelly's) apparently composed by a black singer and with a black stoker as a character. This song was included in Sandburg's *Songbag* and according to the editor was sung by black troops crossing the submarine zone of the Atlantic and in the trenches during the Great War. His version was collected from the singing of a Georgia singer, Bessie Zaban. When the 'icebug' rips the ship's side, Bill a black stoker comes on deck to report water below, only to be told by the captain, 'Go back, Bill, an' shut yo' mouth,/Got forty-eight pumps to keep de water out!' Although Bill is not mentioned again in Zaban's version (the song ends by resembling 'The Great *Titanic*'), the truncated folk structure would seem to suggest that Bill ought to appear three times (following folklore's Law of Three) and that he ought to be the hero of the song. He does reappear in, and is the Trickster hero of, a later, urban black form called 'the *Titanic* Toast' which was especially alive on the streets of Philadelphia.

The 'Toast' could be on a number of subjects and was improvisational; rather than being sung it was rhythmically chanted along its narrative in extensible lines of rhyming couplets. The Toast is related to other black expressions and forms: jive talk, rap, the talking blues, and that verbal game called 'the Dozens'. (Both Moses Asch and Pete Seeger reported that Leadbelly in ordinary conversation would sometimes 'get on a rhyming kick. For a couple hours (sic) on end every sentence that came out of his mouth was rhymed'.) In the *Titanic* Toast, the hero is Shine, a would-be epic figure like John Henry but with humble Trickster elements that relate him to the Travelling Coon and Brer Rabbit. (According to Levine, the name derives from black slang for a very dark-skinned person: 'He's so black he shines', but I wonder if is an ironic self-reference by young urban black men to one stereotype of Uncle Tom, 'Shoeshine'.)

It is Shine, in the words of Roger D. Abrahams:

> who informs the ship's captain about the holes in the hull after the ship crashes with the iceberg. The captain keeps sending him down to pump, and he keeps re-emerging, giving the captain further information on the size of the hole. Finally Shine jumps in the water and begins swimming. He is then offered three temptations from those still on board – money from the captain and sex from the captain's wife and his daughter. All of these he turns down because of the practical demands of his predicament; he is then challenged by the shark and the whale but is able to out-perform them. He swims safely to shore.

Shine's ordeal is a repetition of Bill's:

> Shine went up on deck, said, 'Captain, I was downstairs
> Eating my peas
> Till the water come up to my knees.'
> Captain said, 'Shine, Shine, sit your black ass down.
> I got ninety-nine pumps to pump the water down'.

Shine's triumph is like Jack Johnson's, as in this version: 'when all them white folks went to heaven,/Shine was in Sugar Ray's bar drinking Seagram's Seven'. Most versions of his success could not be recited in, as they used to say, polite company. The *Titanic* Toast is a revenge narrative which in symbolic compensation reverses the black-white power relationship that obtained in the Age of *Titanic* and the decades after. Etheridge Knight the black poet wrote an angrier *Titanic* Toast in our own day of black civil rights agitation, 'Dark Prophecy: I Sing of Shine'.

The black songs of *Titanic* reflect, or rather refract, the American race and class reality at the time the great ship went down with its extraordinary human complement. It is a matter of astonishment that the ship, with no black passengers on board, should be such a creative catalyst after it sank. But then, the black art it provoked is only a part, though perhaps the most surprising part, of the creative response that greeted news of her death. That response extended beyond the Age of *Titanic* into the two generations that followed and the energy of that response has not yet been depleted.

[1] In his testimony to the American hearings, Fifth Officer Lowe distinguished 'listing' (a sideways tilt) from 'tipping' (a bow down motion). Tipping was in the case of a large well-lighted ship at night a more spectacular event.

[2] Paul Heyer in *The Titanic Legacy: Disaster as Media Event and Myth* (1995) has analysed contemporary *Titanic* reportage, particularly by the *New York Times*, as a media phenomenon and milestone.

[3] In the United States, *Titanic* was published as *The Titanic Reader* (2000).

[4] I am reading the Preface to *The Loss of S.S. Titanic: Its Story and Its Lessons* in *The Story of the* Titanic *as Told by Its Survivors* (1960), edited by Jack Winocur, which reproduces the original 1912 text. However, the October 1912 (or second, revised) edition published in London omits the Houghton Mifflin references in its Preface.

[5] Gracie is alluding here to Mary Adams Bulkley, *A Letter Describing the Wreck of the S.S. Ville du Havre, November 23, 1873 from Mrs. Mary Adams Bulkley of Rye, New York to her Mother, Mrs. Adams of Augusta, Georgia: Written at Sea, November 28, 1873* (New York: James A. Anderson, 1873).

[6] The complication, typical of folklore, is that 'The Great *Titanic*' was subsequently sung by many singers, including white ones such as Woody Guthrie and Cisco Houston, and Roy Acuff, under the title of 'When the Great Ship Went Down.' Similar lyrics have been attributed to a WO Smith who drove a horse cab in Durham, North Carolina between 1912 and 1915. The song became very popular just before the Second World War and was sung by soldiers (presumably with jocularly nervous irony) on the troop transports crossing the Atlantic; a version appears in *The Book of Navy Songs* (1955).

[7] However, in another version, entitled 'The *Titanic*,' Astor is correctly identified and plays a champion's role: 'One man, John Jacob Astor,/A man with pluck and brains,/While this great ship was sinkin',/All the women he tried to save.' See *Sing Out!* (Vol.18, nos. 2,3, 1968).

[8] Some caution is advised when discussing Leadbelly's song. In *Leadbelly: A Collection of World-Famous Songs by Huddie Ledbetter* (1959), edited by the Lomaxes, we are told that 'De *Titanic*' has been edited with new additional material by the editors.

[9] Since we have associated Arthur Conan Doyle with *Titanic*, it might of interest that Doyle was approached by letter on December 9, 1909 with an invitation to be a ringside referee at the championship bout between Johnson and Jim Jeffries, Doyle's name having been welcomed by Tex Rickard, the fight's promoter. 'It would indeed rejoice the hearts of the men in this country if you were at the ring side when the negro fighter meets the white man Jeffries for the world's championship.' Engagements and distance caused Doyle regretfully to decline.

sources

Chapter One: A Mechanical Age

Adams, Henry. 1918. *The Education of Henry Adams*. Ed. Ira Nadel. Oxford: Oxford University Press, 1999.

Anon. 1911. "Launch of the *Titantic* [sic]." *International Marine Engineering*: 281-83 (July).

Anon. 1912. "Harland and Wolff's Works at Belfast." *Engineering 94*: 3-12 (July 5), 38-50 (July 12).

Arnold, Matthew. 1868. *Culture and Anarchy*. Cambridge: Cambridge University Press, 1960.

Astor, John Jacob. 1894. *A Journey in Other Worlds: A Romance of the Future*. London: Longmans, Green.

Bardon, Jonathan. 1982. *Belfast: An Illustrated History*. Belfast: Blackstaff Press.

Belford, Barbara. 1996. *Bram Stoker: A Biography of the Author of Dracula*. New York: Alfred A. Knopf.

Bisset, Sir James. 1959. *Tramps and Ladies: My Early Years in Steamers*. New York: Criterion Books.

Butler, Samuel. 1872. *Erewhon, or Over the Range*. Ed. Peter Mudford. London: Penguin Books, 1970. (In his Notes, Mudford quotes Disraeli's *Coningsby*.)

Bradbury, Malcolm and James McFarlane, eds. *Modernism 1890-1930*. Harmondsworth, Middlesex: Penguin Books.

British Commission of Enquiry into the Loss of the S.S. Titanic. May-June, 1912.

Carlyle, Thomas. 1829. "Signs of the Times." *Edinburgh Review 40*: 441-4. Repr. *A Carlyle Reader*. Ed. G.B. Tennyson. New York: Modern Library, 1969.

Chronicle of the 20th century. 1988. Ed.-in-chief, Derrik Mercer. Farnborough, Hampshire: Chronicle Communications.

Chronicle of the 20th Century. 1994. Ed.in-chief, Clifton Daniel. Liberty, MO: JL International Publishing.

Conrad, Joseph. 1912. "Some Reflexions, Seamanlike and Otherwise, on the Loss of the *Titanic*." *The English Review 11*: 304-15.

Conrad, Joseph. 1912. "Some Aspects of the Admirable Inquiry." *The English Review 11*: 581-95. Repr. as "Certain Aspects of the Admirable Inquiry into the Loss of the *Titanic*" in Conrad's *Notes on Life & Letters* (1921).

Dickens, Charles. 1842. Quoted in Maddocks (see below).

Eksteins, Modris. c1989. *Rites of Spring: the Great War and the Birth of the Modern Age*. Toronto: Lester & Orpen Dennys.

Everett, Marshall, ed. 1912. *Wreck and Sinking of the Titanic: The Ocean's Greatest Disaster*. [S.I.]: L.H. Walter.

Fisher, Trevor. 1989. *Portrait of a Decade, 1910-19*. London: B.T. Batsford.

Fletcher, RA. 1913. *Travelling Palaces: Luxury in Passenger Steamships*. London: Sir Isaac Pitman & Sons.

Ford, Boris, ed. *Victorian Britain*. The Cambridge Cultural History of Britain Vol. 7. Cambridge: Cambridge University Press.

Forster, E.M. 1909. "The Machine Stops" in *The New Collected Short Stories*. London: Sidgwick & Jackson.

Forster, E.M. 1910. *Howards End*. London: Edward Arnold.

Freeman, Michael. 1999. *Railways and the Victorian Imagination*. New Haven: Yale University Press.

Grun, Bernard. 1975. *The Timetables of History*. Third Revised Edition. New York: Simon & Schuster, 1991.

Hayes, Carlton J.H. 1941. *A Generation of Materialism, 1871-1900*. New York: Harper & Row.

Hood, A.G., ed. 1911. "The White Star Triple-Screw Atlantic Liners *Olympic* and *Titanic*, 45,000 Tons, the Largest Steamships in the World." Souvenir Number of *The Shipbuilder* 6: 1-130.

Houghton, W.E. 1957. *The Victorian Frame of Mind*. New Haven, Ct.: Yale University Press.

Huxley, T.H. 1887. Quoted in W.E. Houghton, *The Victorian Frame of Mind 1830-1870*. New Haven, Ct.: Yale University Press, 1957.

Illustrated London News. 1912.

Kern, Stephen. 1983. *The Culture of Time and Space, 1880-1918*. Cambridge, Mass.: Harvard University Press.

Le Quesne, A.L. 1982. "Carlyle," in *Victorian Thinkers*. Ed. Keith Thomas. Oxford: Oxford University Press, 1993.

Literary Digest. 1912. New York.

Lord, Walter. 1955. *A Night to Remember*. New York: Holt, Rinehart & Winston. Repr. New York: Bantam, 1956.

Lord, Walter. 1986. *The Night Lives On*. New York: Avon Books.

McCluskie, Tom. 1998. *Anatomy of the* Titanic. London: PRC Publishing.

Maddocks, Melvin, *et al.*, ed. *The Great Liners*. Alexandria, Va.: Time-Life Books, 1978.

Marinetti, F.T. 1972. *Marinetti: Selected Writings*. Eds. R.W. Flint and Arthur A. Coppotelli. London: Secker & Warburg.

Masterman, C.F.G. 1909. *The Condition of England*. London: Methuen, 1912.

Review of Reviews. Christmas Number 1892 ("From the Old World to the New"); *24* (1901); *40* (1909); *41, 42* (1910); *43* (1911); *45* (1912).

Rose, Jonathan. 1986. "The Efficiency Men," in *The Edwardian Temperament, 1895-1919*. Athens, Ohio: Ohio University Press.

Ruskin, John. 1900. *The Complete Works*. Vol. 9: *Fors Clavigera* (vols. 1-4). New York: Kelmscott Society.

Ryves, Reginald. 1912. "The Strength of Large Ships." *Scientific American Supplement*. No. 1900.

Shaw, G.B. 1912. "The Titanic: Some Unmentioned Morals." Letters to the *Daily News*. Repr. Bernard Shaw, *Agitations: Letters to the Press 1875-1950*. Ed. Dan H. Laurence and James Rambeau. New York: Ungar, 1985.

Smiles, Samuel. 1897. *Men of Invention and Industry*. London: John Murray.

Spufford, Francis. 1996. *I May Be Some Time: Ice and the English Imagination*. London: Faber and Faber.

Stead, W.T. 1912. "Character Sketch: Lord Pirrie." *Review of Reviews* 45: 243-49.

Stoker, Bram. 1907. "The World's Greatest Ship-building Yard." *The World's Work* (U.K.), no.54, 647-50.

Swinton, A.A. Campbell. 1907. "The Story of the Steam Turbine and its Inventor." *The World's Work* 10: 266-69.

Trager, James, ed. 1994. *The People's Chronology*. New York: Henry Holt.

Ure, Andrew (1835) and John Fielden (1836) in Alasdair Clayre, ed. *Nature & Industrialization*. Oxford: Oxford University Press and the Open University, 1977.

Weber, Max. 1930. *The Protestant Ethic and the Spirit of Capitalism*. Trans. Talcott Parsons. Intro. Anthony Giddens. London: Routledge, 1992.

Wells, H.G. 1894-1909. *The Country of the Blind and Other Stories*. Ed. Michael Sherborne. New York: Oxford University Press, 1996.

Wells, H.G. 1901. *Anticipations and Other Papers*. London: T. Fisher Unwin, 1924.

White, Alma. 1913. *The Titanic Tragedy–God Speaking to the Nations*. Bound Brook, N.J.: Pentecostal Union.

The World's Work (U.K.) *10* (1907); *19* (1912).

Young, Filson. 1912. *Titanic*. London: Grant Richards.

Chapter Two: The Frozen Deep

Barley, Alfred H. 1922. *The Drayson Problem: His Important Astronomical Discovery*. Exeter: Wm Pollard & Co.

Barley, Alfred H. *et al.* 1927. *The Ice Age: Its Date, Duration, and Astronomical Cause Investigated by the Late Maj.-General A.W. Drayson*. Lewes, Sussex: W.E. Baxter.

Bevis, Richard W. 1999. *The Road to Egdon Heath: The Aesthetics of the Great in Nature*. Montreal: McGill-Queen's University Press.

Bisset, Sir James. 1959. *Tramps and Ladies: My Early Years in Steamers*. New York: Criterion Books.

Borchgrevink, C.E. 1901. *First on the Antarctic Continent, Being an Account of the British Antarctic Expedition 1898-1900*. Montreal: McGill-Queen's University Press, 1980.

Brannan, Robert Louis. 1966. *Under the Management of Mr. Charles Dickens: His Production of "The Frozen Deep."* Ithaca, N.Y.: Cornell University Press.

Canetti, Elias. 1979. *The Tongue Set Free: Remembrance of a European Childhood* in *The Memoirs of Elias Canetti*. Trans. Joachim Neugroschel. New York: Farrar, Straus & Giroux, 1999.

Deacon, Margaret. 1971. *Scientists and the Sea 1650-1900: A Study of Marine Science*. London; Academic Press.

Ellis, Richard. 1996. *Deep Atlantic: Life, Death, and Exploration in the Abyss*. New York: Alfred A. Knopf.

Flint, Kate. 2000. *The Victorians and the Visual Imagination*. Cambridge: Cambridge University Press.

Foster, John Wilson. 1999. *Titanic*. London: Penguin. 2000. *The Titanic Reader*. New York: Viking Penguin.

Gage, John D. and Paul A. Tyler. 1991. *Deep-Sea Biology: A Natural History of Organisms at the Deep-Sea Floor*. Cambridge: Cambridge University Press.

Idyll, C.P. 1971. *Abyss: The Deep Sea and the Creatures that Live in It*. New York: Thomas Y. Crowell.

Illustrated London News. 1912.

Irish News and Belfast Morning News. April 20, 1912.

Linklater, Eric. 1972. *The Voyage of the* Challenger. London: Sphere Books, 1974.

Literary Digest 1912.

Marshall, N.B. 1954. *Aspects of Deep Sea Biology*. London: Hutchinson.

Maxtone-Graham, John. 1988. *Safe Return Doubtful: The Heroic Age of Polar Exploration*. New York: Barnes & Noble.

New York Times. April 16-21, 1912. Special Commemorative Section. April 15, 1998.

Review of Reviews 23 (1901); *40* (1909).

Robins, Elizabeth. 1904. *The Magnetic North*. London: Heinemann.

Robins, Elizabeth. 1908. *Come and Find Me!* London: Heinemann.

Shackleton, Sir Ernest. 1912. "The Future of Exploration." *North American Review* 1, 414-24.

Spufford, Francis. 1996. *I May Be Some Time: Ice and the English Imagination*. London: Faber and Faber.

Thomson, C. Wyville. 1873. *The Depths of the Sea: An Account of the General results of the Dredging Cruises of HMSS* Porcupine *and* Lightning *during the summers of 1868, 1869, and 1870*. London: Macmillan and Co.

Verne, Jules. 1869. *Twenty Thousand Leagues under the Sea*. London: Penguin, 1994.

Wells, H.G. 1894. "Life in the Abyss." Repr. in *H.G. Wells: Early Writings in Science and Science Fiction*, ed. Robert M. Philmus and David Y. Hughes. Berkeley: University of California Press, 1975.

Wilson, Andrew. 1912. *Illustrated London News*. May 11.

Chapter Three: In Memoriam

Beesley, Lawrence. 1912. *The Loss of the R.M.S.* Titanic: *Its Story and Its Lessons*. London: Heinemann.

Biel, Steven. 1996. *Down with the Old Canoe: A Cultural History of the* Titanic *Disaster*. New York: W.W. Norton.

Biel, Steven. 1998. *Titanica: The Disaster of the Century in Poetry, Song, and Prose*. New York: W.W. Norton.

Bown, Mark and Roger Simmons. 1987. *R.M.S.* Titanic: *A Portrait on Old Picture Postcards*. Loggerheads: Brampton Publications.

Bradley, Ian, ed. 1989. *The Penguin Book of Hymns*. London: Penguin.

Bradley, Ian. 1997. *Abide with Me: The World of Victorian Hymns*. London: SCM Press.

British Commission of Enquiry into the Loss of the S.S. Titanic. May-June, 1912.

Cherry-Garrard, Apsley. 1922. *The Worst Journey in the World*. New York: Carroll & Graf, 1989.

Collyer, Charlotte. 1912. Letter repr. in *Titanic Voices*, ed. Donald Hyslop, Alastair Forsyth, Sheila Jemima (1994). "How I was Saved from the *Titanic*." *The Semi-Monthly Magazine*, May 26.

Davie, Michael. 1986. *The* Titanic: *The Full Story of a Tragedy*. London: Bodley Head.

Etude (Philadelphia). June, 1912.

Everett, Marshall, ed. 1912. *Wreck and Sinking of the* Titanic: *The Ocean's Greatest Disaster*. [S.I.]: L.H. Walter.

Gibbs, Philip, ed. 1912. *The Deathless Story of the* Titanic. London: Lloyd's Weekly News. Facs. Reprint, Lloyd's of London Press.

Gracie, Colonel Archibald. 1913. *The Truth about the* Titanic. New York: M. Kennerley.

Harrison, J.F.C. 1990. *Late Victorian Britain 1870-1901*. London: Fontana Press.

Howells, Richard. 1999. *The Myth of the* Titanic. New York: St. Martin's Press.

Illustrated London News. 1912.

Jack, Ian. 1999. "Leonardo's Grave." *Granta* 67, 8-37.

Jeffers, Alan and Rob Gordon. 1998. *Titanic Halifax: A Guide to Sites*. Halifax: Nimbus Publishing.

Lawrence, D.H. 1928. "Hymns in a Man's Life." *Evening News*. Repr. in D.H. Lawrence, *Selected Literary Criticism*. Ed. Anthony Beal. New York: Viking Press, 1966.

Literary Digest. 1912.

Lord, Walter. 1955. *A Night to Remember*. New York: Holt, Rinehart & Winston. Repr. New York: Bantam, 1956.

Lord, Walter. 1986. *The Night Lives On*. New York: Avon Books.

Marshall, Logan, ed. 1912. *Sinking of the Titanic and Great Sea Disasters: A Detailed and Accurate Account of the Most Awful Marine Disaster in History, Constructed from the Real Facts as Obtained from Those on Board Who Survived*. [S.I.]: L.T. Myers.

Mowbray, Jay Henry, ed. 1912. *Sinking of the Titanic: Eyewitness Accounts*. New York: Dover Publications, 1998.

New York Times. April 16-21, 1912. Special Commemorative Section. April 15, 1998.

Review of Reviews 25 (1901); 44 (1911); 45 (1912).

Robins, Elizabeth. 1908. *Come and Find Me!* London: Heinemann.

San Francisco Examiner. April 16, 1912.

Shaw, George Bernard. 1912. "Hymn Singing." *Daily Citizen*, October 26. Repr. in G.B. Shaw, *Agitations: Letters to the Press 1875-1950*. Eds. Dan H. Laurence and James Rambeau. New York: Frederick Ungar, 1985.

Stead, W.T. 1896. *Hymns that have Helped: Being a Collection of Hymns which have been Found most Useful to the Children of Men*. New York: Doubleday and McClure Co., 1897.

Watson, J.R. 1997. *The English Hymn: A Critical and Historical Study*. Oxford: Clarendon Press.

Wilson, Edward. 1972. *Diary of the Terra Nova Expedition to the Antarctic 1910-1912*. New York: Humanities Press.

Chapter Four: The Goblin Footfall

Anon. 1912. "John Bull, Junior–Slacker. The Rubicon of Boyhood, and Some Stepping-Stones." *The World's Work 21*: 15-18.

Appeal to Reason. May 4, 1912. Girard, Kansas.

Barrett, John. 1900. "America's Duty in China." *North American Review*, 171.

Beesley, Lawrence. 1912. *The Loss of the R.M.S. Titanic: Its Story and Its Lessons*. London: Heinemann.

Belfast News-Letter. April 22, 1912.

Beresford, Lord Charles. 1900. "The Future of the Anglo-Saxon Race." *North American Review 171*: 802-810.

Bernard, B., ed. 1900. *Anglo-Saxon Guide to the Paris Exhibition 1900*. London: Boot & Son.

Biel, Steven. 1998. *Titanica: The Disaster of the Century in Poetry, Song, and Prose*. New York: W.W. Norton.

Booth, [General] William. 1890. *In Darkest England and the Way Out*. London, New York: International Headquarters of the Salvation Army.

Boyd-Smith, Peter. 1994. *Titanic from Rare Historical Reports*. Southampton: Steamship Publications.

Bradbury, Malcolm. 1971. *The Social Context of Modern English Literature*. Oxford: Basil Blackwell.

Bryceson, Dave. 1997. *The Titanic Disaster as Reported in the British National Press April-July 1912*. Sparkford, Somerset: Patrick Stephens.

Butler, Daniel Allen. 1998. *"Unsinkable": The Full Story of RMS Titanic*. Mechanicsburg, PA: Stackpole Books.

Carey, John. 1992. *The Intellectuals and the Masses: Pride and Prejudice Among the Literary Intelligentsia 1880-1939*. London: Faber and Faber.

Collyer, Charlotte. 1912. "How I was Saved from the *Titanic.*" *The Semi-Monthly Magazine*, May 26.

Conan Doyle, Arthur. 1912. "Mr. Shaw and the *Titanic.*" *Daily News*, May 20. Reply to Shaw, May 25. Repr. in *The Unknown Conan Doyle: Letters to the Press*. Eds. John Michael Gibson and Richard Lancelyn Green. London: Secker & Warburg, 1986.

Conrad, Joseph. 1912. "Some Reflexions, Seamanlike and Otherwise, on the Loss of the *Titanic.*" *The English Review* 11: 304-15.

Conrad, Joseph. 1912. "Some Aspects of the Admirable Inquiry." *The English Review* 11: 581-95. Repr. as "Certain Aspects of the Admirable Inquiry into the Loss of the *Titanic*" in Conrad's *Notes on Life & Letters* (1921).

Duff Gordon, Lady. 1932. *Discretions and Indiscretions*. New York: Frederick A. Stokes.

Everett, Marshall, ed. 1912. *Wreck and Sinking of the* Titanic: *The Ocean's Greatest Disaster*. [S.I.]: L.H. Walter.

Fletcher, R.A. 1913. *Travelling Palaces: Luxury in Passenger Steamships*. London: Sir Isaac Pitman & Sons.

Forster, E.M. 1939. *What I Believe*. London: Hogarth Press.

Gill, Stephen. 1992. Introduction to George Gissing, *The Nether World*. Oxford: Oxford University Press.

Gissing, George. 1889. *The Nether World: A Novel*. Ed. and Intro. John Goode. Brighton: Harvester Press, 1974. *The Nether World*. Ed. and Intro. Stephen Gill. Oxford: Oxford University Press, 1992.

Gracie, Colonel Archibald. 1913. *The Truth about the* Titanic. New York: M. Kennerley.

Greenslade, William. 1994. *Degeneration, Culture and the Novel 1880-1940*. Cambridge: Cambridge University Press.

Holroyd, Michael. 1989. *Bernard Shaw*. Vol. II: *1898-1918, The Pursuit of Power*. New York: Random House.

Hood, A.G., ed. 1911. "The White Star Triple-Screw Atlantic Liners *Olympic* and *Titanic*, 45,000 Tons, the Largest Steamships in the World." Souvenir Number of *The Shipbuilder* 6: 1-130.

Illustrated London News. 1912.

Ireland, Alleyne. 1900. "Commercial Aspect of the Yellow Peril." *North American Review 171*: 389-400.

Lankester, E. Ray. 1880. *Degeneration: A Chapter in Darwinism*. New York: Humboldt Publishing Co., 1889.

"Launch of the *Titanic.*" *Belfast News-Letter*. June 1, 1911.

Literary Digest. 1912.

London, Jack. 1903. *The People of the Abyss*. New York: Macmillan. Facs. ed. New York: MSS Information Corporation, 1970.

Masterman, C.F.G. 1902. *From the Abyss: Of its Inhabitants by One of Them*. New York: Garland, 1980.

Masterman, C.F.G. 1909. *The Condition of England*. London: Methuen, 1912

New York Times. April 16-21, 1912. Special Commemorative Section. April 15, 1998.

Nordau, Max. 1892, 1895. *Degeneration*. London: Heinemann, 1913.

Ogg, Frederic Austin. 1907. "American Immigration at High Tide." *The World's Work* (U.S.) *14*: 8879-8886.

Pinney, Thomas. 2000. "Ships of Awesome Size: An Unpublished Poem by Rudyard Kipling." *Times Literary Supplement*, September 15.

Review of Reviews 23, 24 (1901); 44 (1911); 45 (1912).

Shaw, George Bernard. 1912. "The *Titanic*: Some Unmentioned Morals." *Daily News*, May 14. Reply to Conan Doyle, May 22. Repr. in G.B. Shaw, *Agitations: Letters to the Press 1875-1950*. Eds. Dan H. Laurence and James Rambeau. New York: Frederick Ungar, 1985.

Shiel, Matthew P. 1898. *The Yellow Danger*. Grant Richards's Colonial Library. London: Grant Richards. Repr. London: Routledge/Thoemmes Press, 1998.

Shutes, Elizabeth W. 1912. "When the *Titanic* Went Down." Repr. in Archibald Gracie, *The Truth about the* Titanic. (See above.)

Stead, Estelle W. 1913. *My Father: Personal & Spiritual Reminiscences*. New York: George H. Doran Company.

Stead, W.T. 1902. *The Americanization of the World*. New York: Garland, 1972.

Thompson, Flora McDonald. 1900. "Retrogression of the American Woman." *North American Review 171*: 748-753.

Tillett, Ben. 1912. Letter to the British Board of Trade. April 18.

Titanic *Disaster: Hearings before a Subcommittee of the Committee on Commerce, United States Senate*, April-May, 1912.

Trant, William. 1912. "Jew and Chinaman." *North American Review*, 1.

Trevelyan, G.M. 1901. "The White Peril." *Nineteenth Century 50*: 1043-1055.

Wanhope, Joshua. 1912. "Asiatic Immigration: How About It?" (Arising from the 1911 National Convention of the American Socialist Party.) *The Masses*.

Wells, H.G. 1894. "Zoological Retrogression." Repr. in *H.G. Wells: Early Writings in Science and Science Fiction*. Eds. R. Philmus and D.Y. Hughes. Berkeley: University of California Press, 1975.

Wells, H.G. 1894. "Life in the Abyss." Repr. in *H.G. Wells: Early Writings in Science and Science Fiction*. Eds. R. Philmus and D.Y. Hughes. Berkeley: University of California Press, 1975.

Wells, H.G. 1894-1909. *The Country of the Blind and Other Stories*. Ed. Michael Sherborne. New York: Oxford University Press, 1996.

Wells, H.G. 1901. *Anticipations and Other Papers*. London: T. Fisher Unwin, 1924.

White, Alma. 1913. *The Titanic Tragedy–God Speaking to the Nations*. Bound Brook, N.J.: Pentecostal Union.

White Star Line Royal Mail Triple-Screw Steamers "Olympic" and "Titanic." Liverpool: White Star Line, 1911. Repr. Cultra, Co. Down: Ulster Folk and Transport Museum, 1987.

Wolf, Nahum. 1912. "Are the Jews an Inferior Race?" *North American Review*, 1.

The World's Work (U.S.) *14* (1907).

The World's Work (U.K.) *21* (1912).

Chapter Five: Baffling Foresight

Beesley, Lawrence. 1912. *The Loss of the R.M.S.* Titanic: *Its Story and Its Lessons*. London: Heinemann.

Bennett, Arnold. 1932. *The Journals of Arnold Bennett, 1911-1921*. Ed. Newman Flower. London: Cassell.

Bisset, Sir James. 1959. *Tramps and Ladies: My Early Years in Steamers*. New York: Criterion Books.

Blavatsky, Mme. 1887-91. Quoted in *1900*. Eds. Mike Jay and Michael Neve. London; Penguin Books, 1999.

Bryceson, Dave. 1997. *The* Titanic *Disaster as Reported in the British National Press April-July 1912*. Sparkford, Somerset: Patrick Stephens.

Coates, James. 1913. *Has W.T. Stead Returned? A Symposium*. London: L.N. Fowler.

Conan Doyle, Sir Arthur. 1924. *Memories and Adventures*. Boston: Little, Brown, and Company.

Conan Doyle, Sir Arthur. 1930. *The Edge of the Unknown*. New York: G.P. Putnam's Sons.

Conan Doyle, Sir Arthur. 1919. "The New Spiritualism." *The Nation*, February 8. Repr. in *The Unknown Conan Doyle: Letters to the Press*. Eds. John Michael Gibson and Richard Lancelyn Green. London: Secker & Warburg, 1986.

Daily Mirror. April 17, 1912.

Doran, George H. 1952. "The Spiritualists." Quoted in *Sir Arthur Conan Doyle: Interviews and Recollections*. Ed. Harold Orel. London: Macmillan, 1991.

Duff Gordon, Lady. 1932. *Discretions and Indiscretions*. New York: Frederick A. Stokes.

Dupre, Catherine. 1976. *John Galsworthy: A Biography*. London: Collins.

Gardner, Martin. 1986. *The Wreck of the* Titanic *Foretold?* New York: Prometheus Books.

Gardiner, Robin and Dan Van der Vat. 1995. *The Riddle of the* Titanic. London: Orion, 1996.

Garnett, Mayn Clew. 1912. "The White Ghost of Disaster." Repr. in *The Wreck of the* Titanic *Foretold?* Ed. Martin Gardner. New York: Prometheus Books, 1986.

Gibbs, Philip, ed. 1912. *The Deathless Story of the* Titanic. London: Lloyd's Weekly News. Facs. Reprint, Lloyd's of London Press.

Goldfarb, Russell M. and Clare R. 1978. *Spiritualism and Nineteenth-Century Letters*. Cranbury, NJ: Associated University Presses.

Gracie, Colonel Archibald. 1913. *The Truth about the* Titanic. New York: M. Kennerley.

Haggard, Sir Rider H. 1926. *The Days of My Life: An Autobiography*. Ed. C.J. Longman. London: Longmans, Green.

Harrison, C.G. 1894. *The Transcendental Universe*. Quoted in *1900*. Eds. Mike Jay and Michael Neve. London: Penguin Books, 1999.

Hill, J. Arthur. 1912. "The Science of the Soul." *The World's Work* 21: 54-57.

Houdini, Harry. 1924. *Houdini: A Magician among the Spirits*. Quoted in *Sir Arthur Conan Doyle: Interviews and Recollections*. Ed. Harold Orel. London: Macmillan, 1991.

Hustak, Alan. 1998. Titanic: *The Canadian Story*. Montreal: Vehicule Press.

Hyslop, Donald, Alastair Forsyth and Sheila Jemima. 1994. *Titanic Voices: Memories from the Fateful Voyage*. Stroud: Sutton, Southampton City Council.

Illustrated London News. 1912.

Irish News and Belfast Morning News. April 4, 19, 1912.

Lombroso, Cesare. 1909. *After Death—What? Spiritistic Phenomena and Their Interpretation*. Trans. W.S. Kennedy. Boston: Small, Maynard & Company.

Lord, Walter. 1955. *A Night to Remember*. New York: Holt, Rinehart & Winston. Repr. New York: Bantam, 1956.

Lord, Walter. 1986. *The Night Lives On*. New York: Avon Books.

Marcus, Geoffrey. 1969. *The Maiden Voyage*. New York: Viking.

Marrot, H.V. 1935. *The Life and Letters of John Galsworthy*. London: Heinemann.

New York Times. April 16-21, 1912. Special Commemorative Section. April 15, 1998.

North Shore News (North Vancouver). April 18, 1999.

Oppenheim, Janet. 1985. *The Other World: Spiritualism and Psychical Research in England, 1850-1914*. Cambridge: Cambridge University Press.

Pound, Reginald. 1952. *Arnold Bennett: A Biography*. London: Heinemann.

Review of Reviews 36 (1907); 40 (1909); 43 (1911); 45 (1912).

Robertson, Morgan. 1898. *Futility*. New York: M.F. Mansfield. 1912. *The Wreck of the*

Titan, Or, Futility. New York: McClure's Magazine and Metropolitan Magazine, 1914.

San Francisco Examiner. April 15, 1912.

Shaw, George Bernard. 1919. Preface to *Heartbreak House*. Quoted in Oppenheim.

Stead, Estelle W. 1913. *My Father: Personal & Spiritual Reminiscences*. New York: George H. Doran Company.

Stead, W.T. 1909. *How I Know that the Dead Return*. Boston: Ball Publishing Co.

"Stead, W.T." 1922. *The Blue Island: Experiences of a New Arrival Beyond the Veil*. Communicated by W.T. Stead. Recorded by Pardoe Woodman and Estelle Stead. London: Rider & Co.

Wallace, Alfred Russel. 1892. Quoted in *Alfred Russel Wallace: An Anthology of his Shorter Writings*. Ed. Charles H Smith. Oxford: Oxford University Press, 1991.

Wells, H.G. 1894-1909. *The Country of the Blind and Other Stories*. Ed. Michael Sherborne. New York: Oxford University Press, 1996.

Williamson, Ellen. 1977. *When We Went First Class*. New York: Doubleday.

The World's Work (U.K.) 19 (1912).

Young, Filson. 1912. *Titanic*. London: Grant Richards.

Chapter Six: From the Old World to the New

Anon. 1911. "The 'Olympic' and the 'Titanic': Two Giant Ocean Steamships." *Scientific American Supplement*. No. 1850 (June).

Anon. 1911. "Launch of the *Titantic* [sic]." *International Marine Engineering*: 281-83 (July).

Anon. 1912. "Harland and Wolff's Works at Belfast." *Engineering 94*: 3-12 (July 5), 38-50 (July 12).

Armstrong, James. 1913. "The Mercantile Fight for the North Atlantic." *The World's Work* (U.K.) *21*: 320-326.

Astor, John Jacob. 1894. *A Journey in Other Worlds: A Romance of the Future*. London: Longmans, Green.

Bardon, Jonathan. 1982. *Belfast: An Illustrated History*. Belfast: Blackstaff Press.

Basbanes, Nicholas A. 1995. *A Gentle Madness: Bibliophiles, Bibliomanes, and the Eternal Passion for Books*. New York: H. Holt and Co.

Biel, Steven. 1996. *Down with the Old Canoe: A Cultural History of the* Titanic *Disaster*. New York: W.W. Norton.

British Commission of Enquiry into the Loss of the S.S. Titanic. May-June, 1912.

Bryceson, Dave. 1997. *The* Titanic *Disaster as Reported in the British National Press April-July 1912*. Sparkford, Somerset: Patrick Stephens.

Buckley, Reginald R. 1912. "Dream Drama and Crowd Drama: From Sophocles to Reinhardt." *The World's Work 19*: 146-155.

Butler, Christopher. 1994. *Early Modernism: Literature, Music and Painting in Europe 1900-1916*. Oxford: Clarendon Press.

Candee, Helen Churchill. 1912. "Sealed Orders." *Collier's Weekly*. May 4, 1912.

Conan Doyle, Sir Arthur. 1924. *Memories and Adventures*. Boston: Little, Brown, and Company.

Conan Doyle, Sir Arthur. 1991. *Interviews and Recollections*. Ed. Harold Orel. London: Macmillan.

Conrad, Joseph. 1912-1916. *The Collected Letters of Joseph Conrad*. Vol. 5: *1912-1916*. Cambridge: Cambridge University Press.

Conrad, Joseph. 1912. "Some Reflexions, Seamanlike and Otherwise, on the Loss of the *Titanic*." *The English Review 11*: 304-15.

Daily Telegraph. April 22, 1912.

Davie, Michael. 1986. *The* Titanic: *The Full Story of a Tragedy*. London: Bodley Head.

Dobson, Alan. 1995. *Anglo-American Relations in the Twentieth Century*. London: Routledge.

Duff Gordon, Lady. 1912. "Newest Summer Fashions." *San Francisco Examiner*. April 14,

Duff Gordon, Lady. 1932. *Discretions and Indiscretions*. New York: Frederick A. Stokes.

Fletcher, R.A. 1913. *Travelling Palaces: Luxury in Passenger Steamships*. London: Sir Isaac Pitman & Sons.

Futrelle, Jacques. 1912. *My Lady's Garter*. The Last Novel. New York: A.L. Burt.

Geller, Judith B. 1998. Titanic: *Women and Children First*. Sparkford: Patrick Stephens.

Gibbs, Philip, ed. 1912. *The Deathless Story of the* Titanic. London: Lloyd's Weekly News. Facs. Reprint, Lloyd's of London Press.

Gilbert, Martin. 1997. *A History of the Twentieth Century*. Vol. 1: *1900-1933*. London: HarperCollins Publishers.

Globe and Mail (Toronto). May 19, 1998.

Gracie, Colonel Archibald. 1913. *The Truth about the* Titanic. New York: M. Kennerley.

Greene, Douglas, ed. 1997. *Detection by Gaslight*. Mineola, New York: Dover Publications.

Hansen, Erik Fosnes. 1996. *Psalm at Journey's End*. Trans. Joan Tate. New York: Farrar, Straus & Giroux.

Hood, A.G., ed. 1911. "The White Star Triple-Screw Atlantic Liners *Olympic* and *Titanic*, 45,000 Tons, the Largest Steamships in the World." Souvenir Number of *The Shipbuilder* 6: 1-130.

Hustak, Alan. 1998. Titanic: *The Canadian Story*. Montreal: Vehicule Press.

Illustrated London News. 1912.

Jordan, Caryl. 1912. "The Alliance and the Entente." *The World's Work* (U.K.) 20: 26-31.

Kaplan, Joel and Sheila Stowell. 1994. *Theatre and Fashion: Oscar Wilde to the Suffragettes*. Cambridge: Cambridge University Press.

Kohfeldt, Mary Lou. 1985. *Lady Gregory: The Woman behind the Irish Renaissance*. New York: Atheneum.

Literary Digest. 1912.

Lord, Walter. 1955. *A Night to Remember*. New York: Holt, Rinehart & Winston. Repr. New York: Bantam, 1956.

Lord, Walter. 1986. *The Night Lives On*. New York: Avon Books.

Marcus, Geoffrey. 1969. *The Maiden Voyage*. New York: Viking.

Marinetti, F.T. 1972. *Marinetti: Selected Writings*. Eds. R.W. Flint and Arthur A. Coppotelli. London: Secker & Warburg.

Marshall, Logan, ed. 1912. *Sinking of the* Titanic *and Great Sea Disasters: A Detailed and Accurate Account of the Most Awful Marine Disaster in History, Constructed from the Real Facts as Obtained from Those on Board Who Survived.* [S.I.]: L.T. Myers.

Moffett, Samuel E. 1901. "How America Really Feels towards England." *The Nineteenth Century and After* 50: 177-189.

New York Times. April 16-21, 1912. Special Commemorative Section. April 15, 1998.

O'Donnell, E.E. 1994. *Father Browne: A Life in Pictures*. Dublin: Wolfhound Press.

O'Donnell, E.E. 1997 *The Last Days of the* Titanic: *Photographs and Mementoes of the Tragic Maiden Voyage*. Niwot, Colo.: Roberts Rinehart Publishers. Dublin: Wolfhound Press.

Pound, Ezra. 1996. *Machine Art & Other Writings: The Lost Thought of the Italian Years*. Ed. Maria Luisa Ardizzone. Durham, NC: Duke University Press.

Reid, B.L. 1968. *The Man from New York: John Quinn and his Friends*. New York: Oxford University Press.

Review of Reviews 23 (1901); *24* (1901).

Rose, Jonathan. 1986. "The Efficiency Men," in *The Edwardian Temperament, 1895-1919*. Athens, Ohio: Ohio University Press.

Saddlemyer, Ann. 1999. Personal Communication.

Seymour, Freddie and Bettina Kyper. 1995. *The Thinking Machine: Discovering the Titanic Talent of a Pioneer American Mystery Author*. Dennisport, MA: Graphic Illusions.

Smith, Terry. 1993. *Making the Modern: Industry, Art, and Design in America*. Chicago: University of Chicago Press.

Stoker, Bram. 1907. "The World's Greatest Ship-building Yard." *The World's Work* (U.K.), no.54, 647-50.

Taft, William H. 1913. "The Monroe Doctrine: Its Limitations and Implications." *The Independent*. December 18, 1913. Repr. in *College Readings in English Prose*. Eds. F.W. Scott and Jacob Zeitlin. New York: Macmillan, 1920.

Times of London. April 22, 1912.

Wade, Wyn Craig. 1979. *The Titanic: End of a Dream*. Harmondsworth: Penguin Books, 1980.

Whitcomb, Ian (conducting the White Star Orchestra). 1997. *Titanic: Music as Heard on the Fateful Voyage*. Santa Monica: Rhino Entertainment Company.

Young, Filson. 1912. *Titanic*. London: Grant Richards.

Zach, Nathan. 1976. "Imagism and Vorticism," in *Modernism 1890-1930*. Eds. Malcolm Bradbury and James McFarlane. Harmondsworth: Penguin Books.

Chapter Seven: Imagining the Titanic

Abrahams, Roger D., 1968 *Deep Down in the Jungle: Negro Narrative Folklore from the Streets of Philadelphia*. Chicago: Aldine Publishing Company.

Anon., ed. 1955. *The Book of Navy Songs*. Annapolis: Trident Society.

Asch, Moses and Alan Lomax, eds. 1962. *The Leadbelly Songbook*. New York: Oak Publications.

Beesley, Lawrence. 1912. *The Loss of the R.M.S. Titanic: Its Story and Its Lessons*. London: Heinemann.

Belfast News-Letter. April 20, 22, 1912.

Biel, Steven. 1996. *Down with the Old Canoe: A Cultural History of the Titanic Disaster*. New York: W.W. Norton.

Candee, Helen Churchill. 1912. "Sealed Orders." *Collier's Weekly*. May 4, 1912.

Collyer, Charlotte. 1912. "How I was Saved from the *Titanic*." *The Semi-Monthly Magazine*, May 26.

Conrad, Joseph. 1912. "Some Aspects of the Admirable Inquiry." *The English Review* 11: 581-95. Repr. as "Certain Aspects of the Admirable Inquiry into the Loss of the *Titanic*" in Conrad's *Notes on Life & Letters* (1921).

Daily Mirror. April 17, 1912.

Conan Doyle, Sir Arthur. 1924. *Memories and Adventures*. Boston: Little, Brown, and Company.

Drew, Edwin. 1912. *The Chief Incidents of the "Titanic" Wreck Treated in Verse: Together with the Lessons of the Disaster*. London: W. Nicholson & Sons.

Foster, John Wilson. 1997. *The Titanic Complex: A Cultural Manifest*. Vancouver: Belcouver Press.

Foster, John Wilson. 1999. *Titanic*. London: Penguin. 2000. *The Titanic Reader*. New York: Viking Penguin.

Friedman, Albert. 1956. *The Viking Book of Folk Ballads of the English-Speaking World*. New York: Viking Press.

Gokturk, Deniz. 2000. "*Atlantis*, or Culture is Sinking! European Auteurs on Seductive Voyages to America 1912-1913." Paper delivered to "Nights to Remember: Memory, Modernity and the Myth of the *Titanic*" Conference Organised by the University of Southampton Film and Media Programme. July 20-23.

Gracie, Colonel Archibald. 1913. *The Truth about the* Titanic. New York: M. Kennerley.

Heyer, Paul. 1995. *The Titanic Legacy: Disaster as Media Event and Myth*. Westport, CT: Praeger.

Illustrated London News. 1912.

Kuntz, Tom, ed. 1998. *The Titanic Disaster Hearings: The Official Transcripts of the 1912 Senate Investigation*. New York: Pocket Books.

Jones, Henry Arthur. 1912. "Arrival Scenes on New York Pier." *Daily Telegraph*, April 20.

Knight, Etheridge. 1980. *Born of a Woman: New and Selected Poems*. Boston: Houghton Mifflin Company.

Levine, Lawrence W. 1977. *Black Culture and Consciousness: Afro-American Folk Thought from Slavery to Freedom*. New York: Oxford University Press.

Literary Digest. 1912.

Lomax, John A. and Alan Lomax, eds. 1941. *Our Singing Country: A Second Volume of American Ballads and Folk Songs*. New York: Macmillan Company.

Lomax, John A. and Alan Lomax, eds. 1959. *Leadbelly: A Collection of World-Famous Songs by Huddie Ledbetter*. New York: Folkways Music Publishers.

Marinetti, F.T. 1972. *Marinetti: Selected Writings*. Eds. R.W. Flint and Arthur A. Coppotelli. London: Secker & Warburg.

Marshall, Logan, ed. 1912. *Sinking of the* Titanic *and Great Sea Disasters: A Detailed and Accurate Account of the Most Awful Marine Disaster in History, Constructed from the Real Facts as Obtained from Those on Board Who Survived*. [S.I.]: L.T. Myers.

Nelson, Graham. 1997. "*The Waste Land* Drafts, 'The Engine' and the Sinking of the *Titanic*." *Notes and Queries*. September: 356-58.

New York Times. April 16-21, 1912. Special Commemorative Section. April 15, 1998.

Niles, Abbe. 1928. "Ballads, Songs and Snatches." *The Bookman* 67: 290-91.

Report of the Committee on Commerce, United States Senate. Report No. 806. 1912. Washington DC.

Review of Reviews 45 (1912).

San Francisco Examiner. April 16, 20, 1912.

Sandburg, Carl. c1927. *The American Songbag*. New York: Harcourt, Brace & Co.

Shutes, Elizabeth W. 1912. "When the *Titanic* Went Down." Repr. in Archibald Gracie, *The Truth about the* Titanic. (See above.)

Silva, Blanca Vanini. 1912. *Solidaridad en el Dolor: Catastrofe del* Titanic. *Poema Filosofico Moral en Tres Partes Y en Romance Heroico*. Ed. Cosme D. Lagos. Barcelona.

Titanic Disaster: Hearings before a Subcommittee of the Committee on Commerce, United States Senate, April-May, 1912.

Titanic Disaster Music. A Listing by Copyright Registration Number, and Showing Names of Authors, Composers, Copyright Proprietors and Publishers, and Dates of Copyright Registration Combining the Original Listings of Joseph C. Hickerson. 1985. American Folklife Center, Archive of Folk Culture. The Library of Congress, Washington DC.

Wade, Wyn Craig. 1979. *The* Titanic: *End of a Dream*. Harmondsworth: Penguin Books, 1986.

Wedel, Michael. 2000. "Creating a Media Event for the Cinema: Interactive Narration in *Titanic: In Nacht und Eis* (Germany 1912)." Paper delivered to "Nights to Remember: Memory, Modernity and the Myth of the *Titanic*" Conference Organised by the University of Southampton Film and Media Programme. July 20-23.

White, Newman I. 1928. *American Negro Folk-Songs*. Cambridge: Harvard University Press.

White, Newman I., ed. 1952. *The Frank C. Brown Collection of North Carolina Folklore*. 5 vols. Durham, North Carolina: Duke University Press.

Williamson, Ellen. 1977. *When We Went First Class*. New York: Doubleday.

Winocur, Jack, ed. 1960. *The Story of the* Titanic *as Told by Its Survivors*. New York: Dover Publications.

Young, Filson. 1912. *Titanic*. London. Grant Richards.

index

Some notable passengers on Titanic: 1. J. Bruce Ismay, 2. A. Peuchen, 3. Major AW Butt, 4. CM Hays, 5. Mrs JJ Astor, 6. Colonel JJ Astor, 7. Lady Cosmo Duff-Gordon, 8. Mr Jack Phillips, 9. Countess of Rothes, 10. Daniel Marvin, 11. Mrs Daniel Marvin, 12. Mr WT Stead, 13, Mr Benjamin Guggenheim, 14. Mr Karl H. Behr, 15. Mr Isidor Straus.